W9-DDM-699
3 4028 07567 9838
HARRIS COUNTY PUBLIC LIBRARY

YA 741.597 Whi
Whitta, Gary
Death, Jr

DISCARDED

$14.99
ocm72150640
12/16/2010

WRITTEN BY
GARY WHITTA

&

ILLUSTRATED BY
TED NAIFEH

ASSISTED BY AARON FARMER AND TRISTAN CRANE

DEATH JR.™

COVER BY ARVIN BAUTISTA

CHAPTER 1 COVER BY DAN BRERETON
CHAPTER 2 COVER BY CHAD PFARR
CHAPTER 3 COVER BY CHRIS BOURASSA

MANAGING EDITOR: NICOLE TANNER
STORY EDITORS: CHRIS CHARLA & MIKE MIKA

DEATH JR. CREATED BY:
MIKE MIKA, TERRI SELTING,
MICAH RUSSO & CHRIS CHARLA

SPECIAL THANKS TO JON GOLDMAN,
DAVID MANN, DOUG HARE, RICHARD HARE,
STEVE SARDEGNA & ANDREW AYRE

IMAGE COMICS, INC.

ERIK LARSEN - PUBLISHER
TODD MCFARLANE - PRESIDENT
MARC SILVESTRI - CEO
JIM VALENTINO - VICE-PRESIDENT

ERIC STEPHENSON - EXECUTIVE DIRECTOR
MARK HAVEN BRITT - DIRECTOR OF MARKETING
THAO LE - ACCOUNTS MANGER
ROSEMARY CAO - ACCOUNTING ASSISTANT
TRACI HUI - ADMINISTRATIVE ASSISTANT
JOE KEATINGE - TRAFFIC MANAGER
ALLEN HUI - PRODUCTION MANAGER
JONATHAN CHAN - PRODUCTION ARTIST
DREW GILL - PRODUCTION ARTIST
CHRIS GIARRUSSO - PRODUCTION ARTIST

WWW.IMAGECOMICS.COM

DEATH, JR., VOL. 2. First Printing. Published by Image Comics, Inc. Office of publication: 1942 University Avenue, Suite 305, Berkeley, California 94704. Copyright © 2007 Backbone Entertainment. Previously published in single magazine form as DEATH, JR., II #1-3. All rights reserved. DEATH, JR.™ (including all prominent characters featured herein), its logo and all character likenesses are trademarks of Backbone Entertainment, unless otherwise noted. Image Comics® is a trademark of Image Comics, Inc. All rights reserved. No part of this publication may be reproduced or transmitted, in any form or by any means (except for short excerpts for review purposes) without the express written permission of Image Comics, Inc. All names, characters, events and locales in this publication are entirely fictional. Any resemblance to actual persons (living or dead), events or places, without satiric intent, is coincidental.

ISBN: 978-1-58240-682-4

PRINTED IN CANADA

BACKBONE ENTERTAINMENT

CHAPTER 1

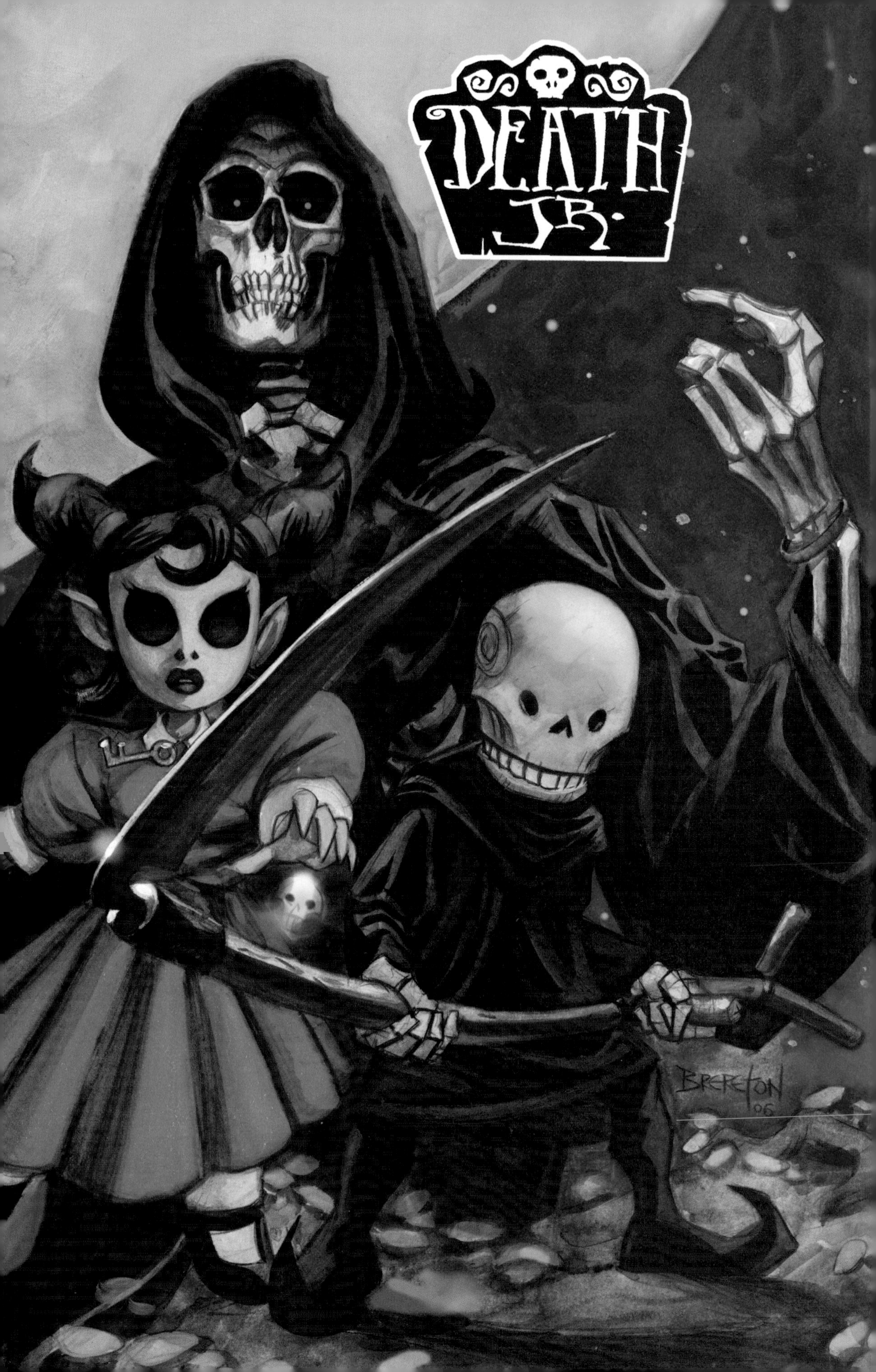
DEATH JR.
BRERETON 06

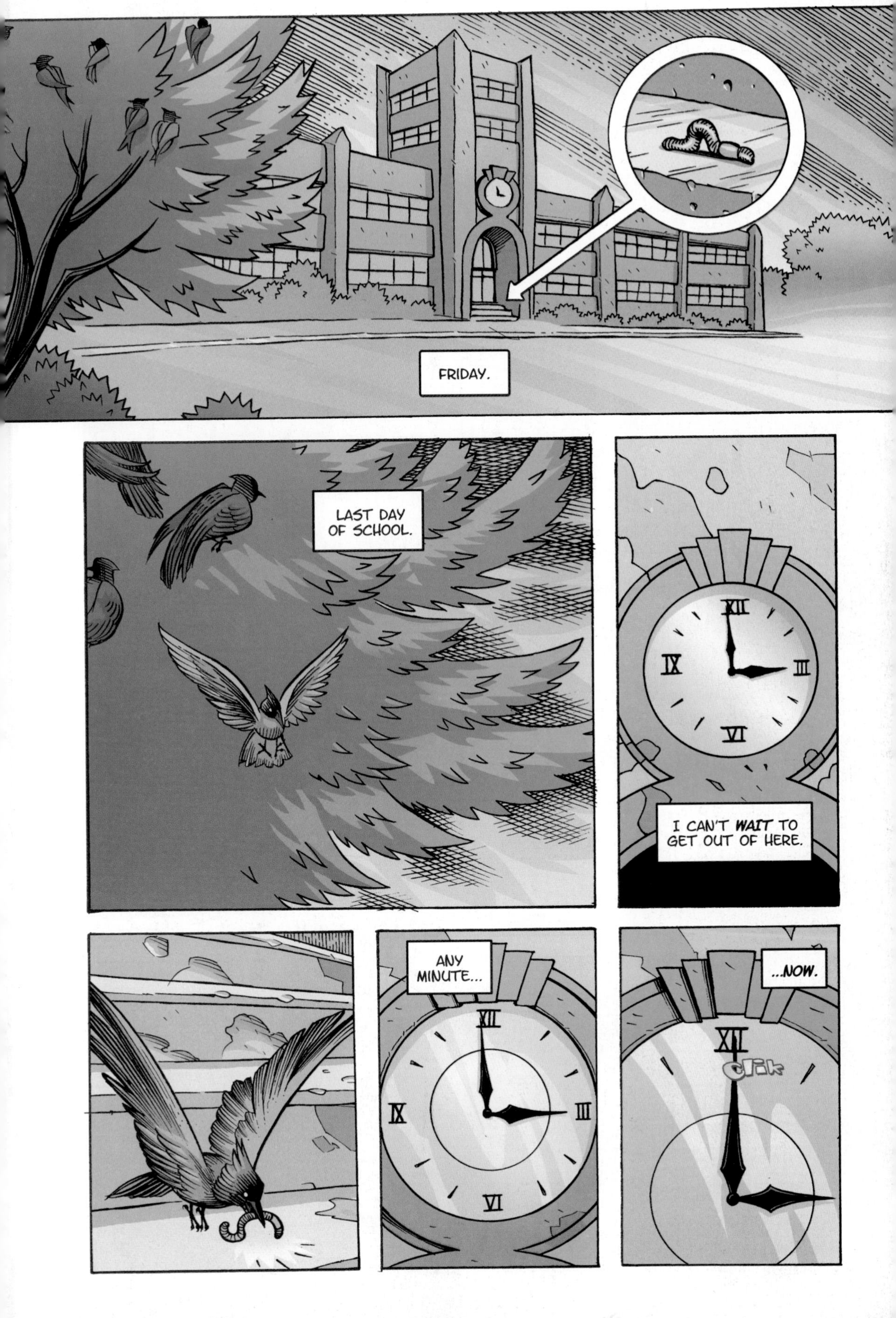
FRIDAY.
LAST DAY OF SCHOOL.
I CAN'T WAIT TO GET OUT OF HERE.
ANY MINUTE...
...NOW.
CLIK

BOY, I TELL YA...

EIGHT WHOLE WEEKS WITH NO TEACHERS, NO HOMEWORK... NOBODY TO TELL ME WHAT TO DO!

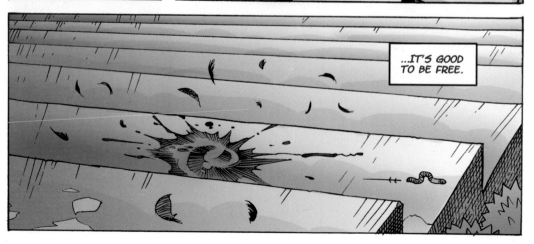

...IT'S GOOD TO BE FREE.

YAY! SUMMERTIME- AND THE LIVING IS *EASY!*

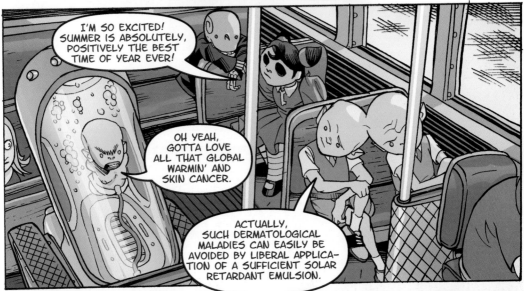

I'M SO *EXCITED!* SUMMER IS ABSOLUTELY, *POSITIVELY* THE BEST TIME OF YEAR EVER!

OH *YEAH,* GOTTA *LOVE* ALL THAT GLOBAL WARMIN' AND SKIN *CANCER.*

ACTUALLY, SUCH DERMATOLOGICAL MALADIES CAN EASILY BE AVOIDED BY LIBERAL APPLICA- TION OF A SUFFICIENT SOLAR RETARDANT EMULSION.

SUNBLOCK.

OH! YES, WHAT *THEY* SAID. I'M LOOKING FORWARD TO WORKING ON MY *TAN.*

TAN? WHAT *EXACTLY* DO YOU DO, TURN DARKER *BLUE?*

IF IT'S ANY OF YOUR BUSINESS...

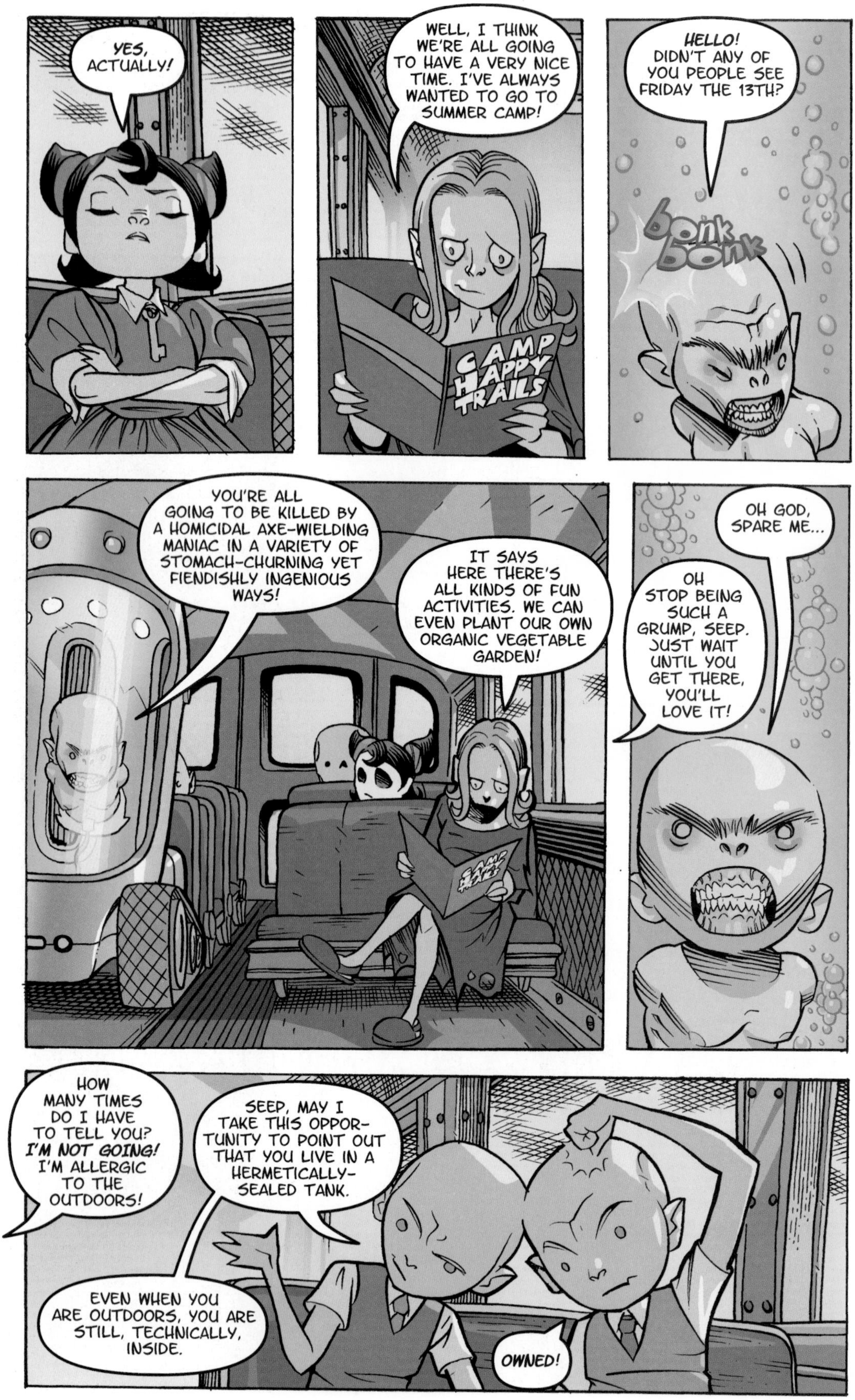

YES, ACTUALLY!
WELL, I THINK WE'RE ALL GOING TO HAVE A VERY NICE TIME. I'VE ALWAYS WANTED TO GO TO SUMMER CAMP!
CAMP HAPPY TRAILS
HELLO! DIDN'T ANY OF YOU PEOPLE SEE FRIDAY THE 13TH?
bonk bonk
YOU'RE ALL GOING TO BE KILLED BY A HOMICIDAL AXE-WIELDING MANIAC IN A VARIETY OF STOMACH-CHURNING YET FIENDISHLY INGENIOUS WAYS!
IT SAYS HERE THERE'S ALL KINDS OF FUN ACTIVITIES. WE CAN EVEN PLANT OUR OWN ORGANIC VEGETABLE GARDEN!
OH GOD, SPARE ME...
OH STOP BEING SUCH A GRUMP, SEEP. JUST WAIT UNTIL YOU GET THERE, YOU'LL LOVE IT!
HOW MANY TIMES DO I HAVE TO TELL YOU? I'M NOT GOING! I'M ALLERGIC TO THE OUTDOORS!
SEEP, MAY I TAKE THIS OPPOR-TUNITY TO POINT OUT THAT YOU LIVE IN A HERMETICALLY-SEALED TANK.
EVEN WHEN YOU ARE OUTDOORS, YOU ARE STILL, TECHNICALLY, INSIDE.
OWNED!

THAT'S NOT THE POINT, BRAINIAC. ME AND NATURE, WE'VE GOT AN AGREEMENT. I DON'T BOTHER IT AND IT DOESN'T BOTHER ME.

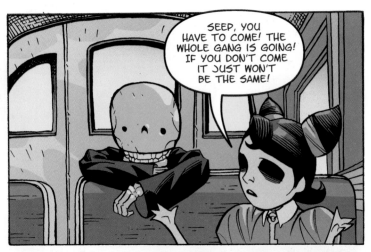

SEEP, YOU HAVE TO COME! THE WHOLE GANG IS GOING! IF YOU DON'T COME IT JUST WON'T BE THE SAME!

WELL WHAT ABOUT DJ? HE'S NOT GOING EITHER!

DON'T BE SILLY! OF COURSE HE'S GOING! HE'S BEEN LOOKING FORWARD TO IT FOR *WEEKS*!

HAVEN'T YOU, DJ?

UH...

WELL,

SEE, THE THING IS...

WHAT!?!

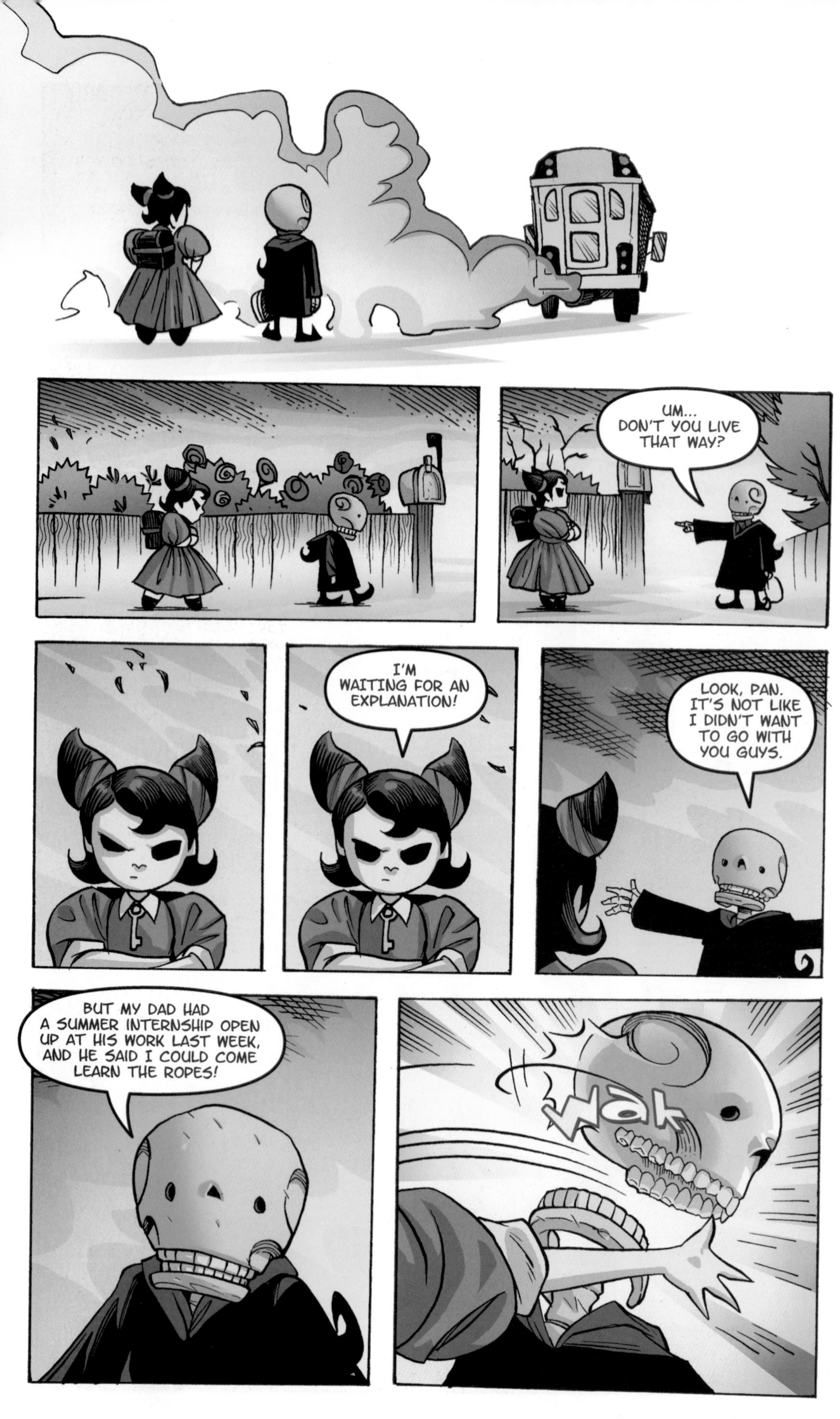
UM...
DON'T YOU LIVE
THAT WAY?
I'M
WAITING FOR AN
EXPLANATION!
LOOK, PAN.
IT'S NOT LIKE
I DIDN'T WANT
TO GO WITH
YOU GUYS.
BUT MY DAD HAD
A SUMMER INTERNSHIP OPEN
UP AT HIS WORK LAST WEEK,
AND HE SAID I COULD COME
LEARN THE ROPES!
WAK

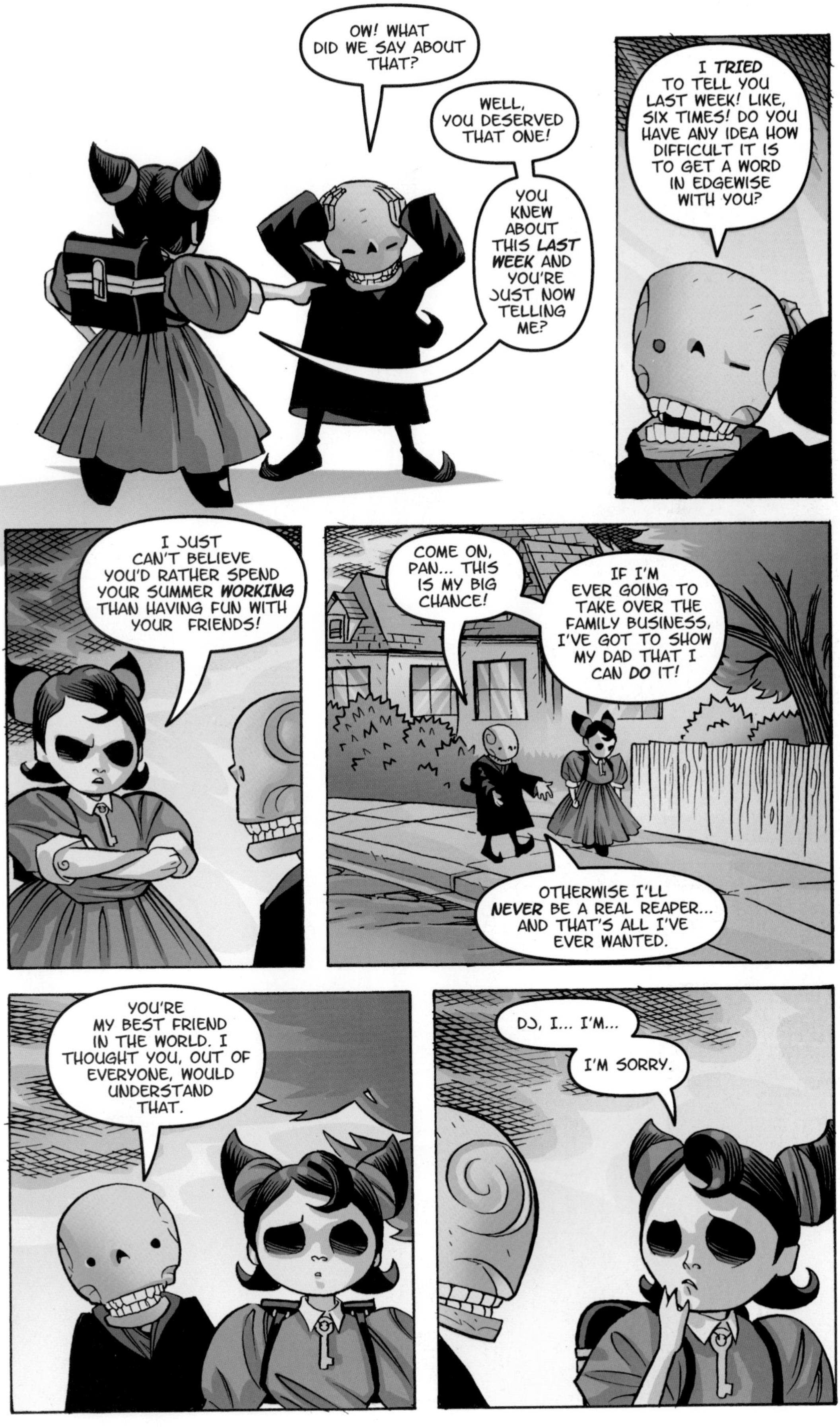
OW! WHAT DID WE SAY ABOUT THAT?
WELL, YOU DESERVED THAT ONE!
YOU KNEW ABOUT THIS LAST WEEK AND YOU'RE JUST NOW TELLING ME?
I TRIED TO TELL YOU LAST WEEK! LIKE, SIX TIMES! DO YOU HAVE ANY IDEA HOW DIFFICULT IT IS TO GET A WORD IN EDGEWISE WITH YOU?
I JUST CAN'T BELIEVE YOU'D RATHER SPEND YOUR SUMMER WORKING THAN HAVING FUN WITH YOUR FRIENDS!
COME ON, PAN... THIS IS MY BIG CHANCE!
IF I'M EVER GOING TO TAKE OVER THE FAMILY BUSINESS, I'VE GOT TO SHOW MY DAD THAT I CAN DO IT!
OTHERWISE I'LL NEVER BE A REAL REAPER... AND THAT'S ALL I'VE EVER WANTED.
YOU'RE MY BEST FRIEND IN THE WORLD. I THOUGHT YOU, OUT OF EVERYONE, WOULD UNDERSTAND THAT.
DJ, I... I'M...
I'M SORRY.

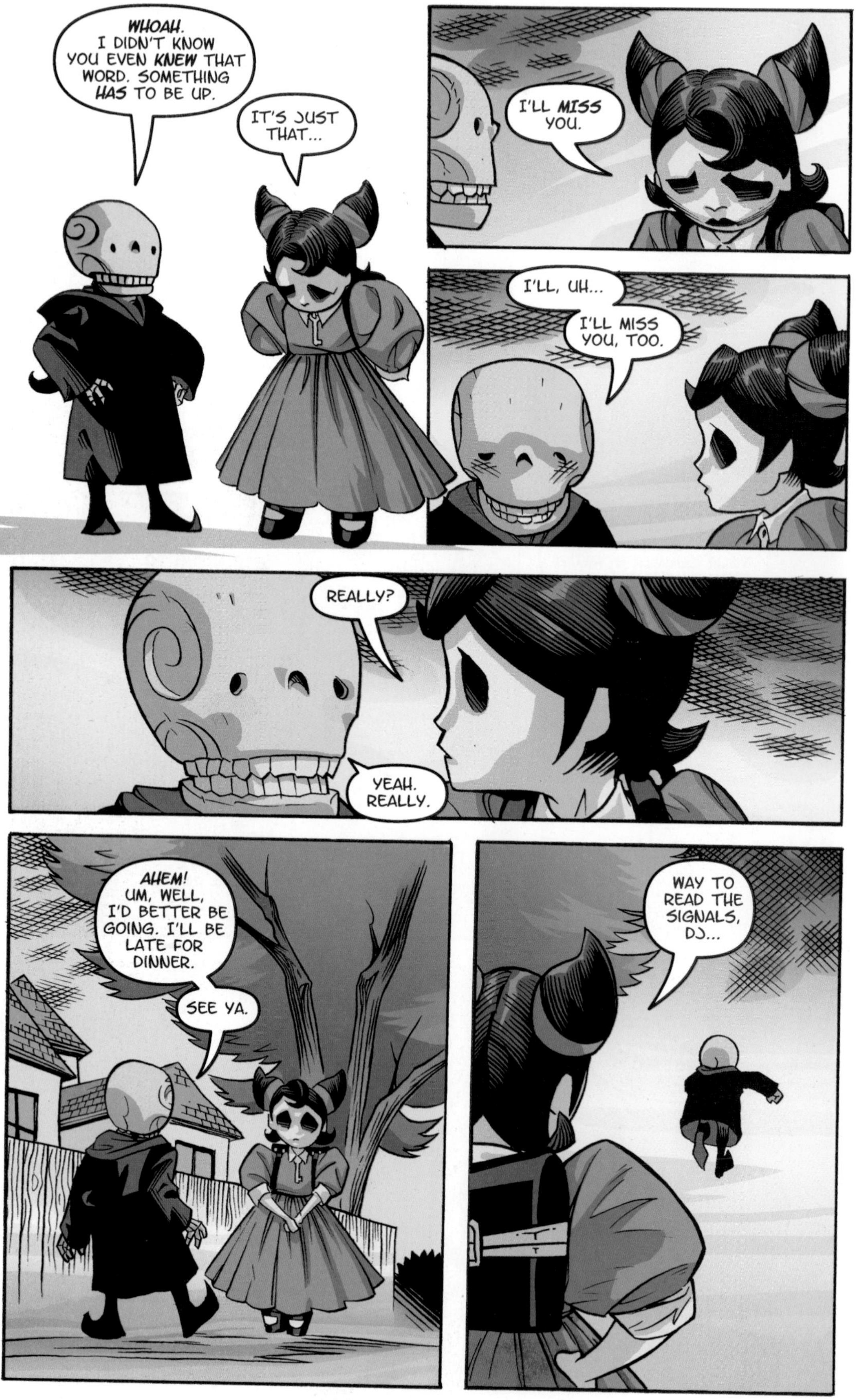
WHOAH. I DIDN'T KNOW YOU EVEN KNEW THAT WORD. SOMETHING HAS TO BE UP.
IT'S JUST THAT...
I'LL MISS YOU.
I'LL, UH...
I'LL MISS YOU, TOO.
REALLY?
YEAH. REALLY.
AHEM! UM, WELL, I'D BETTER BE GOING. I'LL BE LATE FOR DINNER.
SEE YA.
WAY TO READ THE SIGNALS, DJ...

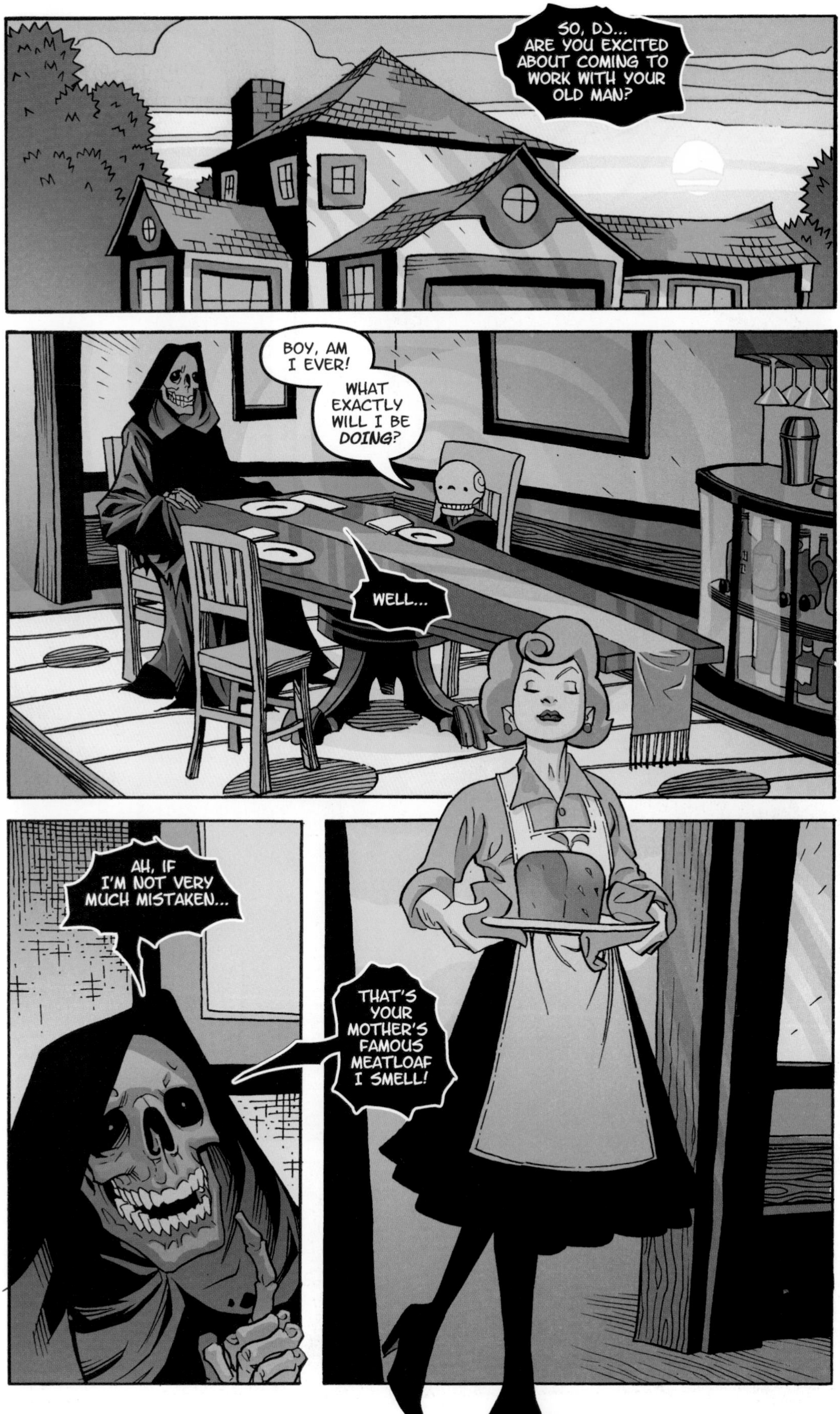
SO, DJ... ARE YOU EXCITED ABOUT COMING TO WORK WITH YOUR OLD MAN?
BOY, AM I EVER!
WHAT EXACTLY WILL I BE DOING?
WELL...
AH, IF I'M NOT VERY MUCH MISTAKEN...
THAT'S YOUR MOTHER'S FAMOUS MEATLOAF I SMELL!

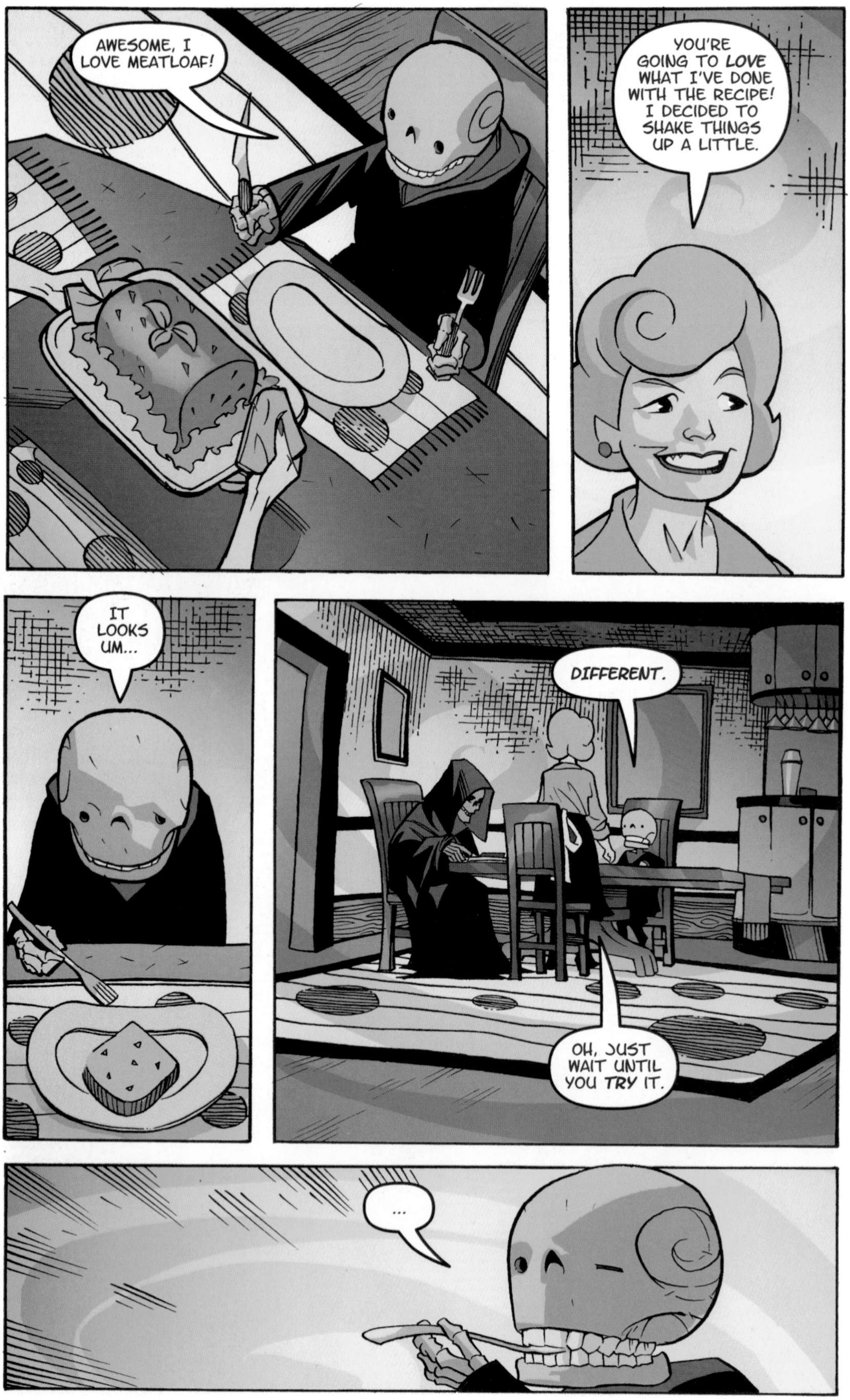
AWESOME, I LOVE MEATLOAF!
YOU'RE GOING TO LOVE WHAT I'VE DONE WITH THE RECIPE! I DECIDED TO SHAKE THINGS UP A LITTLE.
IT LOOKS UM...
DIFFERENT.
OH, JUST WAIT UNTIL YOU TRY IT.
...

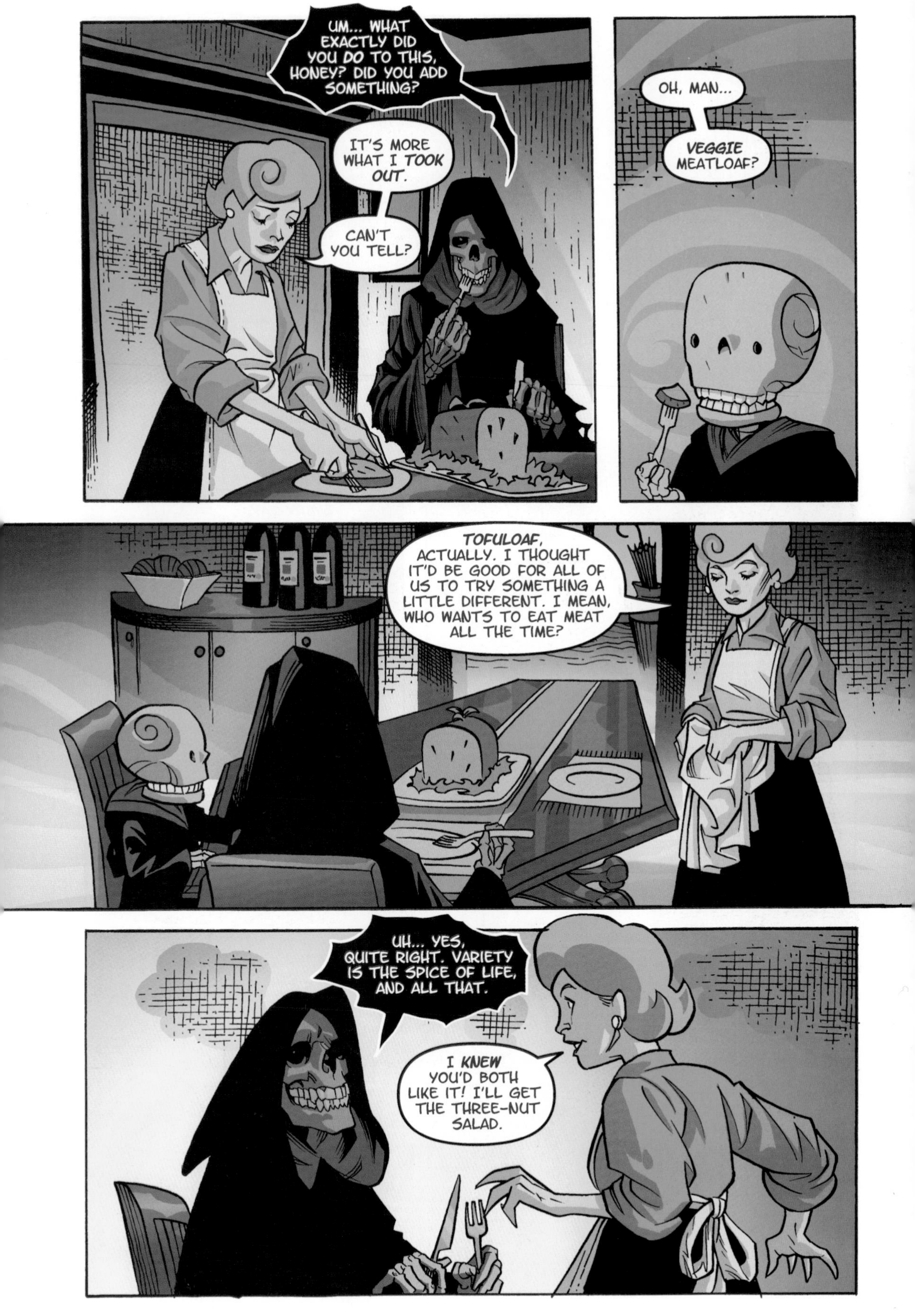
UM... WHAT EXACTLY DID YOU DO TO THIS, HONEY? DID YOU ADD SOMETHING?
IT'S MORE WHAT I TOOK OUT.
CAN'T YOU TELL?
OH, MAN...
VEGGIE MEATLOAF?
TOFULOAF, ACTUALLY. I THOUGHT IT'D BE GOOD FOR ALL OF US TO TRY SOMETHING A LITTLE DIFFERENT. I MEAN, WHO WANTS TO EAT MEAT ALL THE TIME?
UH... YES, QUITE RIGHT. VARIETY IS THE SPICE OF LIFE, AND ALL THAT.
I KNEW YOU'D BOTH LIKE IT! I'LL GET THE THREE-NUT SALAD.

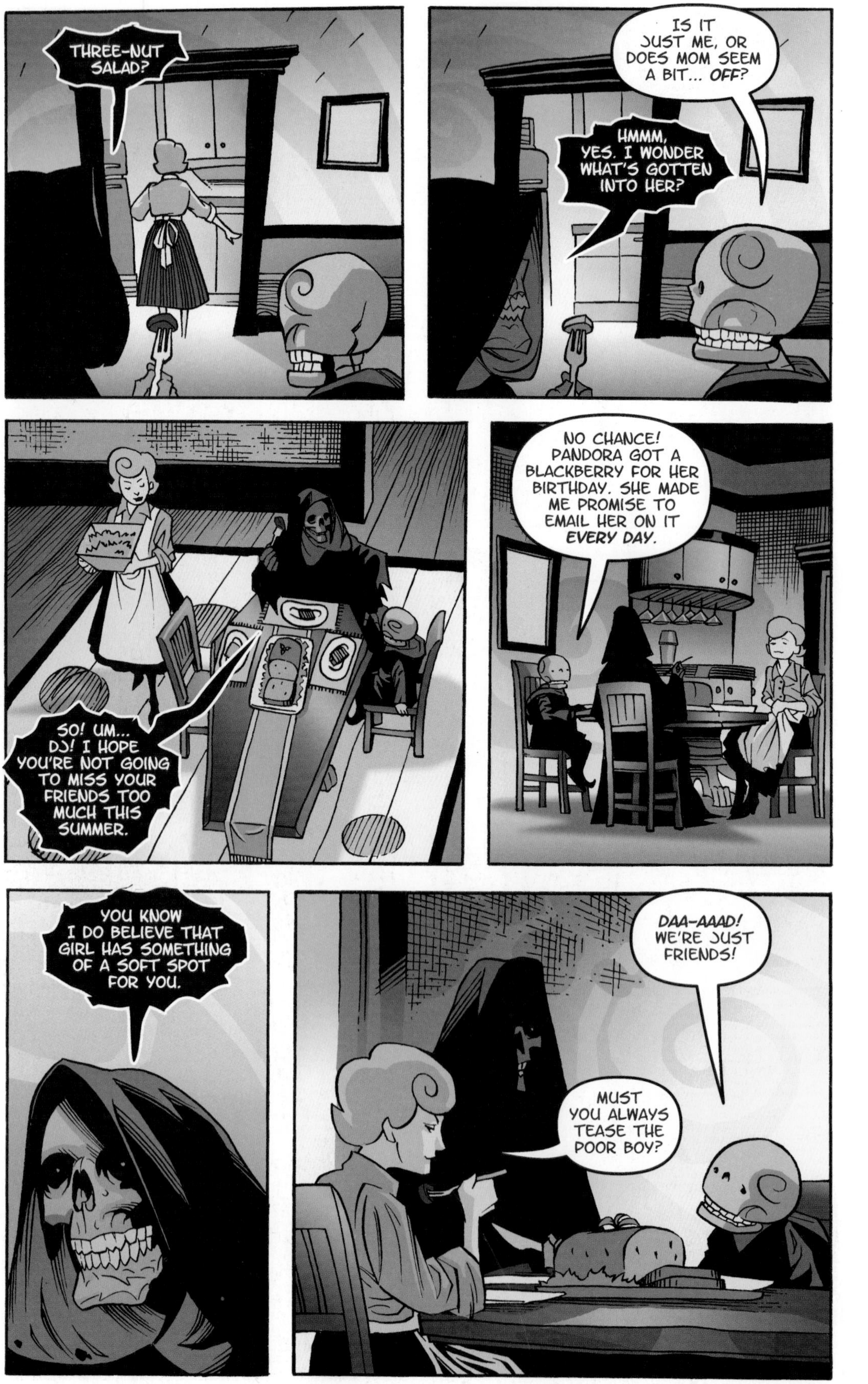
THREE-NUT SALAD?
IS IT JUST ME, OR DOES MOM SEEM A BIT... OFF?
HMMM, YES. I WONDER WHAT'S GOTTEN INTO HER?
SO! UM... DJ! I HOPE YOU'RE NOT GOING TO MISS YOUR FRIENDS TOO MUCH THIS SUMMER.
NO CHANCE! PANDORA GOT A BLACKBERRY FOR HER BIRTHDAY. SHE MADE ME PROMISE TO EMAIL HER ON IT EVERY DAY.
YOU KNOW I DO BELIEVE THAT GIRL HAS SOMETHING OF A SOFT SPOT FOR YOU.
DAA-AAAD! WE'RE JUST FRIENDS!
MUST YOU ALWAYS TEASE THE POOR BOY?

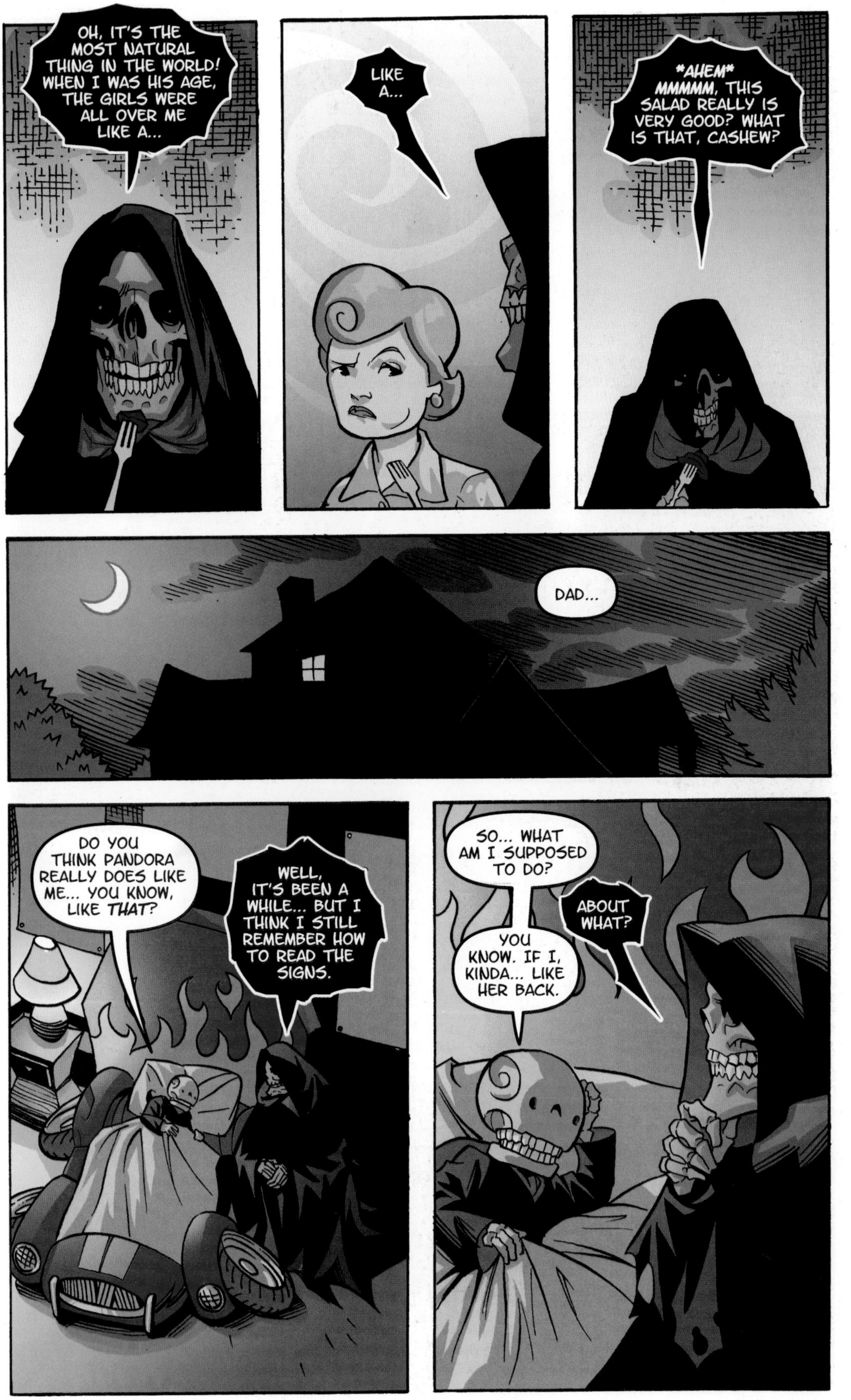
OH, IT'S THE MOST NATURAL THING IN THE WORLD! WHEN I WAS HIS AGE, THE GIRLS WERE ALL OVER ME LIKE A...
LIKE A...
AHEM MMMMM, THIS SALAD REALLY IS VERY GOOD? WHAT IS THAT, CASHEW?
DAD...
DO YOU THINK PANDORA REALLY DOES LIKE ME... YOU KNOW, LIKE THAT?
WELL, IT'S BEEN A WHILE... BUT I THINK I STILL REMEMBER HOW TO READ THE SIGNS.
SO... WHAT AM I SUPPOSED TO DO?
ABOUT WHAT?
YOU KNOW. IF I, KINDA... LIKE HER BACK.

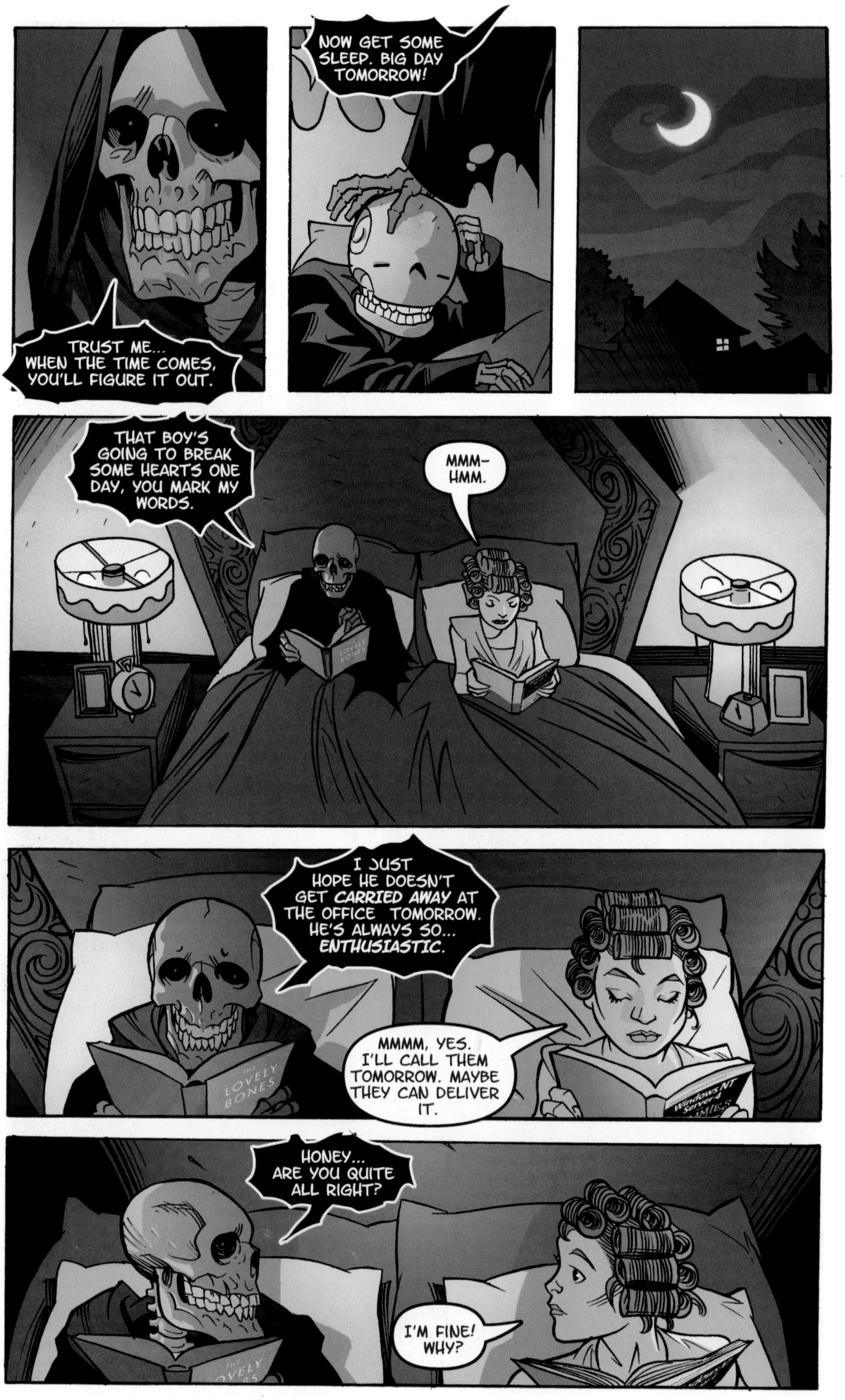

TRUST ME... WHEN THE TIME COMES, YOU'LL FIGURE IT OUT.
NOW GET SOME SLEEP. BIG DAY TOMORROW!
THAT BOY'S GOING TO BREAK SOME HEARTS ONE DAY, YOU MARK MY WORDS.
MMM-HMM.
I JUST HOPE HE DOESN'T GET CARRIED AWAY AT THE OFFICE TOMORROW. HE'S ALWAYS SO... ENTHUSIASTIC.
MMMM, YES. I'LL CALL THEM TOMORROW. MAYBE THEY CAN DELIVER IT.
HONEY... ARE YOU QUITE ALL RIGHT?
I'M FINE! WHY?

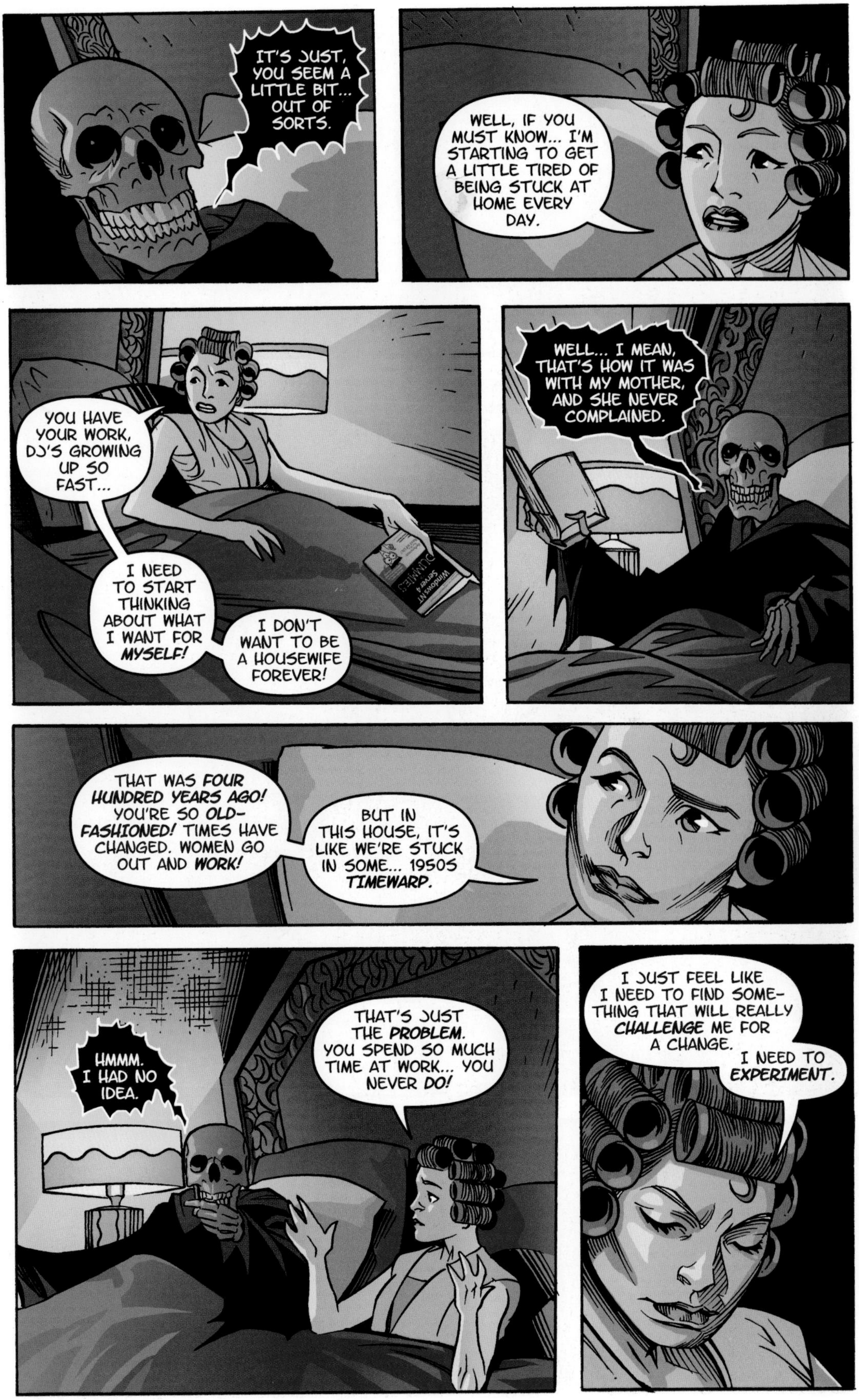
IT'S JUST, YOU SEEM A LITTLE BIT... OUT OF SORTS.
WELL, IF YOU MUST KNOW... I'M STARTING TO GET A LITTLE TIRED OF BEING STUCK AT HOME EVERY DAY.
YOU HAVE YOUR WORK, DJ'S GROWING UP SO FAST...
I NEED TO START THINKING ABOUT WHAT I WANT FOR MYSELF!
I DON'T WANT TO BE A HOUSEWIFE FOREVER!
WELL... I MEAN, THAT'S HOW IT WAS WITH MY MOTHER, AND SHE NEVER COMPLAINED.
THAT WAS FOUR HUNDRED YEARS AGO! YOU'RE SO OLD-FASHIONED! TIMES HAVE CHANGED. WOMEN GO OUT AND WORK!
BUT IN THIS HOUSE, IT'S LIKE WE'RE STUCK IN SOME... 1950S TIMEWARP.
HMMM. I HAD NO IDEA.
THAT'S JUST THE PROBLEM. YOU SPEND SO MUCH TIME AT WORK... YOU NEVER DO!
I JUST FEEL LIKE I NEED TO FIND SOME-THING THAT WILL REALLY CHALLENGE ME FOR A CHANGE.
I NEED TO EXPERIMENT.

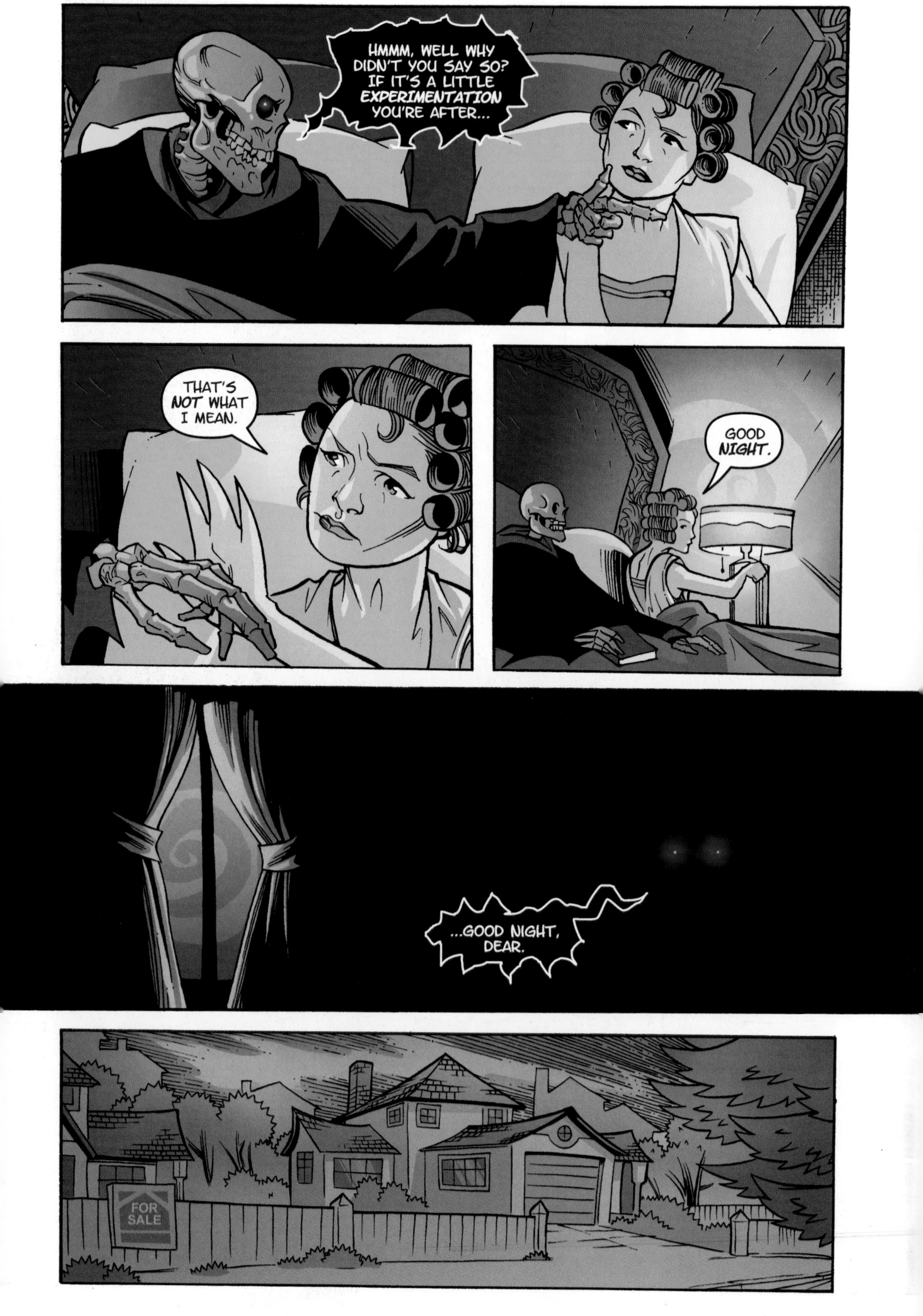
HMMM, WELL WHY DIDN'T YOU SAY SO? IF IT'S A LITTLE EXPERIMENTATION YOU'RE AFTER...
THAT'S NOT WHAT I MEAN.
GOOD NIGHT.
...GOOD NIGHT, DEAR.
FOR SALE

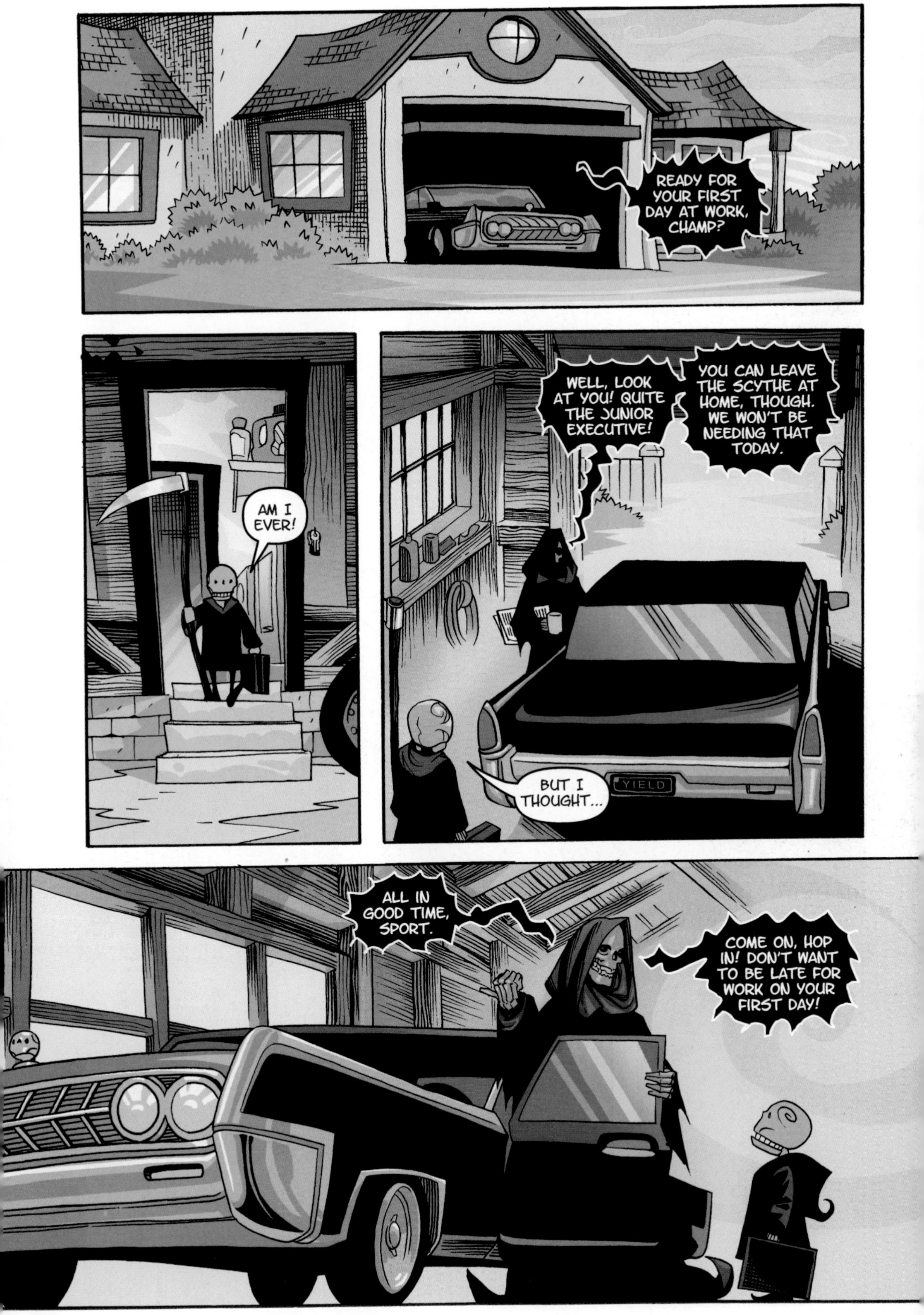
READY FOR YOUR FIRST DAY AT WORK, CHAMP?
AM I EVER!
WELL, LOOK AT YOU! QUITE THE JUNIOR EXECUTIVE!
YOU CAN LEAVE THE SCYTHE AT HOME, THOUGH. WE WON'T BE NEEDING THAT TODAY.
YIELD
BUT I THOUGHT...
ALL IN GOOD TIME, SPORT.
COME ON, HOP IN! DON'T WANT TO BE LATE FOR WORK ON YOUR FIRST DAY!

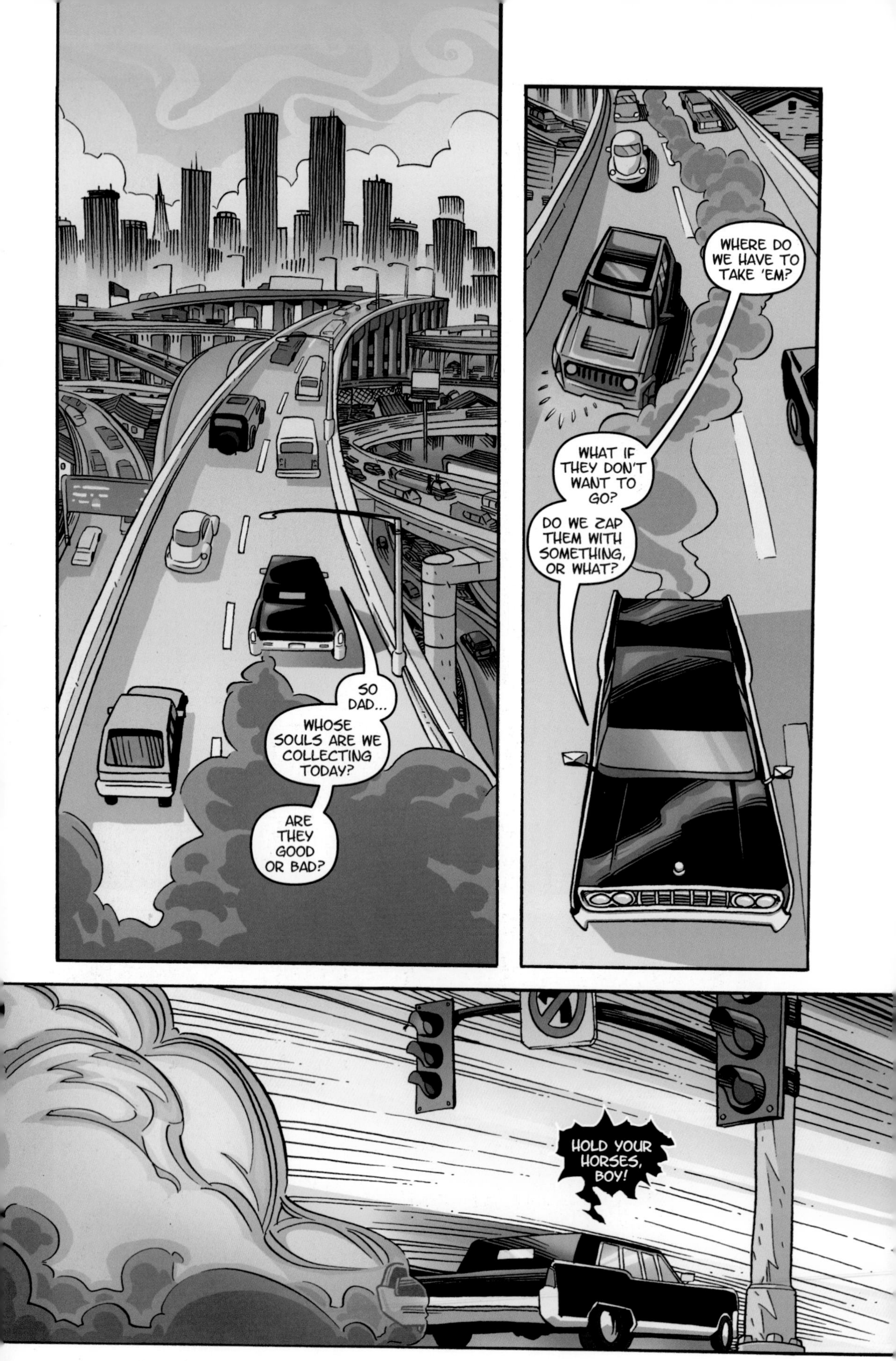
SO DAD...
WHOSE SOULS ARE WE COLLECTING TODAY?
ARE THEY GOOD OR BAD?
WHERE DO WE HAVE TO TAKE 'EM?
WHAT IF THEY DON'T WANT TO GO?
DO WE ZAP THEM WITH SOMETHING, OR WHAT?
HOLD YOUR HORSES, BOY!

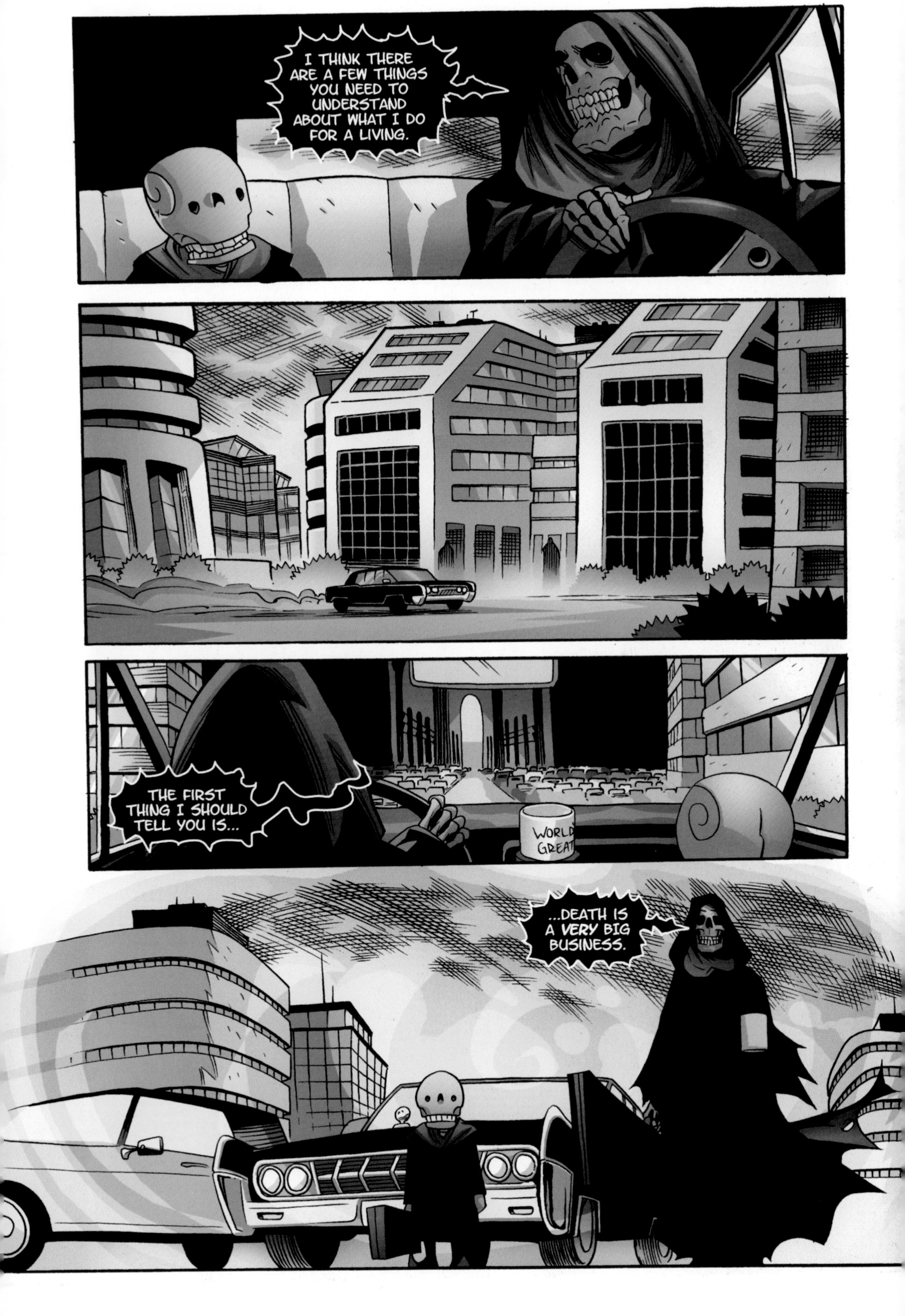
I THINK THERE ARE A FEW THINGS YOU NEED TO UNDERSTAND ABOUT WHAT I DO FOR A LIVING.
THE FIRST THING I SHOULD TELL YOU IS...
WORLD GREAT
...DEATH IS A **VERY** BIG BUSINESS.

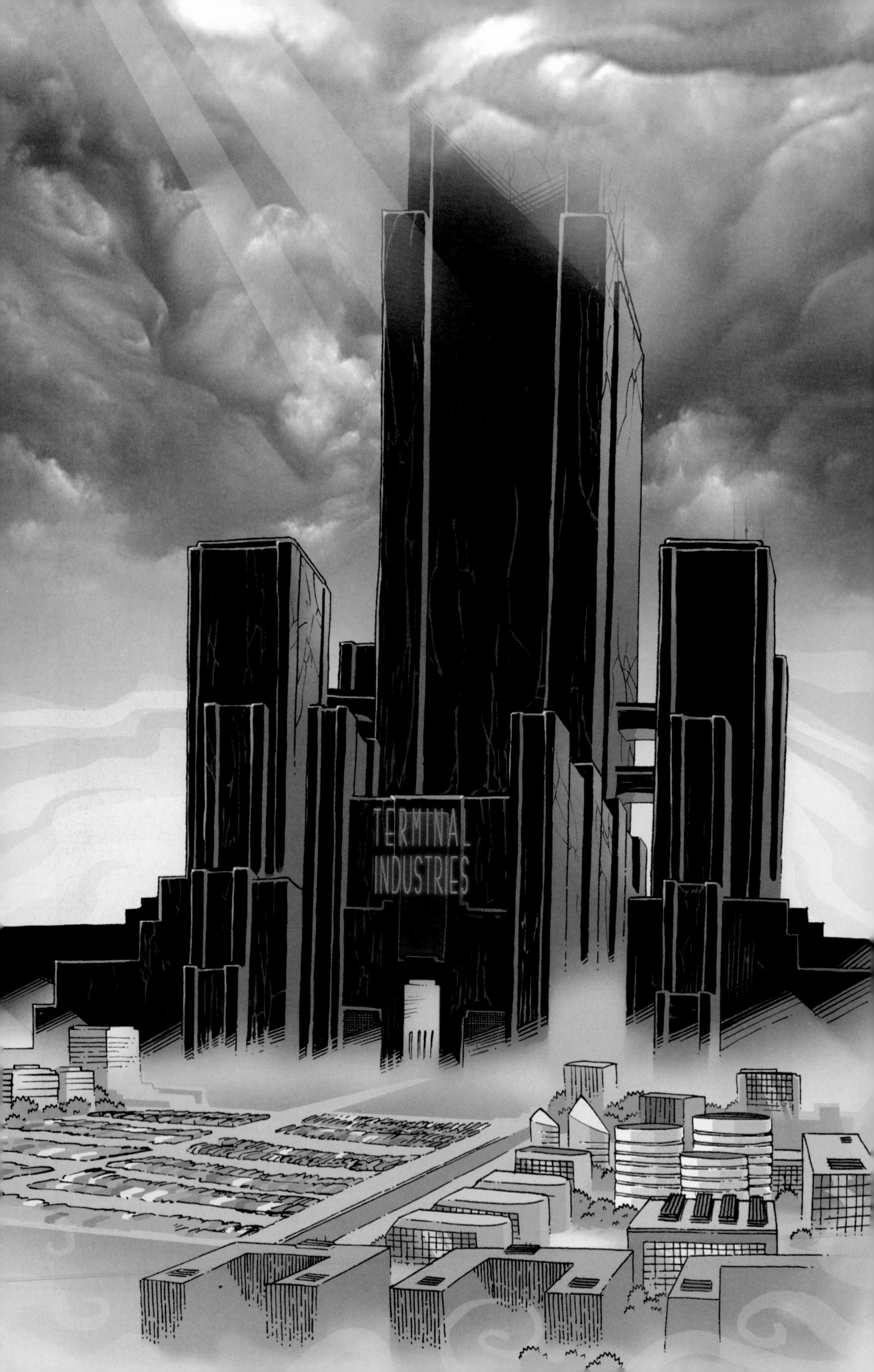
TERMINAL INDUSTRIES

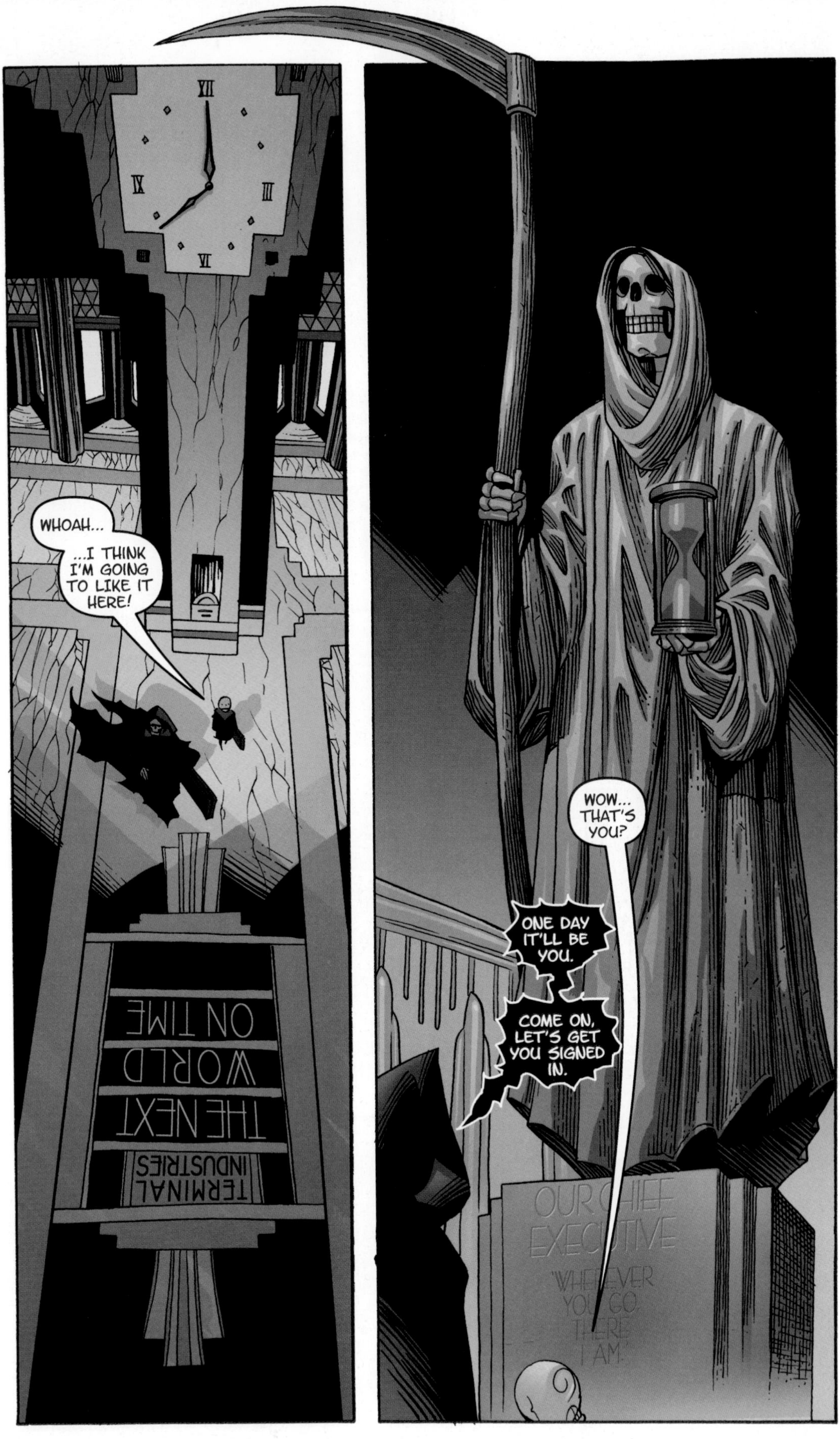

WHOAH...
...I THINK I'M GOING TO LIKE IT HERE!
TERMINAL INDUSTRIES
THE NEXT WORLD ON TIME
WOW... THAT'S YOU?
ONE DAY IT'LL BE YOU.
COME ON, LET'S GET YOU SIGNED IN.
OUR CHIEF EXECUTIVE
"WHEREVER YOU GO, THERE I AM."

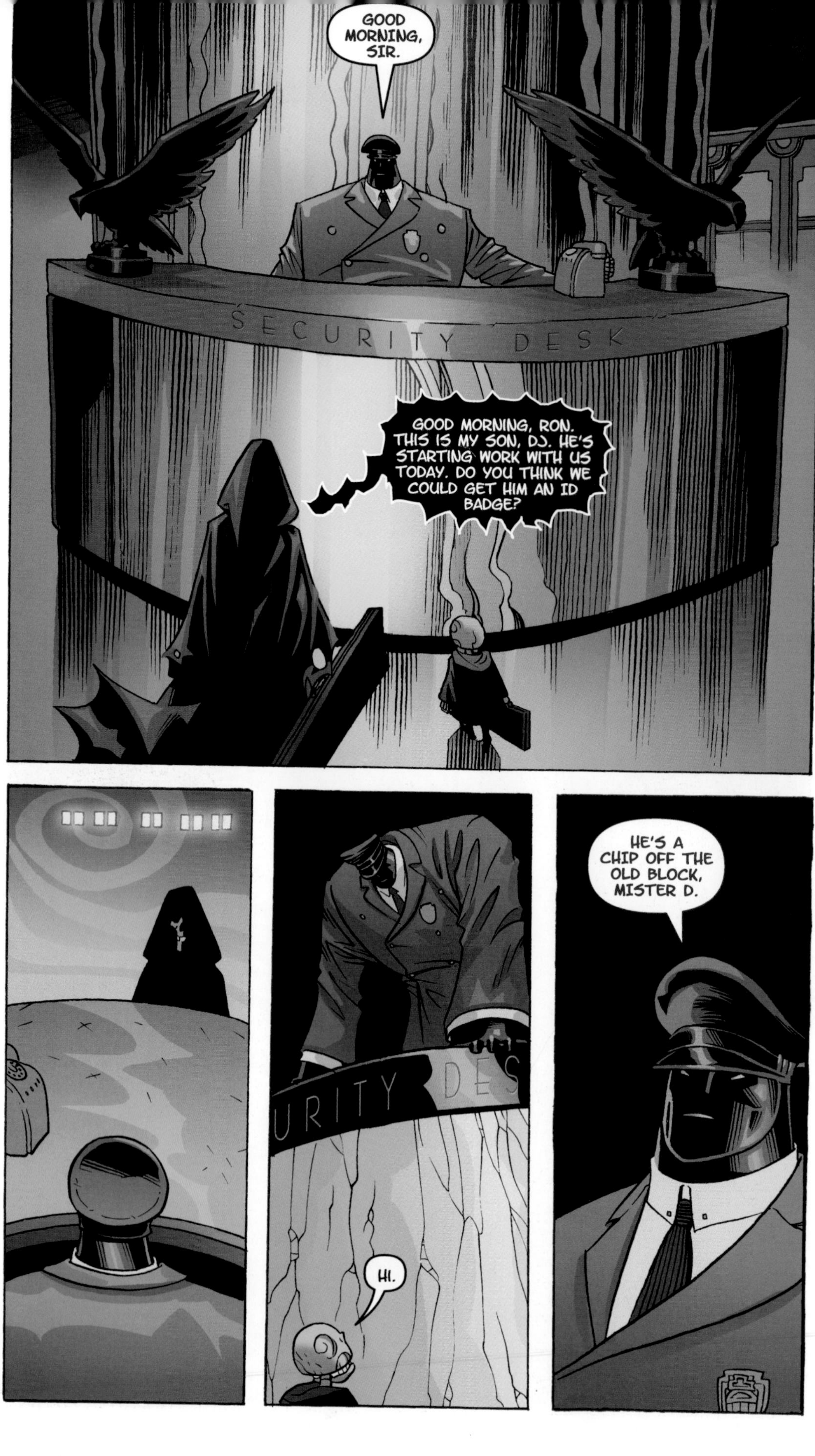
GOOD MORNING, SIR.
SECURITY DESK
GOOD MORNING, RON. THIS IS MY SON, DJ. HE'S STARTING WORK WITH US TODAY. DO YOU THINK WE COULD GET HIM AN ID BADGE?
URITY DES
HI.
HE'S A CHIP OFF THE OLD BLOCK, MISTER D.

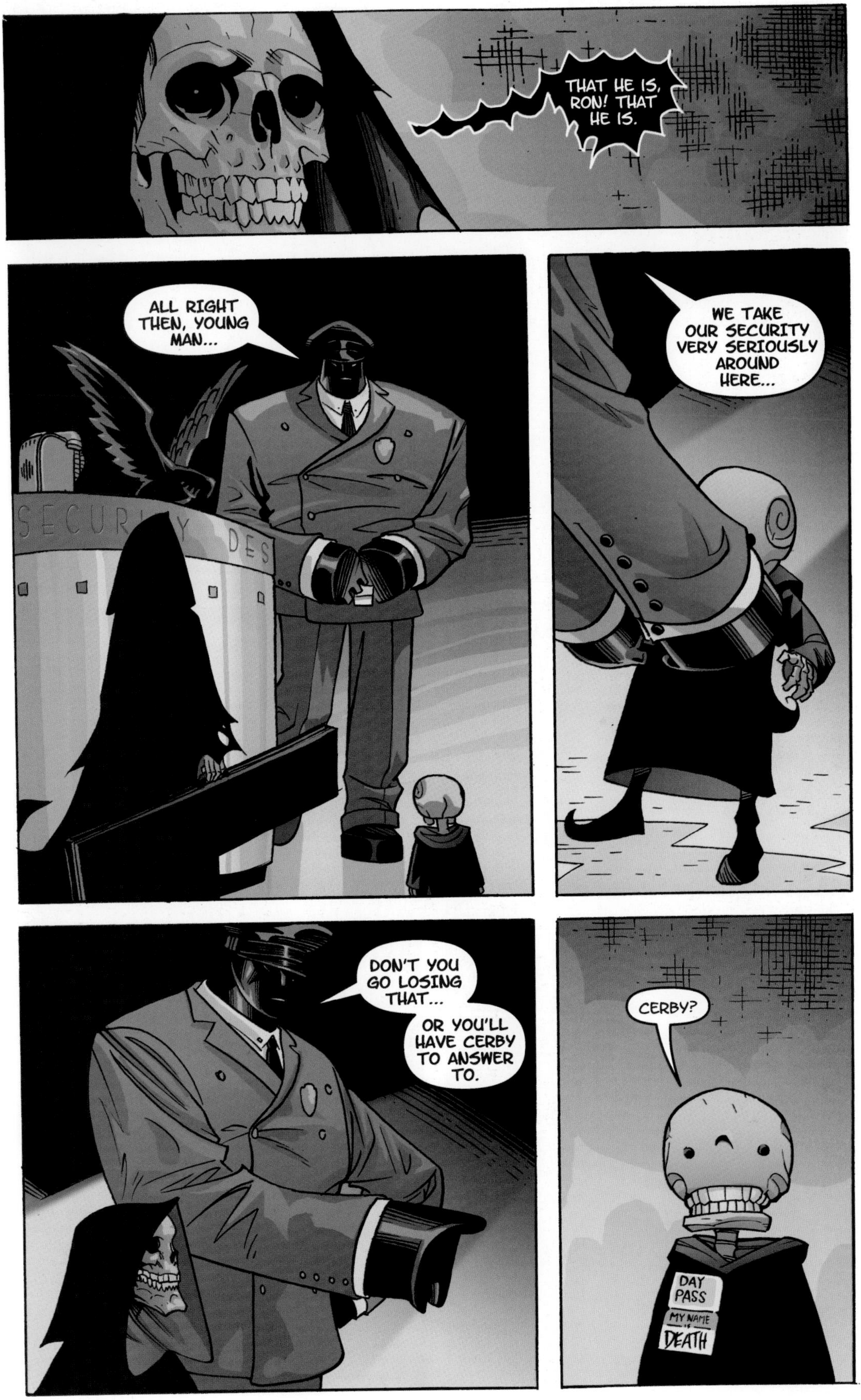
THAT HE IS, RON! THAT HE IS.
ALL RIGHT THEN, YOUNG MAN...
SECURITY DES
WE TAKE OUR SECURITY VERY SERIOUSLY AROUND HERE...
DON'T YOU GO LOSING THAT...
OR YOU'LL HAVE CERBY TO ANSWER TO.
CERBY?
DAY PASS
MY NAME IS
DEATH

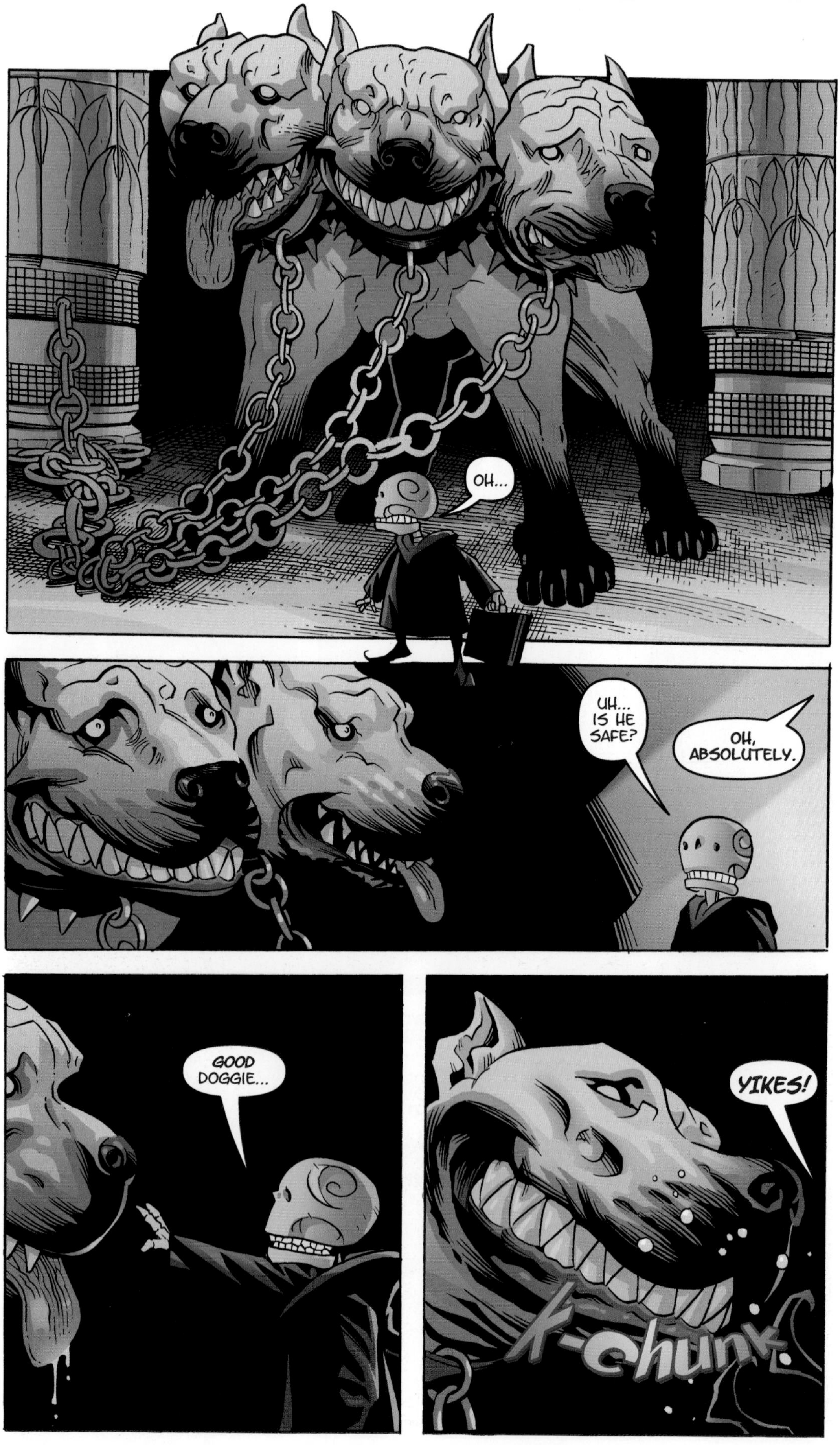
OH...
UH... IS HE SAFE?
OH, ABSOLUTELY.
GOOD DOGGIE...
YIKES!
K-CHUNK

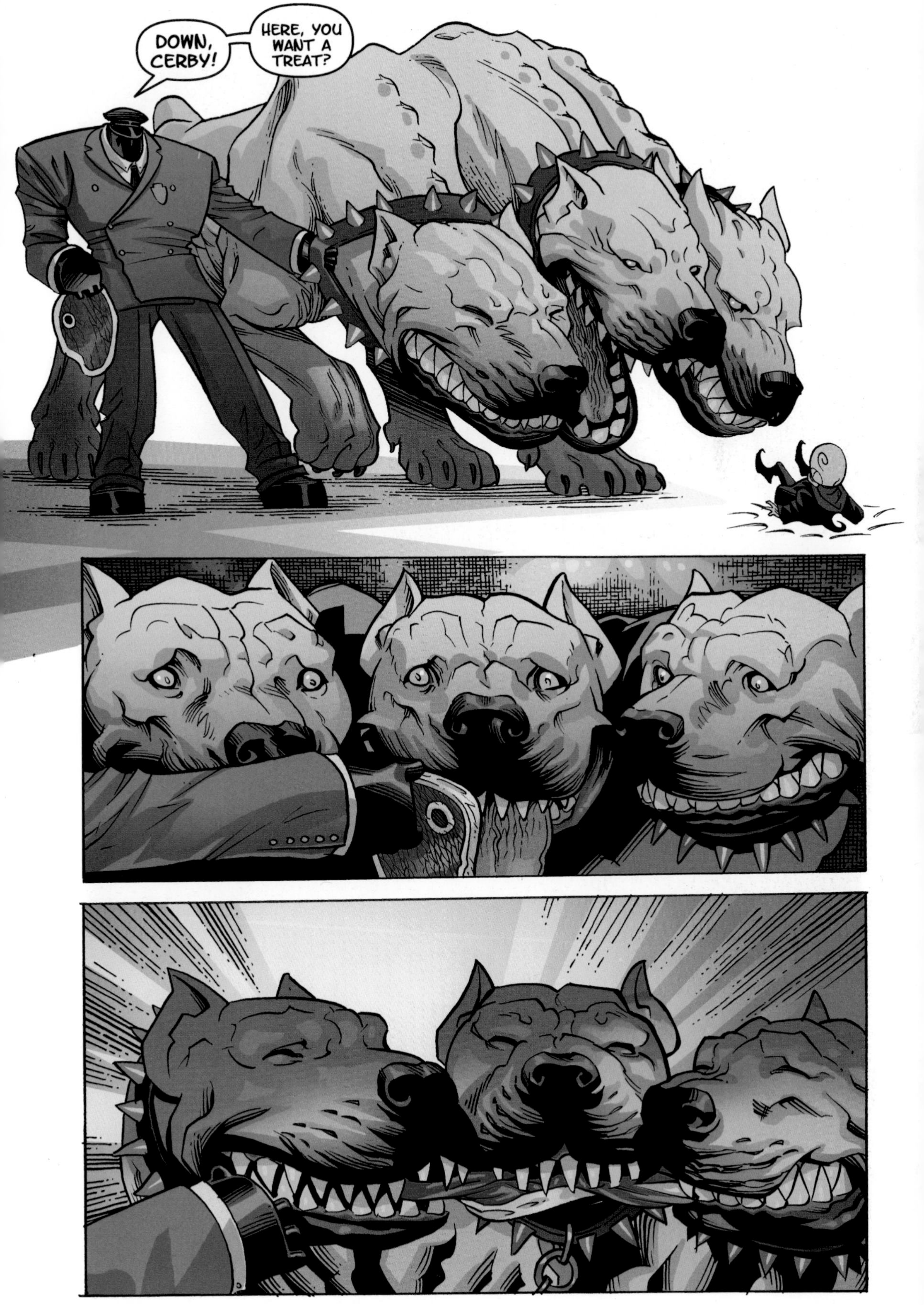
DOWN, CERBY!
HERE, YOU WANT A TREAT?

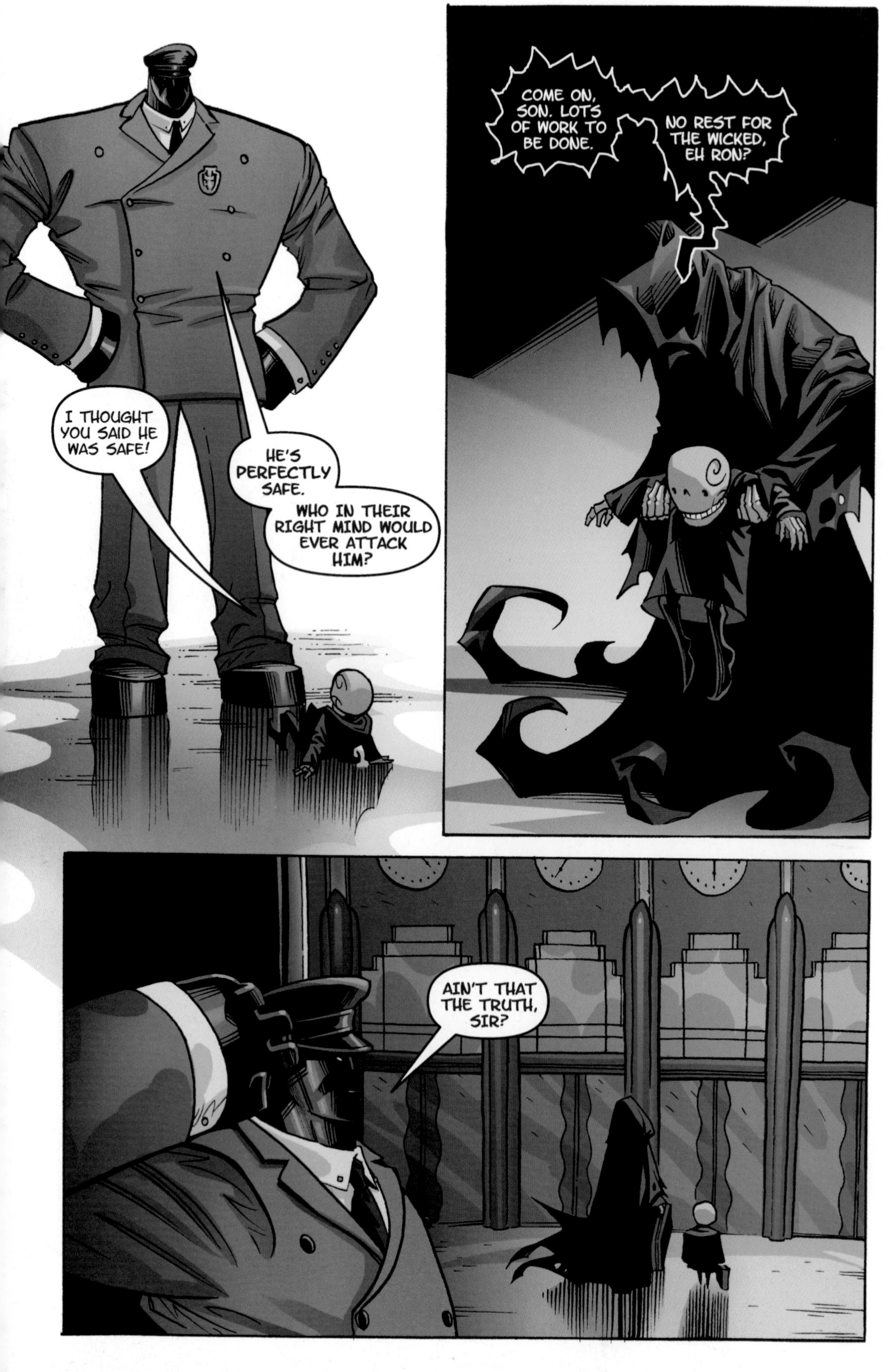
I THOUGHT YOU SAID HE WAS SAFE!
HE'S PERFECTLY SAFE.
WHO IN THEIR RIGHT MIND WOULD EVER ATTACK HIM?
COME ON, SON. LOTS OF WORK TO BE DONE.
NO REST FOR THE WICKED, EH RON?
AIN'T THAT THE TRUTH, SIR?

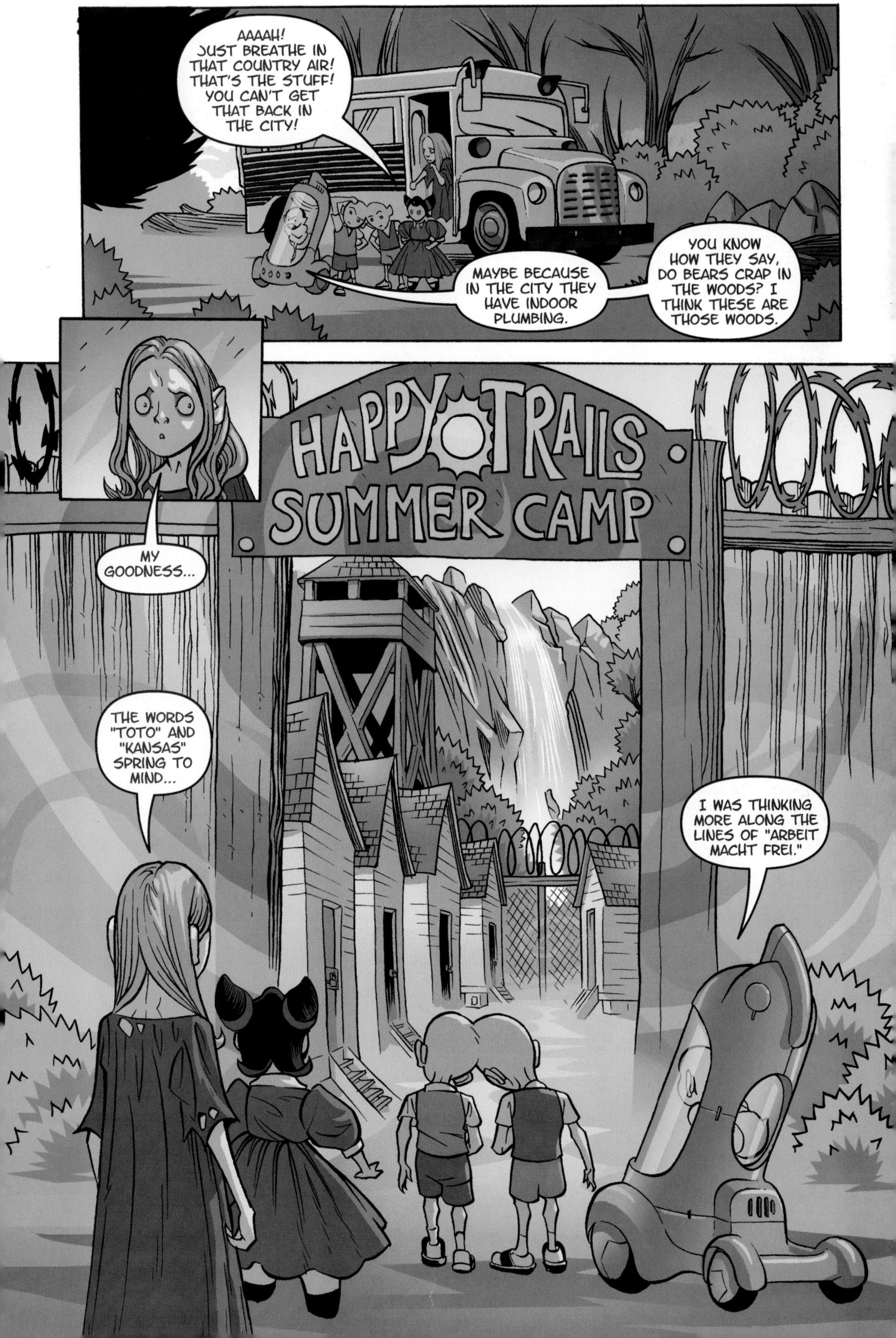
AAAAH! JUST BREATHE IN THAT COUNTRY AIR! THAT'S THE STUFF! YOU CAN'T GET THAT BACK IN THE CITY!
MAYBE BECAUSE IN THE CITY THEY HAVE INDOOR PLUMBING.
YOU KNOW HOW THEY SAY, DO BEARS CRAP IN THE WOODS? I THINK THESE ARE THOSE WOODS.
MY GOODNESS...
HAPPY TRAILS SUMMER CAMP
THE WORDS "TOTO" AND "KANSAS" SPRING TO MIND...
I WAS THINKING MORE ALONG THE LINES OF "ARBEIT MACHT FREI."

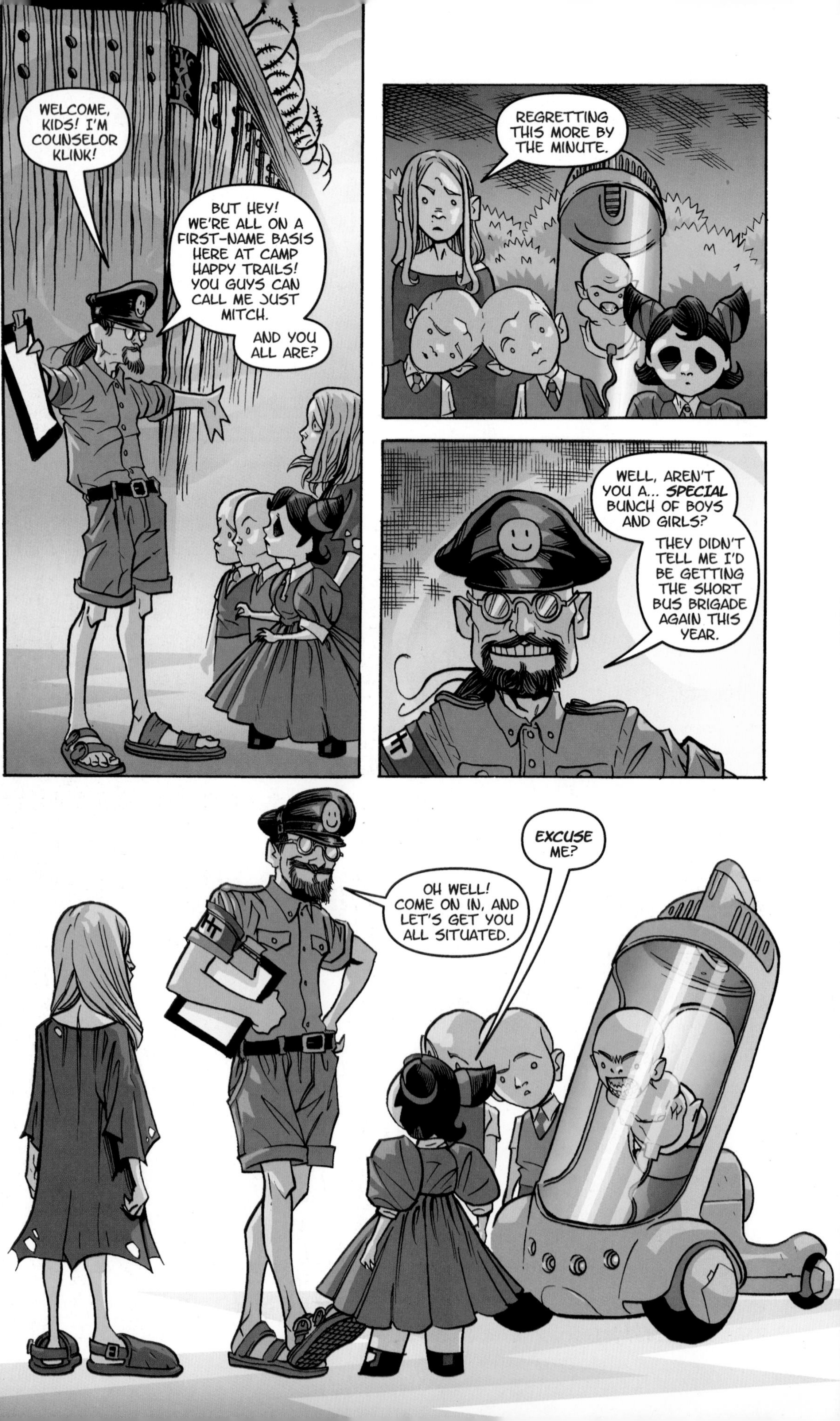
WELCOME, KIDS! I'M COUNSELOR KLINK!
BUT HEY! WE'RE ALL ON A FIRST-NAME BASIS HERE AT CAMP HAPPY TRAILS! YOU GUYS CAN CALL ME JUST MITCH.
AND YOU ALL ARE?
REGRETTING THIS MORE BY THE MINUTE.
WELL, AREN'T YOU A... SPECIAL BUNCH OF BOYS AND GIRLS?
THEY DIDN'T TELL ME I'D BE GETTING THE SHORT BUS BRIGADE AGAIN THIS YEAR.
OH WELL! COME ON IN, AND LET'S GET YOU ALL SITUATED.
EXCUSE ME?

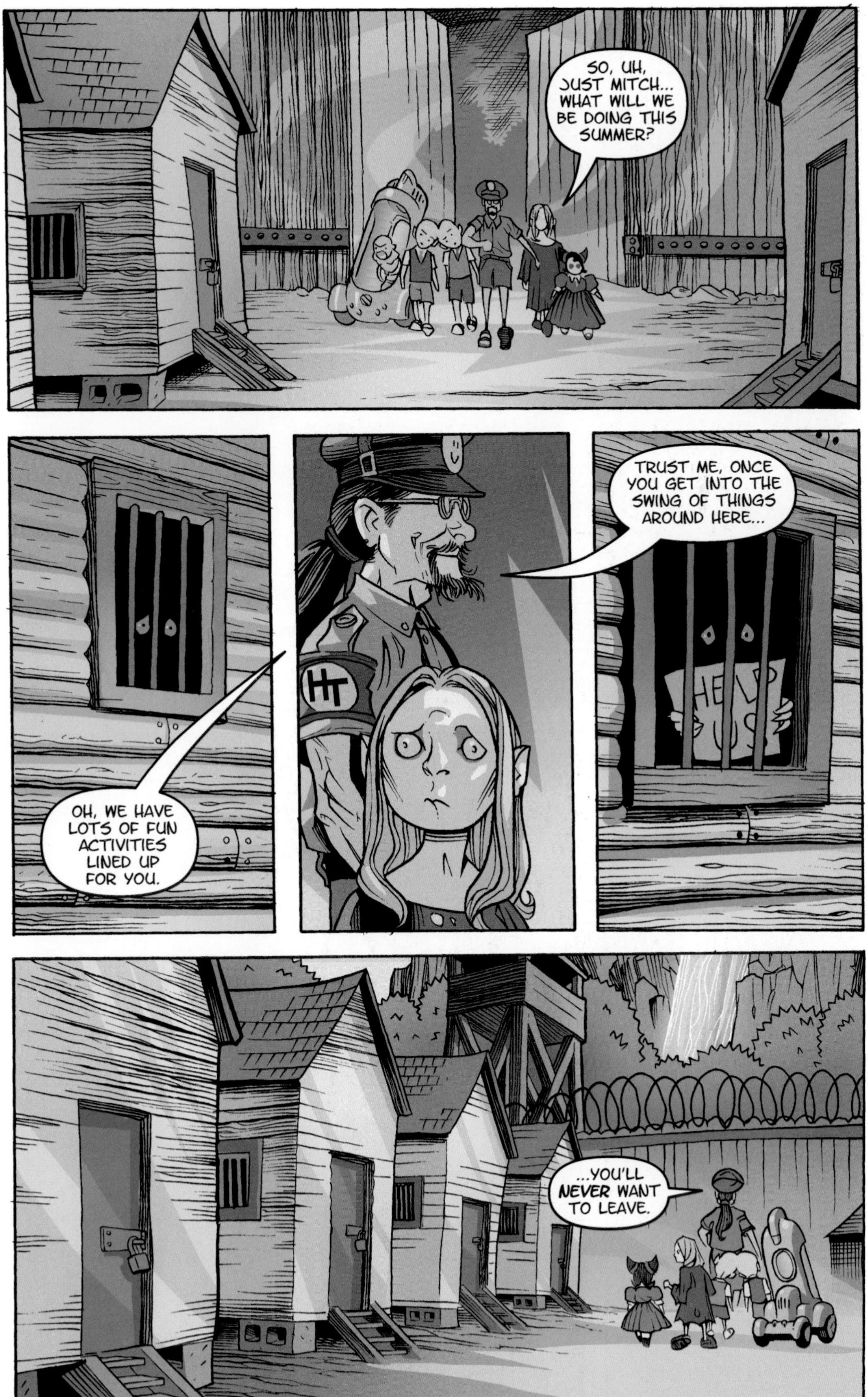
SO, UH, JUST MITCH... WHAT WILL WE BE DOING THIS SUMMER?
OH, WE HAVE LOTS OF FUN ACTIVITIES LINED UP FOR YOU.
TRUST ME, ONCE YOU GET INTO THE SWING OF THINGS AROUND HERE...
...YOU'LL **NEVER** WANT TO LEAVE.

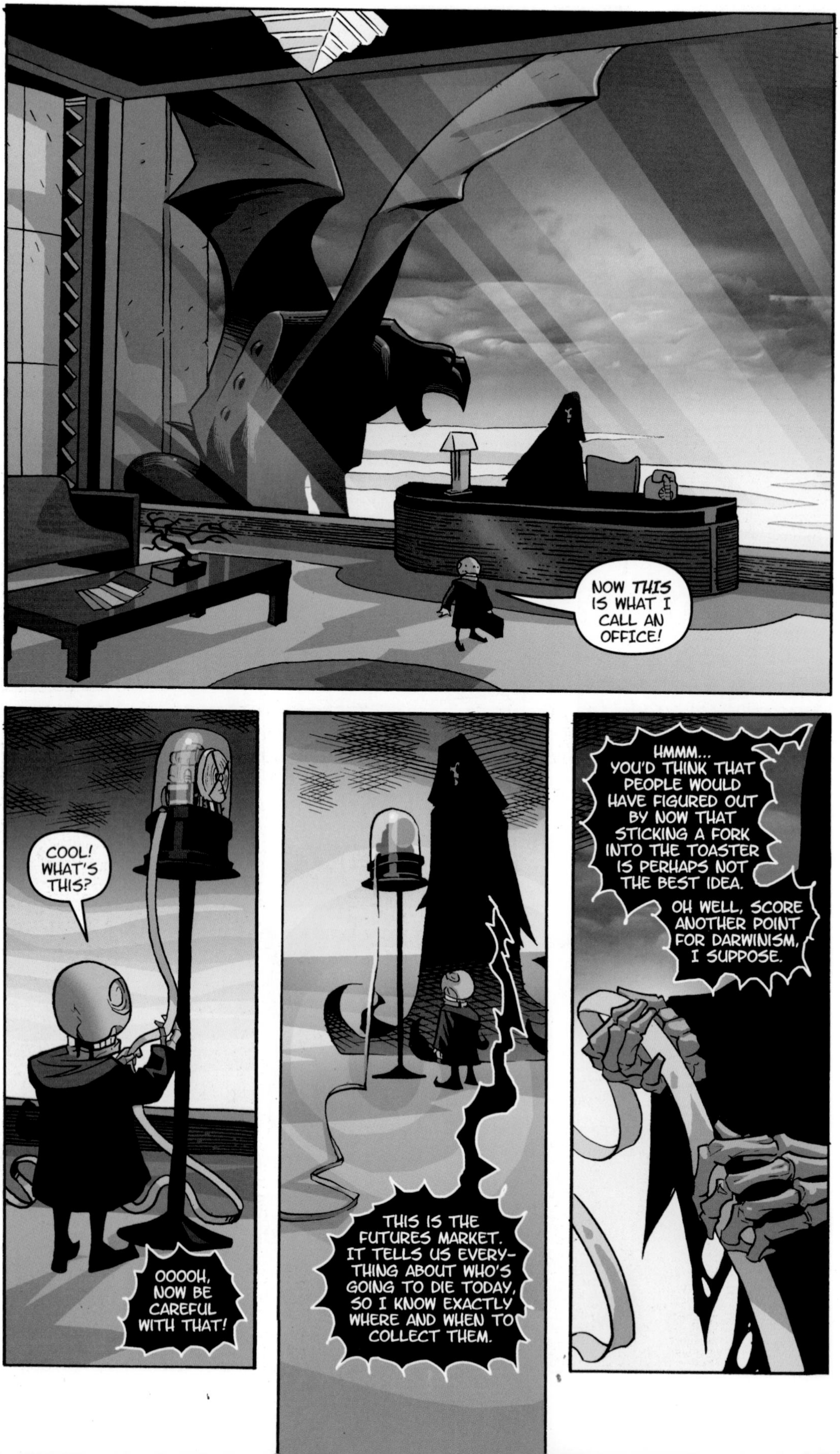
NOW THIS IS WHAT I CALL AN OFFICE!
COOL! WHAT'S THIS?
OOOOH, NOW BE CAREFUL WITH THAT!
THIS IS THE FUTURES MARKET. IT TELLS US EVERY-THING ABOUT WHO'S GOING TO DIE TODAY, SO I KNOW EXACTLY WHERE AND WHEN TO COLLECT THEM.
HMMM... YOU'D THINK THAT PEOPLE WOULD HAVE FIGURED OUT BY NOW THAT STICKING A FORK INTO THE TOASTER IS PERHAPS NOT THE BEST IDEA.
OH WELL, SCORE ANOTHER POINT FOR DARWINISM, I SUPPOSE.

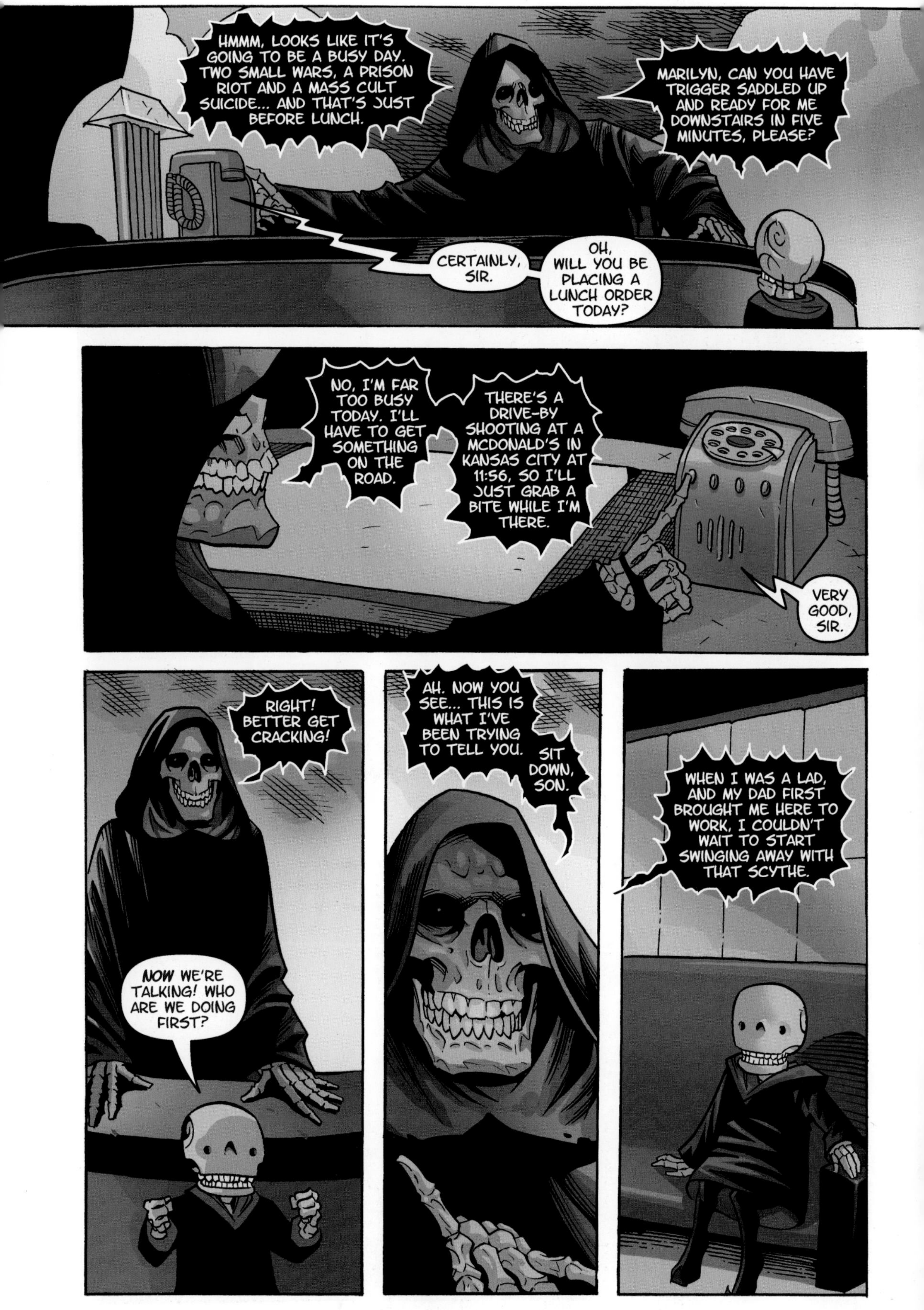
HMMM, LOOKS LIKE IT'S GOING TO BE A BUSY DAY. TWO SMALL WARS, A PRISON RIOT AND A MASS CULT SUICIDE... AND THAT'S JUST BEFORE LUNCH.
MARILYN, CAN YOU HAVE TRIGGER SADDLED UP AND READY FOR ME DOWNSTAIRS IN FIVE MINUTES, PLEASE?
CERTAINLY, SIR.
OH, WILL YOU BE PLACING A LUNCH ORDER TODAY?
NO, I'M FAR TOO BUSY TODAY. I'LL HAVE TO GET SOMETHING ON THE ROAD.
THERE'S A DRIVE-BY SHOOTING AT A MCDONALD'S IN KANSAS CITY AT 11:56, SO I'LL JUST GRAB A BITE WHILE I'M THERE.
VERY GOOD, SIR.
RIGHT! BETTER GET CRACKING!
NOW WE'RE TALKING! WHO ARE WE DOING FIRST?
AH. NOW YOU SEE... THIS IS WHAT I'VE BEEN TRYING TO TELL YOU.
SIT DOWN, SON.
WHEN I WAS A LAD, AND MY DAD FIRST BROUGHT ME HERE TO WORK, I COULDN'T WAIT TO START SWINGING AWAY WITH THAT SCYTHE.

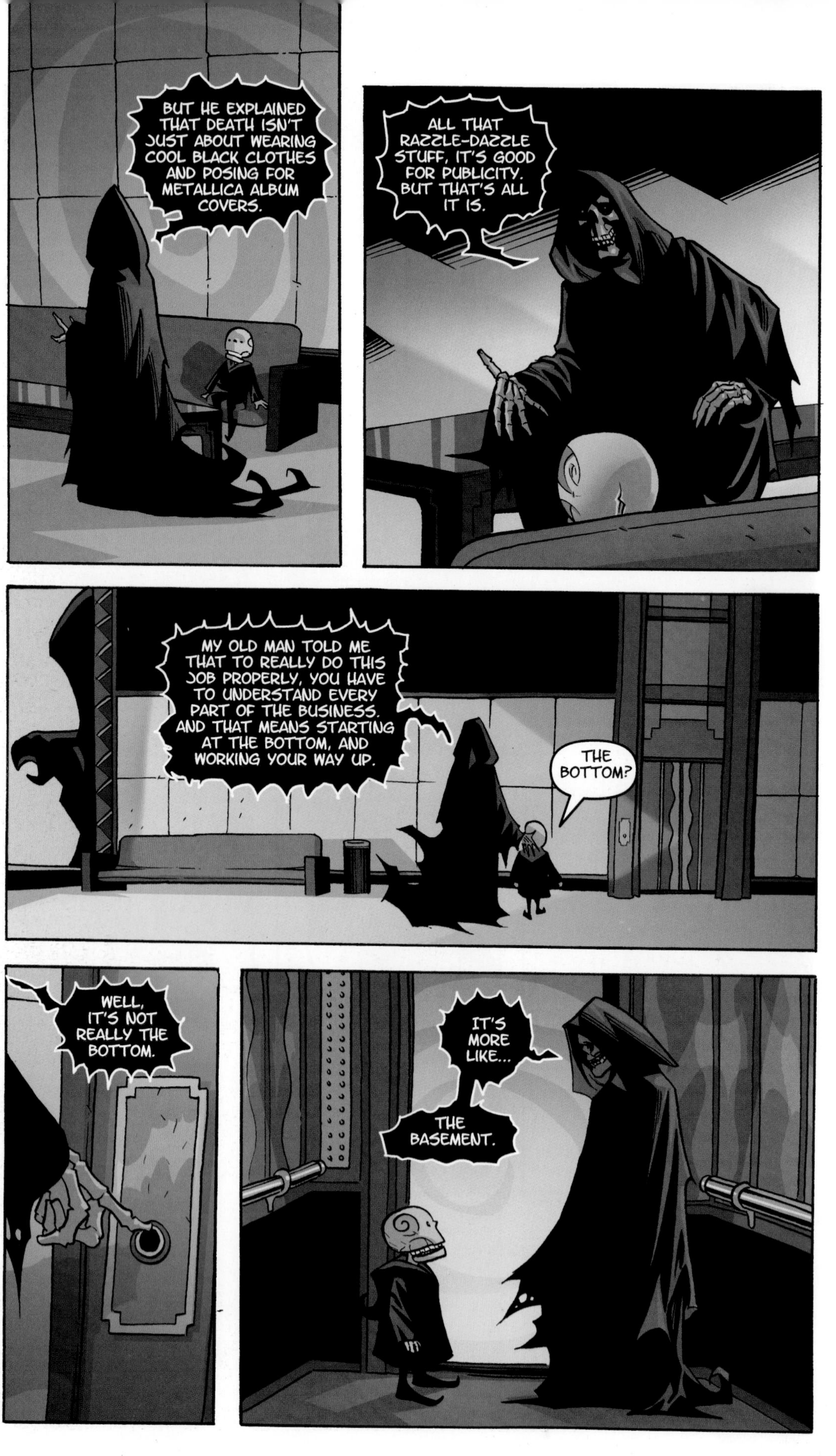
BUT HE EXPLAINED THAT DEATH ISN'T JUST ABOUT WEARING COOL BLACK CLOTHES AND POSING FOR METALLICA ALBUM COVERS.
ALL THAT RAZZLE-DAZZLE STUFF, IT'S GOOD FOR PUBLICITY. BUT THAT'S ALL IT IS.
MY OLD MAN TOLD ME THAT TO REALLY DO THIS JOB PROPERLY, YOU HAVE TO UNDERSTAND EVERY PART OF THE BUSINESS. AND THAT MEANS STARTING AT THE BOTTOM, AND WORKING YOUR WAY UP.
THE BOTTOM?
WELL, IT'S NOT REALLY THE BOTTOM.
IT'S MORE LIKE...
THE BASEMENT.

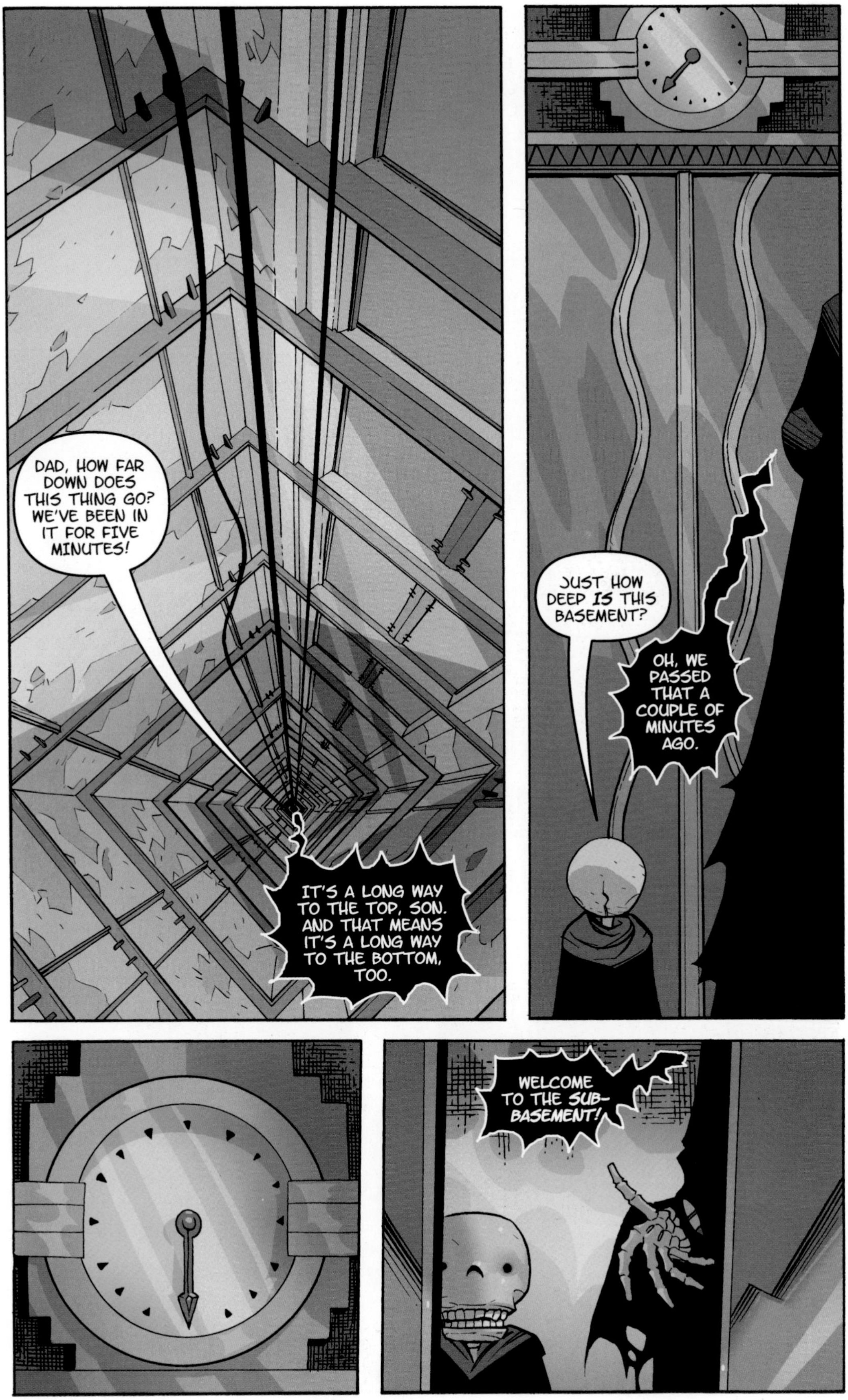
DAD, HOW FAR DOWN DOES THIS THING GO? WE'VE BEEN IN IT FOR FIVE MINUTES!
IT'S A LONG WAY TO THE TOP, SON. AND THAT MEANS IT'S A LONG WAY TO THE BOTTOM, TOO.
JUST HOW DEEP IS THIS BASEMENT?
OH, WE PASSED THAT A COUPLE OF MINUTES AGO.
WELCOME TO THE SUB-BASEMENT!

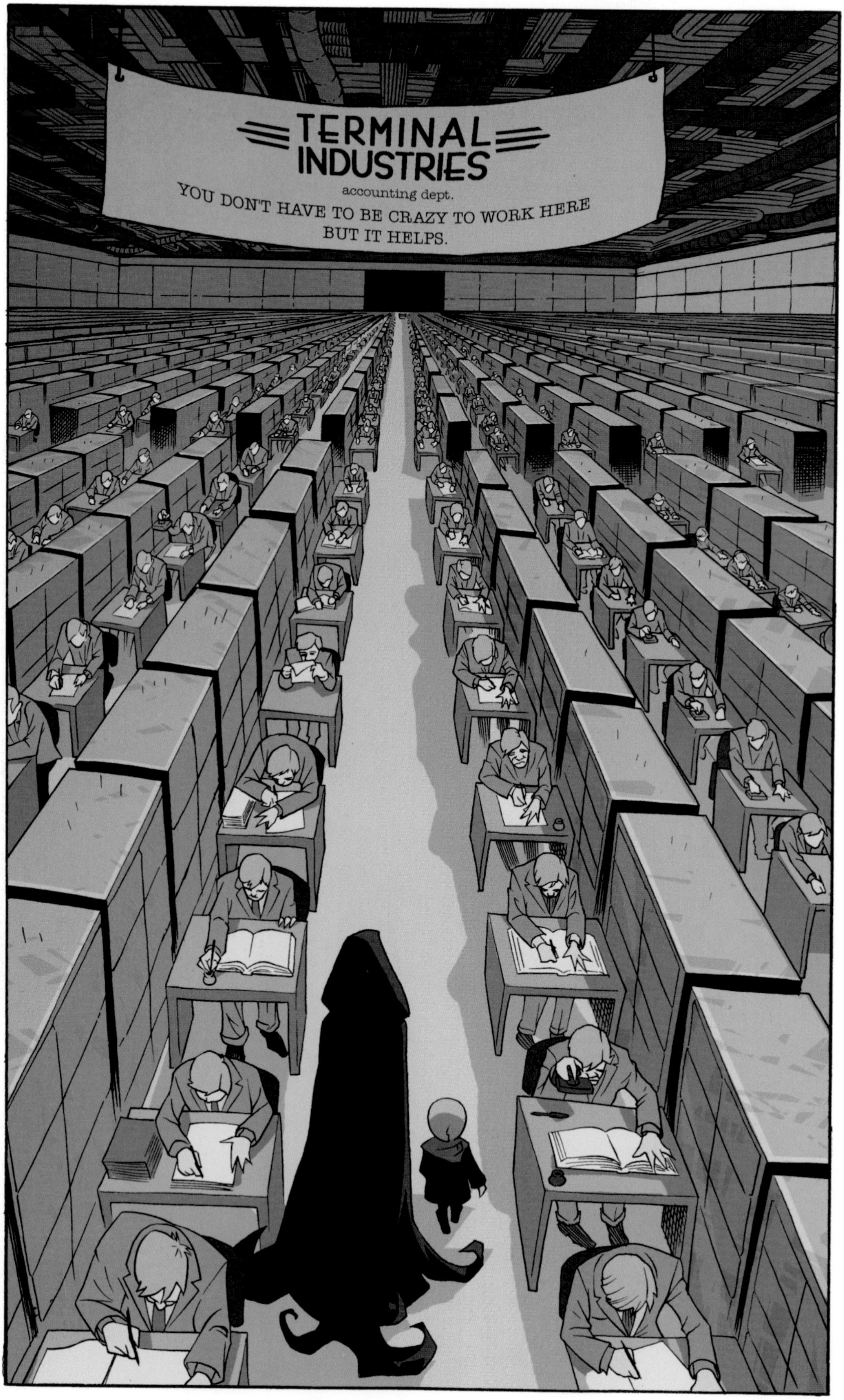
TERMINAL INDUSTRIES
accounting dept.
YOU DON'T HAVE TO BE CRAZY TO WORK HERE
BUT IT HELPS.

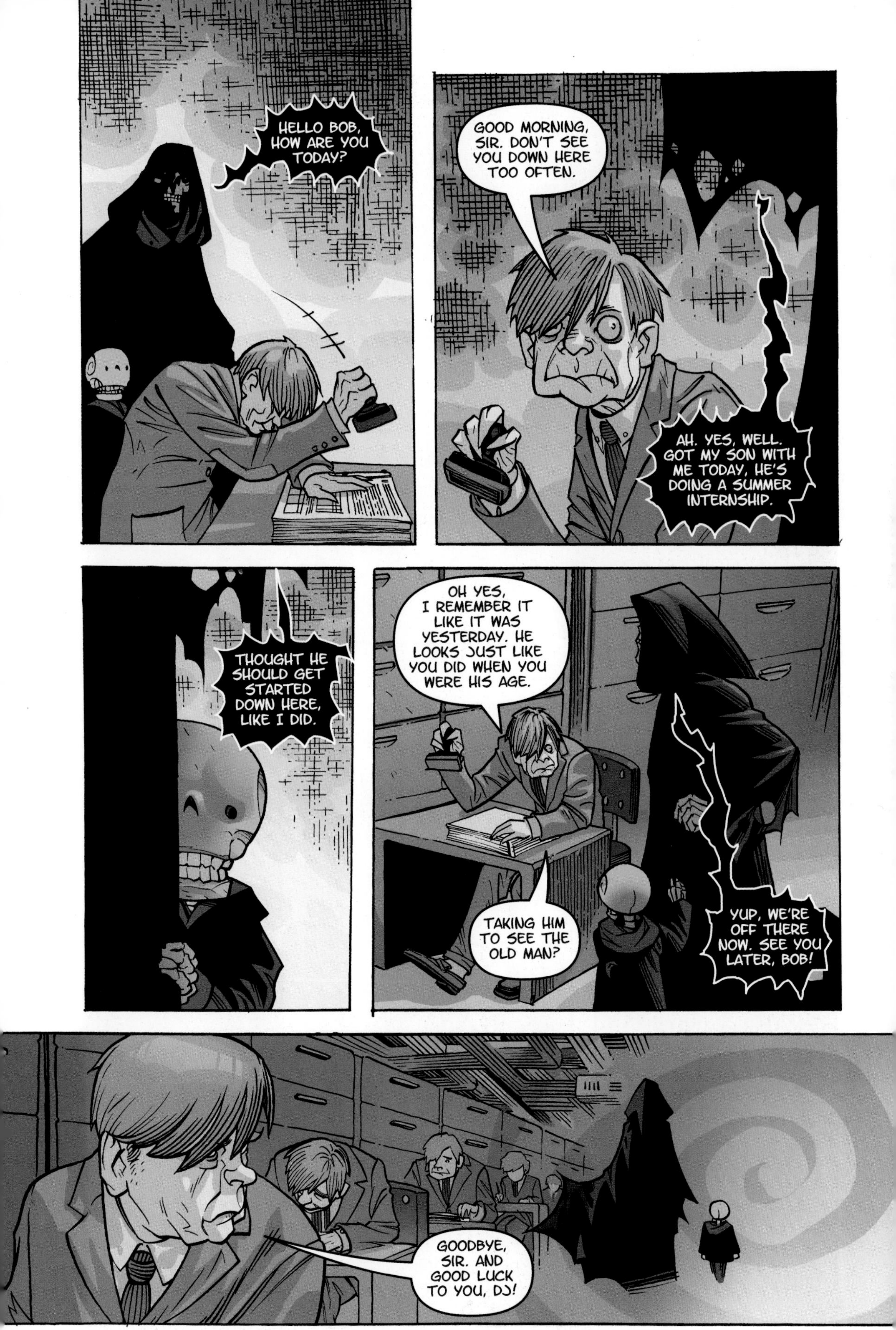
HELLO BOB, HOW ARE YOU TODAY?
GOOD MORNING, SIR. DON'T SEE YOU DOWN HERE TOO OFTEN.
AH. YES, WELL. GOT MY SON WITH ME TODAY, HE'S DOING A SUMMER INTERNSHIP.
THOUGHT HE SHOULD GET STARTED DOWN HERE, LIKE I DID.
OH YES, I REMEMBER IT LIKE IT WAS YESTERDAY. HE LOOKS JUST LIKE YOU DID WHEN YOU WERE HIS AGE.
TAKING HIM TO SEE THE OLD MAN?
YUP, WE'RE OFF THERE NOW. SEE YOU LATER, BOB!
GOODBYE, SIR. AND GOOD LUCK TO YOU, DJ!

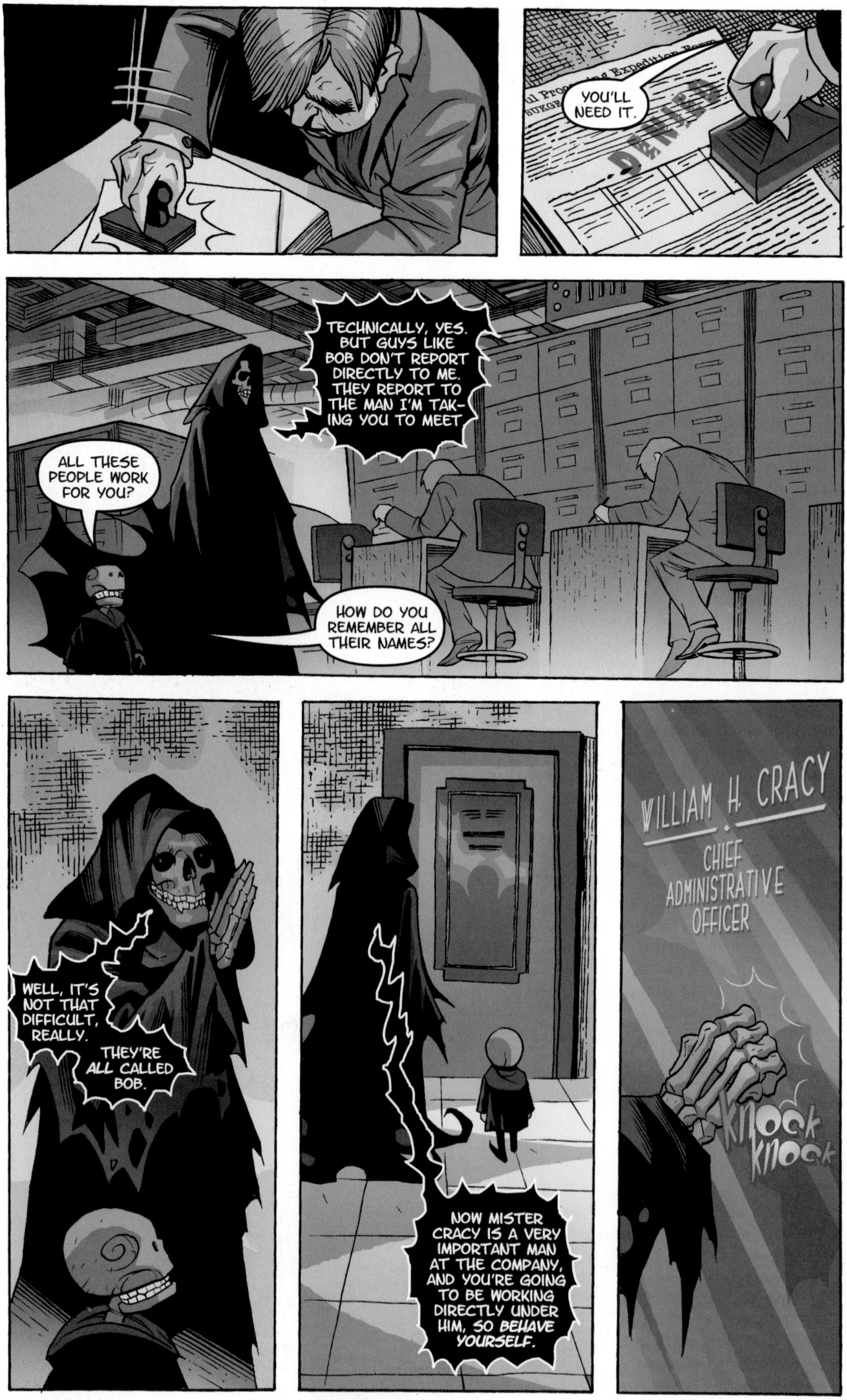
YOU'LL NEED IT.
ALL THESE PEOPLE WORK FOR YOU?
TECHNICALLY, YES. BUT GUYS LIKE BOB DON'T REPORT DIRECTLY TO ME. THEY REPORT TO THE MAN I'M TAKING YOU TO MEET
HOW DO YOU REMEMBER ALL THEIR NAMES?
WELL, IT'S NOT THAT DIFFICULT, REALLY.
THEY'RE ALL CALLED BOB.
NOW MISTER CRACY IS A VERY IMPORTANT MAN AT THE COMPANY, AND YOU'RE GOING TO BE WORKING DIRECTLY UNDER HIM, SO BEHAVE YOURSELF.
WILLIAM H. CRACY
CHIEF ADMINISTRATIVE OFFICER
knock knock

SKRITCH

SKRITCH
SKRITCH

COME.

SKRITCH
SKRITCH

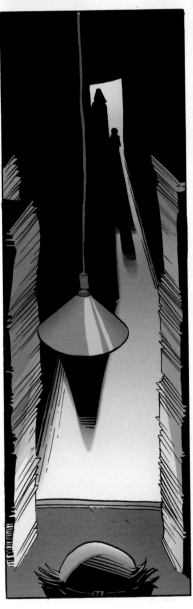

AHEM
BILL, THIS
IS MY—

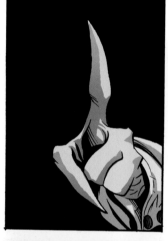

AH! NEW BLOOD, I SEE.

BILL, I'D LIKE YOU TO MEET YOUR NEW DEPUTY ASSISTANT CLERK. HE'LL BE INTERNING WITH THE FIRM OVER THE SUMMER, GETTING A FEEL FOR THE FAMILY BUSINESS.

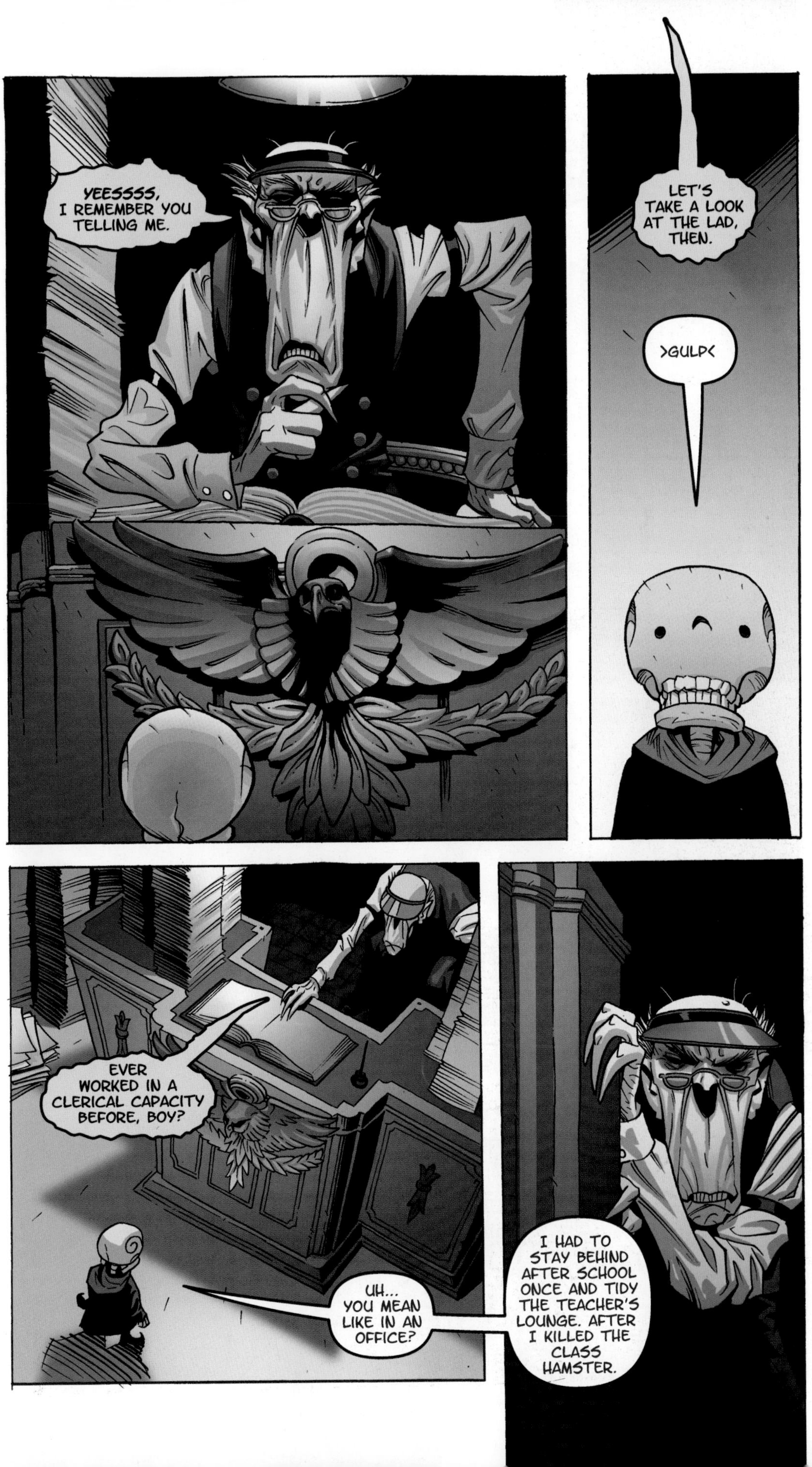
YEESSSS, I REMEMBER YOU TELLING ME.
LET'S TAKE A LOOK AT THE LAD, THEN.
>GULP<
EVER WORKED IN A CLERICAL CAPACITY BEFORE, BOY?
UH... YOU MEAN LIKE IN AN OFFICE?
I HAD TO STAY BEHIND AFTER SCHOOL ONCE AND TIDY THE TEACHER'S LOUNGE. AFTER I KILLED THE CLASS HAMSTER.

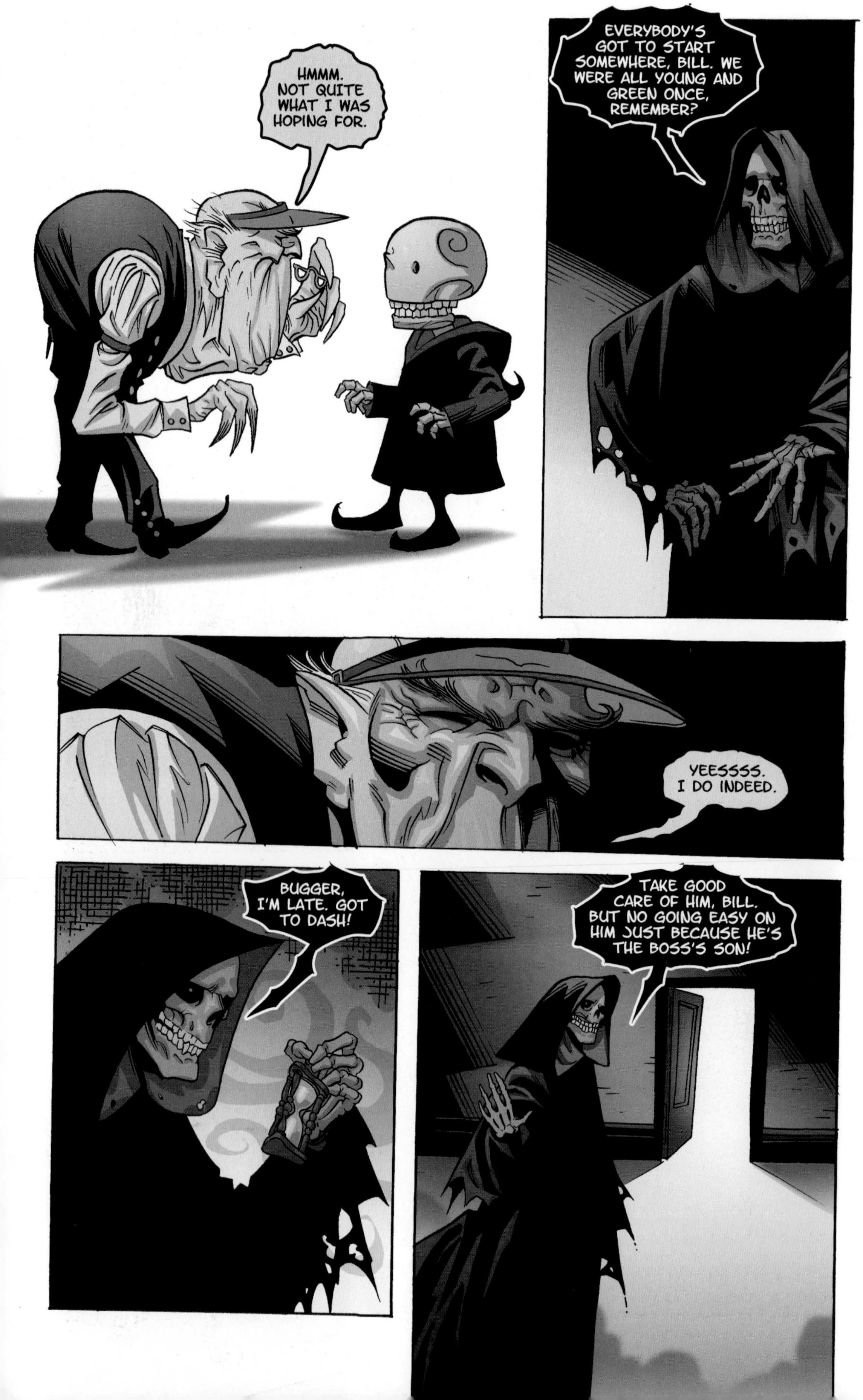
HMMM. NOT QUITE WHAT I WAS HOPING FOR.
EVERYBODY'S GOT TO START SOMEWHERE, BILL. WE WERE ALL YOUNG AND GREEN ONCE, REMEMBER?
YEESSSS. I DO INDEED.
BUGGER, I'M LATE. GOT TO DASH!
TAKE GOOD CARE OF HIM, BILL. BUT NO GOING EASY ON HIM JUST BECAUSE HE'S THE BOSS'S SON!

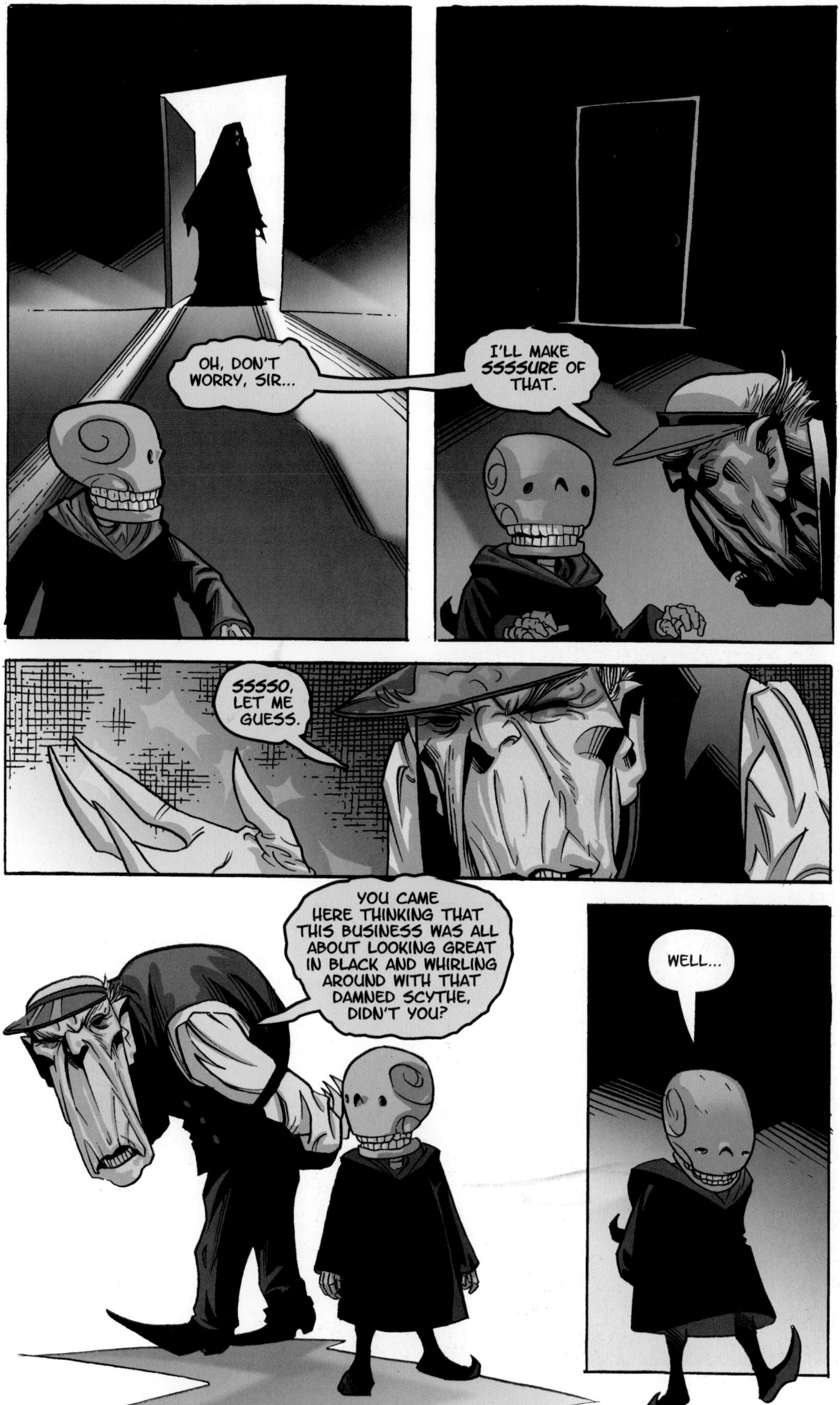
OH, DON'T WORRY, SIR...
I'LL MAKE SSSSURE OF THAT.
SSSSO, LET ME GUESS.
YOU CAME HERE THINKING THAT THIS BUSINESS WAS ALL ABOUT LOOKING GREAT IN BLACK AND WHIRLING AROUND WITH THAT DAMNED SCYTHE, DIDN'T YOU?
WELL...

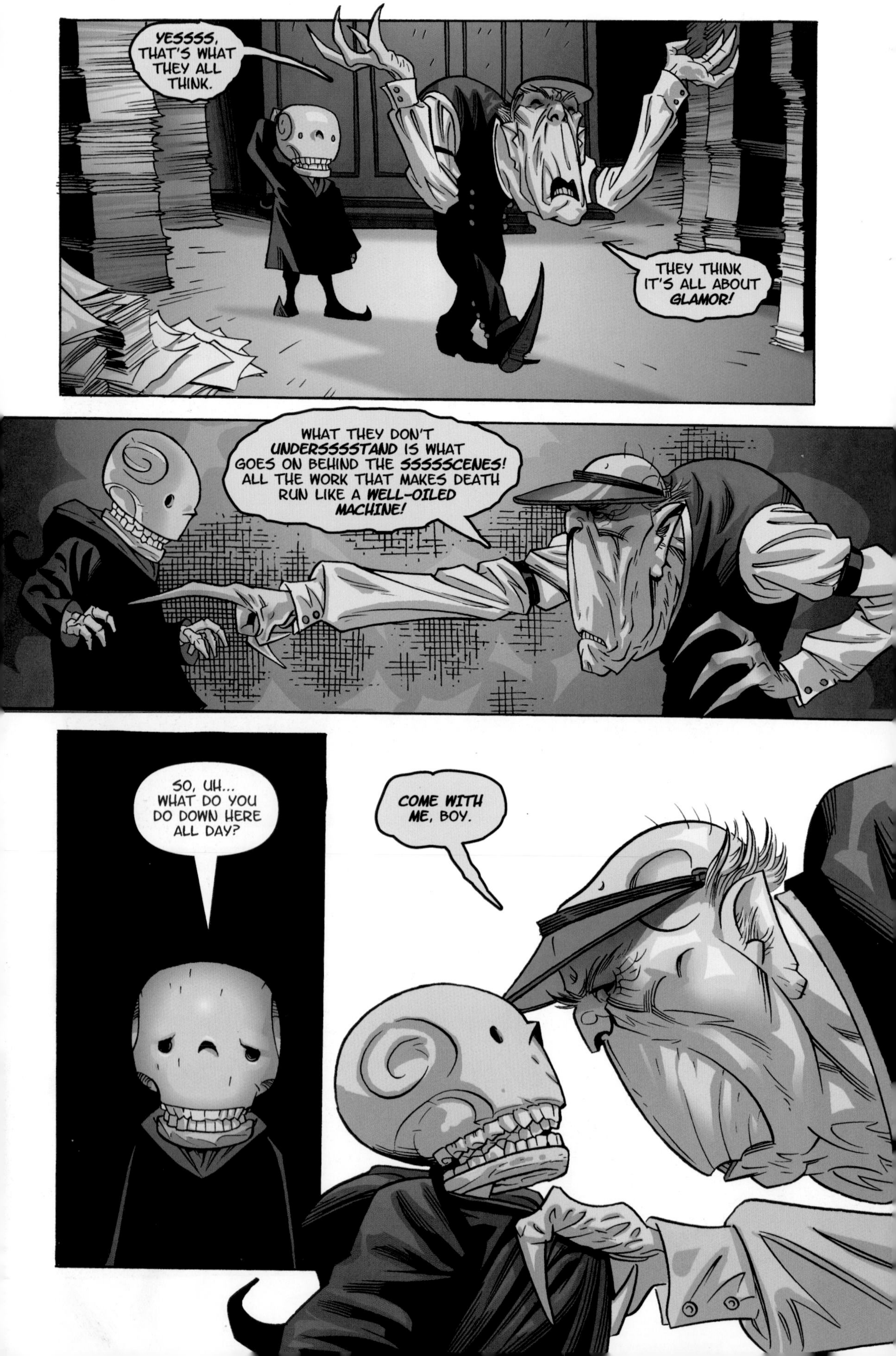
YESSSS, THAT'S WHAT THEY ALL THINK.
THEY THINK IT'S ALL ABOUT GLAMOR!
WHAT THEY DON'T UNDERSSSSTAND IS WHAT GOES ON BEHIND THE SSSSSCENES! ALL THE WORK THAT MAKES DEATH RUN LIKE A WELL-OILED MACHINE!
SO, UH... WHAT DO YOU DO DOWN HERE ALL DAY?
COME WITH ME, BOY.

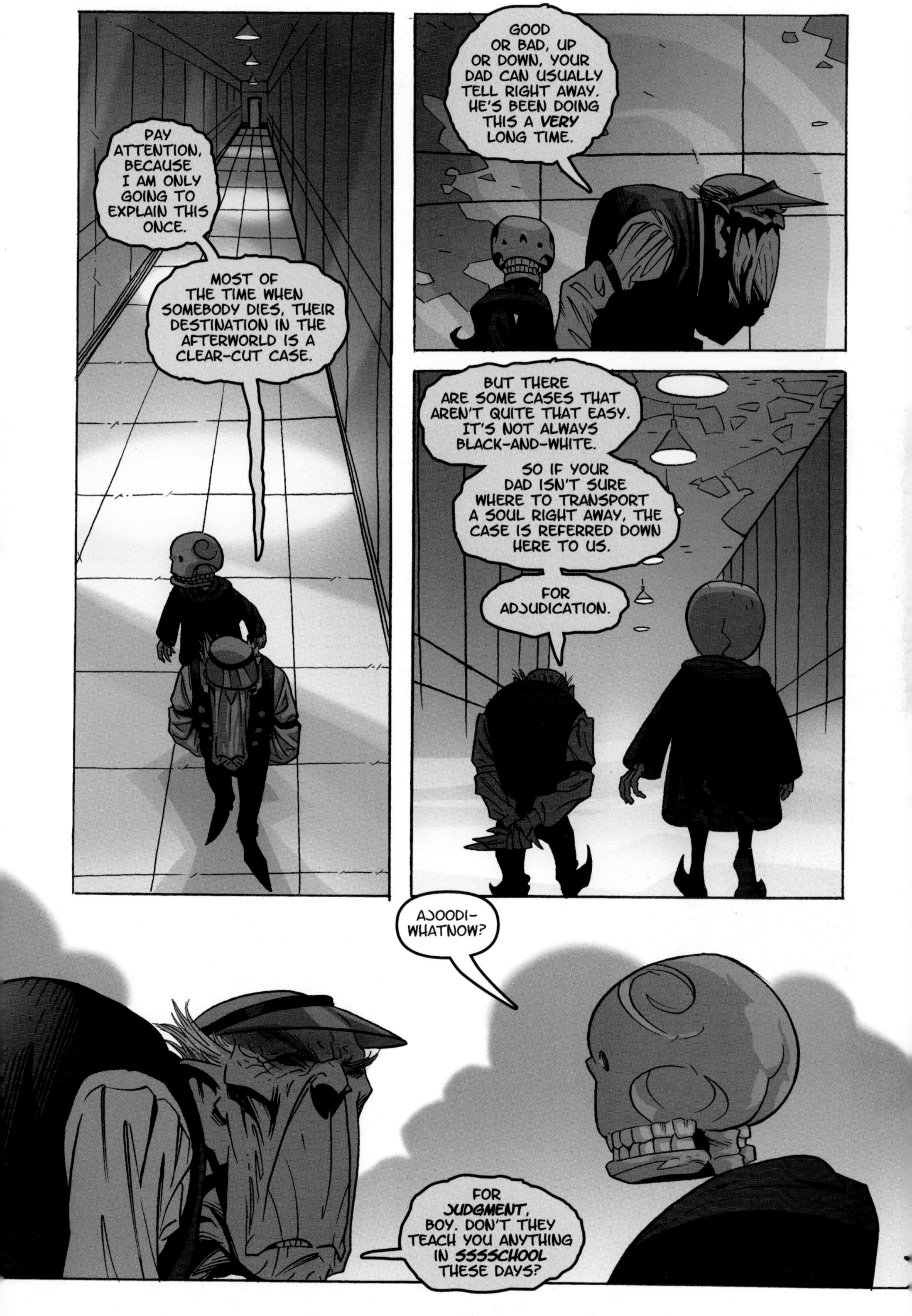
PAY ATTENTION, BECAUSE I AM ONLY GOING TO EXPLAIN THIS ONCE.
MOST OF THE TIME WHEN SOMEBODY DIES, THEIR DESTINATION IN THE AFTERWORLD IS A CLEAR-CUT CASE.
GOOD OR BAD, UP OR DOWN, YOUR DAD CAN USUALLY TELL RIGHT AWAY. HE'S BEEN DOING THIS A VERY LONG TIME.
BUT THERE ARE SOME CASES THAT AREN'T QUITE THAT EASY. IT'S NOT ALWAYS BLACK-AND-WHITE.
SO IF YOUR DAD ISN'T SURE WHERE TO TRANSPORT A SOUL RIGHT AWAY, THE CASE IS REFERRED DOWN HERE TO US.
FOR ADJUDICATION.
AJOODI-WHATNOW?
FOR JUDGMENT, BOY. DON'T THEY TEACH YOU ANYTHING IN SSSSCHOOL THESE DAYS?

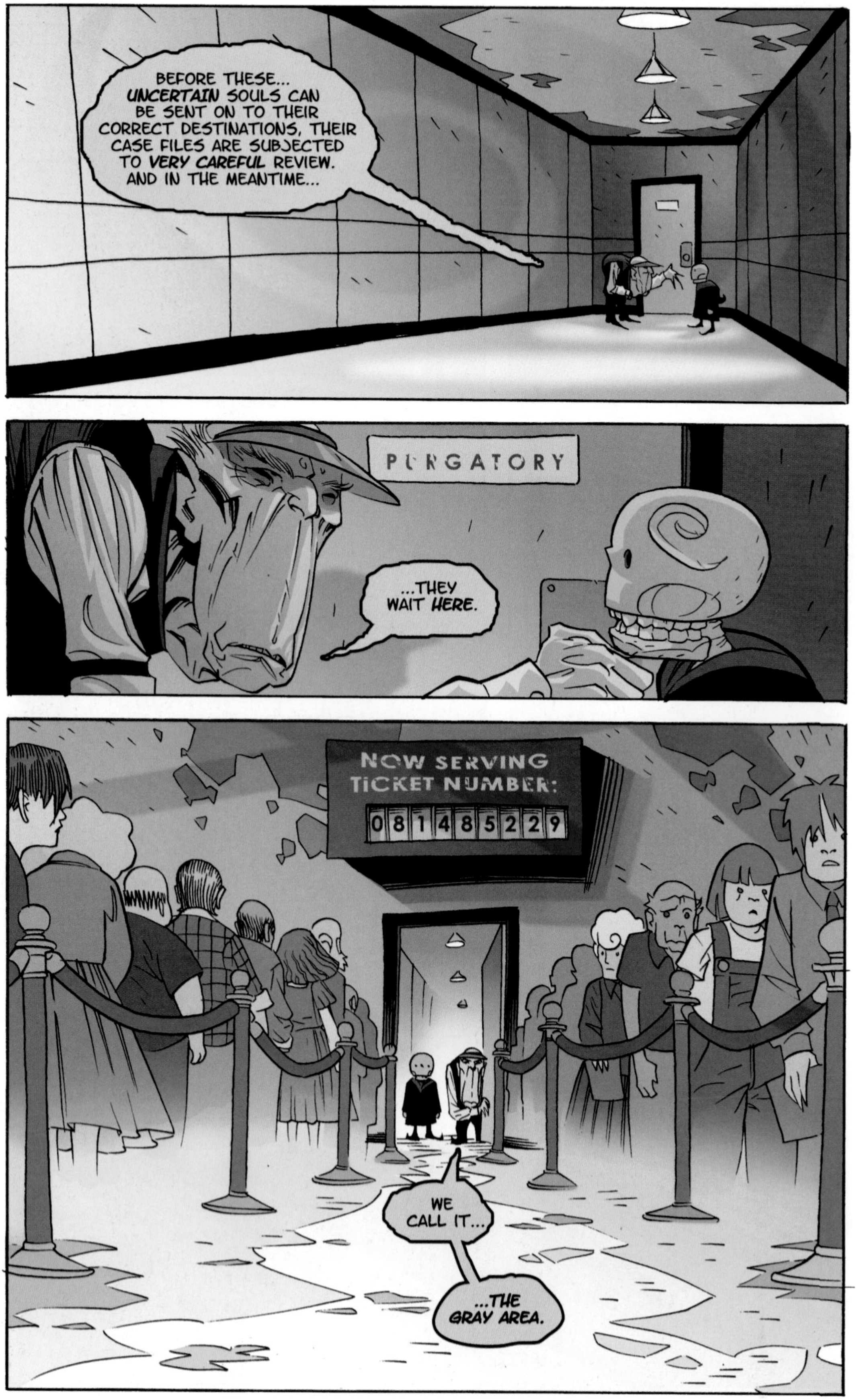
BEFORE THESE... UNCERTAIN SOULS CAN BE SENT ON TO THEIR CORRECT DESTINATIONS, THEIR CASE FILES ARE SUBJECTED TO VERY CAREFUL REVIEW. AND IN THE MEANTIME...
PURGATORY
...THEY WAIT HERE.
NOW SERVING TICKET NUMBER:
0814852229
WE CALL IT...
...THE GRAY AREA.

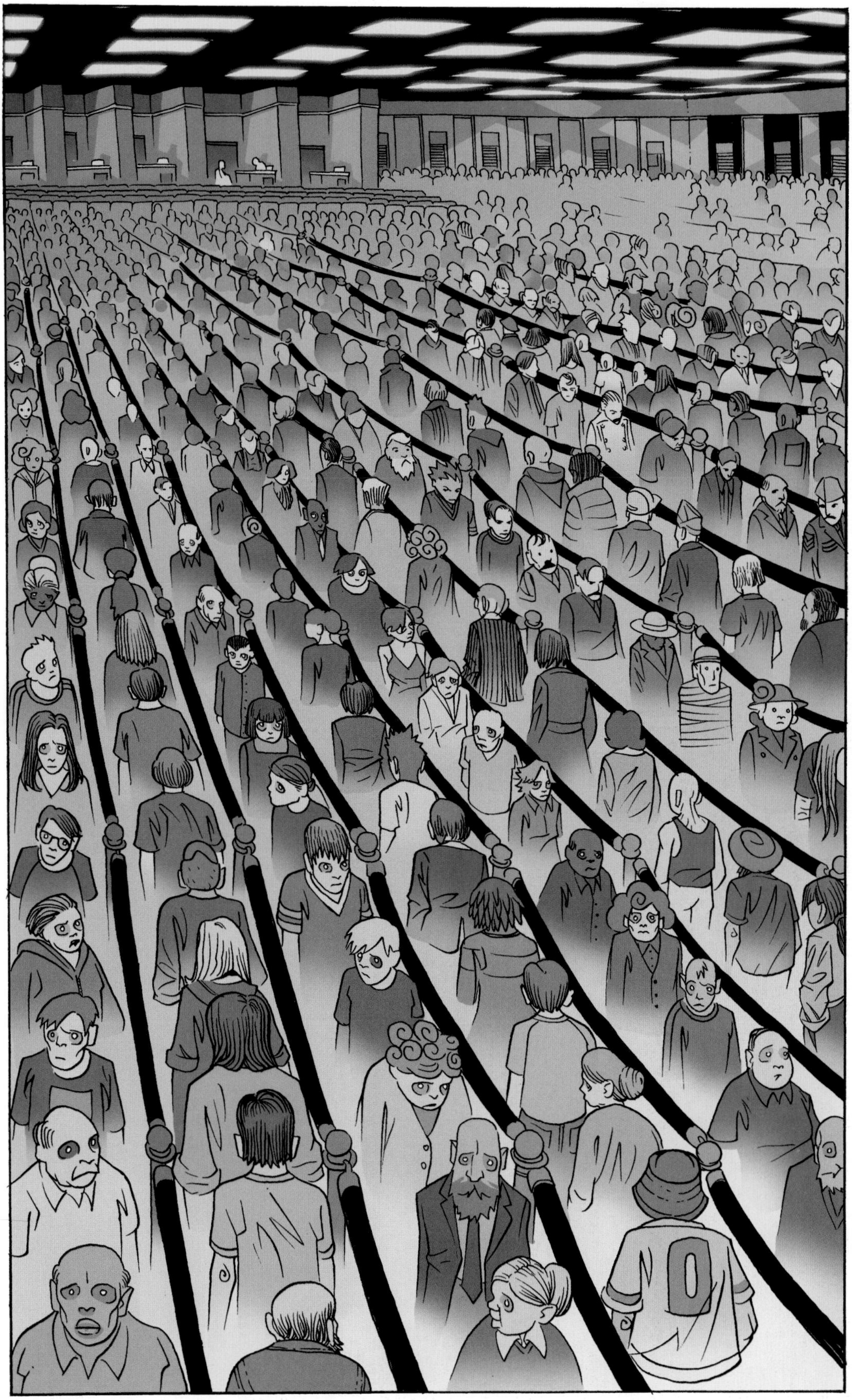
0

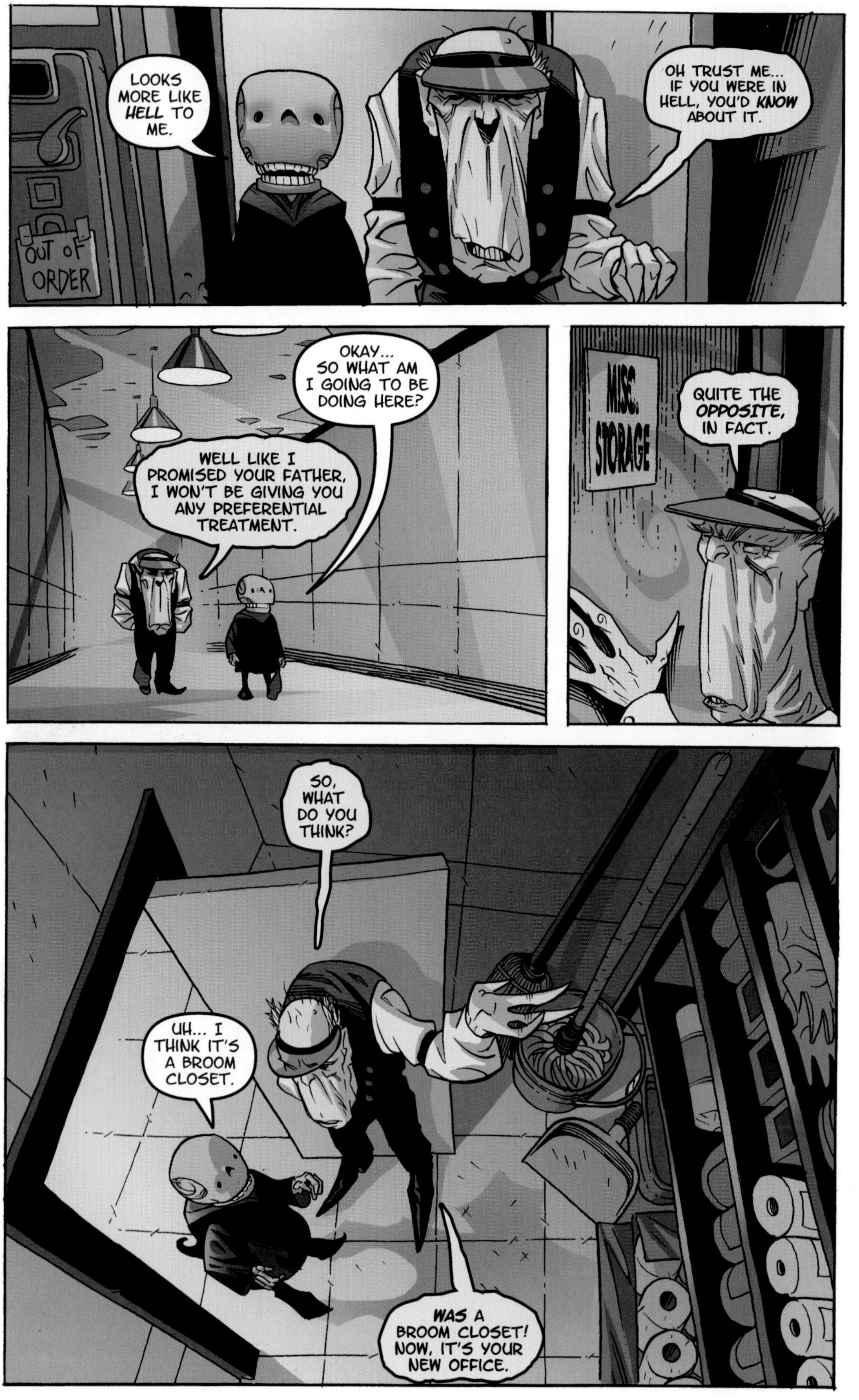
OUT OF ORDER
LOOKS MORE LIKE HELL TO ME.
OH TRUST ME... IF YOU WERE IN HELL, YOU'D KNOW ABOUT IT.
OKAY... SO WHAT AM I GOING TO BE DOING HERE?
WELL LIKE I PROMISED YOUR FATHER, I WON'T BE GIVING YOU ANY PREFERENTIAL TREATMENT.
MISC. STORAGE
QUITE THE OPPOSITE, IN FACT.
SO, WHAT DO YOU THINK?
UH... I THINK IT'S A BROOM CLOSET.
WAS A BROOM CLOSET! NOW, IT'S YOUR NEW OFFICE.

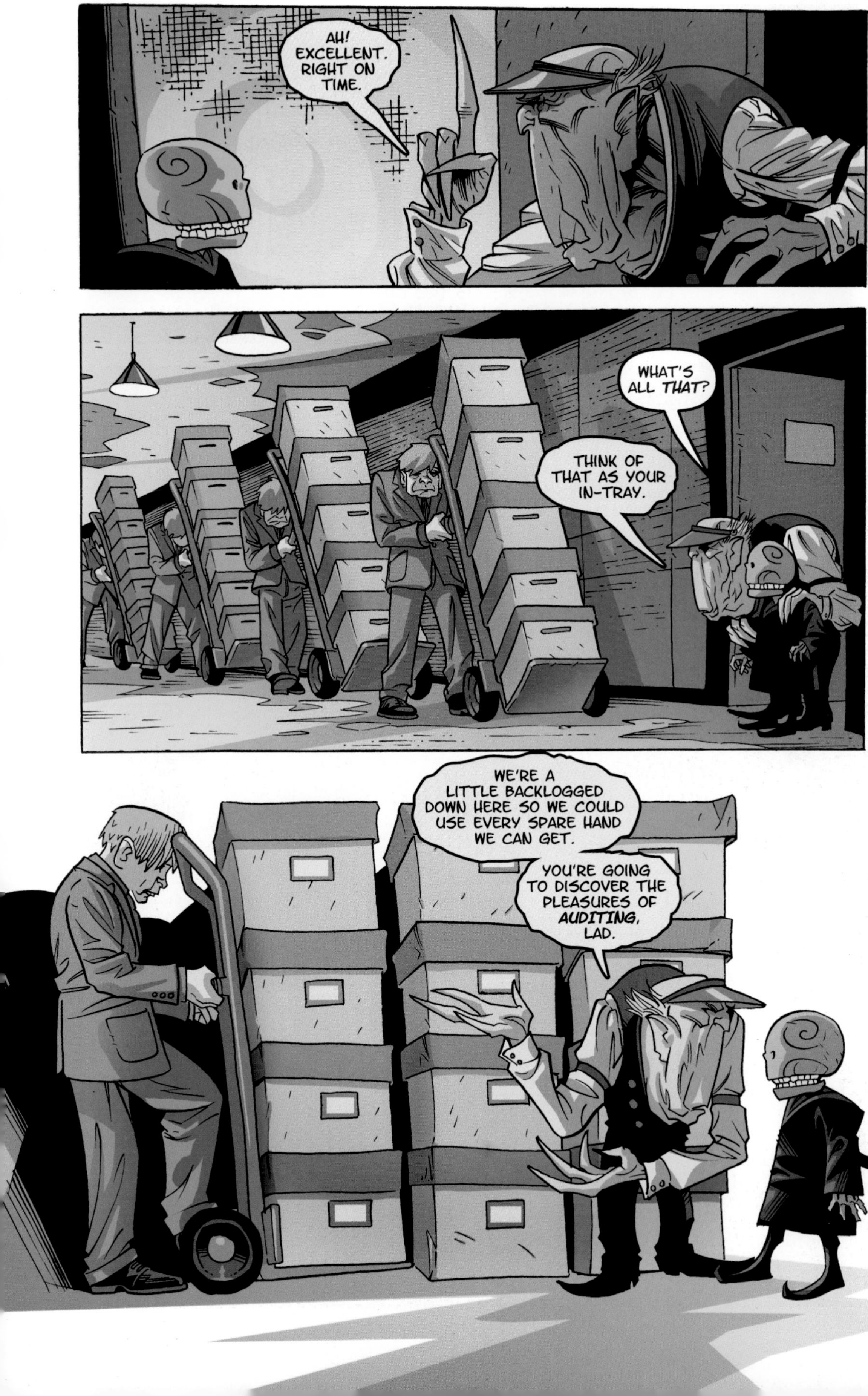
AH! EXCELLENT. RIGHT ON TIME.
WHAT'S ALL *THAT*?
THINK OF THAT AS YOUR IN-TRAY.
WE'RE A LITTLE BACKLOGGED DOWN HERE SO WE COULD USE EVERY SPARE HAND WE CAN GET.
YOU'RE GOING TO DISCOVER THE PLEASURES OF *AUDITING*, LAD.

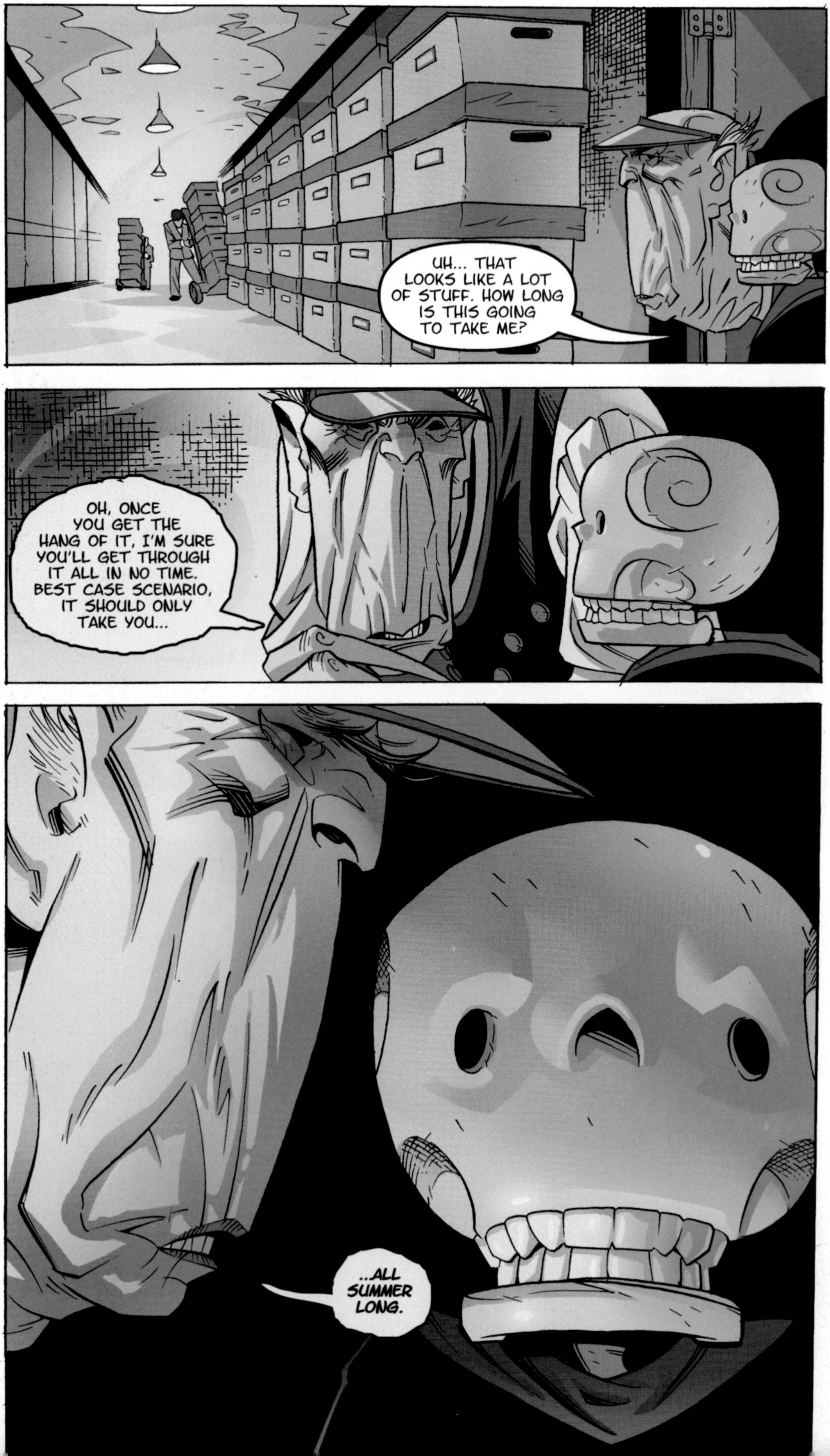
UH... THAT LOOKS LIKE A LOT OF STUFF. HOW LONG IS THIS GOING TO TAKE ME?
OH, ONCE YOU GET THE HANG OF IT, I'M SURE YOU'LL GET THROUGH IT ALL IN NO TIME. BEST CASE SCENARIO, IT SHOULD ONLY TAKE YOU...
...ALL SUMMER LONG.

CHAPTER 2

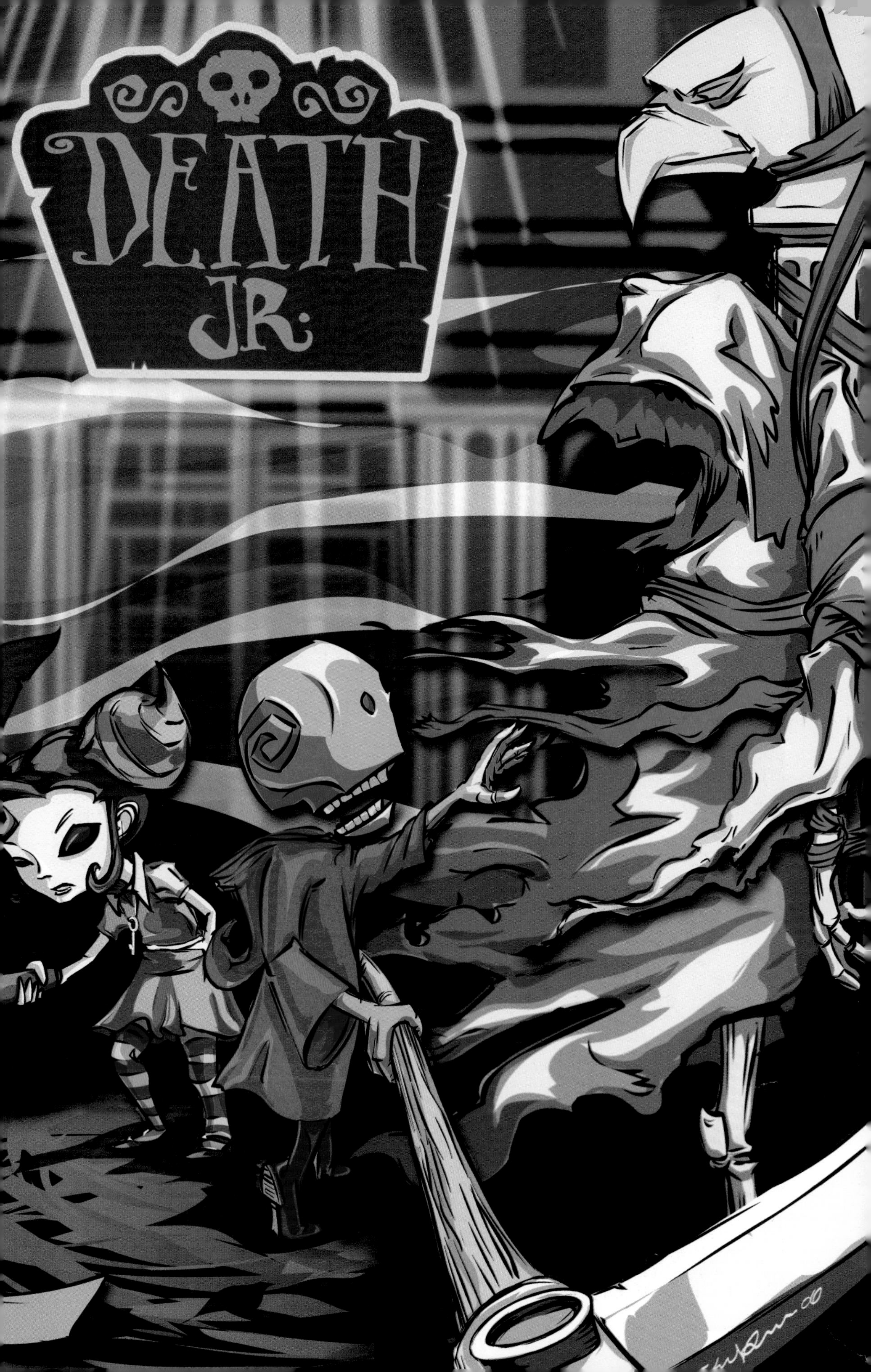
DEATH
JR.

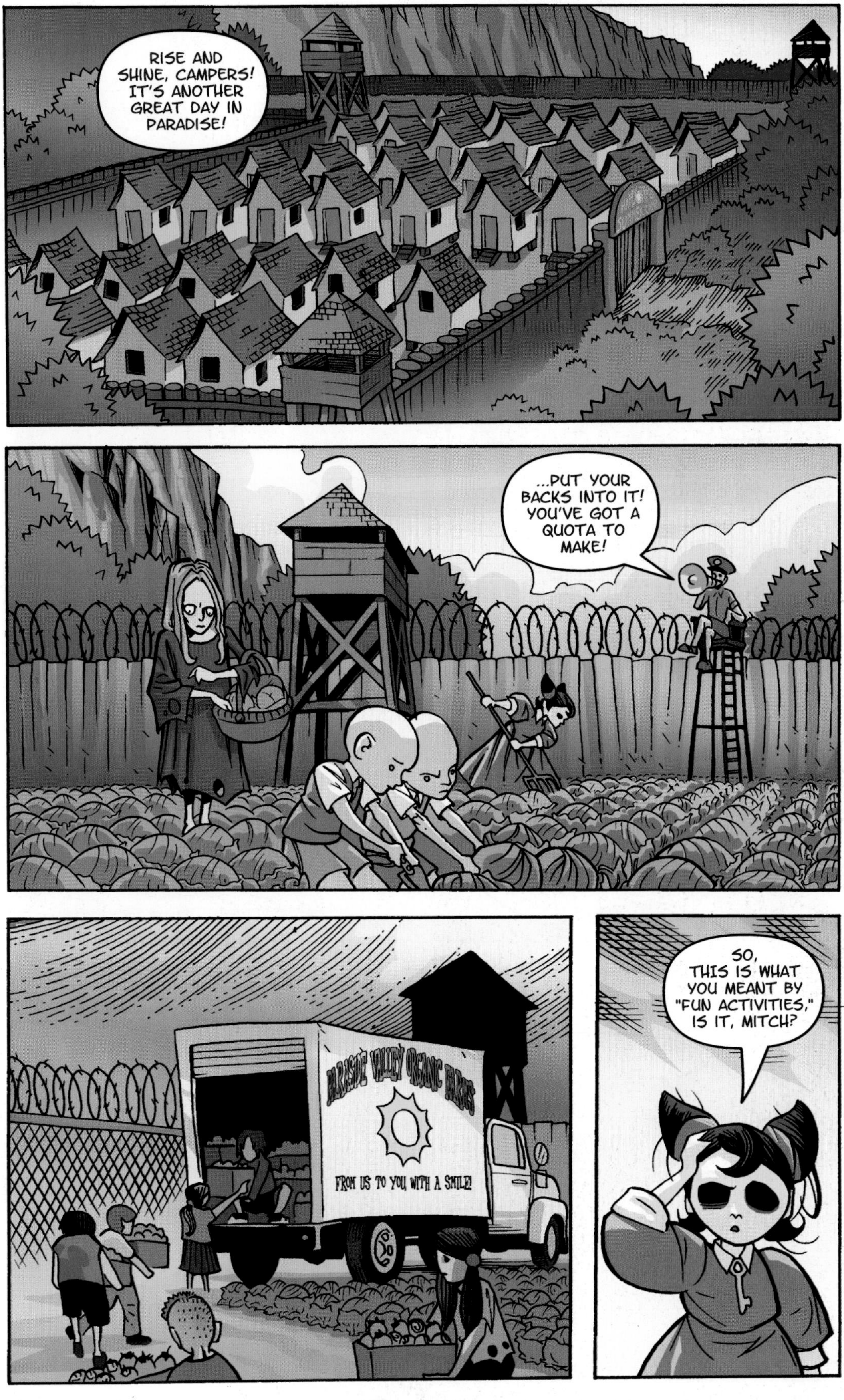
RISE AND SHINE, CAMPERS! IT'S ANOTHER GREAT DAY IN PARADISE!
...PUT YOUR BACKS INTO IT! YOU'VE GOT A QUOTA TO MAKE!
PARADISE VALLEY ORGANIC FARMS
FROM US TO YOU, WITH A SMILE!
SO, THIS IS WHAT YOU MEANT BY "FUN ACTIVITIES," IS IT, MITCH?

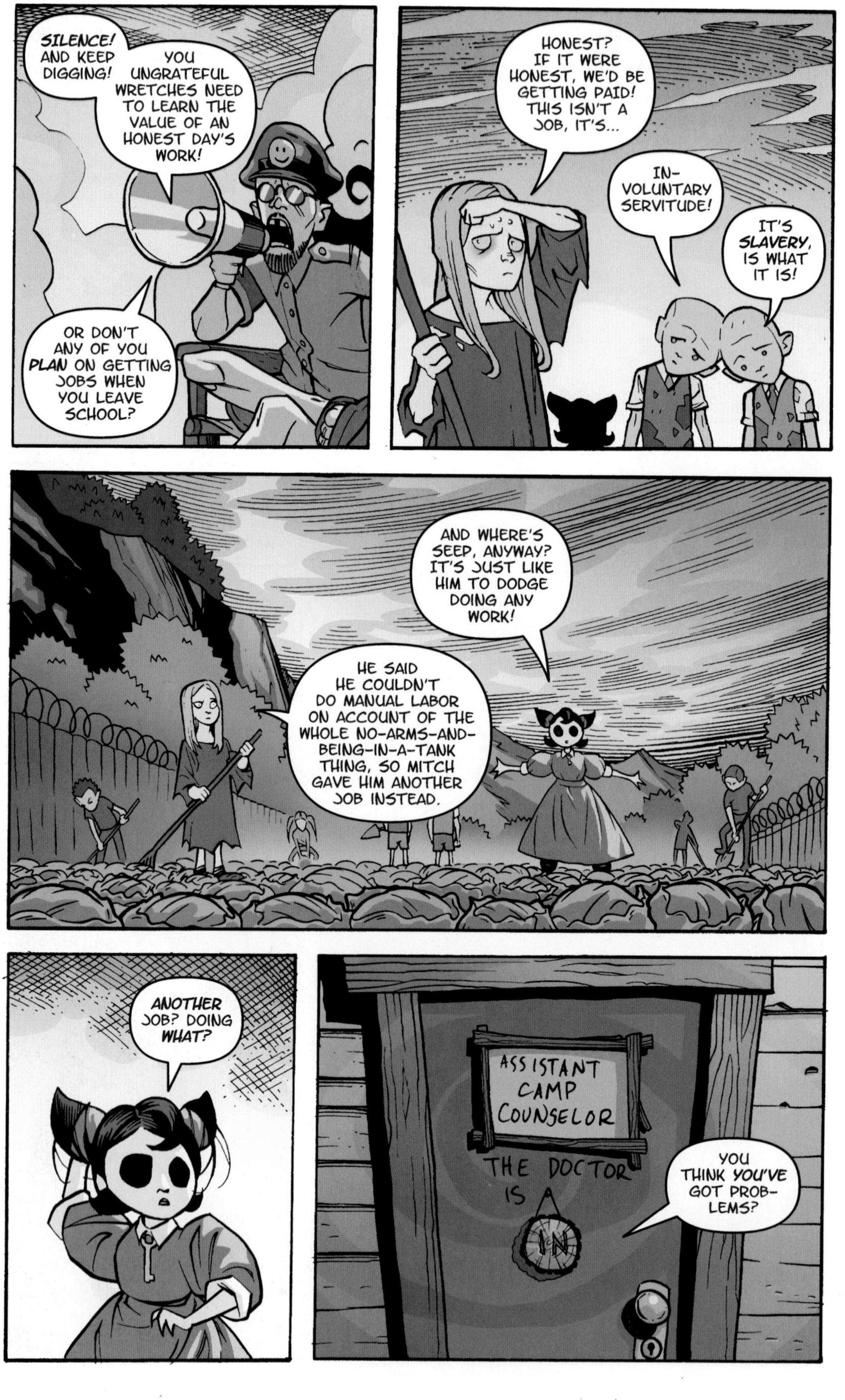
SILENCE! AND KEEP DIGGING!
YOU UNGRATEFUL WRETCHES NEED TO LEARN THE VALUE OF AN HONEST DAY'S WORK!
OR DON'T ANY OF YOU PLAN ON GETTING JOBS WHEN YOU LEAVE SCHOOL?
HONEST? IF IT WERE HONEST, WE'D BE GETTING PAID! THIS ISN'T A JOB, IT'S...
IN-VOLUNTARY SERVITUDE!
IT'S SLAVERY, IS WHAT IT IS!
AND WHERE'S SEEP, ANYWAY? IT'S JUST LIKE HIM TO DODGE DOING ANY WORK!
HE SAID HE COULDN'T DO MANUAL LABOR ON ACCOUNT OF THE WHOLE NO-ARMS-AND-BEING-IN-A-TANK THING, SO MITCH GAVE HIM ANOTHER JOB INSTEAD.
ANOTHER JOB? DOING WHAT?
ASSISTANT CAMP COUNSELOR
THE DOCTOR IS
IN
YOU THINK YOU'VE GOT PROB-LEMS?

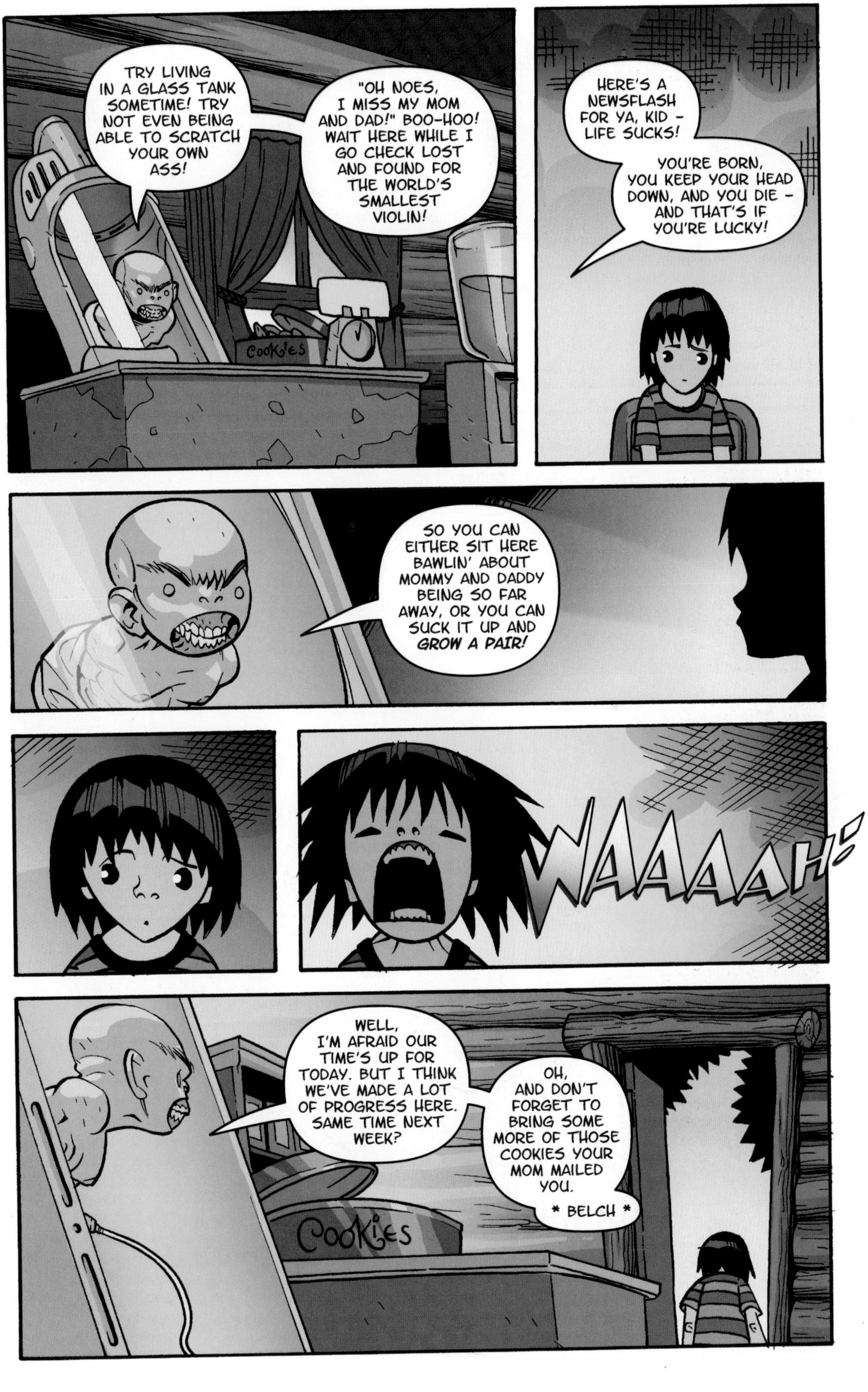
TRY LIVING IN A GLASS TANK SOMETIME! TRY NOT EVEN BEING ABLE TO SCRATCH YOUR OWN ASS!
"OH NOES, I MISS MY MOM AND DAD!" BOO-HOO! WAIT HERE WHILE I GO CHECK LOST AND FOUND FOR THE WORLD'S SMALLEST VIOLIN!
COOKIES
HERE'S A NEWSFLASH FOR YA, KID - LIFE SUCKS!
YOU'RE BORN, YOU KEEP YOUR HEAD DOWN, AND YOU DIE - AND THAT'S IF YOU'RE LUCKY!
SO YOU CAN EITHER SIT HERE BAWLIN' ABOUT MOMMY AND DADDY BEING SO FAR AWAY, OR YOU CAN SUCK IT UP AND *GROW A PAIR!*
WAAAAAH!
WELL, I'M AFRAID OUR TIME'S UP FOR TODAY. BUT I THINK WE'VE MADE A LOT OF PROGRESS HERE. SAME TIME NEXT WEEK?
OH, AND DON'T FORGET TO BRING SOME MORE OF THOSE COOKIES YOUR MOM MAILED YOU.
* BELCH *
COOKIES

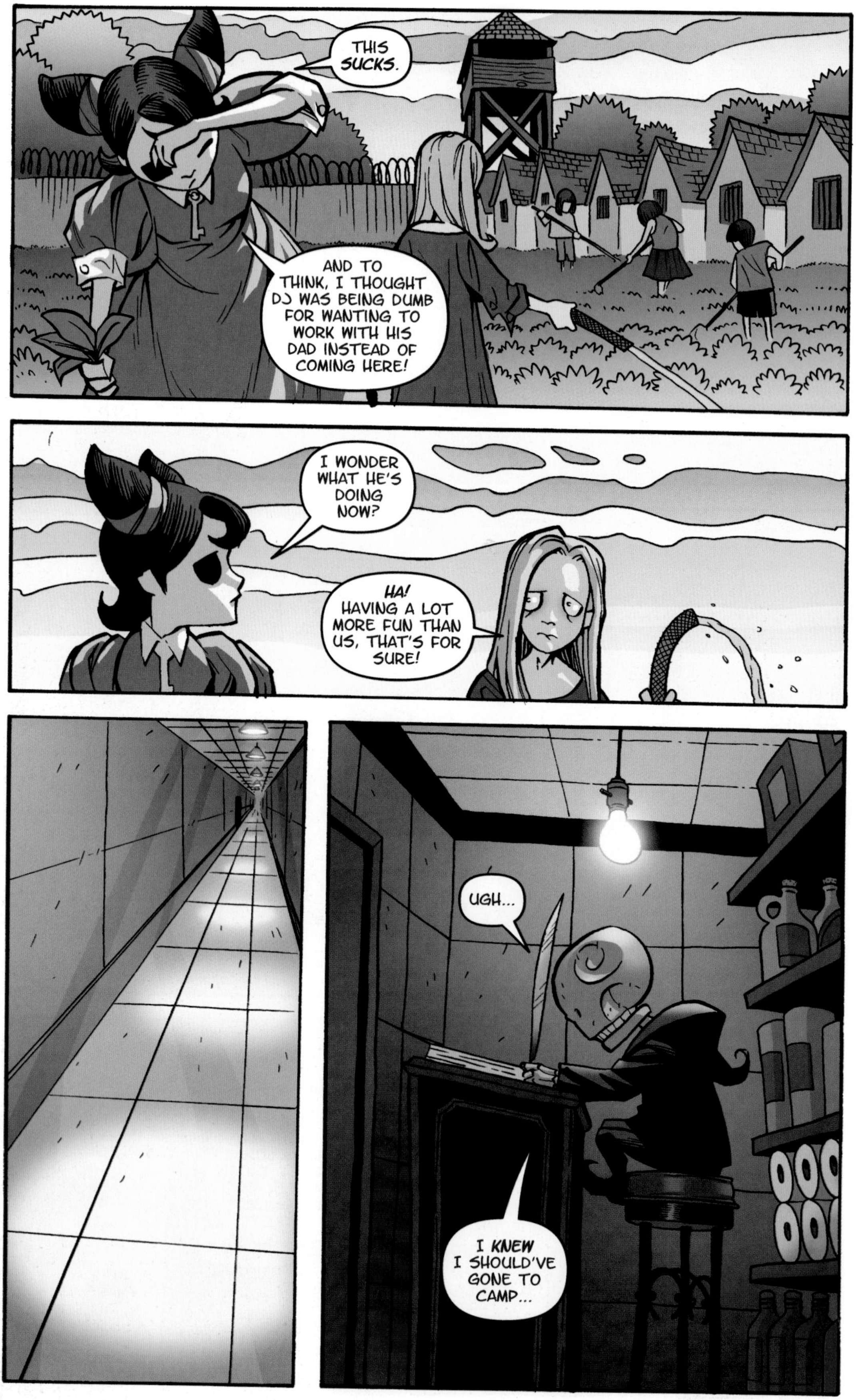
THIS SUCKS.
AND TO THINK, I THOUGHT DJ WAS BEING DUMB FOR WANTING TO WORK WITH HIS DAD INSTEAD OF COMING HERE!
I WONDER WHAT HE'S DOING NOW?
HA! HAVING A LOT MORE FUN THAN US, THAT'S FOR SURE!
UGH...
I KNEW I SHOULD'VE GONE TO CAMP...

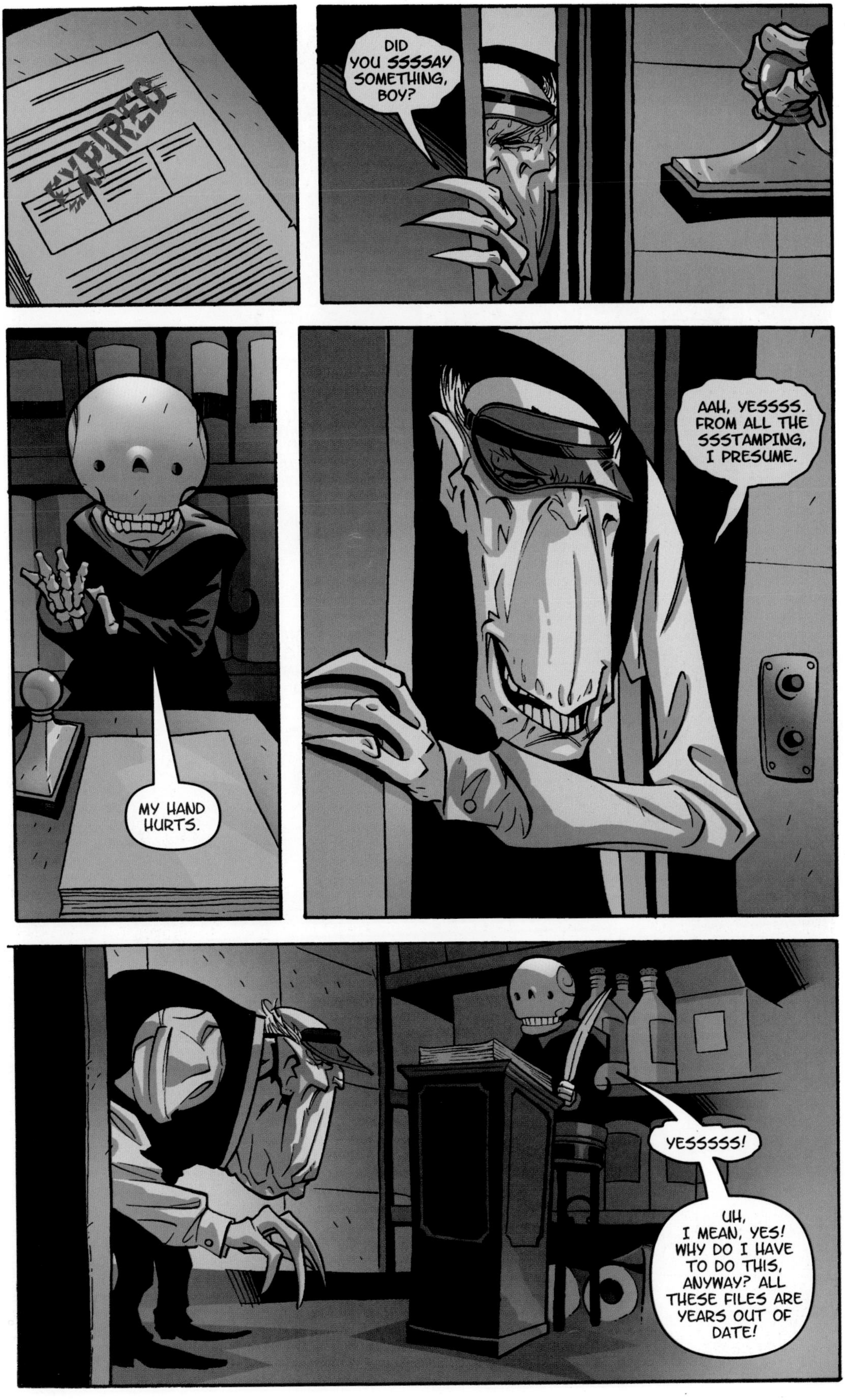
EXPIRED
DID YOU SSSSAY SOMETHING, BOY?
MY HAND HURTS.
AAH, YESSSS. FROM ALL THE SSSTAMPING, I PRESUME.
YESSSSS!
UH, I MEAN, YES! WHY DO I HAVE TO DO THIS, ANYWAY? ALL THESE FILES ARE YEARS OUT OF DATE!

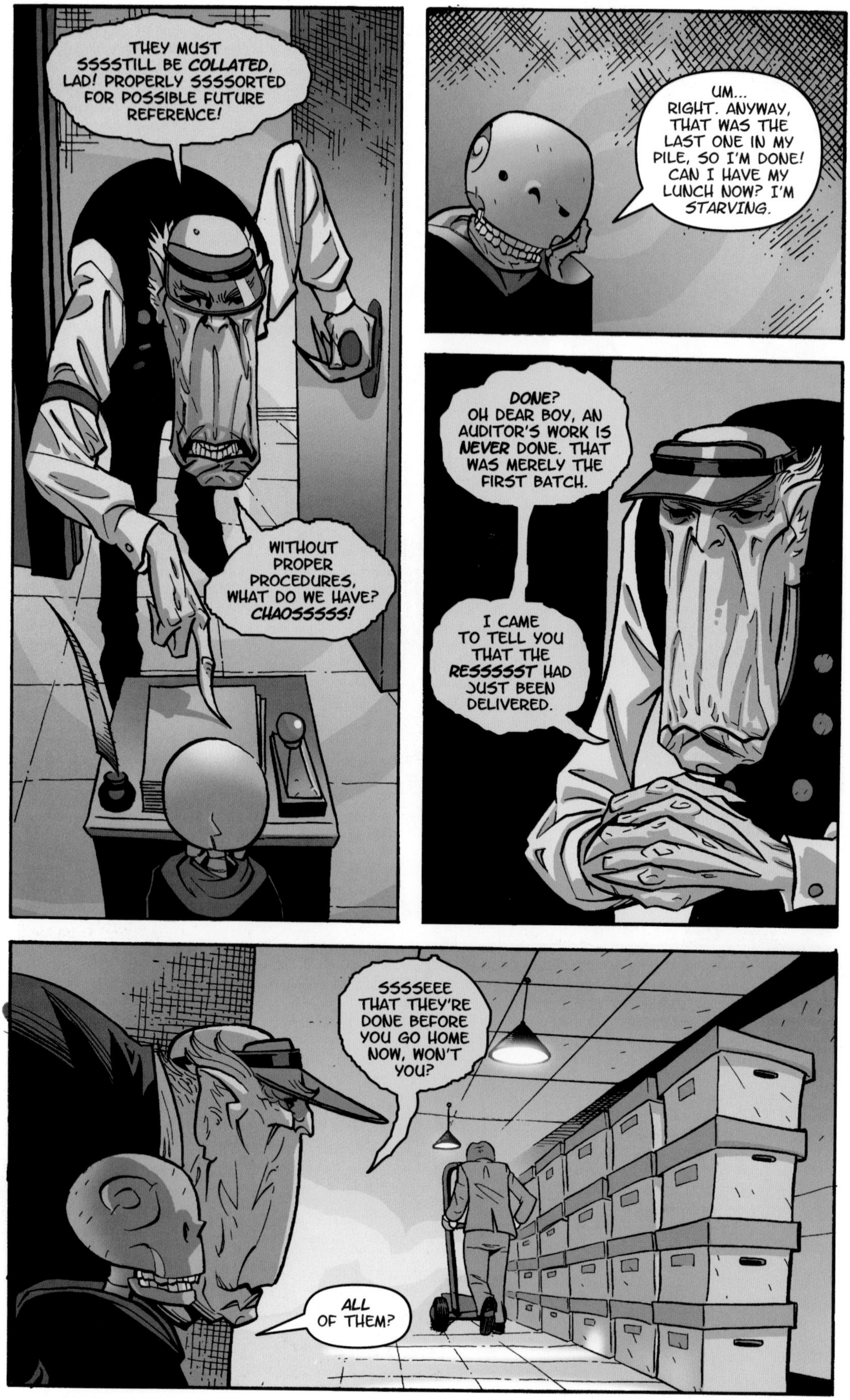
THEY MUST SSSSTILL BE COLLATED, LAD! PROPERLY SSSSORTED FOR POSSIBLE FUTURE REFERENCE!
WITHOUT PROPER PROCEDURES, WHAT DO WE HAVE? CHAOSSSSS!
UM... RIGHT. ANYWAY, THAT WAS THE LAST ONE IN MY PILE, SO I'M DONE! CAN I HAVE MY LUNCH NOW? I'M STARVING.
DONE? OH DEAR BOY, AN AUDITOR'S WORK IS NEVER DONE. THAT WAS MERELY THE FIRST BATCH.
I CAME TO TELL YOU THAT THE RESSSSST HAD JUST BEEN DELIVERED.
SSSSEEE THAT THEY'RE DONE BEFORE YOU GO HOME NOW, WON'T YOU?
ALL OF THEM?

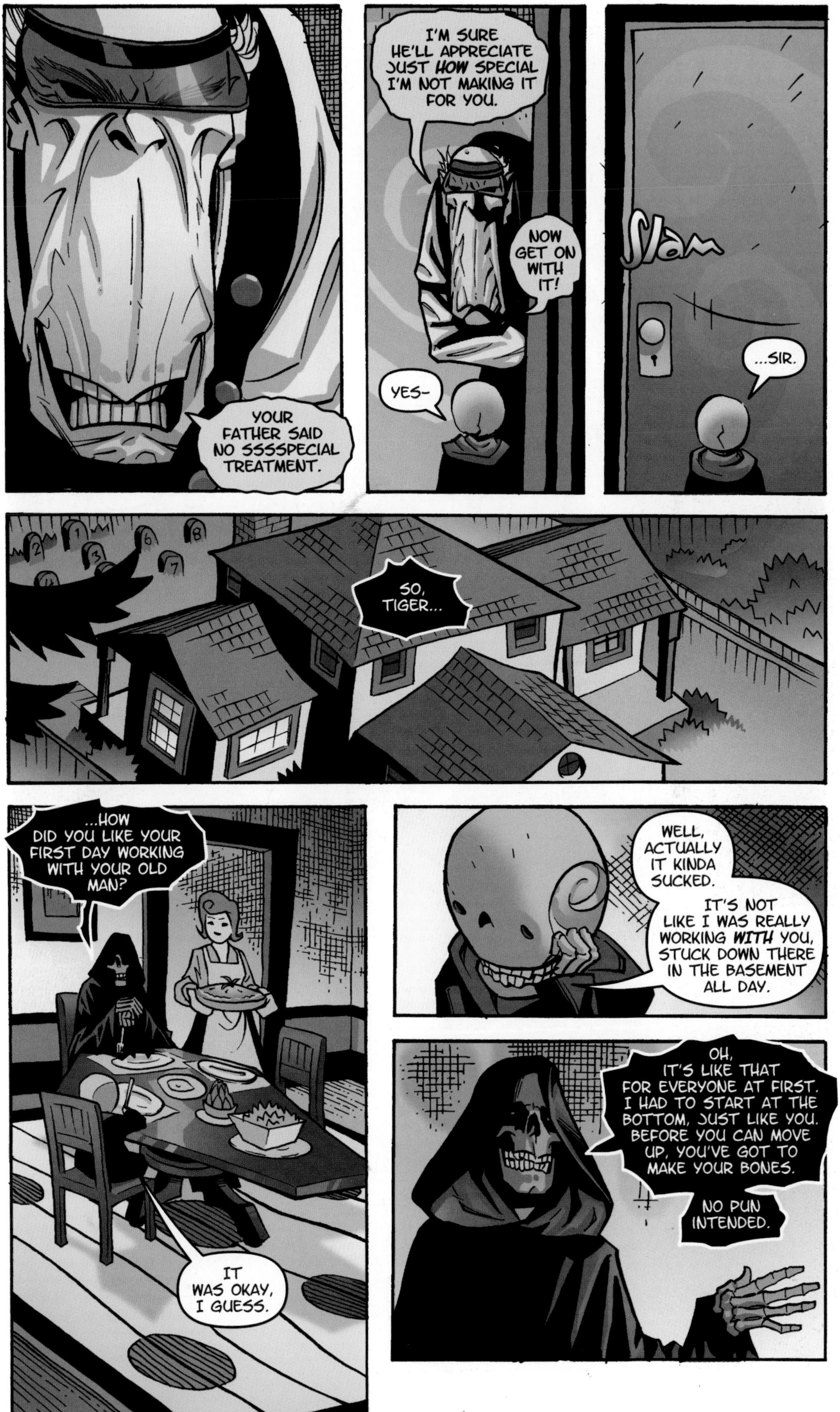
YOUR FATHER SAID NO SSSSPECIAL TREATMENT.
I'M SURE HE'LL APPRECIATE JUST **HOW** SPECIAL I'M NOT MAKING IT FOR YOU.
NOW GET ON WITH IT!
YES-
SLAM
...SIR.
SO, TIGER...
...HOW DID YOU LIKE YOUR FIRST DAY WORKING WITH YOUR OLD MAN?
IT WAS OKAY, I GUESS.
WELL, ACTUALLY IT KINDA SUCKED.
IT'S NOT LIKE I WAS REALLY WORKING **WITH** YOU, STUCK DOWN THERE IN THE BASEMENT ALL DAY.
OH, IT'S LIKE THAT FOR EVERYONE AT FIRST. I HAD TO START AT THE BOTTOM, JUST LIKE YOU. BEFORE YOU CAN MOVE UP, YOU'VE GOT TO MAKE YOUR BONES.
NO PUN INTENDED.

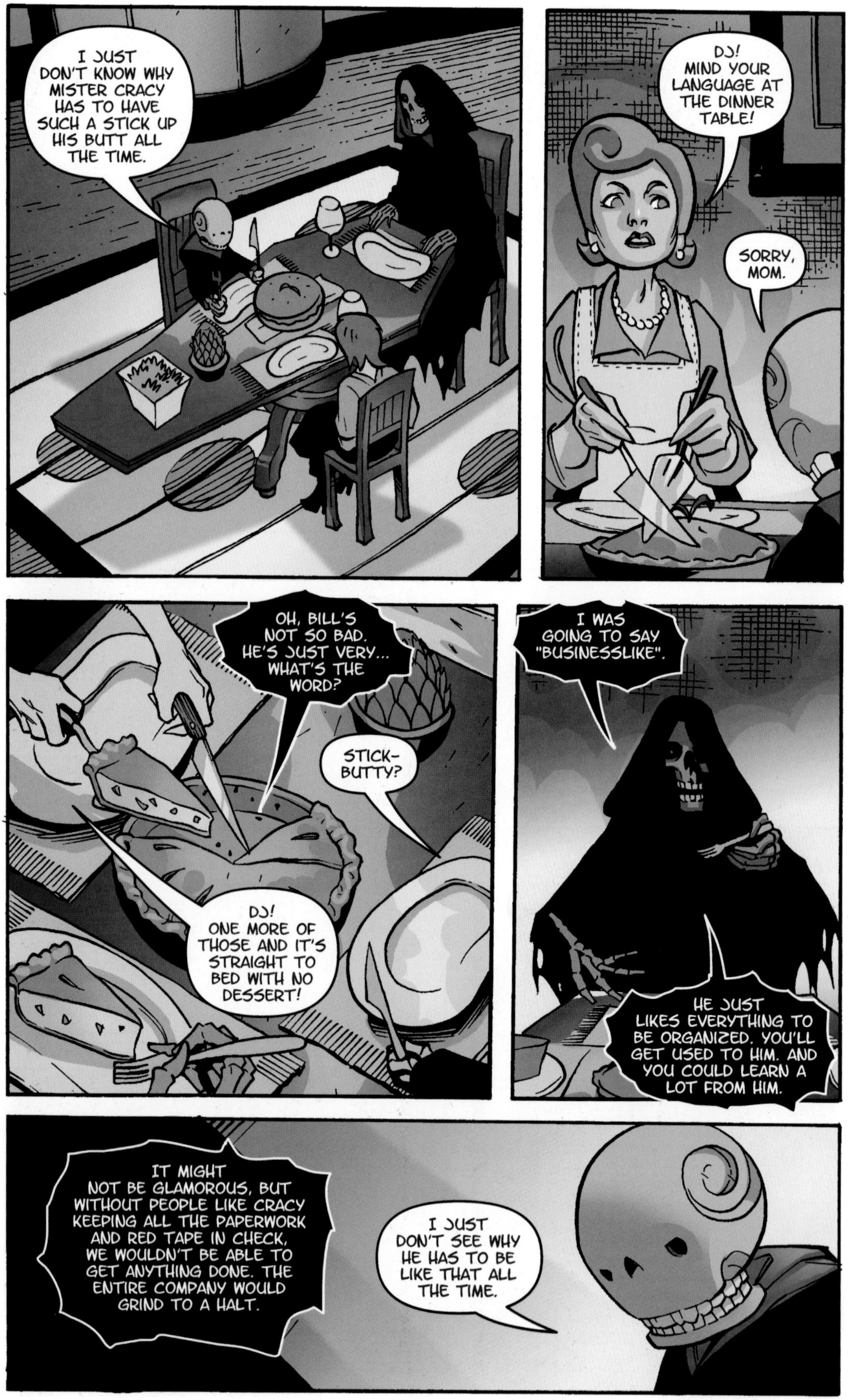
I JUST DON'T KNOW WHY MISTER CRACY HAS TO HAVE SUCH A STICK UP HIS BUTT ALL THE TIME.
DJ! MIND YOUR LANGUAGE AT THE DINNER TABLE!
SORRY, MOM.
OH, BILL'S NOT SO BAD. HE'S JUST VERY... WHAT'S THE WORD?
STICK-BUTTY?
DJ! ONE MORE OF THOSE AND IT'S STRAIGHT TO BED WITH NO DESSERT!
I WAS GOING TO SAY "BUSINESSLIKE".
HE JUST LIKES EVERYTHING TO BE ORGANIZED. YOU'LL GET USED TO HIM. AND YOU COULD LEARN A LOT FROM HIM.
IT MIGHT NOT BE GLAMOROUS, BUT WITHOUT PEOPLE LIKE CRACY KEEPING ALL THE PAPERWORK AND RED TAPE IN CHECK, WE WOULDN'T BE ABLE TO GET ANYTHING DONE. THE ENTIRE COMPANY WOULD GRIND TO A HALT.
I JUST DON'T SEE WHY HE HAS TO BE LIKE THAT ALL THE TIME.

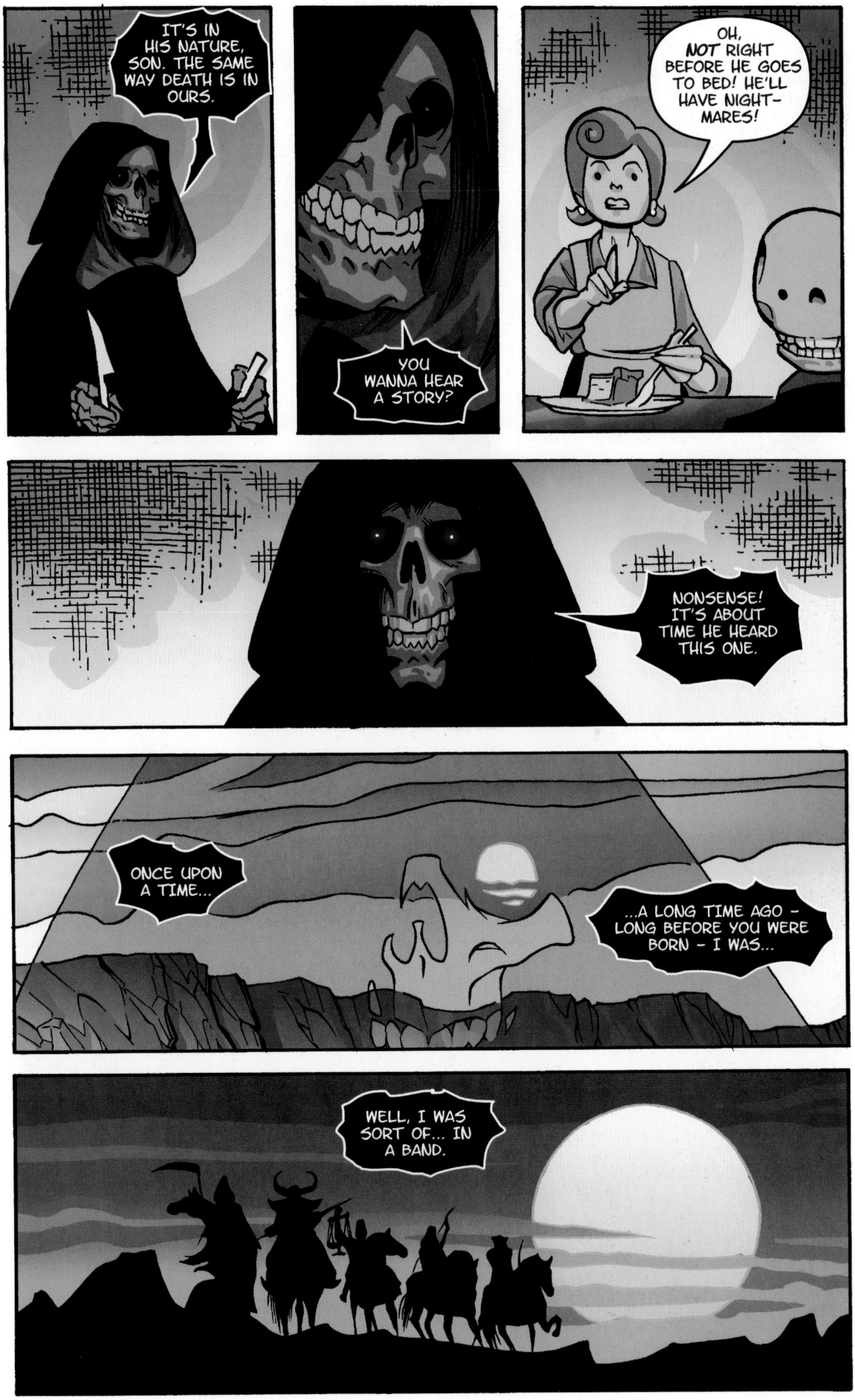
IT'S IN HIS NATURE, SON. THE SAME WAY DEATH IS IN OURS.
YOU WANNA HEAR A STORY?
OH, NOT RIGHT BEFORE HE GOES TO BED! HE'LL HAVE NIGHT-MARES!
NONSENSE! IT'S ABOUT TIME HE HEARD THIS ONE.
ONCE UPON A TIME...
...A LONG TIME AGO - LONG BEFORE YOU WERE BORN - I WAS...
WELL, I WAS SORT OF... IN A BAND.

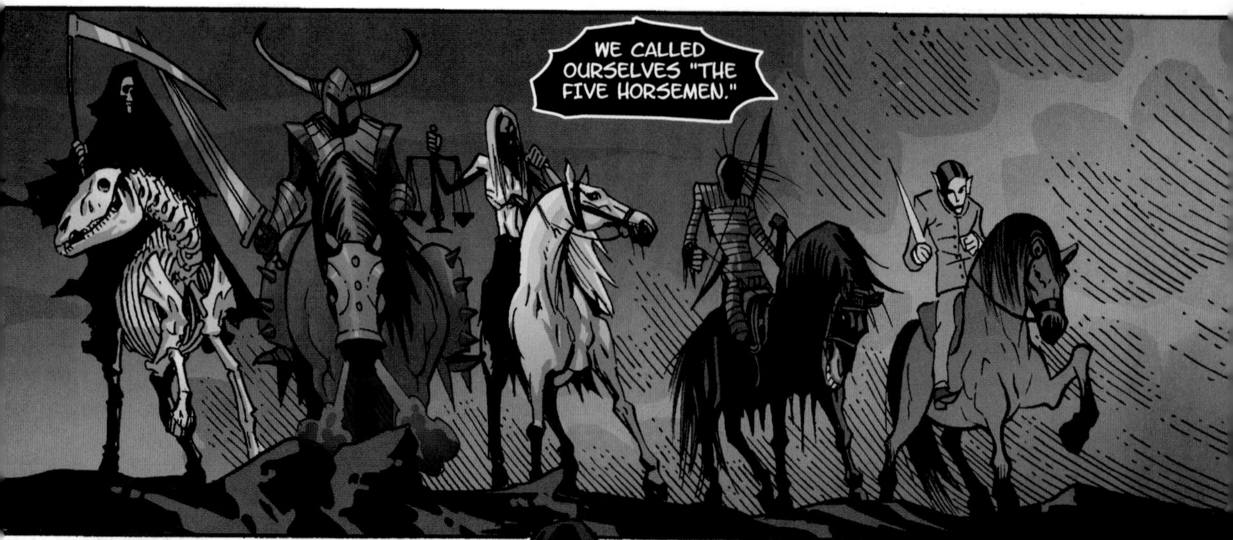
WE CALLED OURSELVES "THE FIVE HORSEMEN."

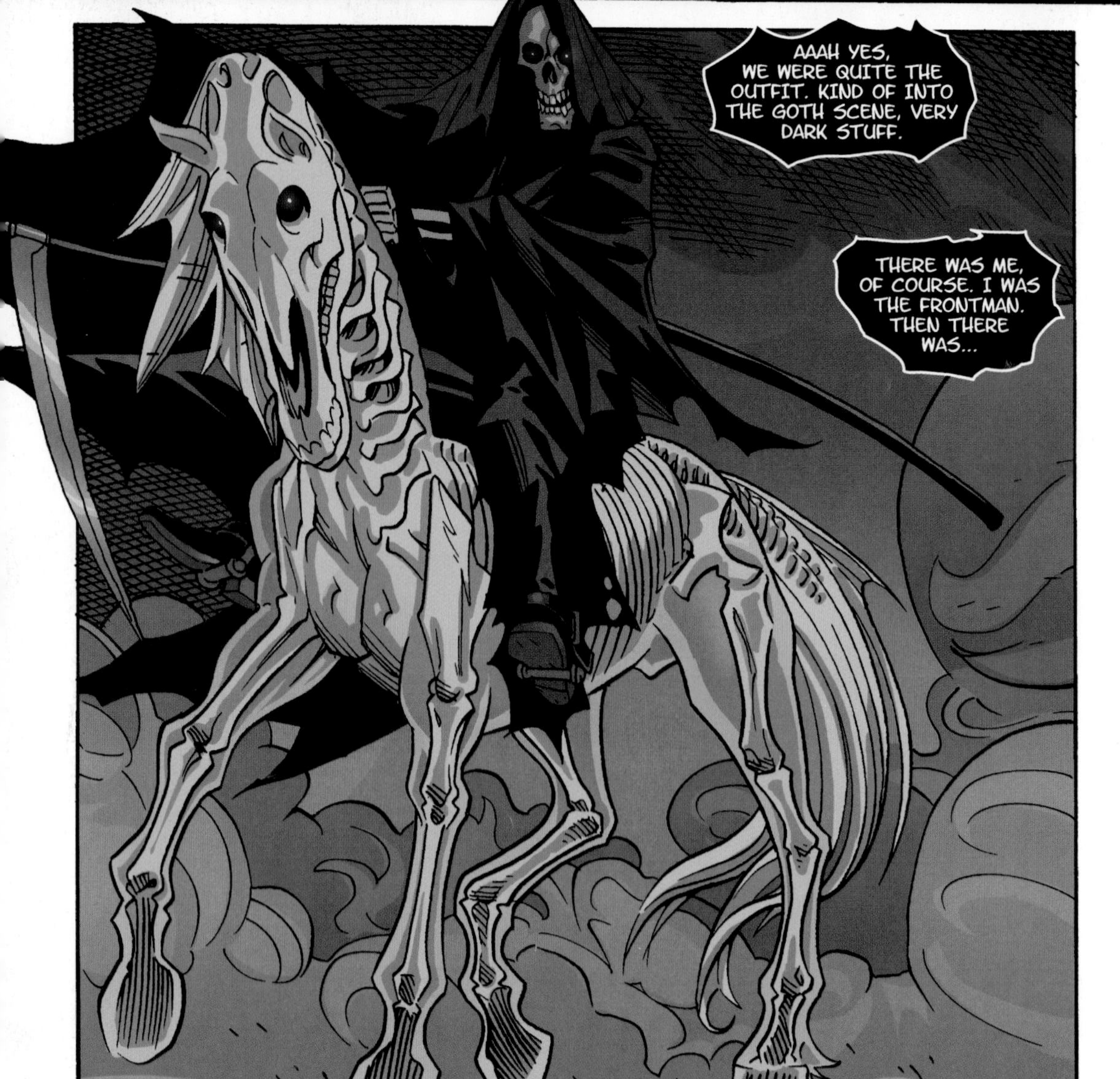
AAAH YES, WE WERE QUITE THE OUTFIT. KIND OF INTO THE GOTH SCENE, VERY DARK STUFF.
THERE WAS ME, OF COURSE. I WAS THE FRONTMAN. THEN THERE WAS...

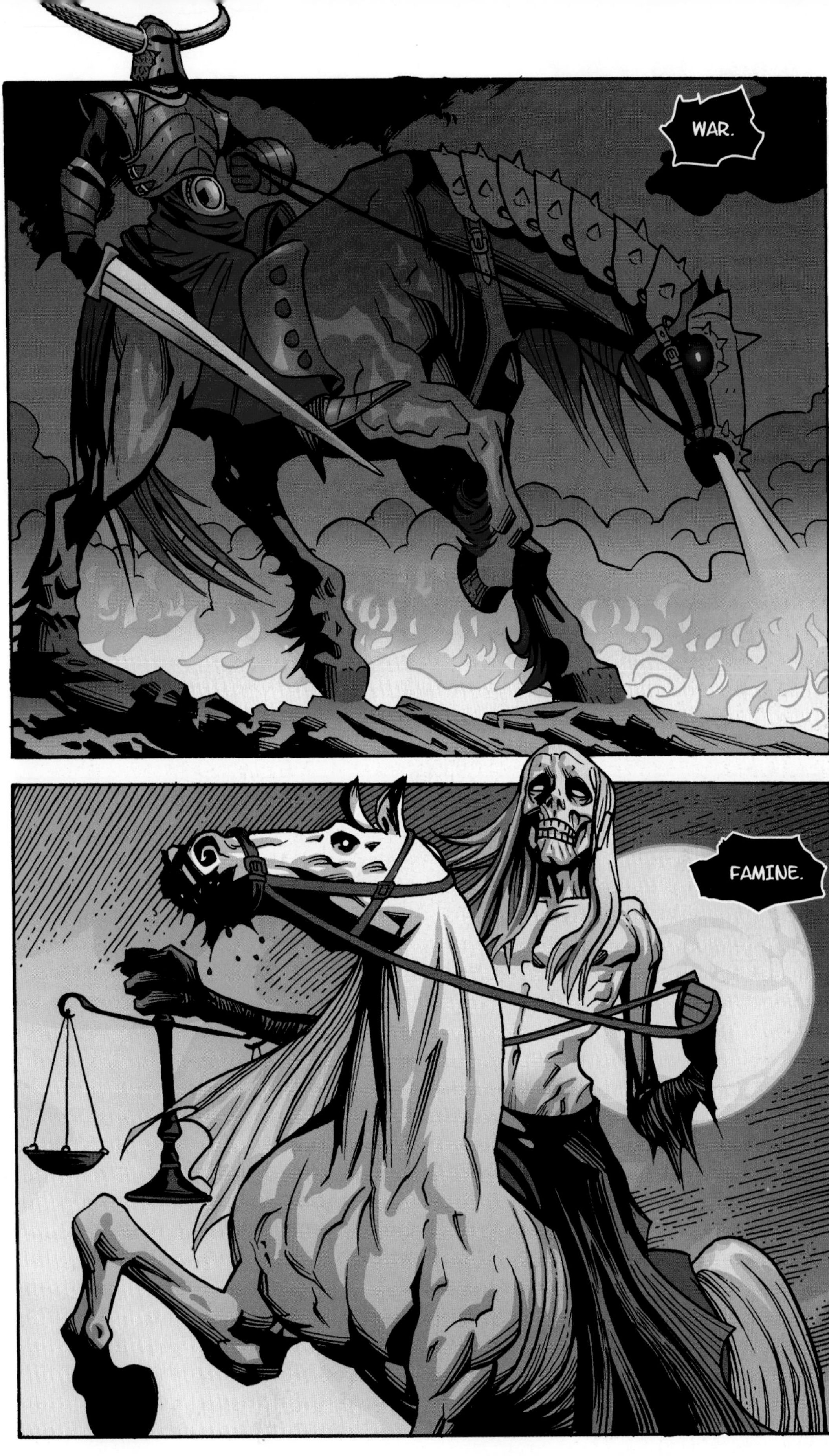
WAR.
FAMINE.

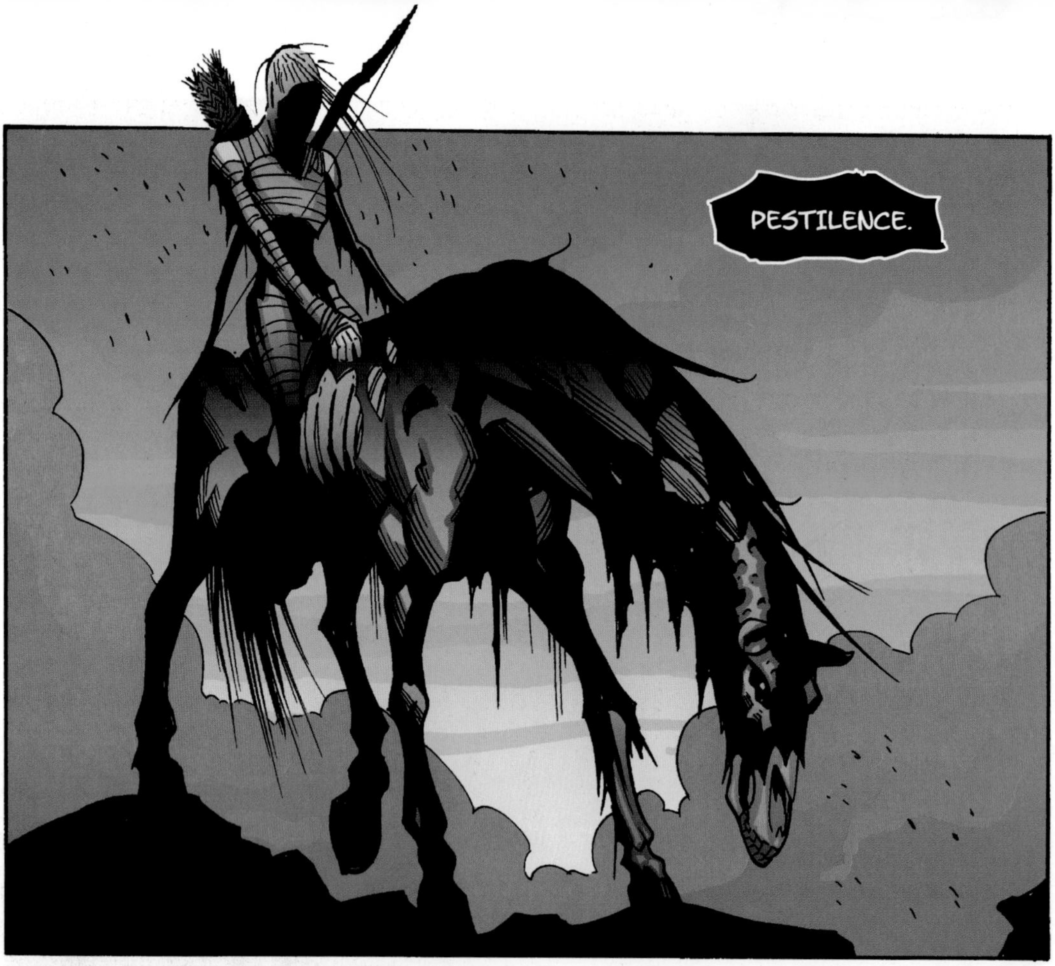
PESTILENCE.

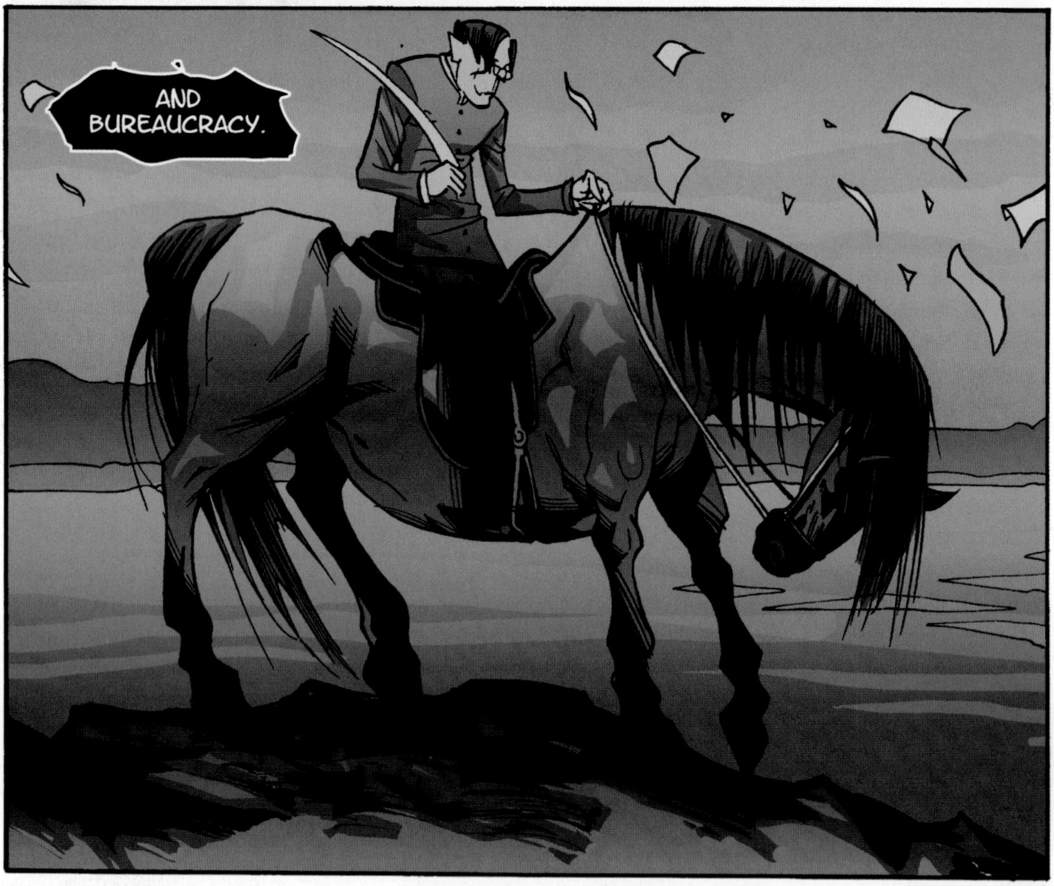
AND BUREAUCRACY.

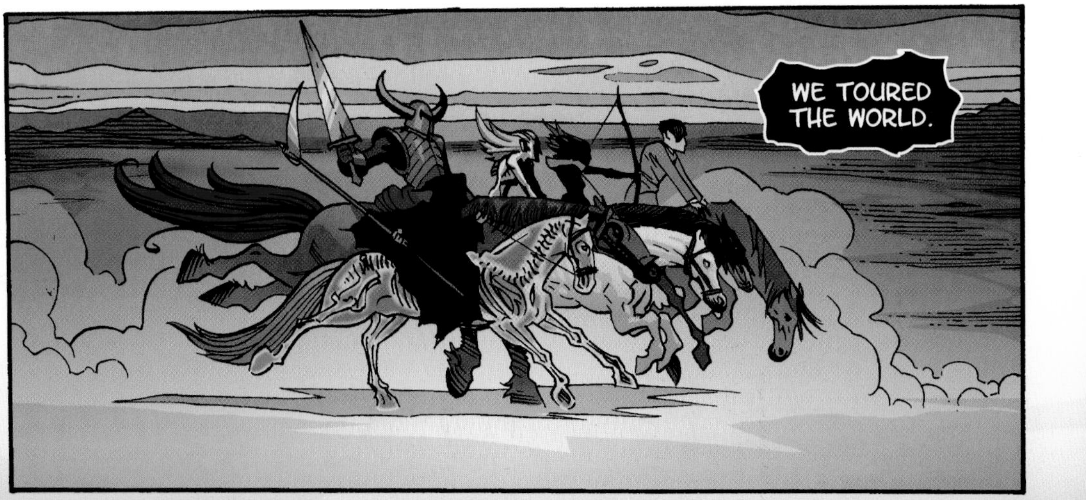
WE TOURED THE WORLD.

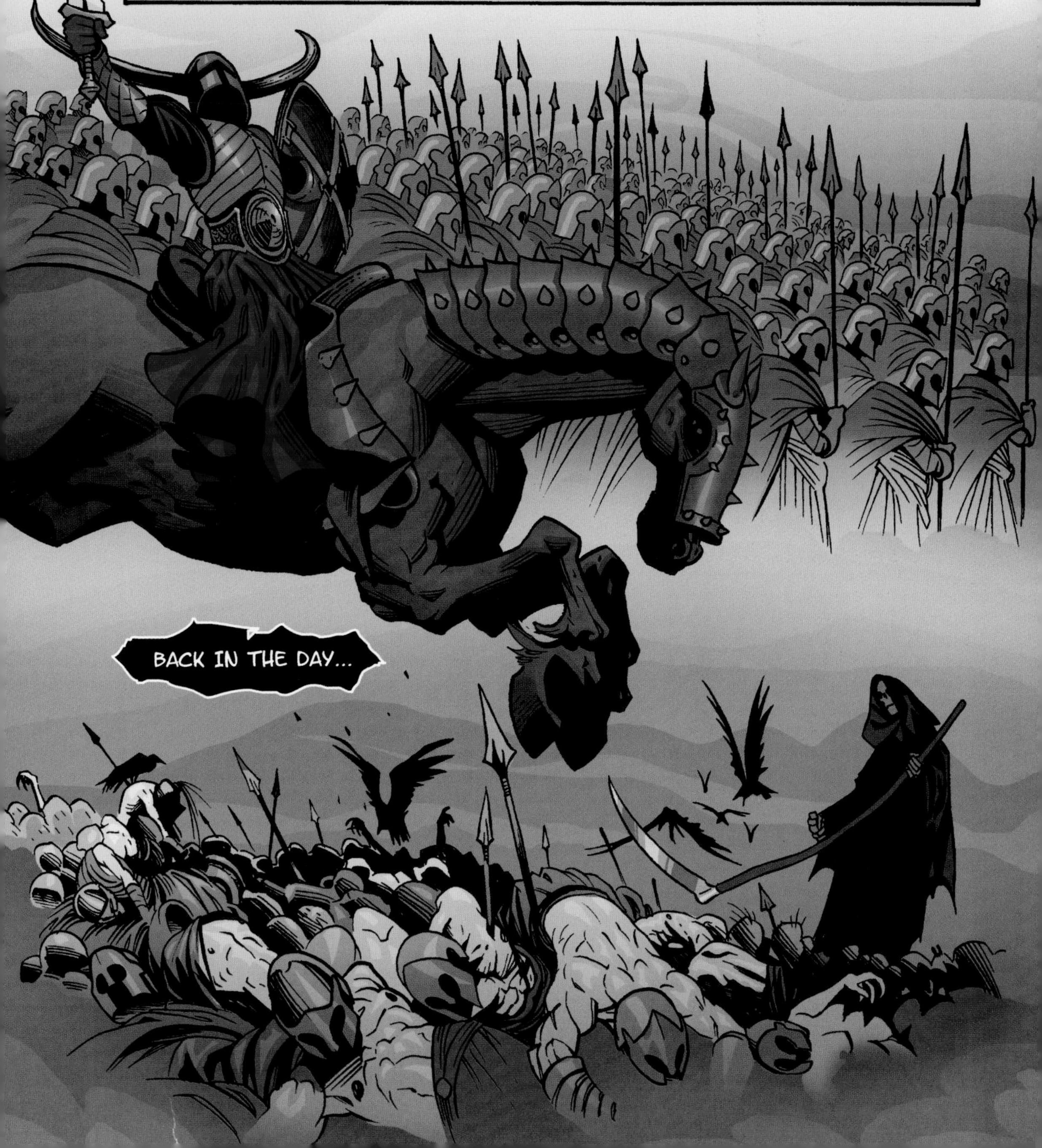
BACK IN THE DAY...

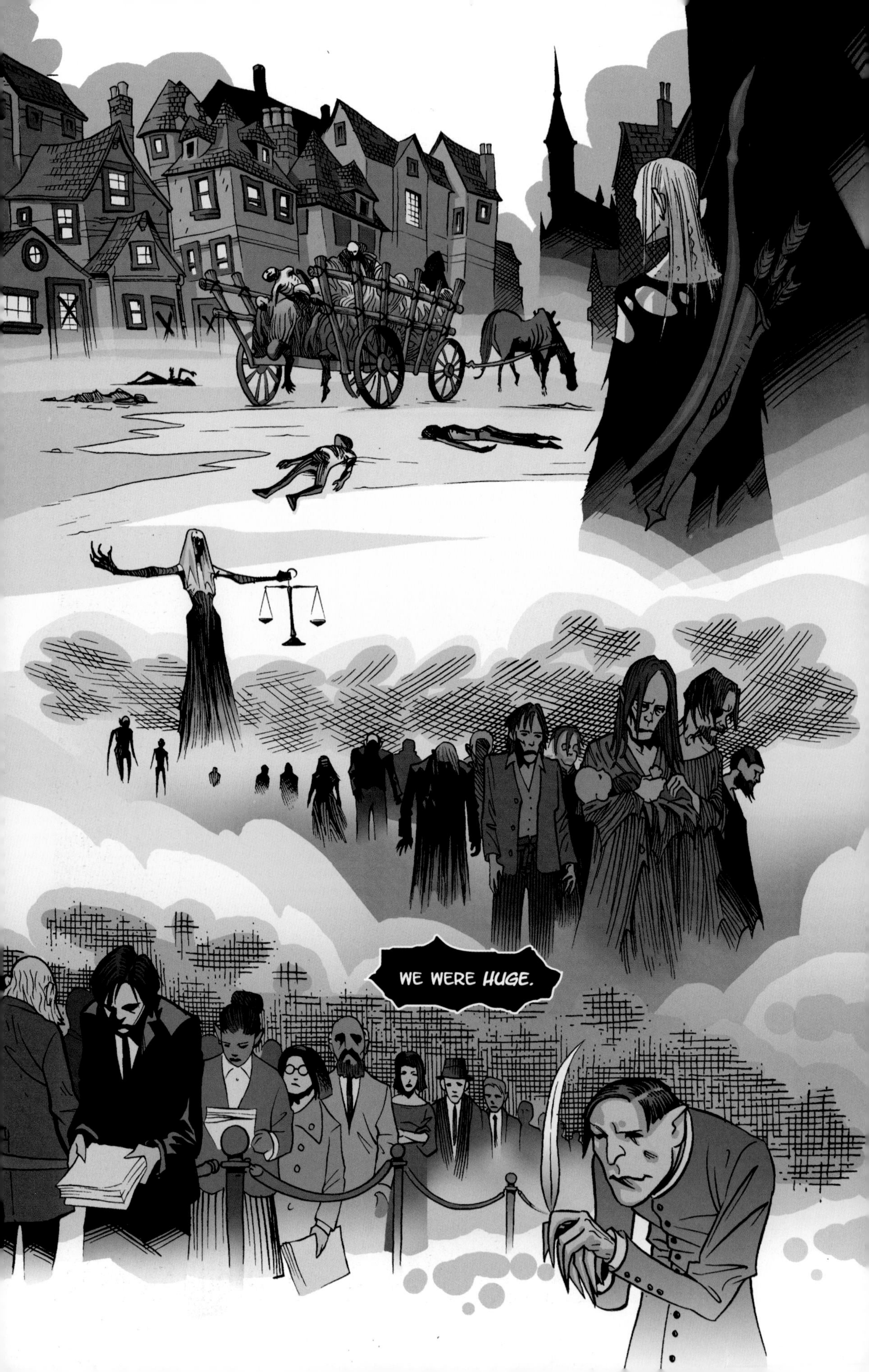
WE WERE HUGE.

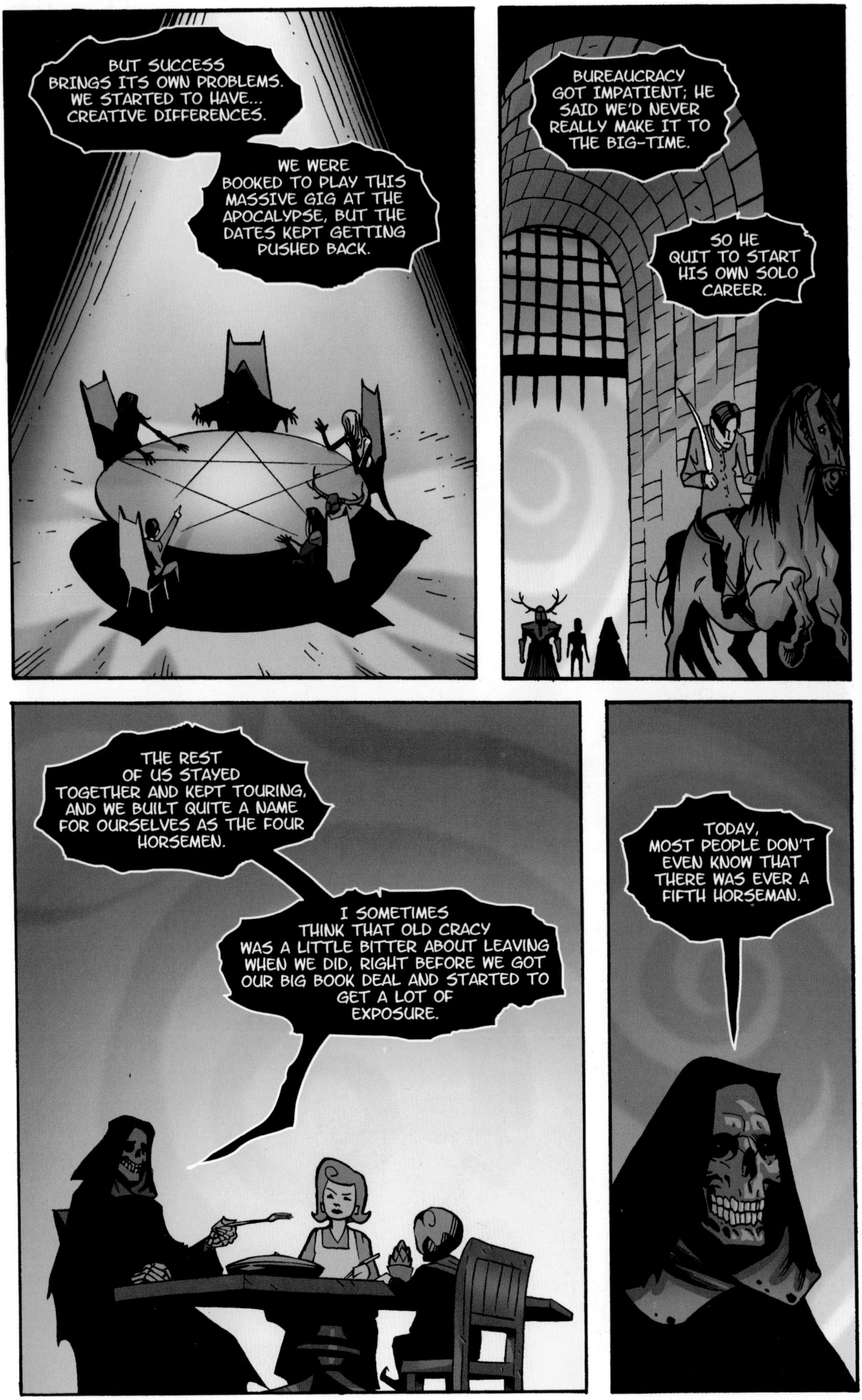
BUT SUCCESS BRINGS ITS OWN PROBLEMS. WE STARTED TO HAVE... CREATIVE DIFFERENCES.
WE WERE BOOKED TO PLAY THIS MASSIVE GIG AT THE APOCALYPSE, BUT THE DATES KEPT GETTING PUSHED BACK.
BUREAUCRACY GOT IMPATIENT; HE SAID WE'D NEVER REALLY MAKE IT TO THE BIG-TIME.
SO HE QUIT TO START HIS OWN SOLO CAREER.
THE REST OF US STAYED TOGETHER AND KEPT TOURING, AND WE BUILT QUITE A NAME FOR OURSELVES AS THE FOUR HORSEMEN.
I SOMETIMES THINK THAT OLD CRACY WAS A LITTLE BITTER ABOUT LEAVING WHEN WE DID, RIGHT BEFORE WE GOT OUR BIG BOOK DEAL AND STARTED TO GET A LOT OF EXPOSURE.
TODAY, MOST PEOPLE DON'T EVEN KNOW THAT THERE WAS EVER A FIFTH HORSEMAN.

WAIT... BUREAUCRACY. THAT'S... MISTER CRACY?

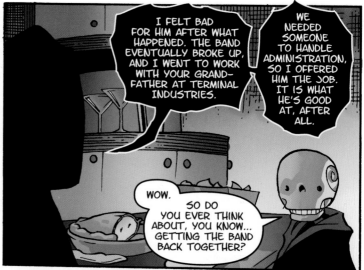

I FELT BAD FOR HIM AFTER WHAT HAPPENED. THE BAND EVENTUALLY BROKE UP, AND I WENT TO WORK WITH YOUR GRAND-FATHER AT TERMINAL INDUSTRIES.

WE NEEDED SOMEONE TO HANDLE ADMINISTRATION, SO I OFFERED HIM THE JOB. IT IS WHAT HE'S GOOD AT, AFTER ALL.

WOW.

SO DO YOU EVER THINK ABOUT, YOU KNOW... GETTING THE BAND BACK TOGETHER?

AAH, WELL SOMETIMES I THINK...

AHEM. NO, NOT AT ALL.

THAT WAS A LONG TIME AGO, WE WERE ALL MUCH YOUNGER BACK THEN. YOUNG AND RECKLESS. WE'VE ALL GOT FAMILIES NOW.

RESPONSIBILITIES.

SSSSSTILL WORKING HARD, I SEE?

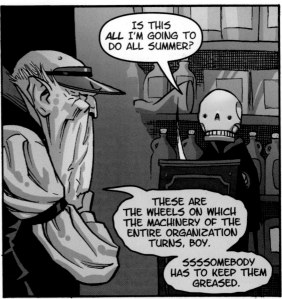

IS THIS ALL I'M GOING TO DO ALL SUMMER?

THESE ARE THE WHEELS ON WHICH THE MACHINERY OF THE ENTIRE ORGANIZATION TURNS, BOY.

SSSSOMEBODY HAS TO KEEP THEM GREASED.

I KNOW, BUT IT'S JUST SO *BORING*! ISN'T THERE *ANYTHING* ELSE I CAN DO?

HMMMM.

YOU KNOW, THERE IS SOMETHING YOU COULD HELP US WITH.

YEAH?

PERHAPSSSSS.

ON SECOND THOUGHT, PERHAPS NOT. IT'S A LOT OF RESPONSIBILITY. REALLY SOMETHING FOR A MORE SENIOR EMPLOYEE. FORGET I EVER MENTIONED IT.

NO, NO! I CAN DO IT! I JUST NEED A CHANCE TO *PROVE* MYSELF!

WELL, I DON'T KNOW...

PLEEEEAASE?

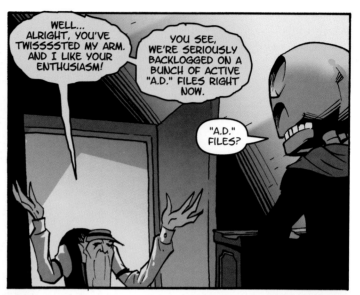

WELL... ALRIGHT, YOU'VE TWISSSSTED MY ARM. AND I LIKE YOUR ENTHUSIASM!

YOU SEE, WE'RE SERIOUSLY BACKLOGGED ON A BUNCH OF ACTIVE "A.D." FILES RIGHT NOW.

"A.D." FILES?

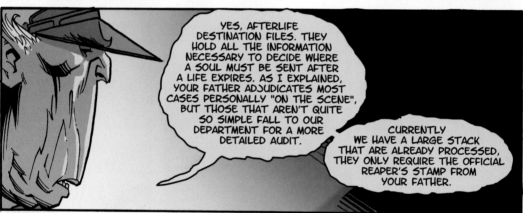

YES, AFTERLIFE DESTINATION FILES. THEY HOLD ALL THE INFORMATION NECESSARY TO DECIDE WHERE A SOUL MUST BE SENT AFTER A LIFE EXPIRES. AS I EXPLAINED, YOUR FATHER ADJUDICATES MOST CASES PERSONALLY "ON THE SCENE", BUT THOSE THAT AREN'T QUITE SO SIMPLE FALL TO OUR DEPARTMENT FOR A MORE DETAILED AUDIT.

CURRENTLY WE HAVE A LARGE STACK THAT ARE ALREADY PROCESSED, THEY ONLY REQUIRE THE OFFICIAL REAPER'S STAMP FROM YOUR FATHER.

THEY JUST NEED TO BE STAMPED?

YES, WE'VE BEEN WAITING TO SEND THEM UP TO HIS OFFICE FOR SEVERAL DAYS NOW. BUT HE'S BEEN SO BUSY LATELY...

THOSE POOR SOULS WILL JUST HAVE TO WAIT IN PURGATORY UNTIL HE CAN GET TO THEM.

UNLESS...

UNLESS WHAT?

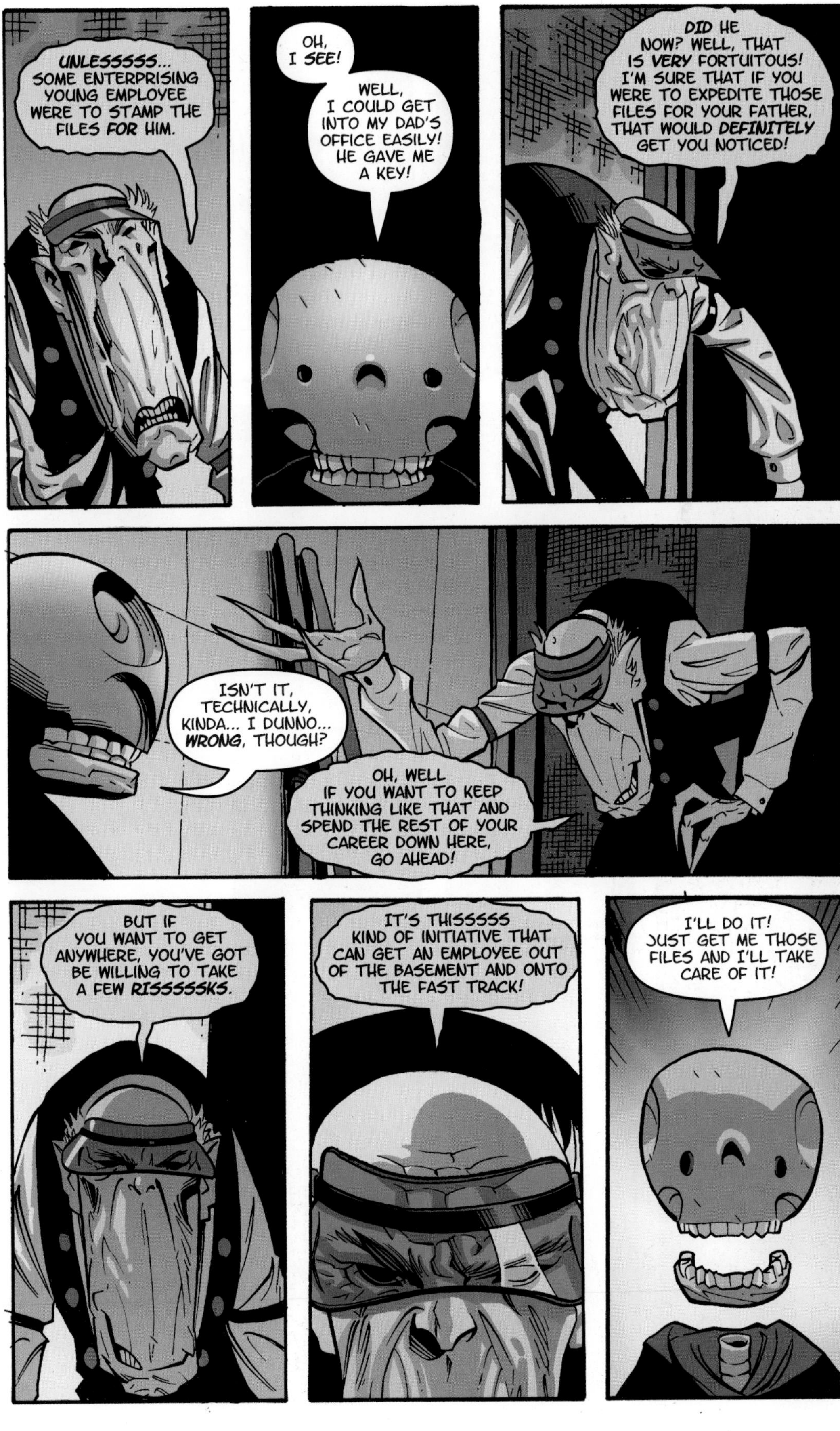
UNLESSSSS... SOME ENTERPRISING YOUNG EMPLOYEE WERE TO STAMP THE FILES FOR HIM.
OH, I SEE!
WELL, I COULD GET INTO MY DAD'S OFFICE EASILY! HE GAVE ME A KEY!
DID HE NOW? WELL, THAT IS VERY FORTUITOUS! I'M SURE THAT IF YOU WERE TO EXPEDITE THOSE FILES FOR YOUR FATHER, THAT WOULD DEFINITELY GET YOU NOTICED!
ISN'T IT, TECHNICALLY, KINDA... I DUNNO... WRONG, THOUGH?
OH, WELL IF YOU WANT TO KEEP THINKING LIKE THAT AND SPEND THE REST OF YOUR CAREER DOWN HERE, GO AHEAD!
BUT IF YOU WANT TO GET ANYWHERE, YOU'VE GOT BE WILLING TO TAKE A FEW RISSSSSKS.
IT'S THISSSSS KIND OF INITIATIVE THAT CAN GET AN EMPLOYEE OUT OF THE BASEMENT AND ONTO THE FAST TRACK!
I'LL DO IT! JUST GET ME THOSE FILES AND I'LL TAKE CARE OF IT!

WELL AS LUCK WOULD HAVE IT, I JUST SO HAPPEN TO HAVE THEM...

...RIGHT HERE.

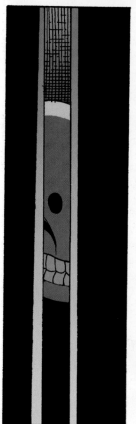

THERE IT IS.

MISTER CRACY IS RIGHT.

IT'S ALL ABOUT INITIATIVE.

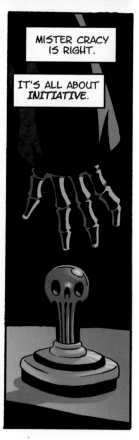

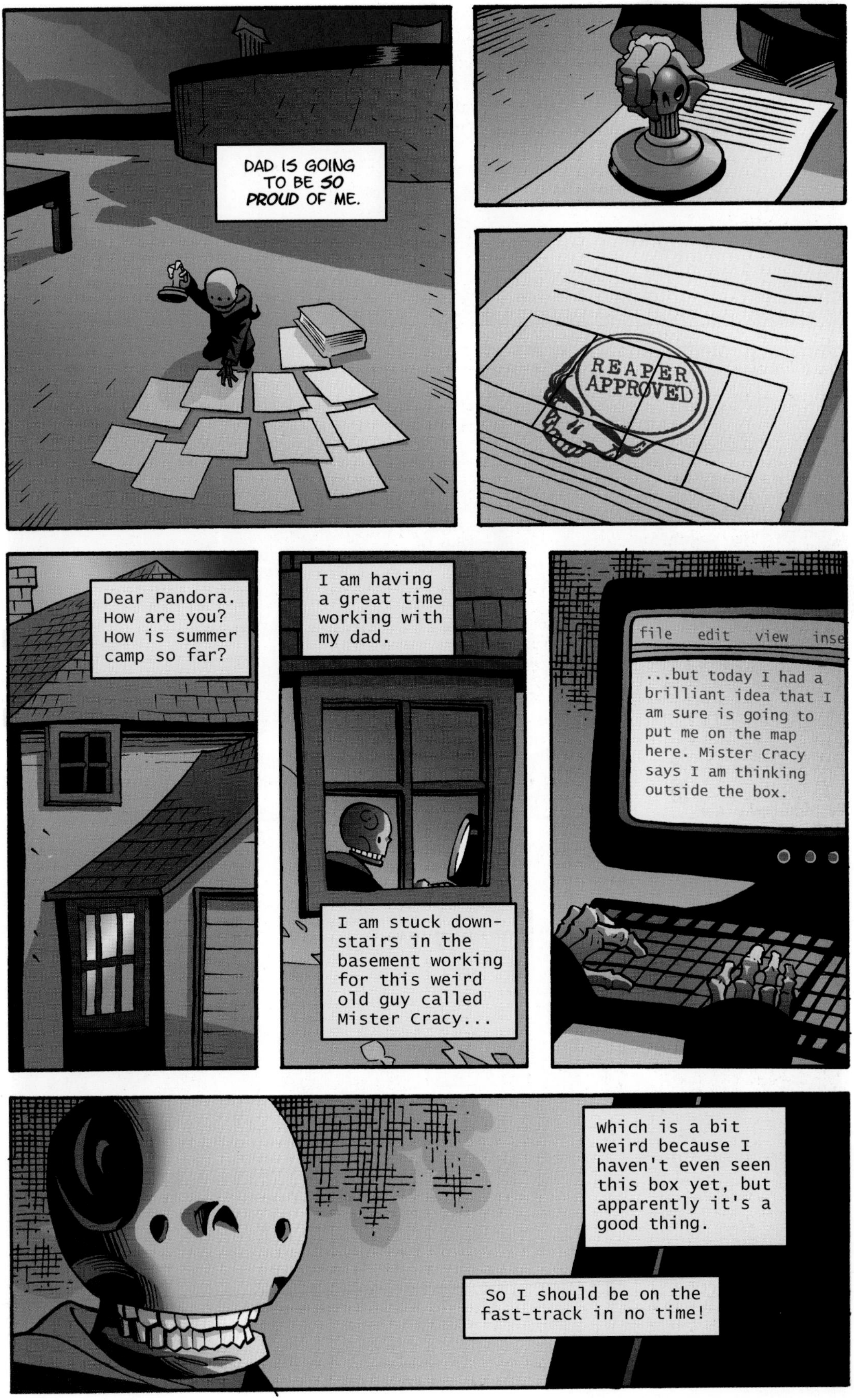
DAD IS GOING TO BE SO PROUD OF ME.
REAPER APPROVED
Dear Pandora. How are you? How is summer camp so far?
I am having a great time working with my dad.
I am stuck down-stairs in the basement working for this weird old guy called Mister Cracy...
file edit view inse
...but today I had a brilliant idea that I am sure is going to put me on the map here. Mister Cracy says I am thinking outside the box.
Which is a bit weird because I haven't even seen this box yet, but apparently it's a good thing.
So I should be on the fast-track in no time!

Anyway, I hope you and the gang are enjoying camp.
Say hi to everyone for me.

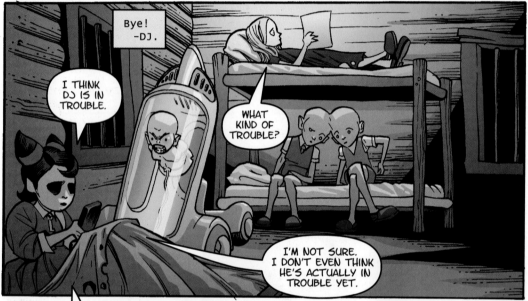

Bye!
-DJ.

I THINK DJ IS IN TROUBLE.

WHAT KIND OF TROUBLE?

I'M NOT SURE. I DON'T EVEN THINK HE'S ACTUALLY IN TROUBLE YET.

JUST THAT... HE'S ABOUT TO BE, SOON.

WHY DO YOU SAY THAT?

I DON'T KNOW... JUST A FEELING.

SOMETHING HE SAID IN THIS EMAIL.

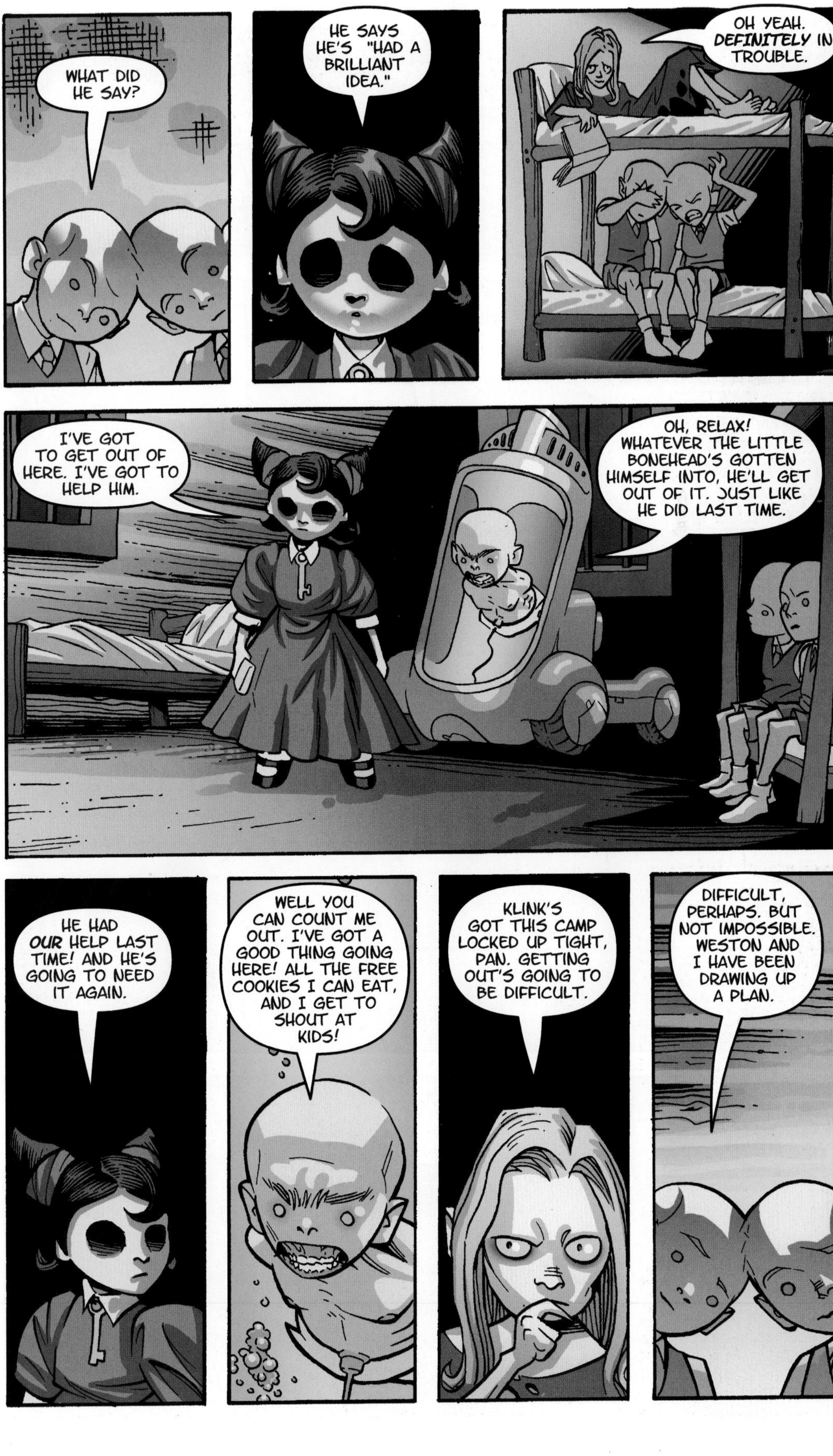
WHAT DID HE SAY?
HE SAYS HE'S "HAD A BRILLIANT IDEA."
OH YEAH. DEFINITELY IN TROUBLE.
I'VE GOT TO GET OUT OF HERE. I'VE GOT TO HELP HIM.
OH, RELAX! WHATEVER THE LITTLE BONEHEAD'S GOTTEN HIMSELF INTO, HE'LL GET OUT OF IT. JUST LIKE HE DID LAST TIME.
HE HAD OUR HELP LAST TIME! AND HE'S GOING TO NEED IT AGAIN.
WELL YOU CAN COUNT ME OUT. I'VE GOT A GOOD THING GOING HERE! ALL THE FREE COOKIES I CAN EAT, AND I GET TO SHOUT AT KIDS!
KLINK'S GOT THIS CAMP LOCKED UP TIGHT, PAN. GETTING OUT'S GOING TO BE DIFFICULT.
DIFFICULT, PERHAPS. BUT NOT IMPOSSIBLE. WESTON AND I HAVE BEEN DRAWING UP A PLAN.

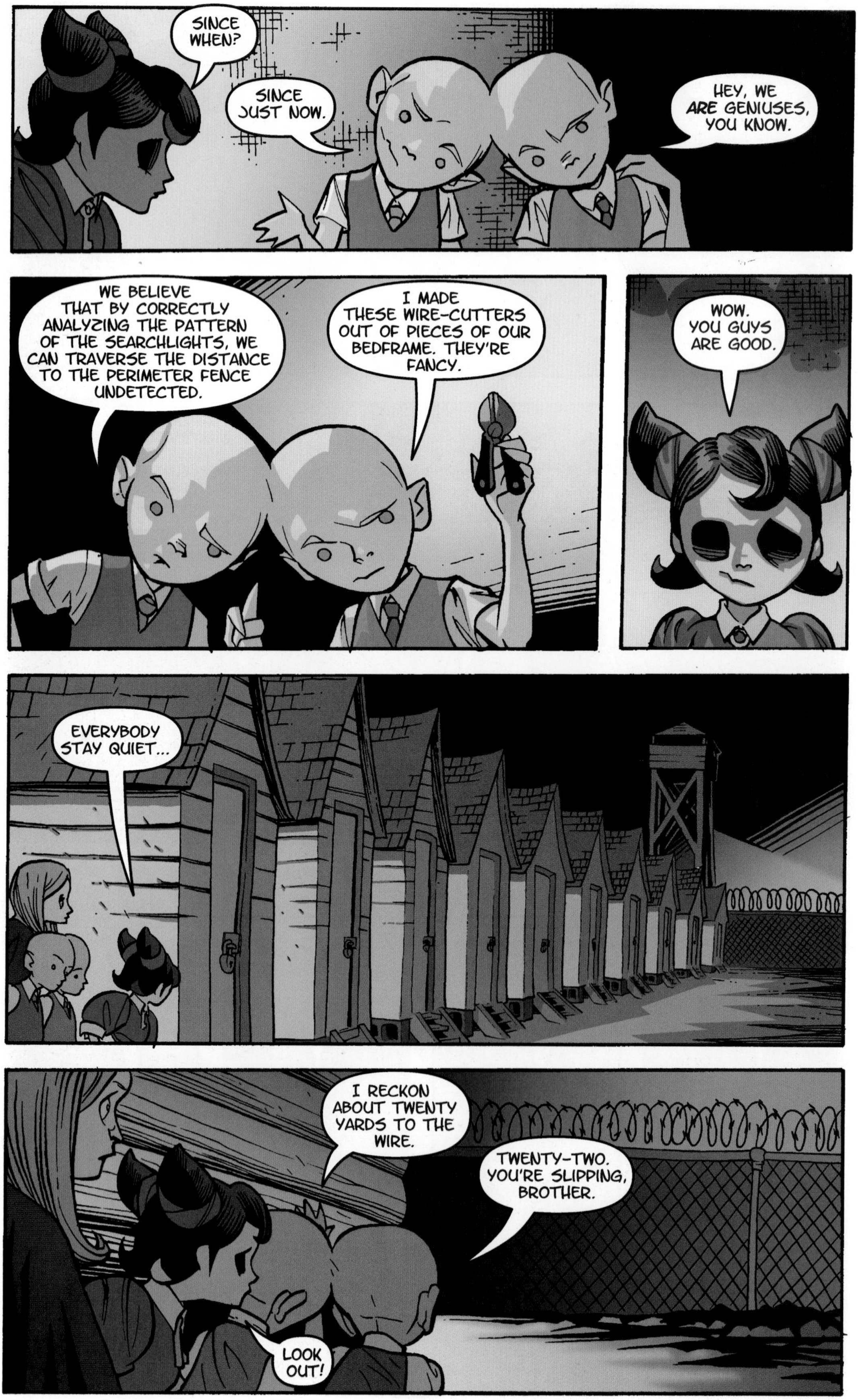
SINCE WHEN?
SINCE JUST NOW.
HEY, WE ARE GENIUSES, YOU KNOW.
WE BELIEVE THAT BY CORRECTLY ANALYZING THE PATTERN OF THE SEARCHLIGHTS, WE CAN TRAVERSE THE DISTANCE TO THE PERIMETER FENCE UNDETECTED.
I MADE THESE WIRE-CUTTERS OUT OF PIECES OF OUR BEDFRAME. THEY'RE FANCY.
WOW. YOU GUYS ARE GOOD.
EVERYBODY STAY QUIET...
I RECKON ABOUT TWENTY YARDS TO THE WIRE.
TWENTY-TWO. YOU'RE SLIPPING, BROTHER.
LOOK OUT!

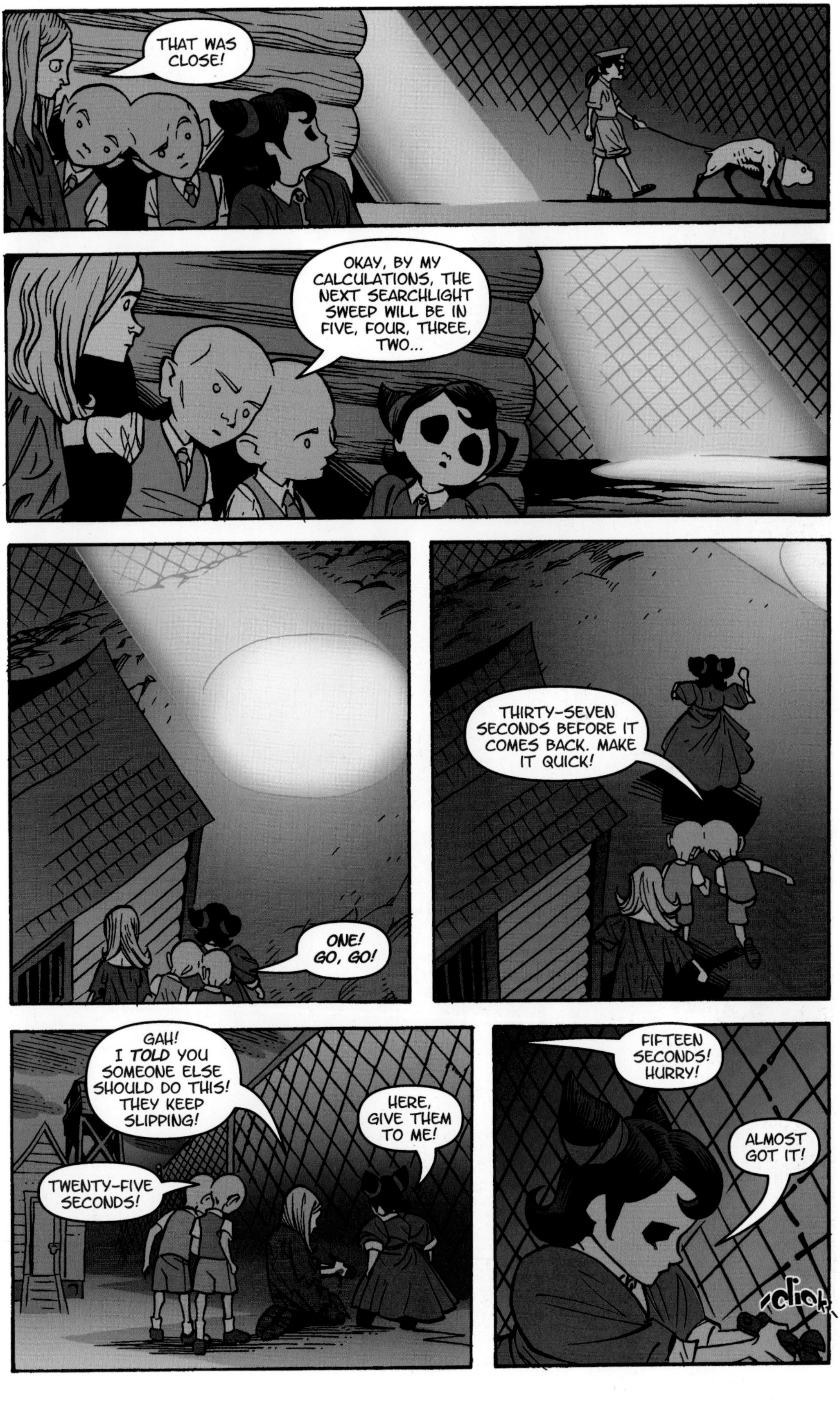
THAT WAS CLOSE!
OKAY, BY MY CALCULATIONS, THE NEXT SEARCHLIGHT SWEEP WILL BE IN FIVE, FOUR, THREE, TWO...
ONE! GO, GO!
THIRTY-SEVEN SECONDS BEFORE IT COMES BACK. MAKE IT QUICK!
GAH! I TOLD YOU SOMEONE ELSE SHOULD DO THIS! THEY KEEP SLIPPING!
TWENTY-FIVE SECONDS!
HERE, GIVE THEM TO ME!
FIFTEEN SECONDS! HURRY!
ALMOST GOT IT!
click

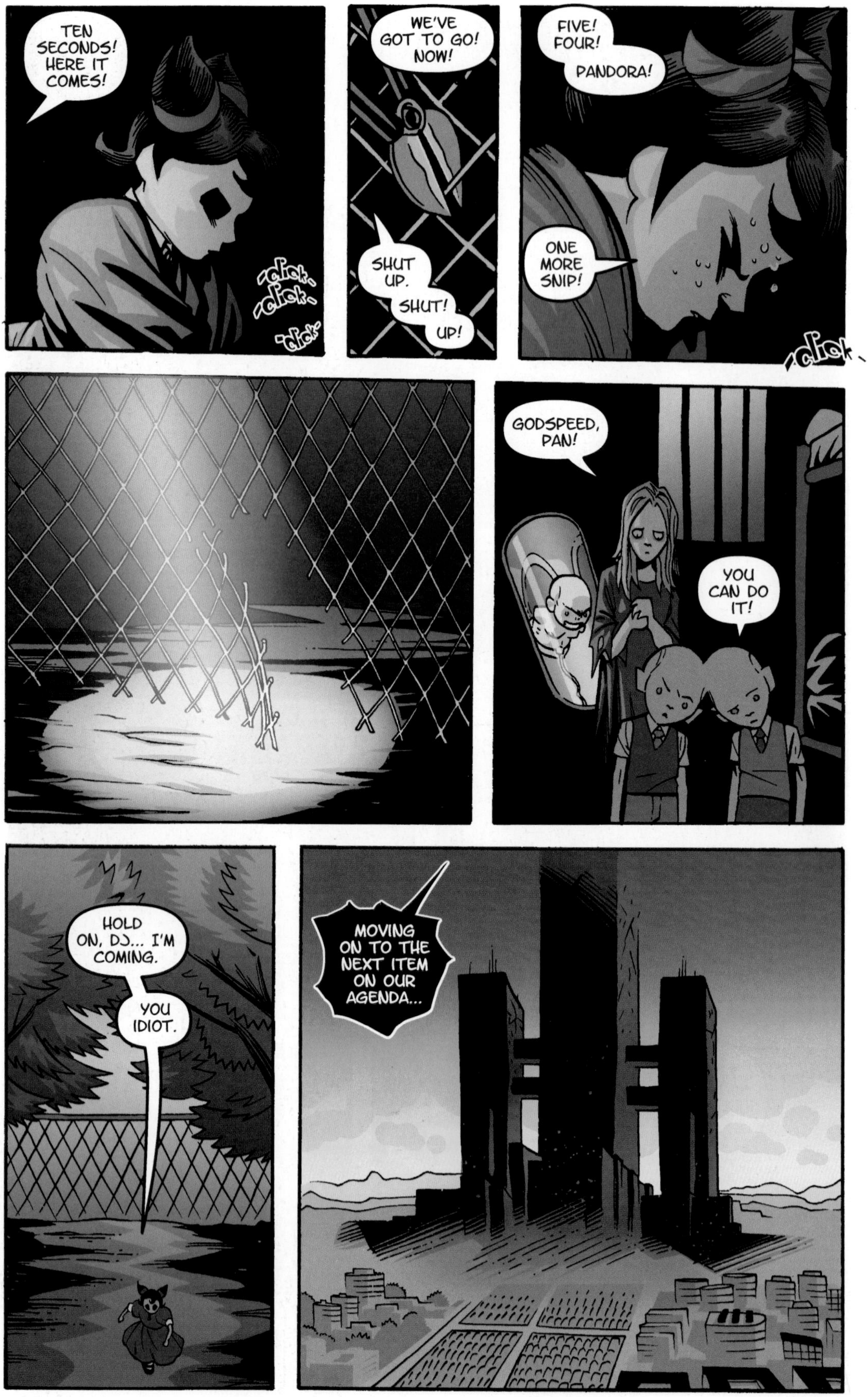

TEN SECONDS! HERE IT COMES!
-click- -click- -click-
WE'VE GOT TO GO! NOW!
SHUT UP.
SHUT!
UP!
FIVE! FOUR!
PANDORA!
ONE MORE SNIP!
-click-
GODSPEED, PAN!
YOU CAN DO IT!
HOLD ON, DJ... I'M COMING.
YOU IDIOT.
MOVING ON TO THE NEXT ITEM ON OUR AGENDA...

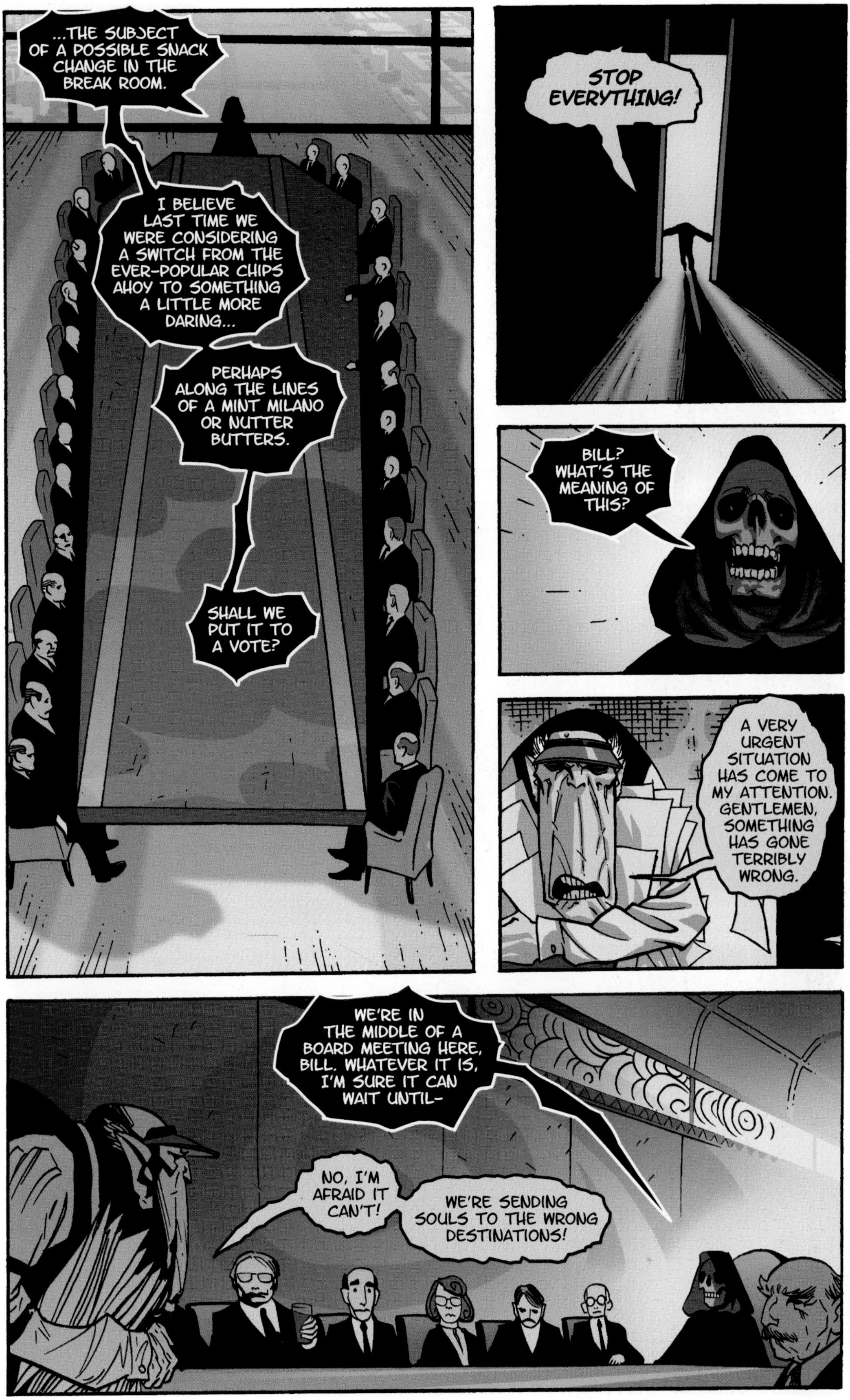
...THE SUBJECT OF A POSSIBLE SNACK CHANGE IN THE BREAK ROOM.
I BELIEVE LAST TIME WE WERE CONSIDERING A SWITCH FROM THE EVER-POPULAR CHIPS AHOY TO SOMETHING A LITTLE MORE DARING...
PERHAPS ALONG THE LINES OF A MINT MILANO OR NUTTER BUTTERS.
SHALL WE PUT IT TO A VOTE?
STOP EVERYTHING!
BILL? WHAT'S THE MEANING OF THIS?
A VERY URGENT SITUATION HAS COME TO MY ATTENTION. GENTLEMEN, SOMETHING HAS GONE TERRIBLY WRONG.
WE'RE IN THE MIDDLE OF A BOARD MEETING HERE, BILL. WHATEVER IT IS, I'M SURE IT CAN WAIT UNTIL-
NO, I'M AFRAID IT CAN'T!
WE'RE SENDING SOULS TO THE WRONG DESTINATIONS!

...*WHAT* DID YOU SAY?

I TOOK THE LIBERTY OF PULLING SOME OF THE FOOTAGE FROM OUR AFTERLIFE SECURITY CAMERAS.

IF YOU'D ALL PLEASE DIRECT YOUR ATTENTIONS TO THE MONITOR...

THIS IS MRS GLADYS CAMPBELL OF PEORIA, ILLINOIS.

AS PART OF HER PERSONALIZED AFTERLIFE PACKAGE, SHE HAS BEEN REWARDED WITH A DAILY ROUND OF GOLF WITH 1930S GOLF LEGEND BOBBY JONES.

THE ONLY PROBLEM IS, MRS CAMPBELL ALWAYS HATED GOLF AND SO ASSUMES SHE HAS BEEN SENT TO SOME KIND OF PERSONALIZED HELL.

IN A SIMILAR CASE...

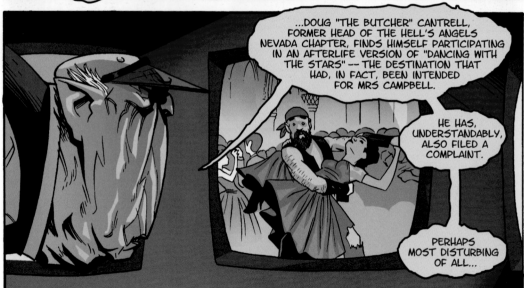

...DOUG "THE BUTCHER" CANTRELL, FORMER HEAD OF THE HELL'S ANGELS NEVADA CHAPTER, FINDS HIMSELF PARTICIPATING IN AN AFTERLIFE VERSION OF "DANCING WITH THE STARS" -- THE DESTINATION THAT HAD, IN FACT, BEEN INTENDED FOR MRS CAMPBELL.

HE HAS, UNDERSTANDABLY, ALSO FILED A COMPLAINT.

PERHAPS MOST DISTURBING OF ALL...

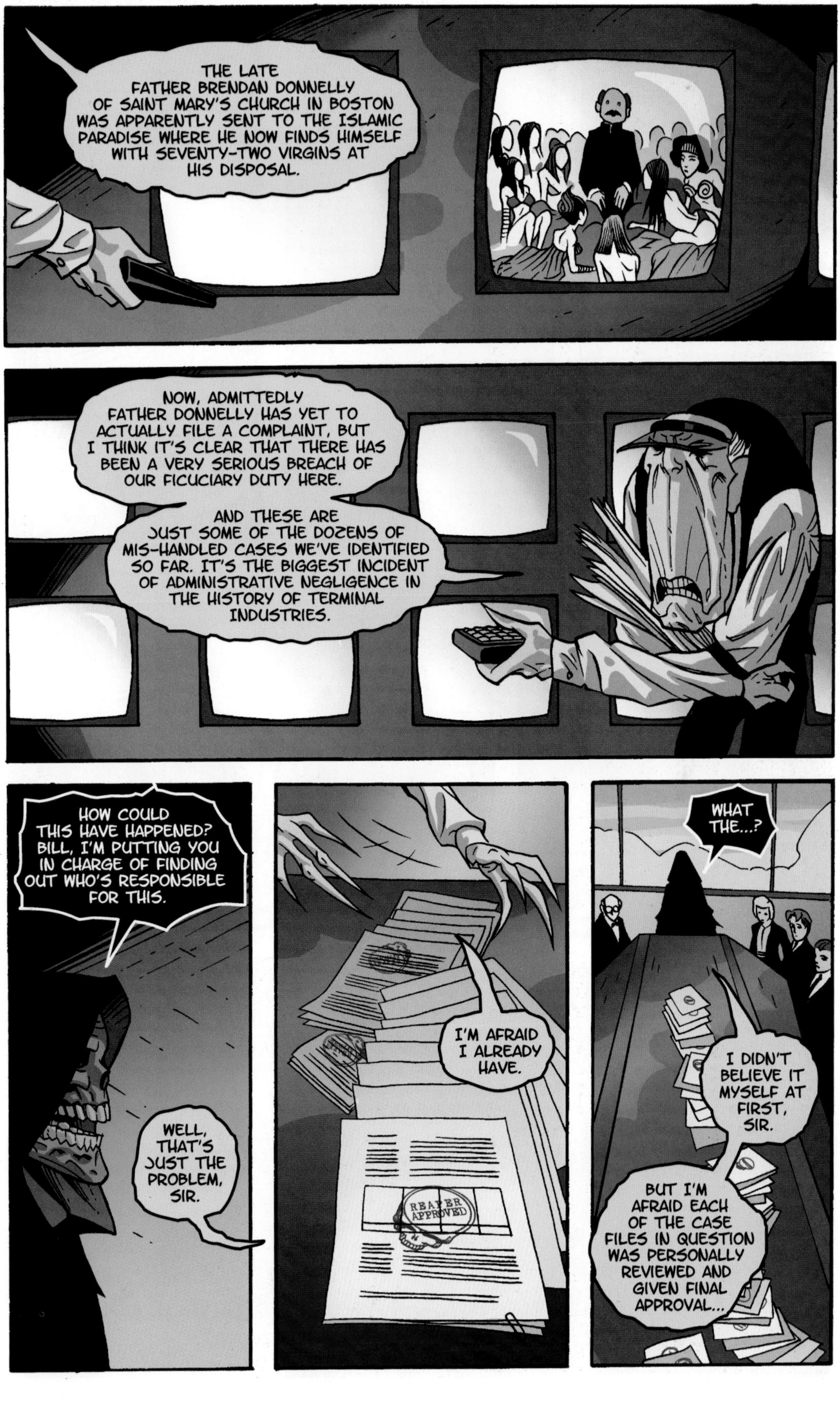
THE LATE FATHER BRENDAN DONNELLY OF SAINT MARY'S CHURCH IN BOSTON WAS APPARENTLY SENT TO THE ISLAMIC PARADISE WHERE HE NOW FINDS HIMSELF WITH SEVENTY-TWO VIRGINS AT HIS DISPOSAL.
NOW, ADMITTEDLY FATHER DONNELLY HAS YET TO ACTUALLY FILE A COMPLAINT, BUT I THINK IT'S CLEAR THAT THERE HAS BEEN A VERY SERIOUS BREACH OF OUR FICUCIARY DUTY HERE.
AND THESE ARE JUST SOME OF THE DOZENS OF MIS-HANDLED CASES WE'VE IDENTIFIED SO FAR. IT'S THE BIGGEST INCIDENT OF ADMINISTRATIVE NEGLIGENCE IN THE HISTORY OF TERMINAL INDUSTRIES.
HOW COULD THIS HAVE HAPPENED? BILL, I'M PUTTING YOU IN CHARGE OF FINDING OUT WHO'S RESPONSIBLE FOR THIS.
WELL, THAT'S JUST THE PROBLEM, SIR.
I'M AFRAID I ALREADY HAVE.
REAPER APPROVED
WHAT THE...?
I DIDN'T BELIEVE IT MYSELF AT FIRST, SIR.
BUT I'M AFRAID EACH OF THE CASE FILES IN QUESTION WAS PERSONALLY REVIEWED AND GIVEN FINAL APPROVAL...

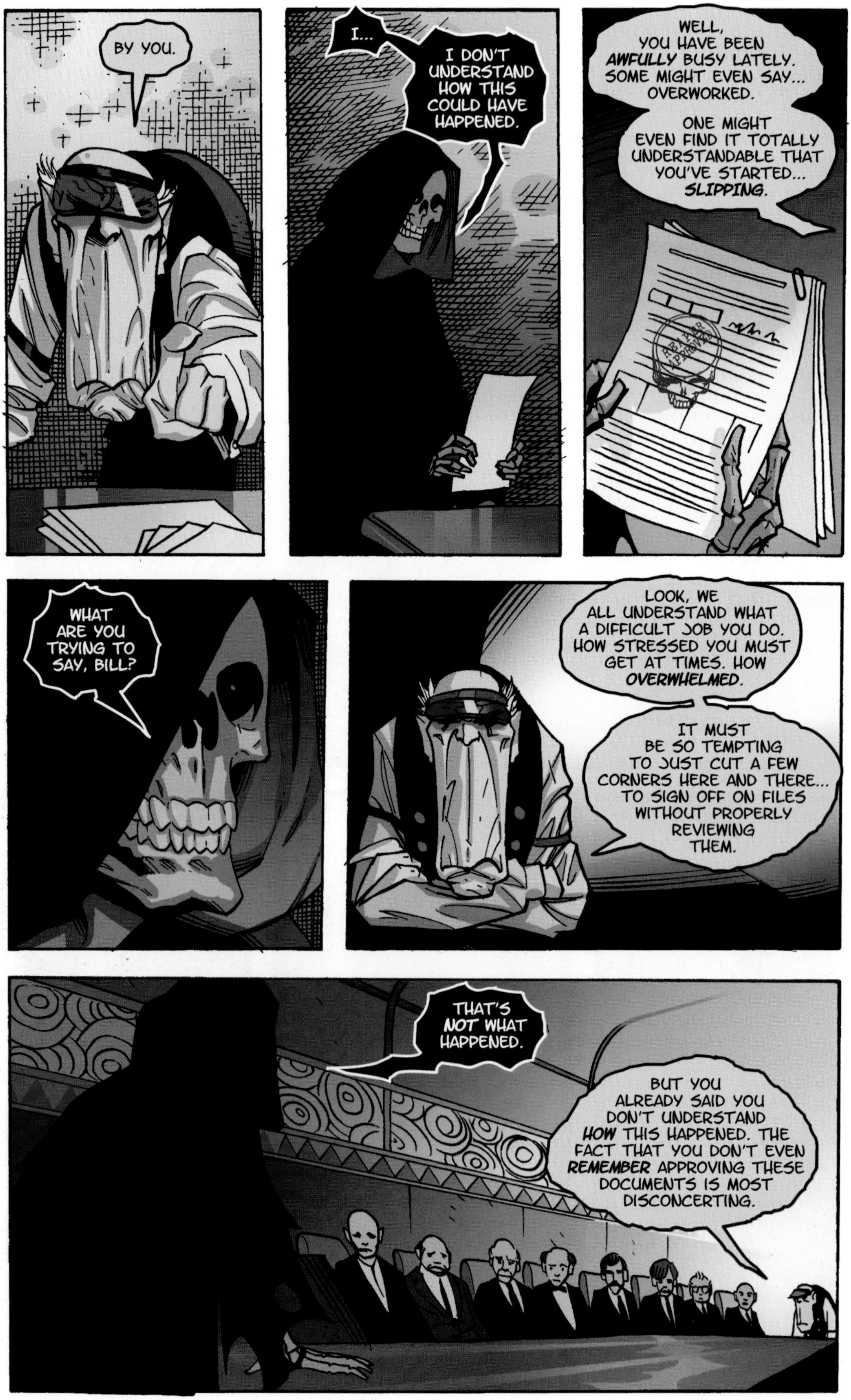

BY YOU.
I...
I DON'T UNDERSTAND HOW THIS COULD HAVE HAPPENED.
WELL, YOU HAVE BEEN AWFULLY BUSY LATELY. SOME MIGHT EVEN SAY... OVERWORKED.
ONE MIGHT EVEN FIND IT TOTALLY UNDERSTANDABLE THAT YOU'VE STARTED... SLIPPING.
WHAT ARE YOU TRYING TO SAY, BILL?
LOOK, WE ALL UNDERSTAND WHAT A DIFFICULT JOB YOU DO. HOW STRESSED YOU MUST GET AT TIMES. HOW OVERWHELMED.
IT MUST BE SO TEMPTING TO JUST CUT A FEW CORNERS HERE AND THERE... TO SIGN OFF ON FILES WITHOUT PROPERLY REVIEWING THEM.
THAT'S NOT WHAT HAPPENED.
BUT YOU ALREADY SAID YOU DON'T UNDERSTAND HOW THIS HAPPENED. THE FACT THAT YOU DON'T EVEN REMEMBER APPROVING THESE DOCUMENTS IS MOST DISCONCERTING.

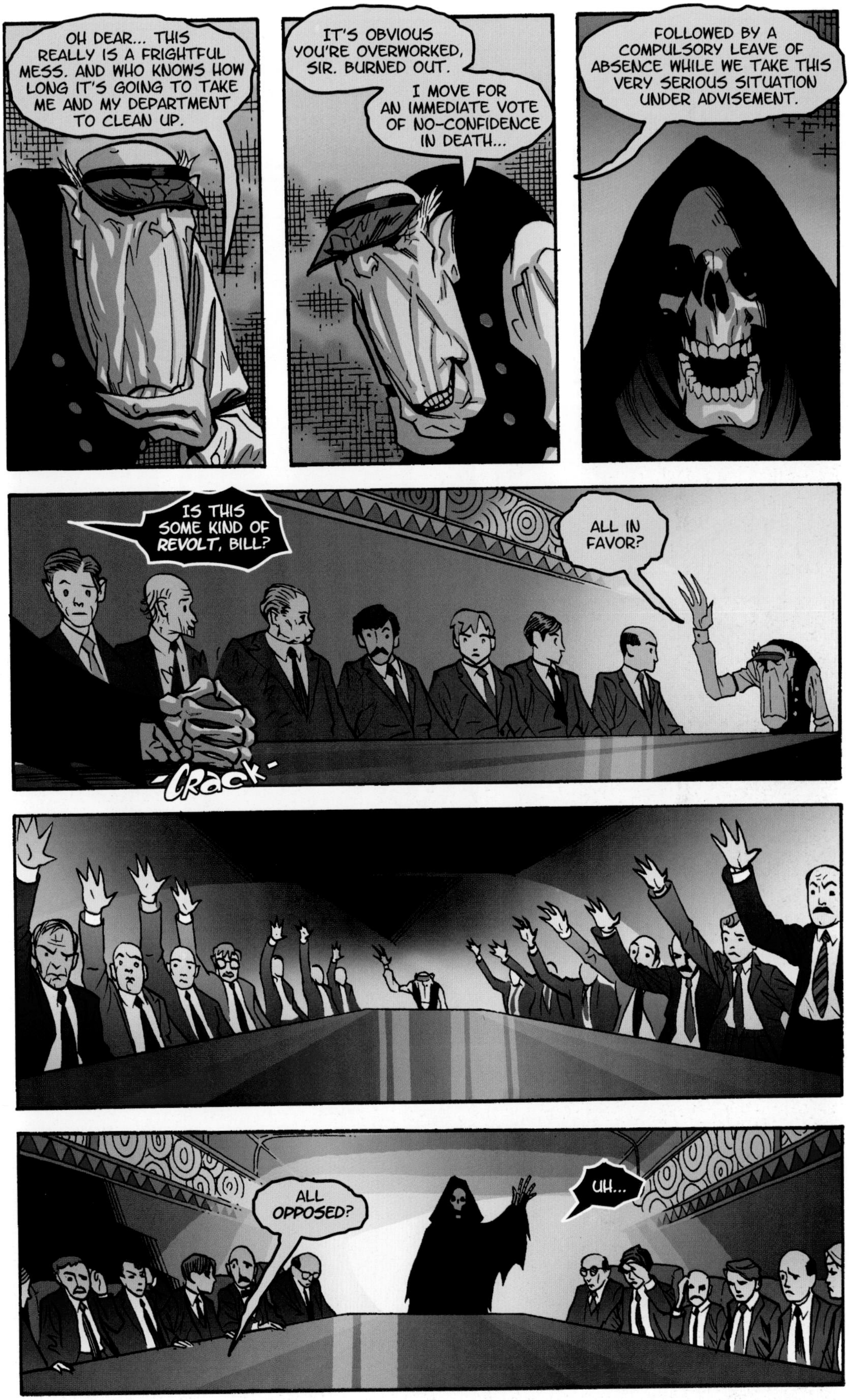
OH DEAR... THIS REALLY IS A FRIGHTFUL MESS. AND WHO KNOWS HOW LONG IT'S GOING TO TAKE ME AND MY DEPARTMENT TO CLEAN UP.
IT'S OBVIOUS YOU'RE OVERWORKED, SIR. BURNED OUT.
I MOVE FOR AN IMMEDIATE VOTE OF NO-CONFIDENCE IN DEATH...
FOLLOWED BY A COMPULSORY LEAVE OF ABSENCE WHILE WE TAKE THIS VERY SERIOUS SITUATION UNDER ADVISEMENT.
IS THIS SOME KIND OF REVOLT, BILL?
ALL IN FAVOR?
-CRACK-
ALL OPPOSED?
UH...

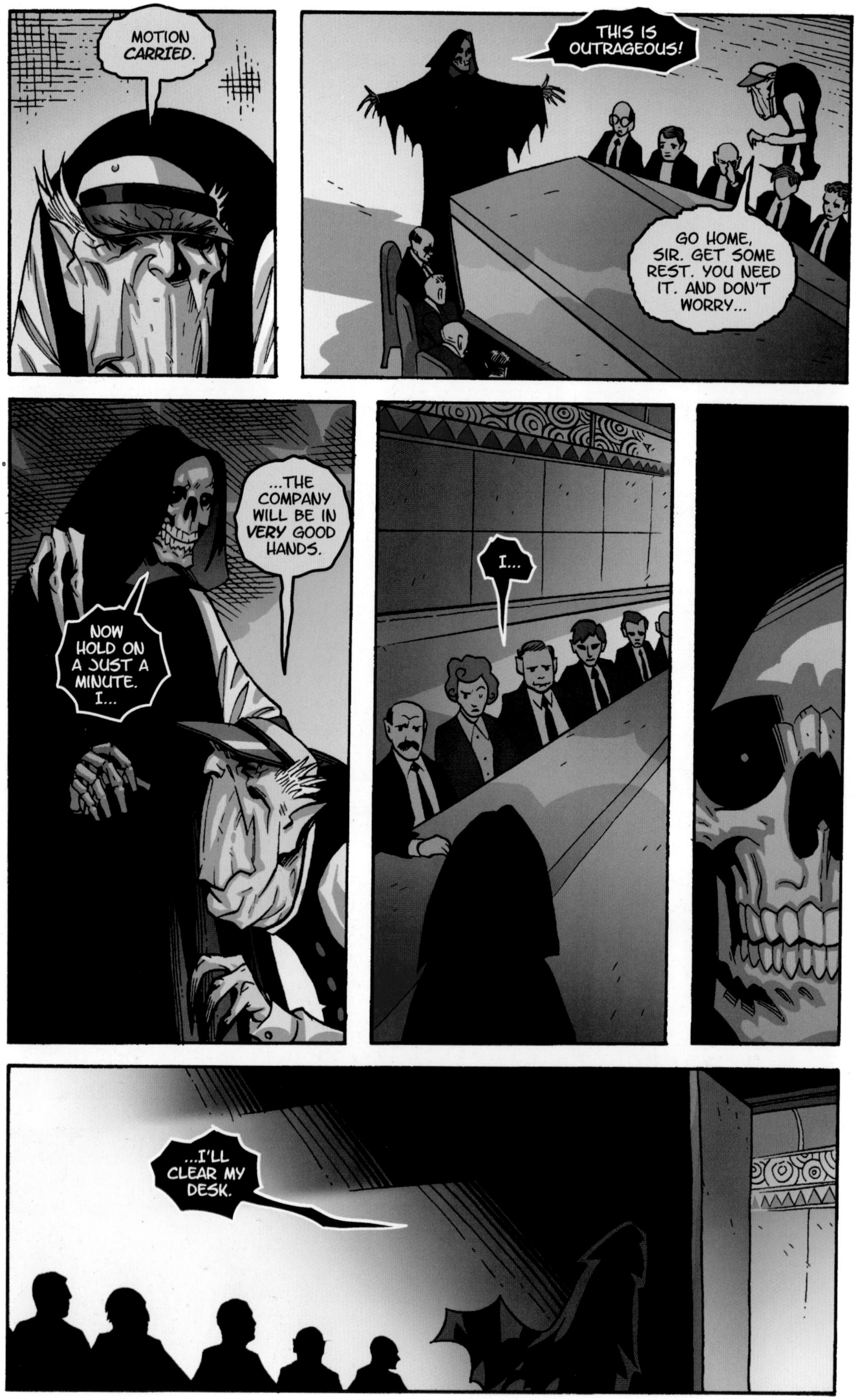
MOTION CARRIED.
THIS IS OUTRAGEOUS!
GO HOME, SIR. GET SOME REST. YOU NEED IT. AND DON'T WORRY...
...THE COMPANY WILL BE IN VERY GOOD HANDS.
NOW HOLD ON A JUST A MINUTE. I...
I...
...I'LL CLEAR MY DESK.

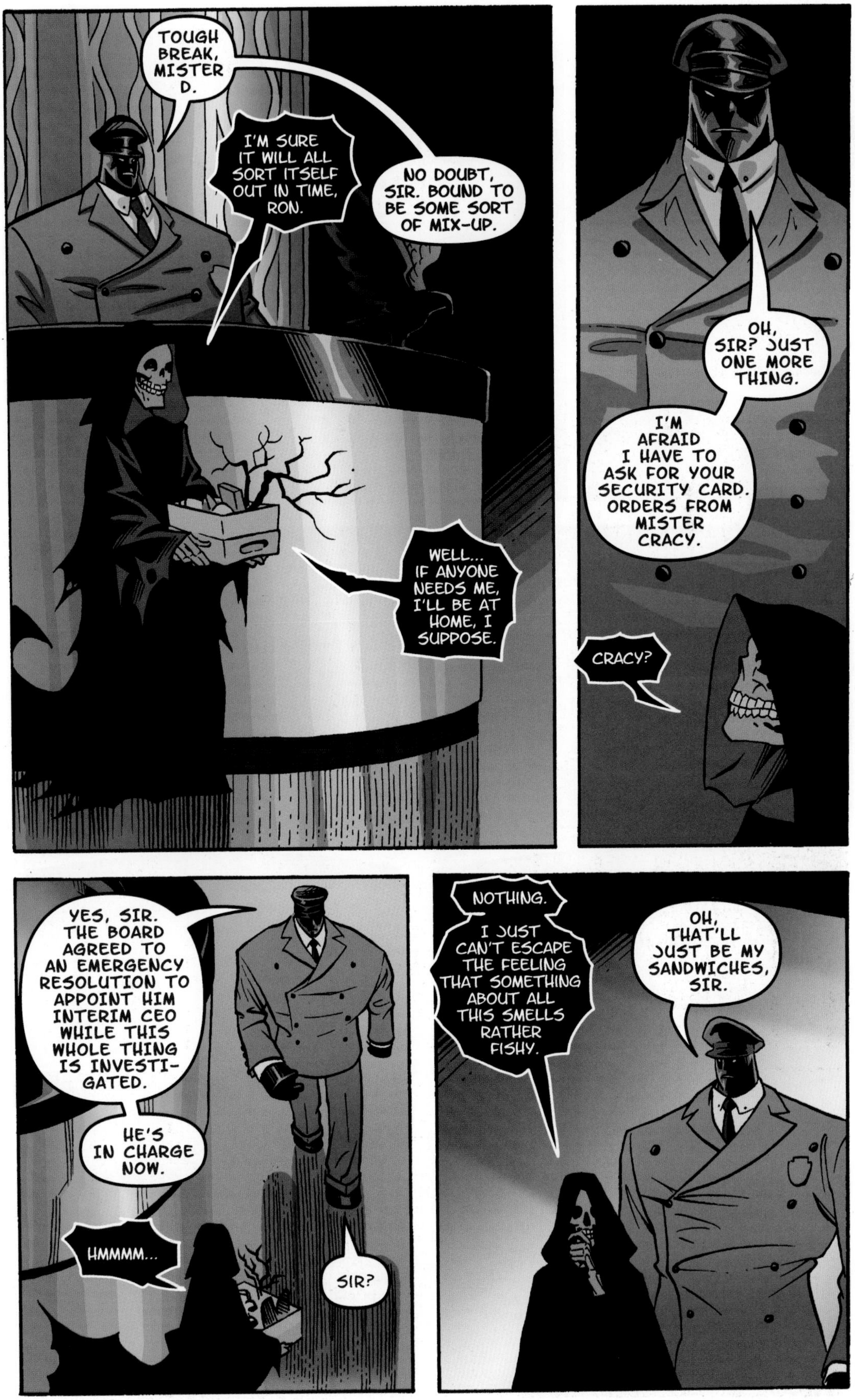
TOUGH BREAK, MISTER D.
I'M SURE IT WILL ALL SORT ITSELF OUT IN TIME, RON.
NO DOUBT, SIR. BOUND TO BE SOME SORT OF MIX-UP.
WELL... IF ANYONE NEEDS ME, I'LL BE AT HOME, I SUPPOSE.
OH, SIR? JUST ONE MORE THING.
I'M AFRAID I HAVE TO ASK FOR YOUR SECURITY CARD. ORDERS FROM MISTER CRACY.
CRACY?
YES, SIR. THE BOARD AGREED TO AN EMERGENCY RESOLUTION TO APPOINT HIM INTERIM CEO WHILE THIS WHOLE THING IS INVESTI-GATED.
HE'S IN CHARGE NOW.
HMMMM...
SIR?
NOTHING.
I JUST CAN'T ESCAPE THE FEELING THAT SOMETHING ABOUT ALL THIS SMELLS RATHER FISHY.
OH, THAT'LL JUST BE MY SANDWICHES, SIR.

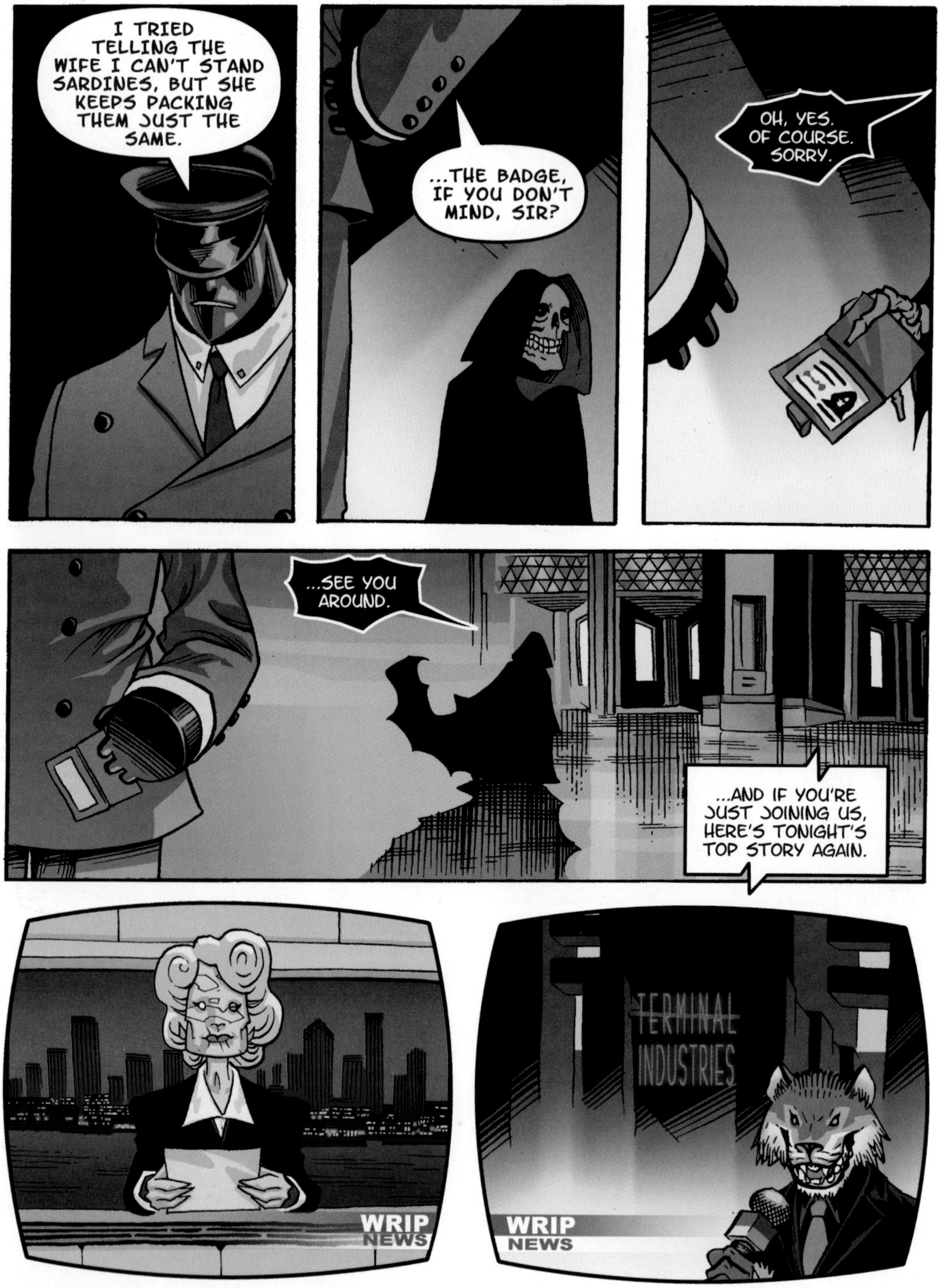
I TRIED TELLING THE WIFE I CAN'T STAND SARDINES, BUT SHE KEEPS PACKING THEM JUST THE SAME.
...THE BADGE, IF YOU DON'T MIND, SIR?
OH, YES. OF COURSE. SORRY.
...SEE YOU AROUND.
...AND IF YOU'RE JUST JOINING US, HERE'S TONIGHT'S TOP STORY AGAIN.
WRIP NEWS
TERMINAL INDUSTRIES
WRIP NEWS

FOLLOWING ALLEGATIONS OF GROSS NEGLIGENCE AND CORPORATE MISMANAGEMENT THAT HAS LEFT THE AFTERLIFE IN CHAOS, THE GRIM REAPER HIMSELF WAS TODAY SUSPENDED INDEFINITELY AS CEO OF TERMINAL INDUSTRIES BY THE COMPANY'S BOARD OF DIRECTORS. WRIP'S BILL LYCANTHROPE HAS THIS REPORT.

BUTTONWILLOW, DEATH HAS LEFT THE BUILDING. I'M STANDING OUTSIDE THE HEADQUARTERS OF TERMINAL INDUSTRIES, WHERE JUST AN HOUR AGO A SURPRISING BOARDROOM REVOLT RESULTED IN THE REMOVAL OF THE GRIM REAPER AS CHIEF EXECUTIVE OFFICER.

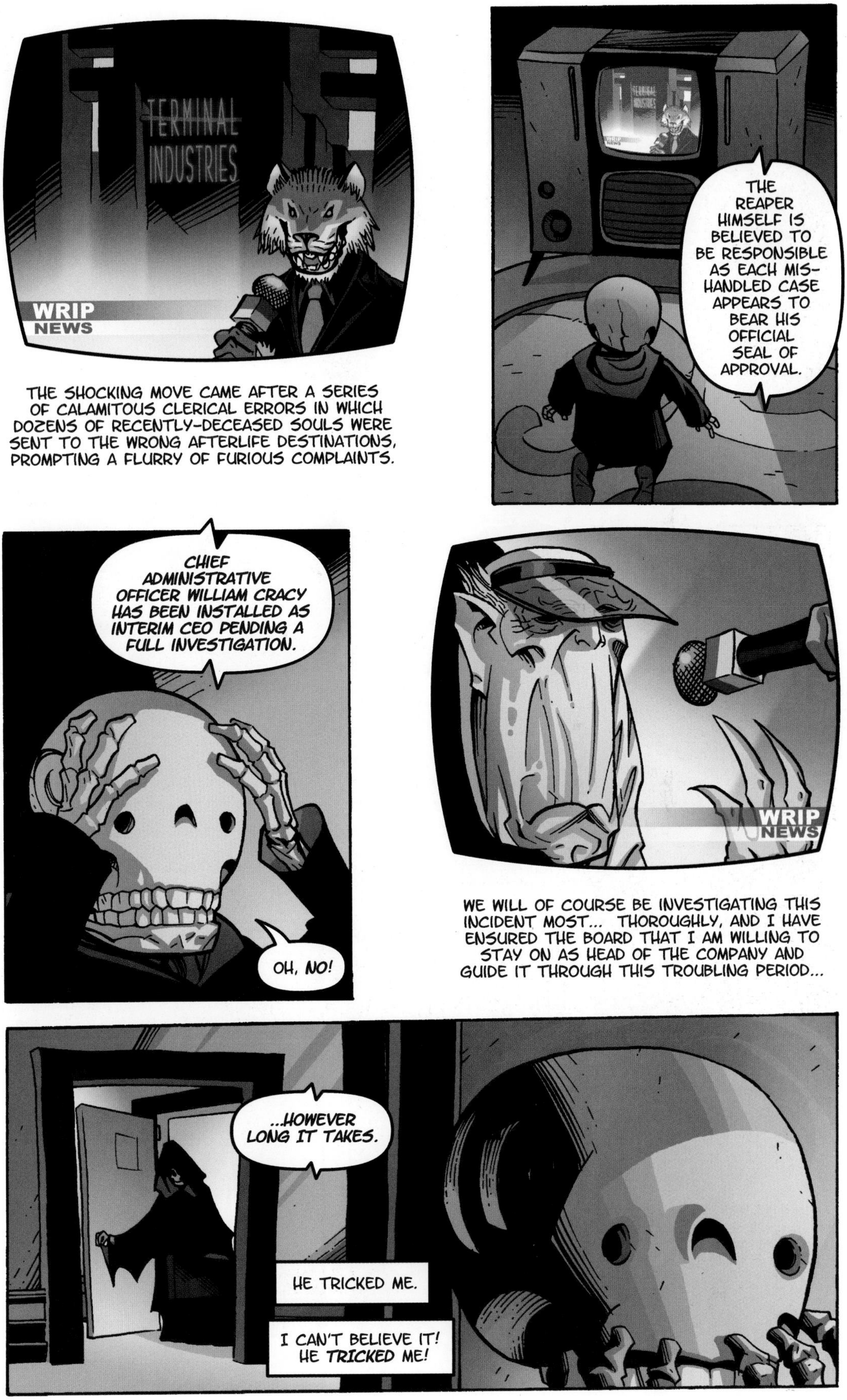
TERMINAL
INDUSTRIES
WRIP
NEWS
THE SHOCKING MOVE CAME AFTER A SERIES OF CALAMITOUS CLERICAL ERRORS IN WHICH DOZENS OF RECENTLY-DECEASED SOULS WERE SENT TO THE WRONG AFTERLIFE DESTINATIONS, PROMPTING A FLURRY OF FURIOUS COMPLAINTS.
THE REAPER HIMSELF IS BELIEVED TO BE RESPONSIBLE AS EACH MIS-HANDLED CASE APPEARS TO BEAR HIS OFFICIAL SEAL OF APPROVAL.
CHIEF ADMINISTRATIVE OFFICER WILLIAM CRACY HAS BEEN INSTALLED AS INTERIM CEO PENDING A FULL INVESTIGATION.
OH, NO!
WRIP
NEWS
WE WILL OF COURSE BE INVESTIGATING THIS INCIDENT MOST... THOROUGHLY, AND I HAVE ENSURED THE BOARD THAT I AM WILLING TO STAY ON AS HEAD OF THE COMPANY AND GUIDE IT THROUGH THIS TROUBLING PERIOD...
...HOWEVER LONG IT TAKES.
HE TRICKED ME.
I CAN'T BELIEVE IT! HE TRICKED ME!

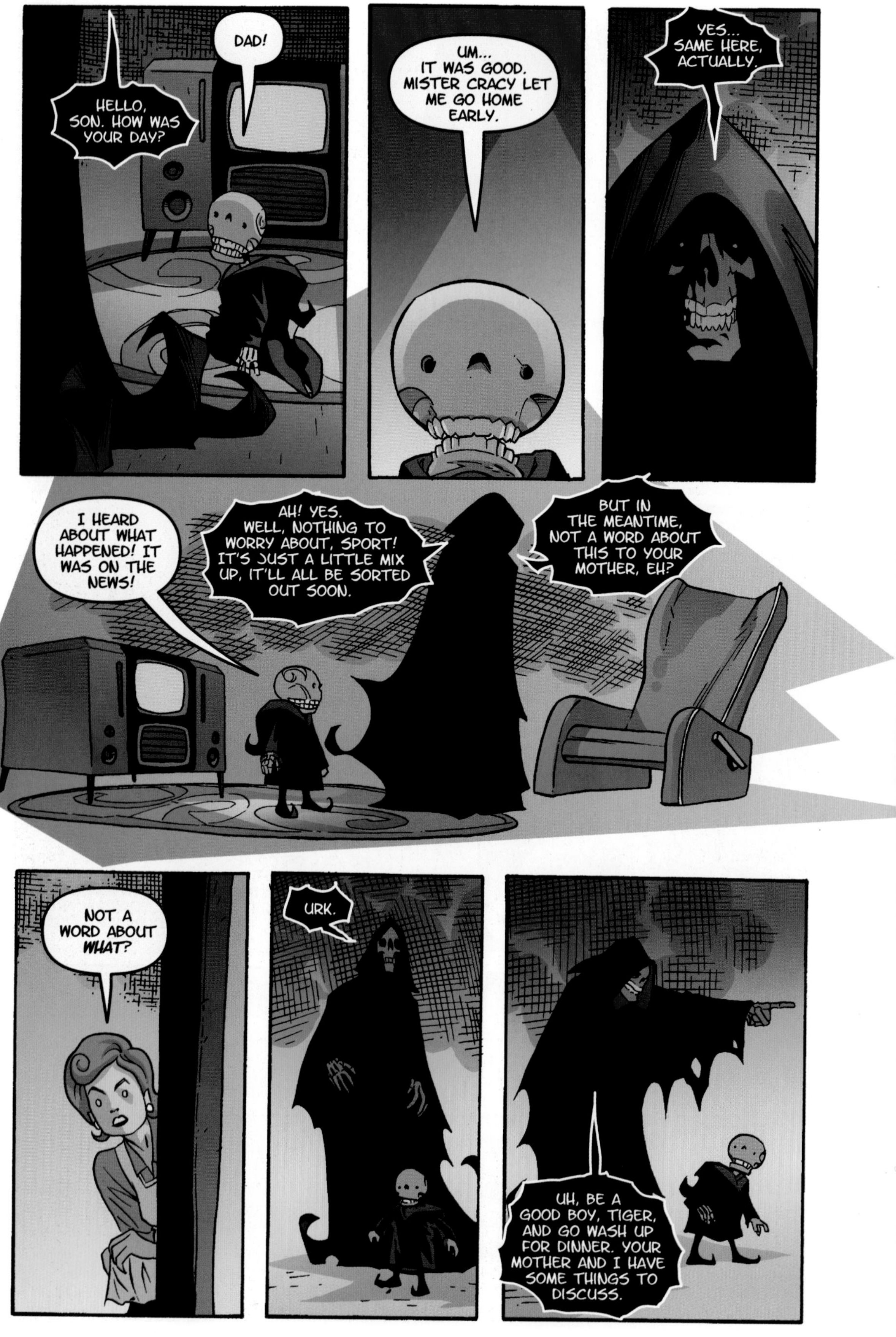
HELLO, SON. HOW WAS YOUR DAY?
DAD!
UM... IT WAS GOOD. MISTER CRACY LET ME GO HOME EARLY.
YES... SAME HERE, ACTUALLY.
I HEARD ABOUT WHAT HAPPENED! IT WAS ON THE NEWS!
AH! YES. WELL, NOTHING TO WORRY ABOUT, SPORT! IT'S JUST A LITTLE MIX UP, IT'LL ALL BE SORTED OUT SOON.
BUT IN THE MEANTIME, NOT A WORD ABOUT THIS TO YOUR MOTHER, EH?
NOT A WORD ABOUT *WHAT*?
URK.
UH, BE A GOOD BOY, TIGER, AND GO WASH UP FOR DINNER. YOUR MOTHER AND I HAVE SOME THINGS TO DISCUSS.

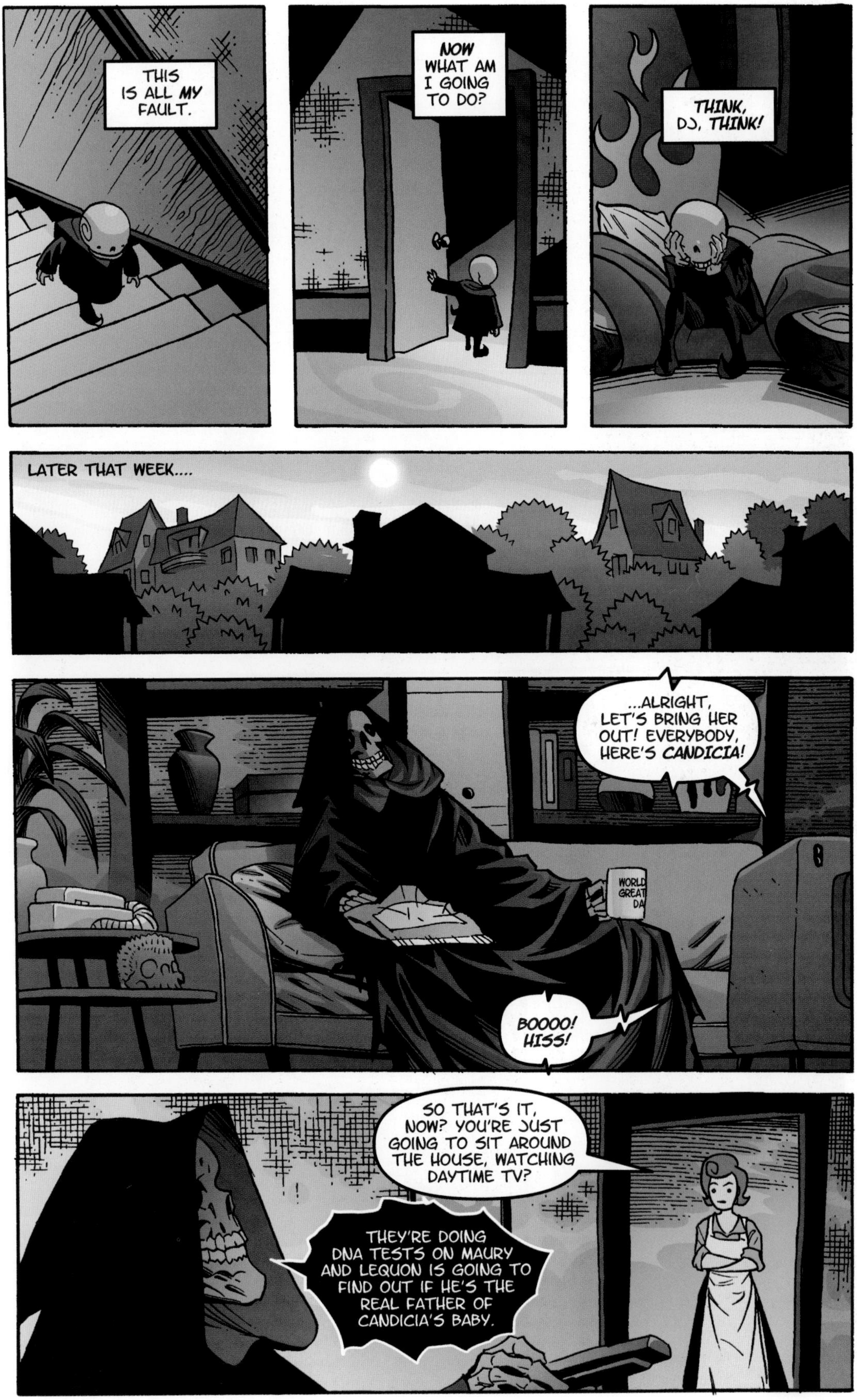
THIS IS ALL MY FAULT.
NOW WHAT AM I GOING TO DO?
THINK, DJ, THINK!
LATER THAT WEEK....
...ALRIGHT, LET'S BRING HER OUT! EVERYBODY, HERE'S CANDICIA!
BOOOO! HISS!
SO THAT'S IT, NOW? YOU'RE JUST GOING TO SIT AROUND THE HOUSE, WATCHING DAYTIME TV?
THEY'RE DOING DNA TESTS ON MAURY AND LEQUON IS GOING TO FIND OUT IF HE'S THE REAL FATHER OF CANDICIA'S BABY.

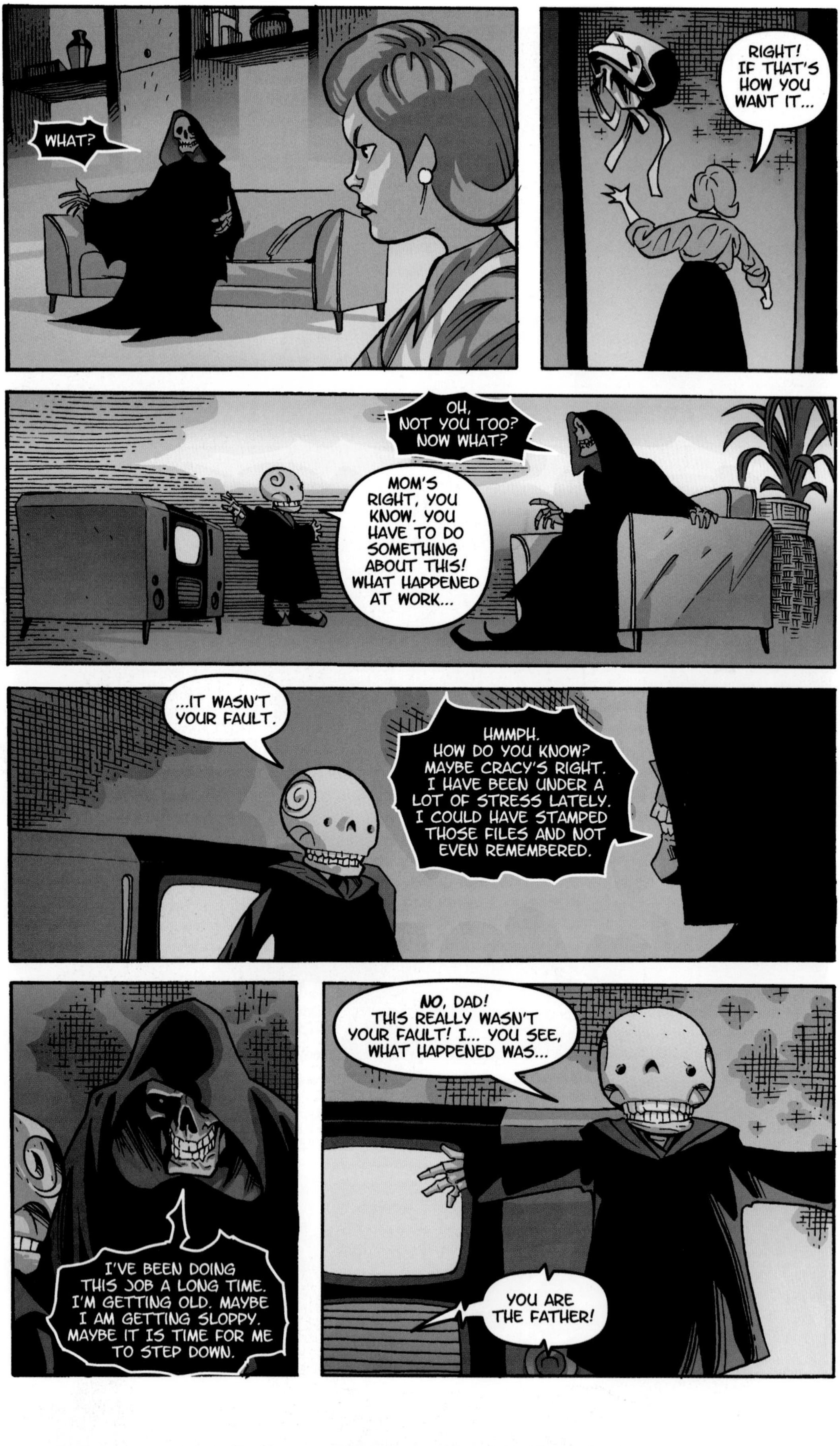
WHAT?
RIGHT! IF THAT'S HOW YOU WANT IT...
OH, NOT YOU TOO? NOW WHAT?
MOM'S RIGHT, YOU KNOW. YOU HAVE TO DO SOMETHING ABOUT THIS! WHAT HAPPENED AT WORK...
...IT WASN'T YOUR FAULT.
HMMPH. HOW DO YOU KNOW? MAYBE CRACY'S RIGHT. I HAVE BEEN UNDER A LOT OF STRESS LATELY. I COULD HAVE STAMPED THOSE FILES AND NOT EVEN REMEMBERED.
I'VE BEEN DOING THIS JOB A LONG TIME. I'M GETTING OLD. MAYBE I AM GETTING SLOPPY. MAYBE IT IS TIME FOR ME TO STEP DOWN.
NO, DAD! THIS REALLY WASN'T YOUR FAULT! I... YOU SEE, WHAT HAPPENED WAS...
YOU ARE THE FATHER!

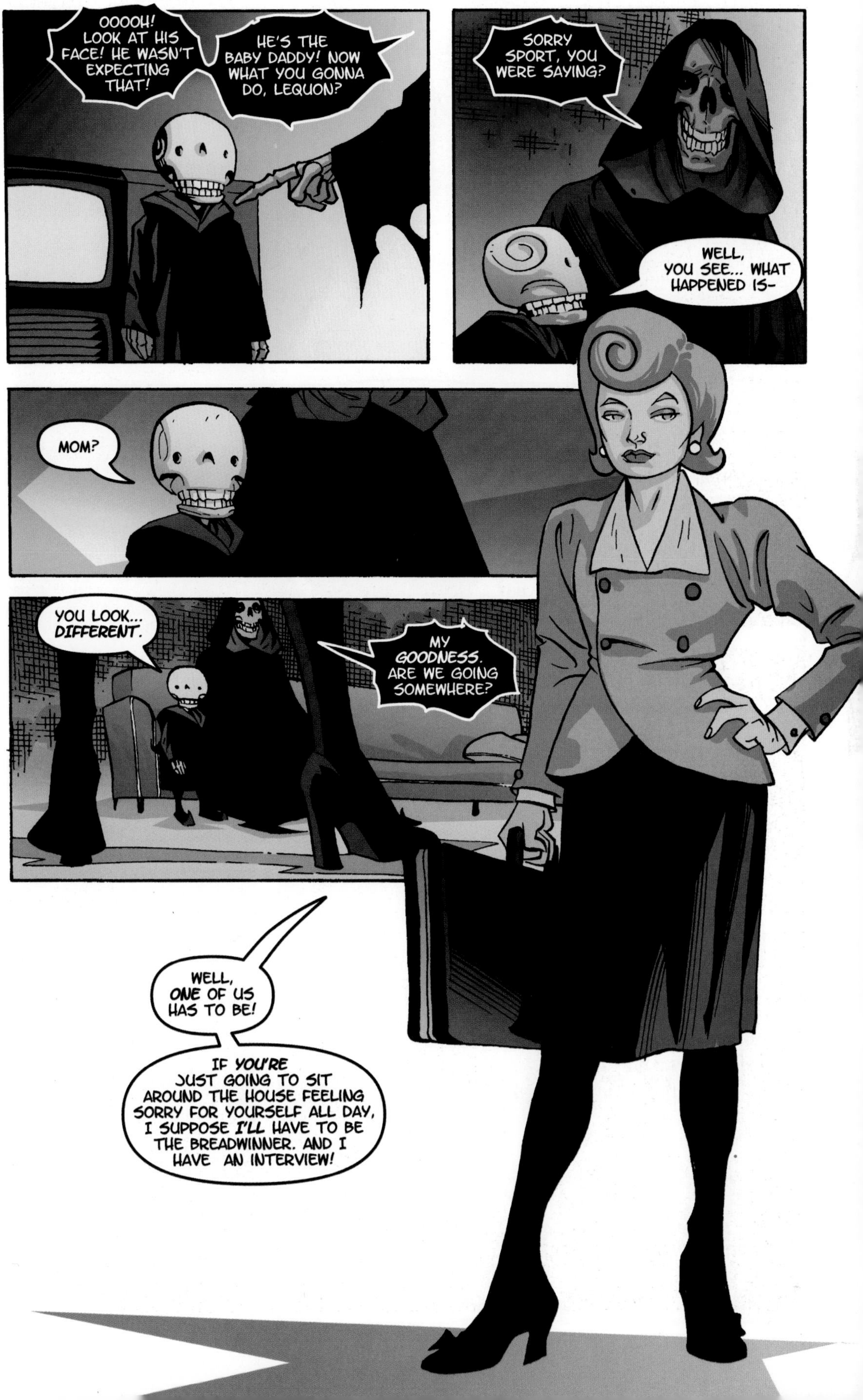
OOOOH! LOOK AT HIS FACE! HE WASN'T EXPECTING THAT!
HE'S THE BABY DADDY! NOW WHAT YOU GONNA DO, LEQUON?
SORRY SPORT, YOU WERE SAYING?
WELL, YOU SEE... WHAT HAPPENED IS-
MOM?
YOU LOOK... DIFFERENT.
MY GOODNESS. ARE WE GOING SOMEWHERE?
WELL, ONE OF US HAS TO BE!
IF YOU'RE JUST GOING TO SIT AROUND THE HOUSE FEELING SORRY FOR YOURSELF ALL DAY, I SUPPOSE I'LL HAVE TO BE THE BREADWINNER. AND I HAVE AN INTERVIEW!

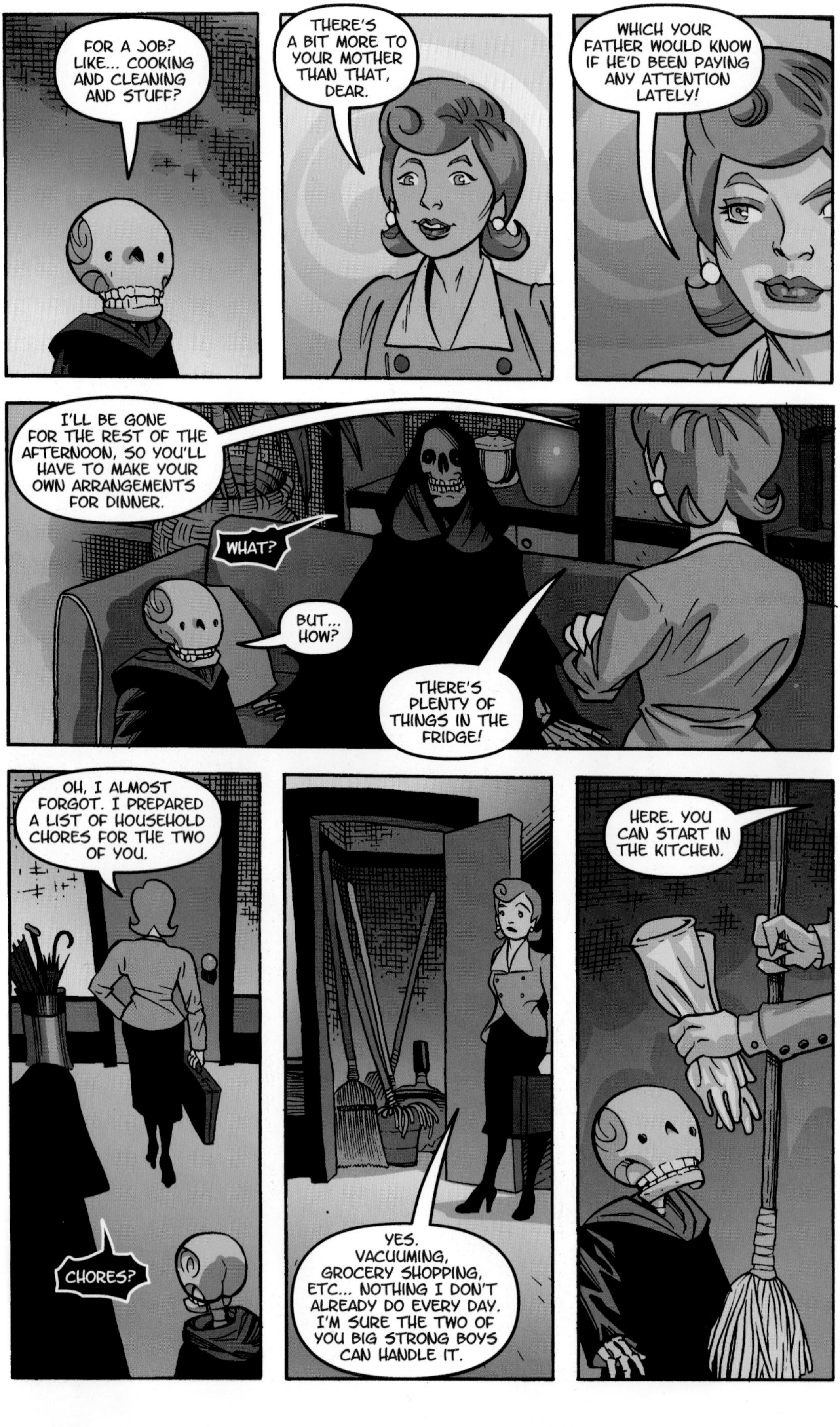
FOR A JOB? LIKE... COOKING AND CLEANING AND STUFF?
THERE'S A BIT MORE TO YOUR MOTHER THAN THAT, DEAR.
WHICH YOUR FATHER WOULD KNOW IF HE'D BEEN PAYING ANY ATTENTION LATELY!
I'LL BE GONE FOR THE REST OF THE AFTERNOON, SO YOU'LL HAVE TO MAKE YOUR OWN ARRANGEMENTS FOR DINNER.
WHAT?
BUT... HOW?
THERE'S PLENTY OF THINGS IN THE FRIDGE!
OH, I ALMOST FORGOT. I PREPARED A LIST OF HOUSEHOLD CHORES FOR THE TWO OF YOU.
CHORES?
YES. VACUUMING, GROCERY SHOPPING, ETC... NOTHING I DON'T ALREADY DO EVERY DAY. I'M SURE THE TWO OF YOU BIG STRONG BOYS CAN HANDLE IT.
HERE. YOU CAN START IN THE KITCHEN.

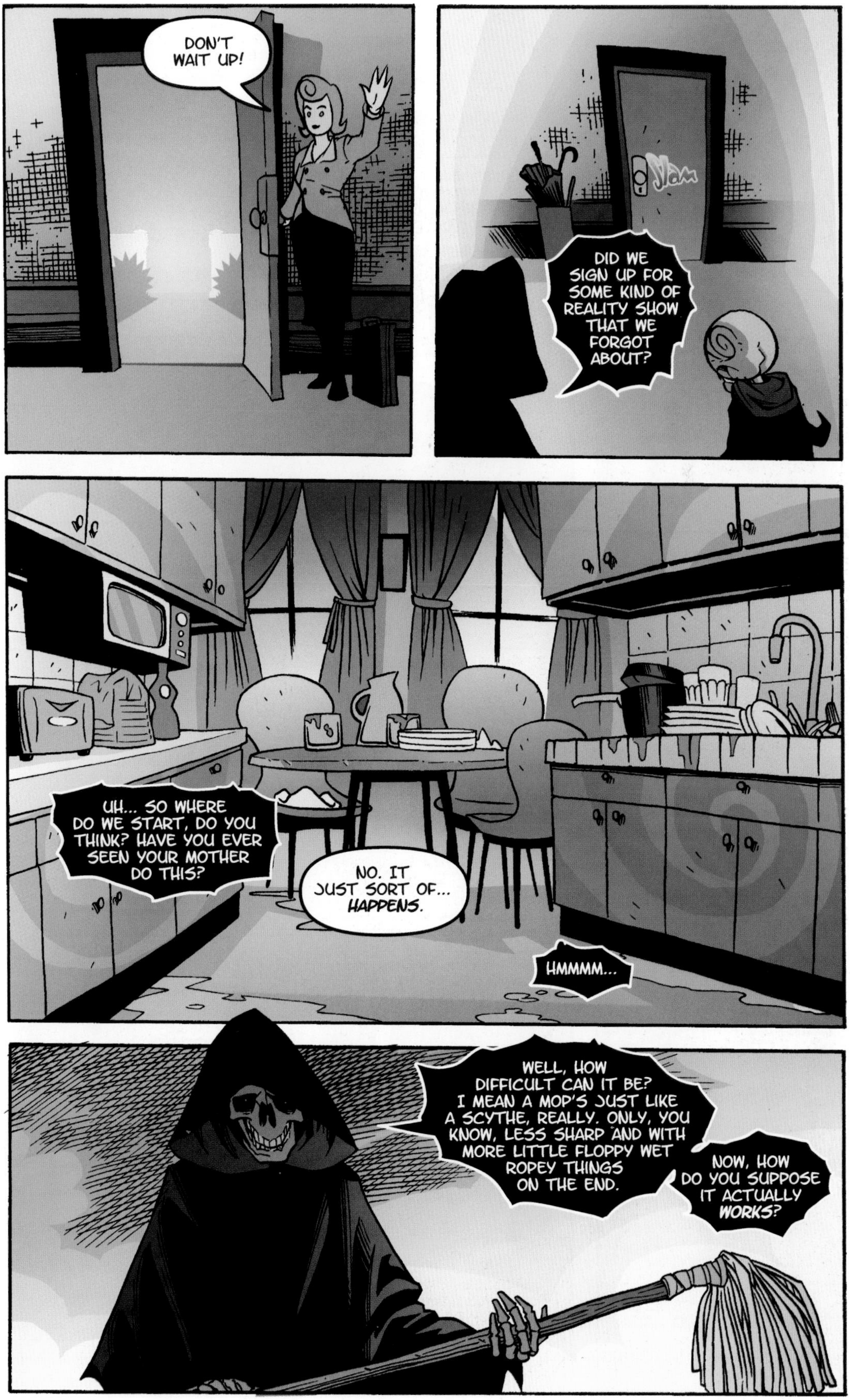
DON'T WAIT UP!
SLAM
DID WE SIGN UP FOR SOME KIND OF REALITY SHOW THAT WE FORGOT ABOUT?
UH... SO WHERE DO WE START, DO YOU THINK? HAVE YOU EVER SEEN YOUR MOTHER DO THIS?
NO. IT JUST SORT OF... HAPPENS.
HMMMM...
WELL, HOW DIFFICULT CAN IT BE? I MEAN A MOP'S JUST LIKE A SCYTHE, REALLY. ONLY, YOU KNOW, LESS SHARP AND WITH MORE LITTLE FLOPPY WET ROPEY THINGS ON THE END.
NOW, HOW DO YOU SUPPOSE IT ACTUALLY WORKS?

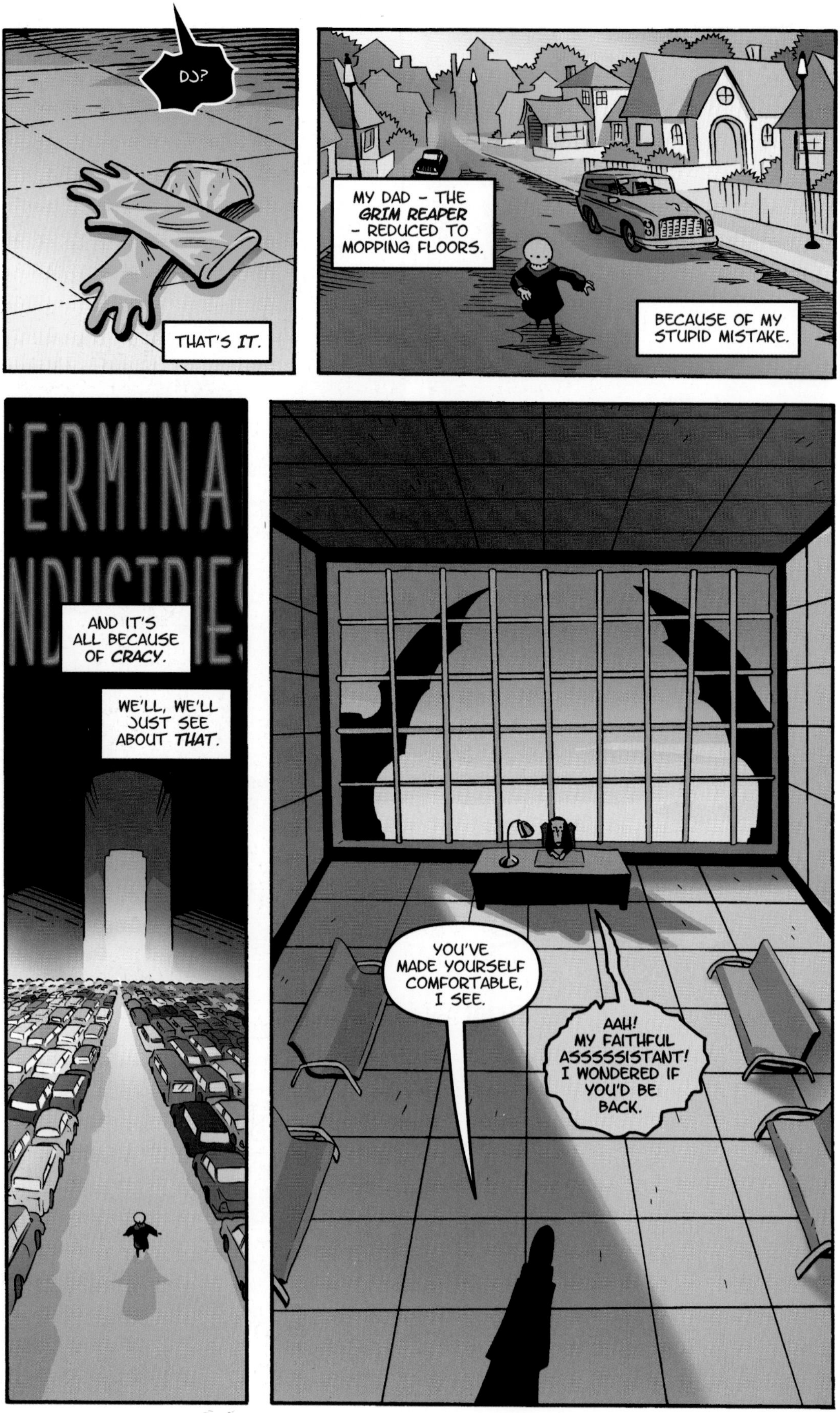
DJ?
THAT'S IT.
MY DAD – THE GRIM REAPER – REDUCED TO MOPPING FLOORS.
BECAUSE OF MY STUPID MISTAKE.
ERMINA
NDUSTRIES
AND IT'S ALL BECAUSE OF CRACY.
WE'LL, WE'LL JUST SEE ABOUT THAT.
YOU'VE MADE YOURSELF COMFORTABLE, I SEE.
AAH! MY FAITHFUL ASSSSSISTANT! I WONDERED IF YOU'D BE BACK.

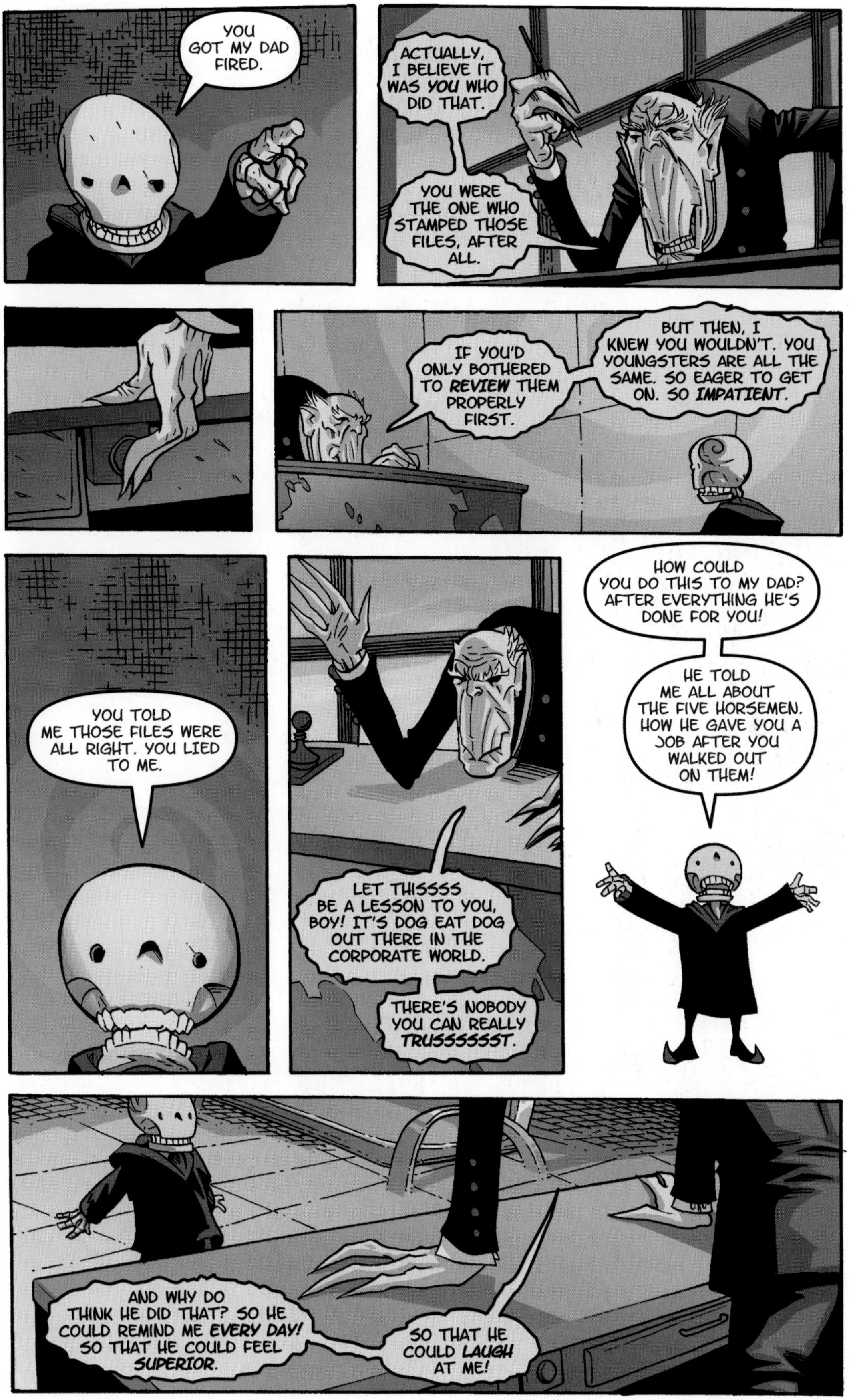
YOU GOT MY DAD FIRED.
ACTUALLY, I BELIEVE IT WAS *YOU* WHO DID THAT.
YOU WERE THE ONE WHO STAMPED THOSE FILES, AFTER ALL.
IF YOU'D ONLY BOTHERED TO *REVIEW* THEM PROPERLY FIRST.
BUT THEN, I KNEW YOU WOULDN'T. YOU YOUNGSTERS ARE ALL THE SAME. SO EAGER TO GET ON. SO *IMPATIENT*.
YOU TOLD ME THOSE FILES WERE ALL RIGHT. YOU LIED TO ME.
LET THISSSS BE A LESSON TO YOU, BOY! IT'S DOG EAT DOG OUT THERE IN THE CORPORATE WORLD.
THERE'S NOBODY YOU CAN REALLY **TRUSSSSSST**.
HOW COULD YOU DO THIS TO MY DAD? AFTER EVERYTHING HE'S DONE FOR YOU!
HE TOLD ME ALL ABOUT THE FIVE HORSEMEN. HOW HE GAVE YOU A JOB AFTER YOU WALKED OUT ON THEM!
AND WHY DO THINK HE DID THAT? SO HE COULD REMIND ME *EVERY DAY!* SO THAT HE COULD FEEL **SUPERIOR**.
SO THAT HE COULD *LAUGH* AT ME!

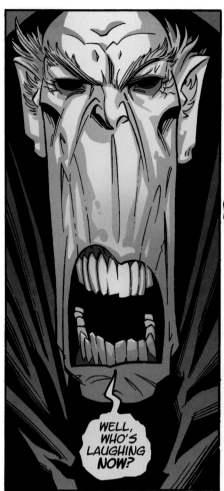

WELL, WHO'S LAUGHING NOW?

I'M GOING TO TELL MY DAD!

THEN WE'LL SEE!

OH, ARE YOU? THAT WOULD BE *AWFULLY* BRAVE OF YOU. I MEAN, YOU'D HAVE TO TELL HIM THAT ALL OF THIS IS *YOUR* FAULT, WOULDN'T YOU?

I IMAGINE HE'D BE *TERRIBLY* DISAPPOINTED IN YOU. I WONDER IF HE'D EVER TRUST YOU AGAIN?

AH, THERE YOU ARE, RON. SEE OUR GUEST OUT, WOULD YOU?

RON... IT'S DJ! REMEMBER ME?

YOU'VE GOT TO HELP ME!

CRACY FRAMED MY DAD! HE'S EVIL! I CAN PROVE IT!

I'LL MAKE SURE HE FINDS THE EXIT, SIR.

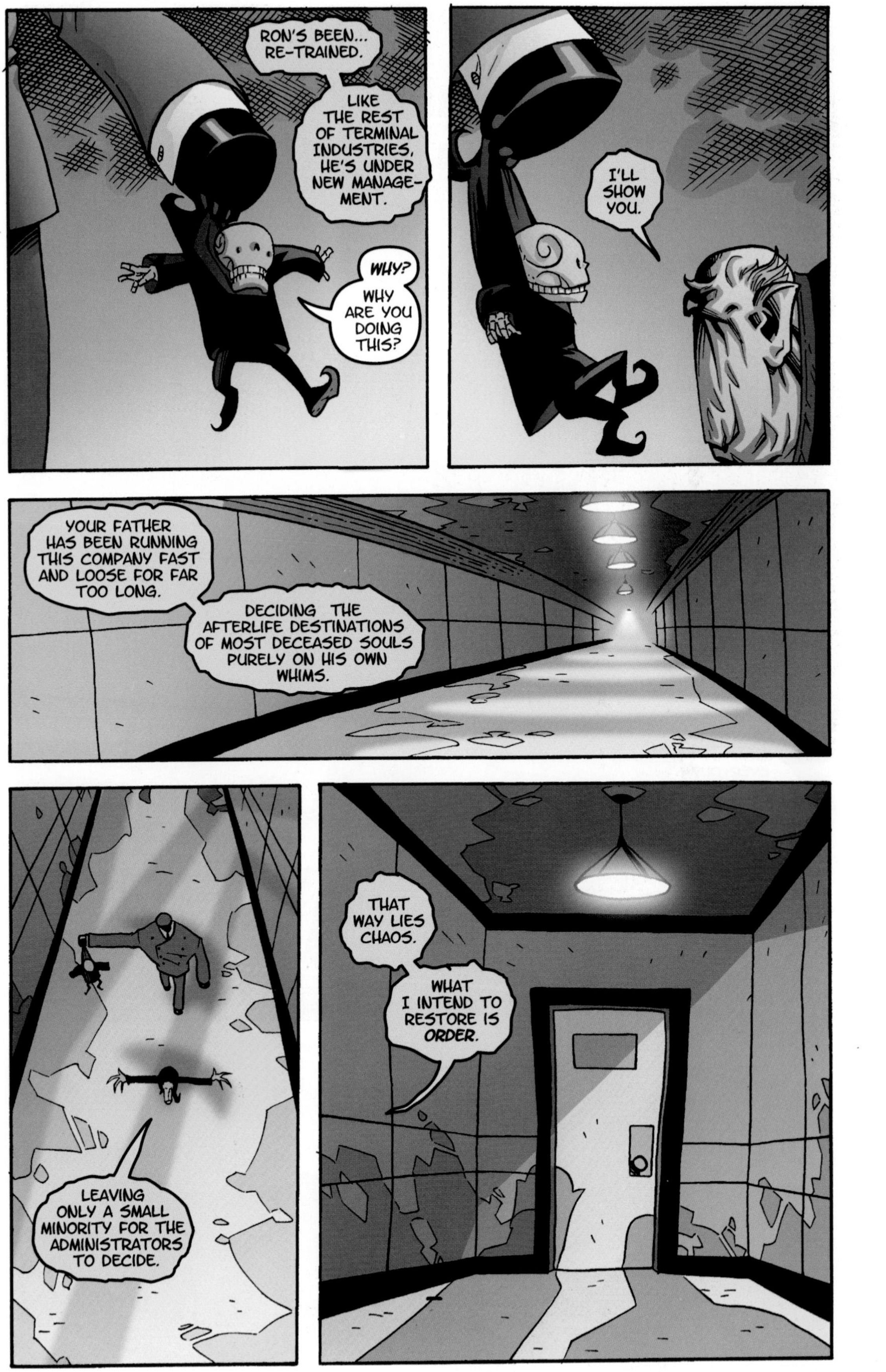
RON'S BEEN... RE-TRAINED.
LIKE THE REST OF TERMINAL INDUSTRIES, HE'S UNDER NEW MANAGE-MENT.
WHY? WHY ARE YOU DOING THIS?
I'LL SHOW YOU.
YOUR FATHER HAS BEEN RUNNING THIS COMPANY FAST AND LOOSE FOR FAR TOO LONG.
DECIDING THE AFTERLIFE DESTINATIONS OF MOST DECEASED SOULS PURELY ON HIS OWN WHIMS.
LEAVING ONLY A SMALL MINORITY FOR THE ADMINISTRATORS TO DECIDE.
THAT WAY LIES CHAOS.
WHAT I INTEND TO RESTORE IS *ORDER*.

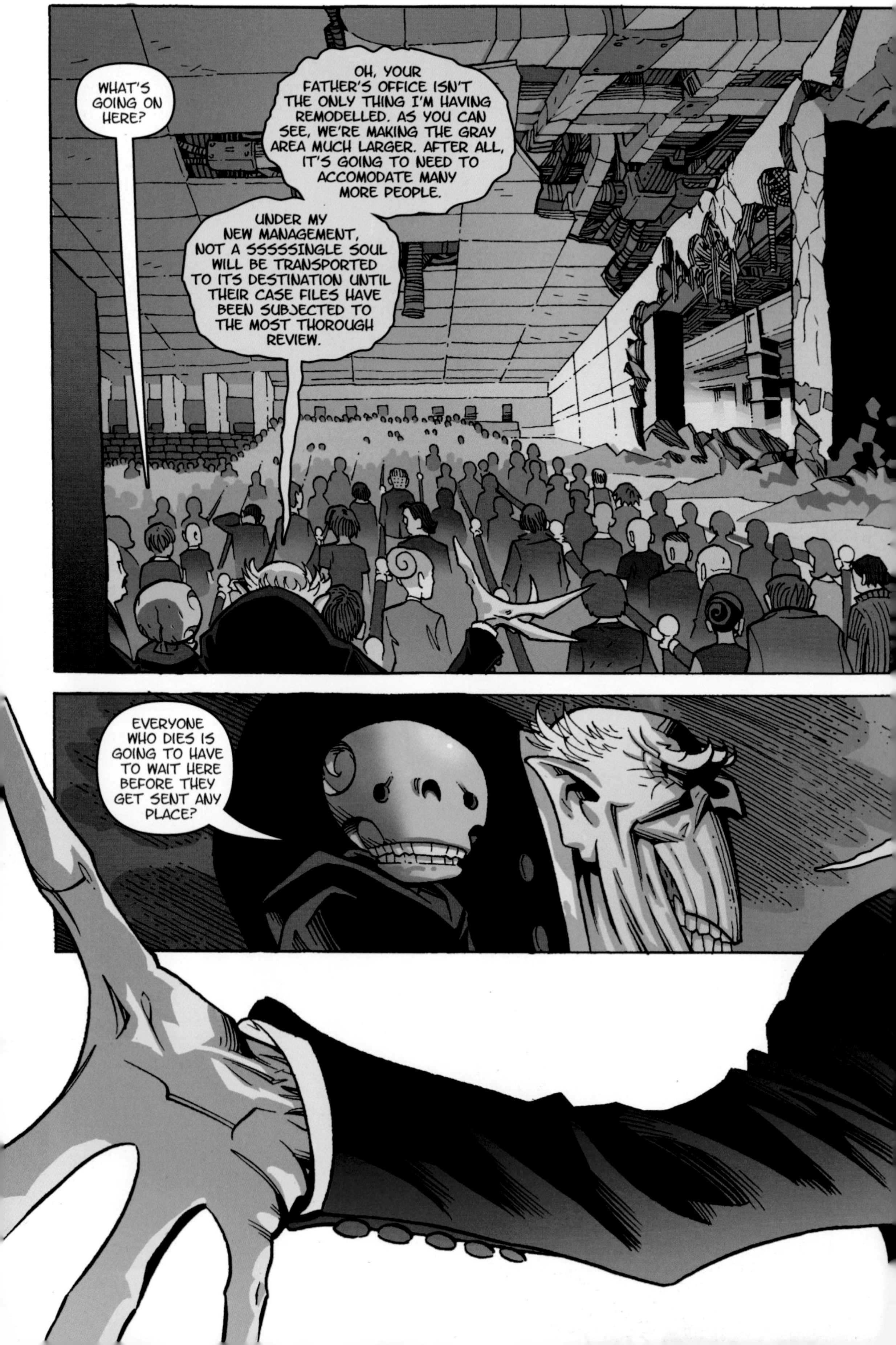
WHAT'S GOING ON HERE?
OH, YOUR FATHER'S OFFICE ISN'T THE ONLY THING I'M HAVING REMODELLED. AS YOU CAN SEE, WE'RE MAKING THE GRAY AREA MUCH LARGER. AFTER ALL, IT'S GOING TO NEED TO ACCOMODATE MANY MORE PEOPLE.
UNDER MY NEW MANAGEMENT, NOT A SSSSSINGLE SOUL WILL BE TRANSPORTED TO ITS DESTINATION UNTIL THEIR CASE FILES HAVE BEEN SUBJECTED TO THE MOST THOROUGH REVIEW.
EVERYONE WHO DIES IS GOING TO HAVE TO WAIT HERE BEFORE THEY GET SENT ANY PLACE?

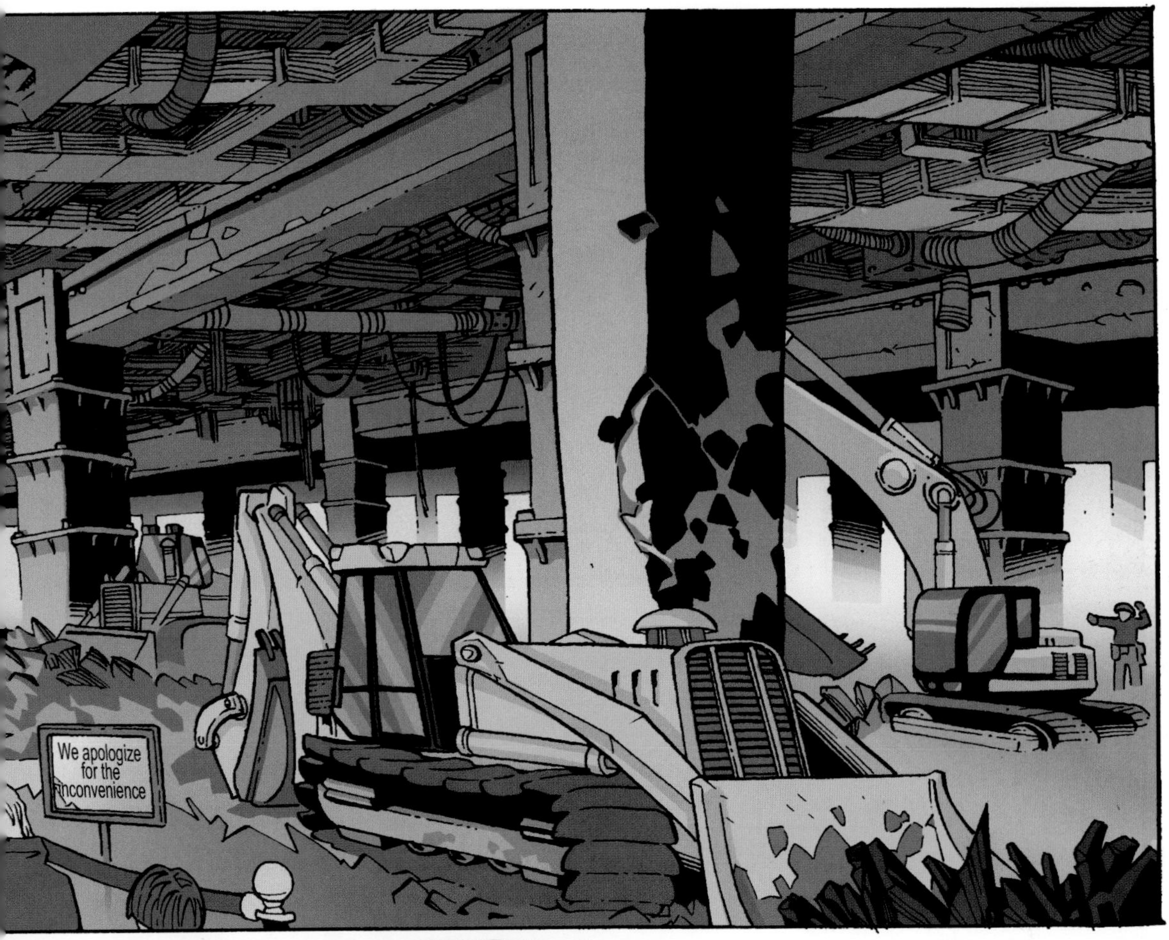
We apologize for the inconvenience

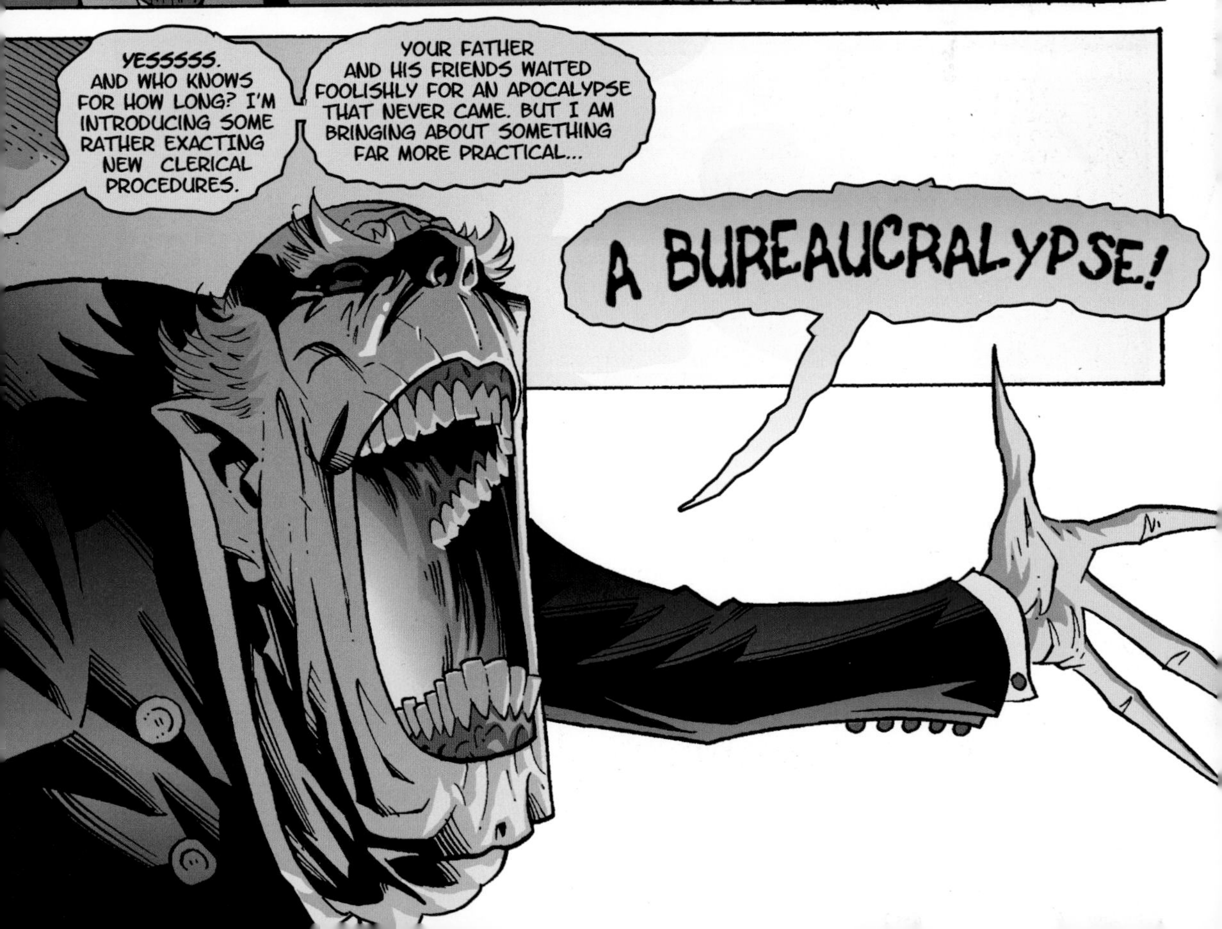
YESSSSS. AND WHO KNOWS FOR HOW LONG? I'M INTRODUCING SOME RATHER EXACTING NEW CLERICAL PROCEDURES.
YOUR FATHER AND HIS FRIENDS WAITED FOOLISHLY FOR AN APOCALYPSE THAT NEVER CAME. BUT I AM BRINGING ABOUT SOMETHING FAR MORE PRACTICAL...
A BUREAUCRALYPSE!

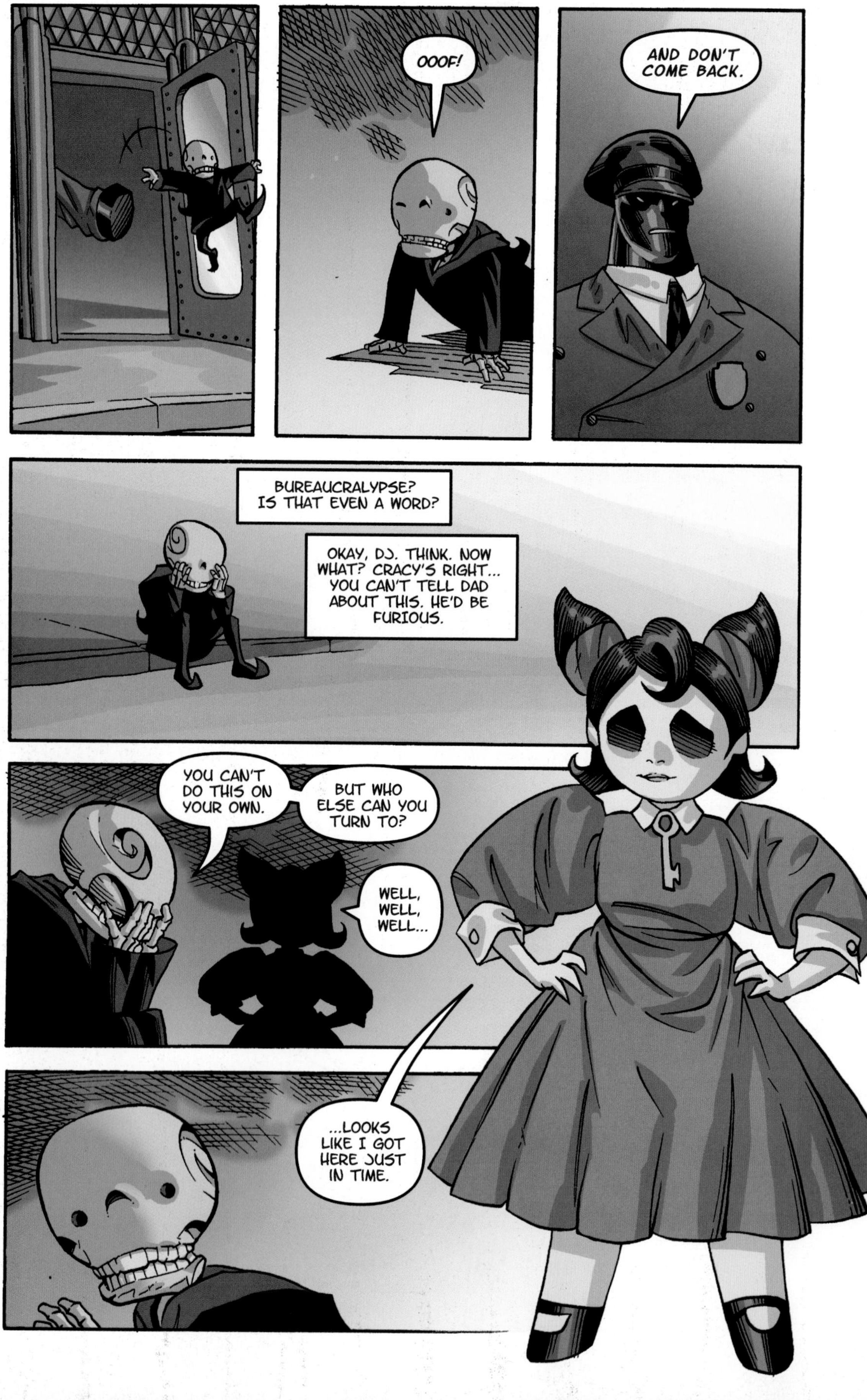
OOOF!
AND DON'T COME BACK.
BUREAUCRALYPSE? IS THAT EVEN A WORD?
OKAY, DJ. THINK. NOW WHAT? CRACY'S RIGHT... YOU CAN'T TELL DAD ABOUT THIS. HE'D BE FURIOUS.
YOU CAN'T DO THIS ON YOUR OWN.
BUT WHO ELSE CAN YOU TURN TO?
WELL, WELL, WELL...
...LOOKS LIKE I GOT HERE JUST IN TIME.

CHAPTER 3

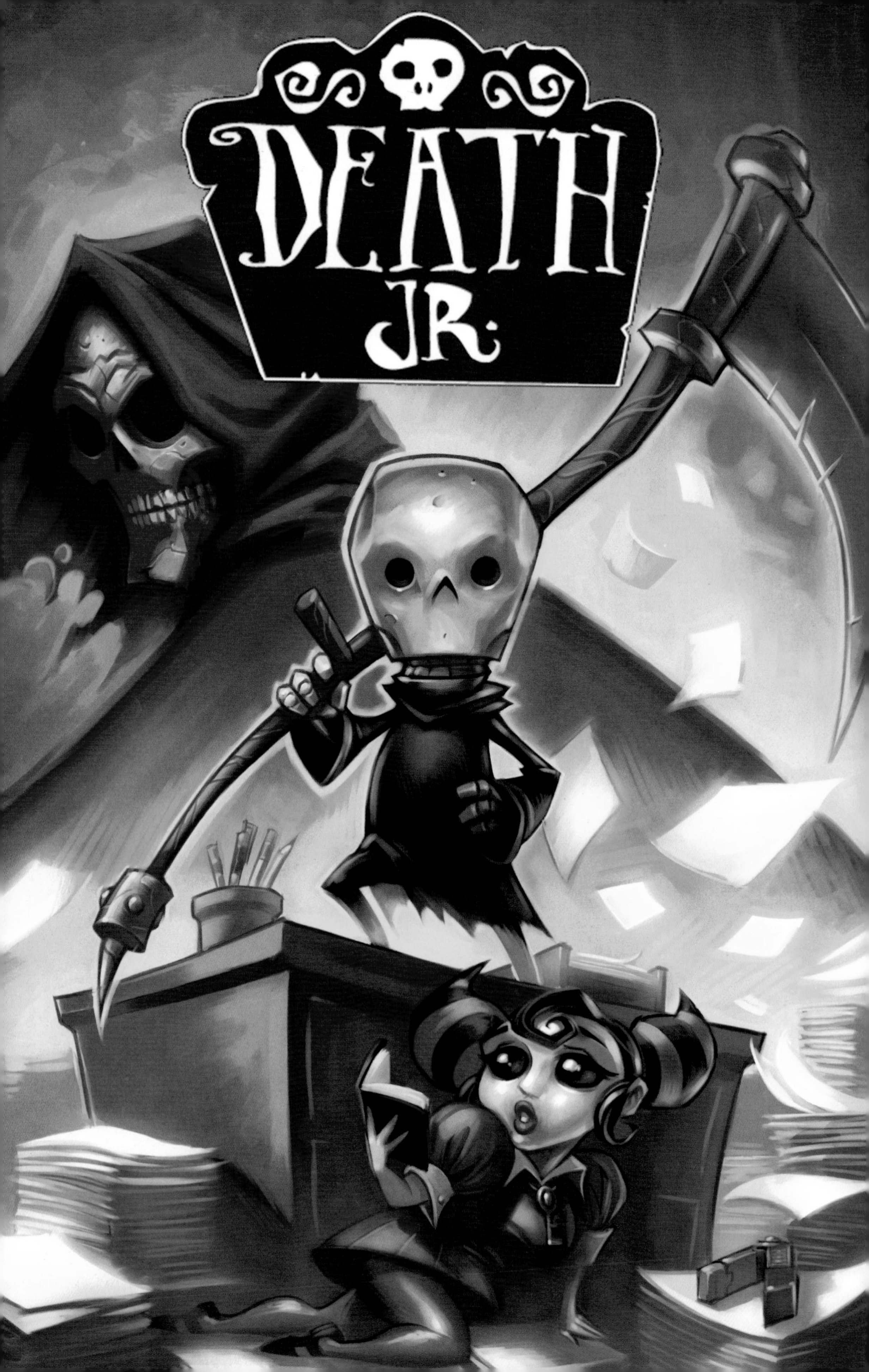
DEATH
JR.

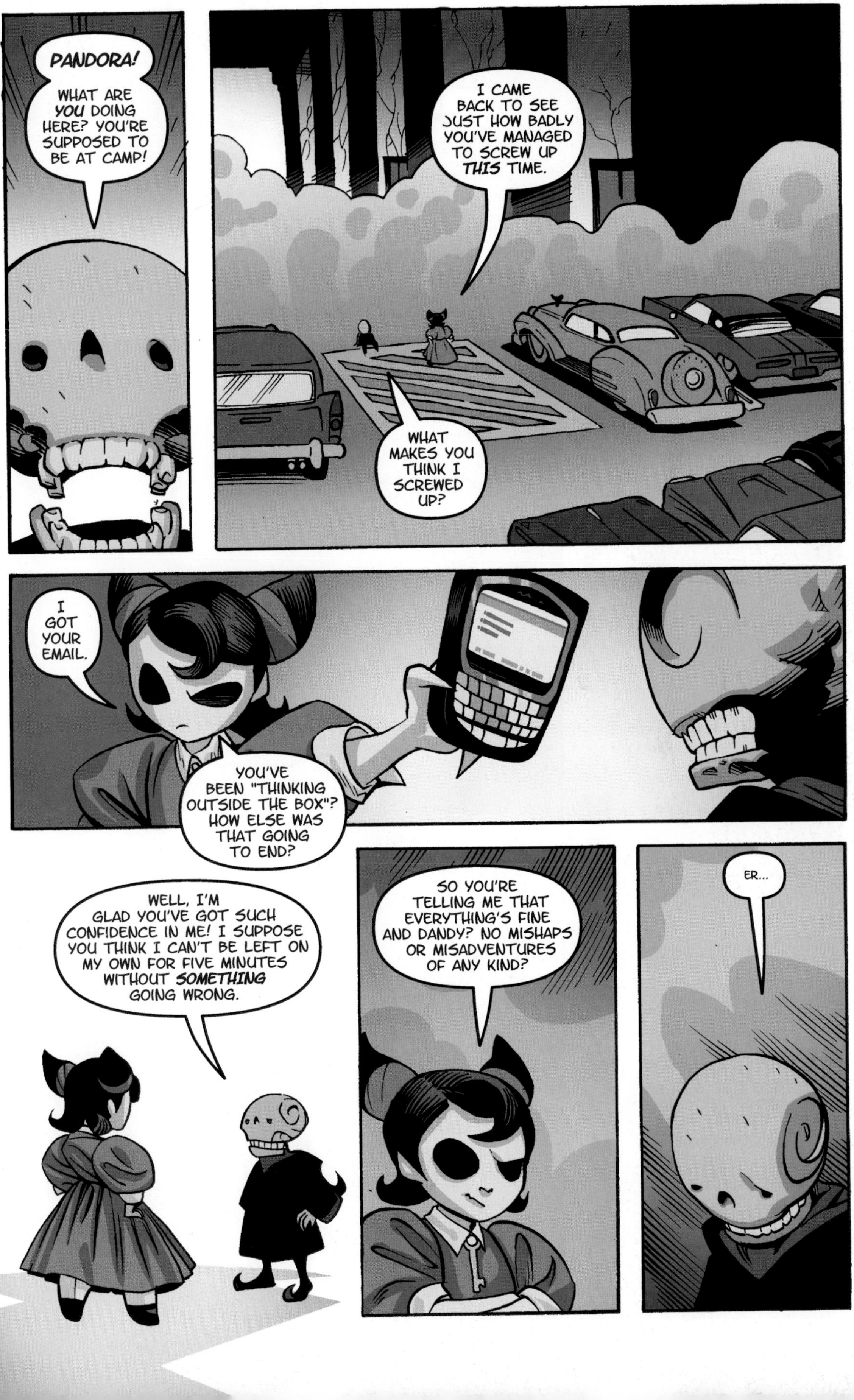
PANDORA!
WHAT ARE YOU DOING HERE? YOU'RE SUPPOSED TO BE AT CAMP!
I CAME BACK TO SEE JUST HOW BADLY YOU'VE MANAGED TO SCREW UP THIS TIME.
WHAT MAKES YOU THINK I SCREWED UP?
I GOT YOUR EMAIL.
YOU'VE BEEN "THINKING OUTSIDE THE BOX"? HOW ELSE WAS THAT GOING TO END?
WELL, I'M GLAD YOU'VE GOT SUCH CONFIDENCE IN ME! I SUPPOSE YOU THINK I CAN'T BE LEFT ON MY OWN FOR FIVE MINUTES WITHOUT SOMETHING GOING WRONG.
SO YOU'RE TELLING ME THAT EVERYTHING'S FINE AND DANDY? NO MISHAPS OR MISADVENTURES OF ANY KIND?
ER...

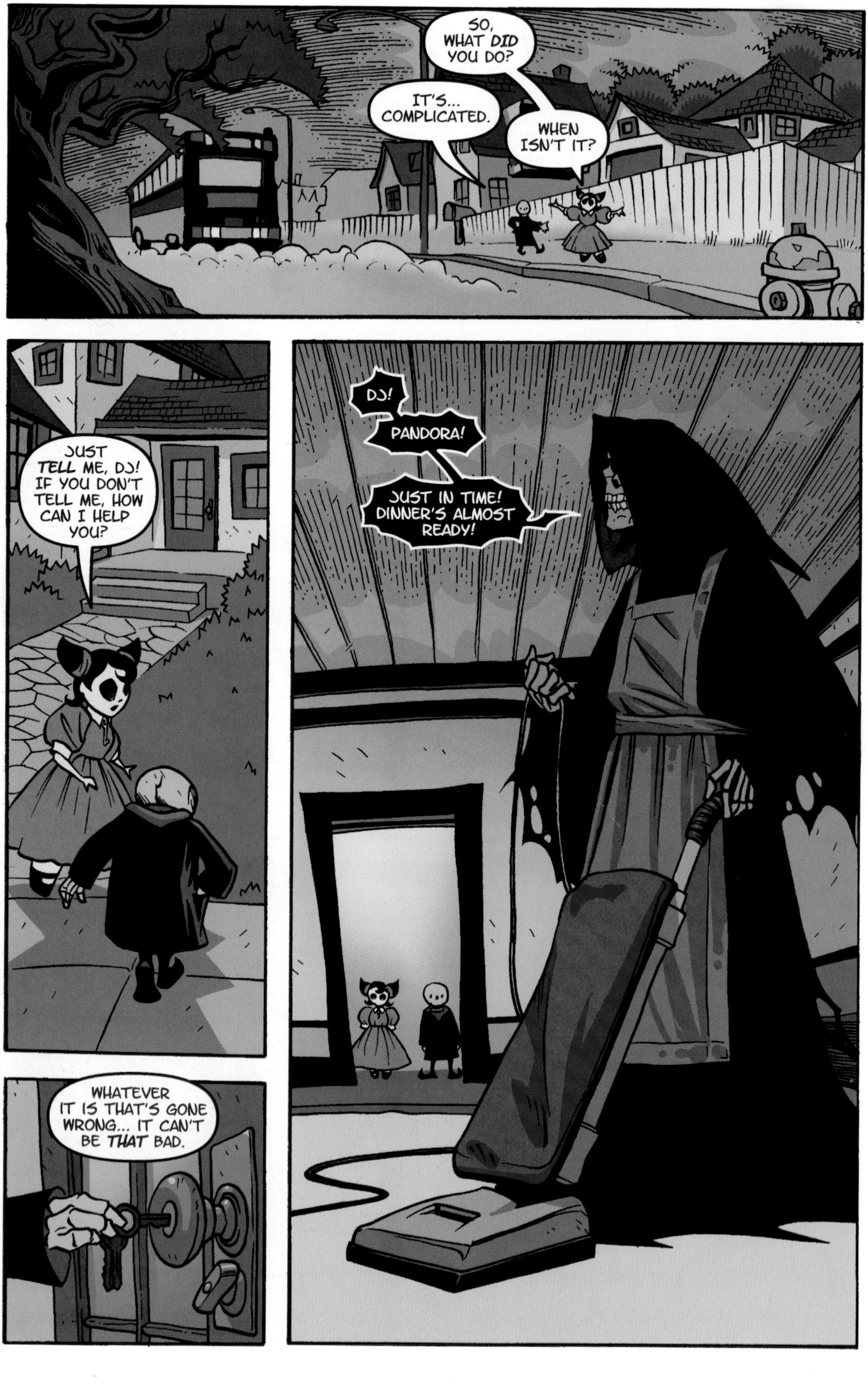
SO, WHAT DID YOU DO?
IT'S... COMPLICATED.
WHEN ISN'T IT?
JUST TELL ME, DJ! IF YOU DON'T TELL ME, HOW CAN I HELP YOU?
WHATEVER IT IS THAT'S GONE WRONG... IT CAN'T BE THAT BAD.
DJ!
PANDORA!
JUST IN TIME! DINNER'S ALMOST READY!

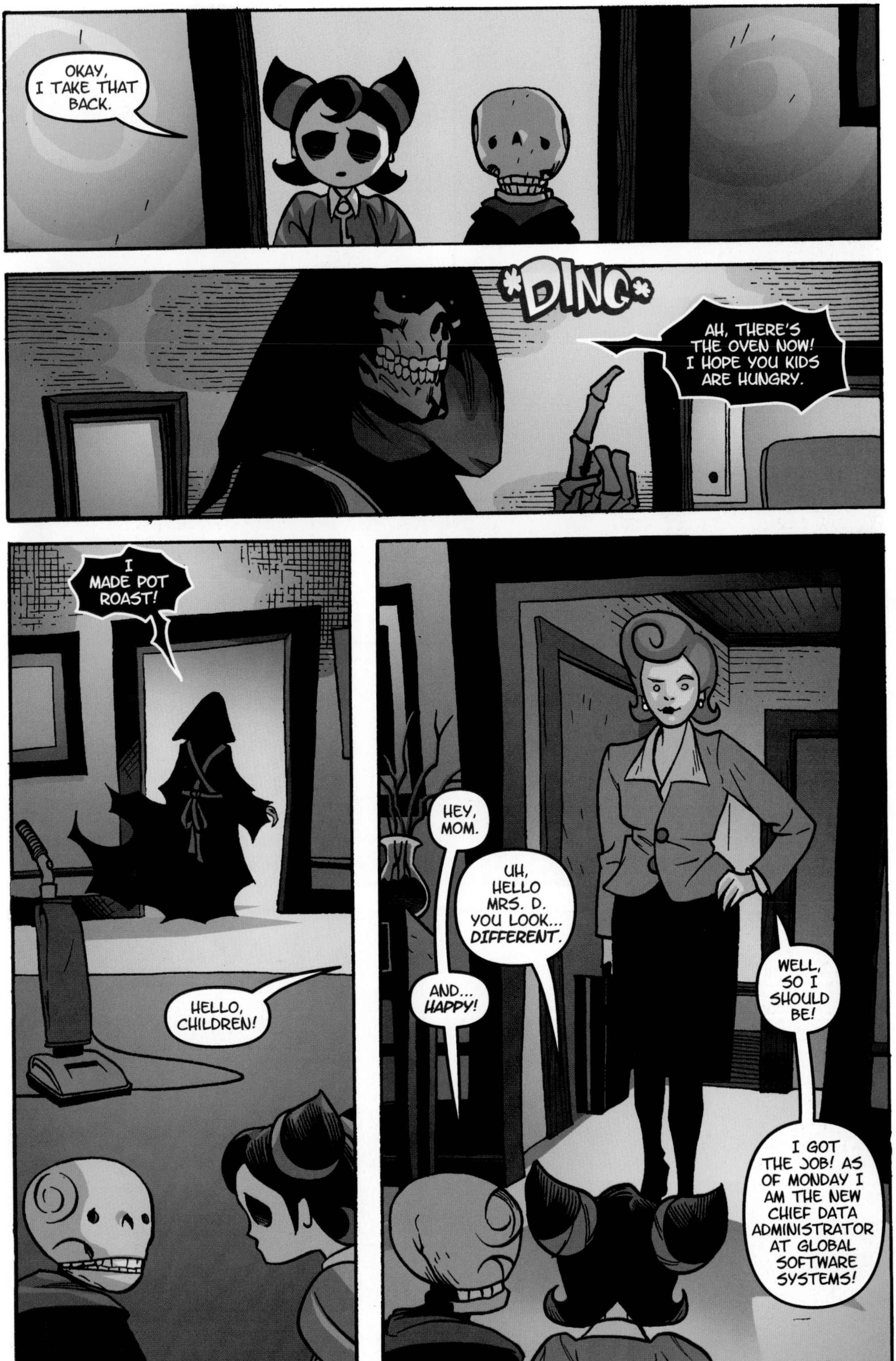
OKAY, I TAKE THAT BACK.
DING
AH, THERE'S THE OVEN NOW! I HOPE YOU KIDS ARE HUNGRY.
I MADE POT ROAST!
HELLO, CHILDREN!
HEY, MOM.
UH, HELLO MRS. D. YOU LOOK... DIFFERENT.
AND... HAPPY!
WELL, SO I SHOULD BE!
I GOT THE JOB! AS OF MONDAY I AM THE NEW CHIEF DATA ADMINISTRATOR AT GLOBAL SOFTWARE SYSTEMS!

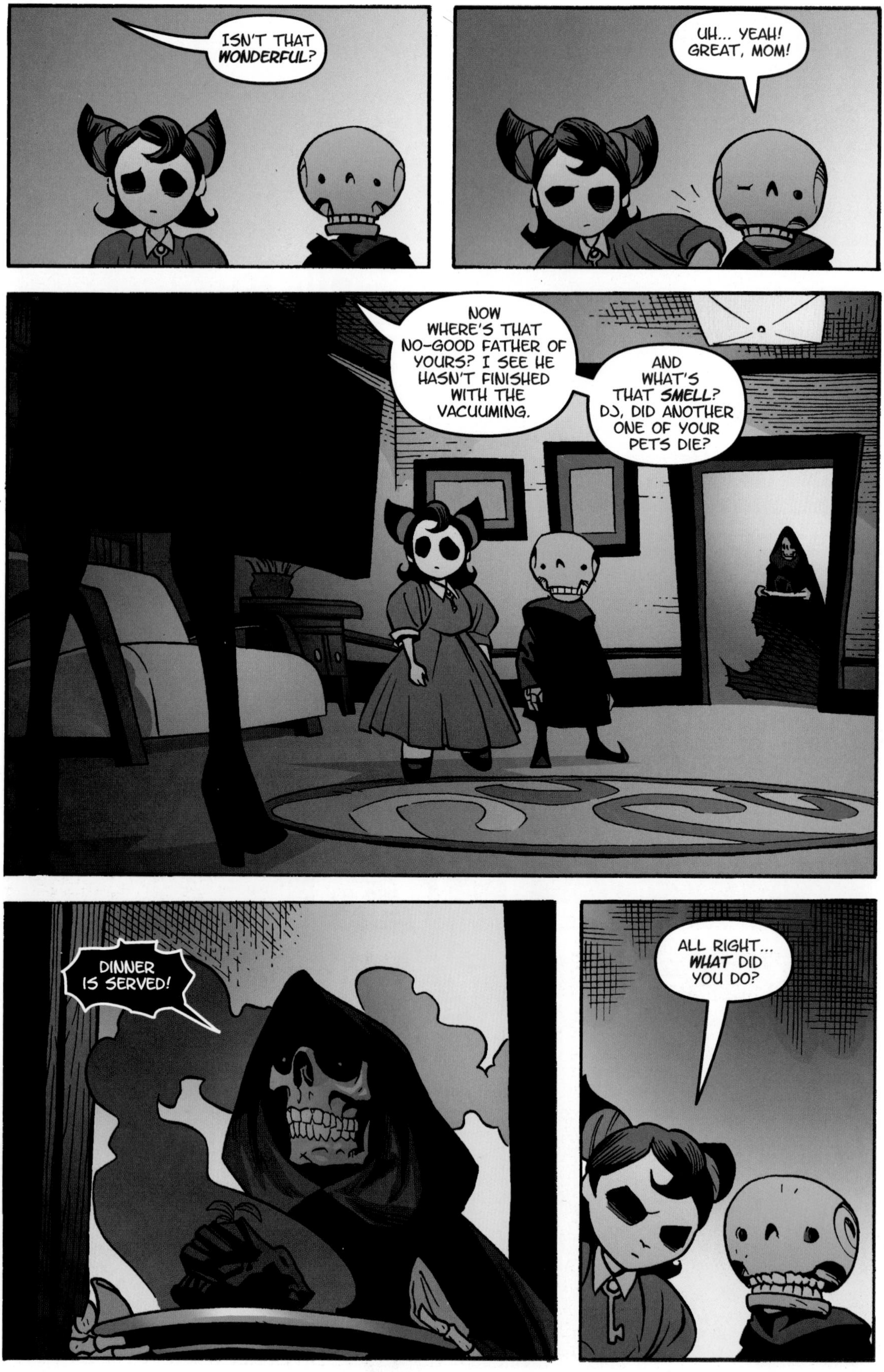
ISN'T THAT WONDERFUL?
UH... YEAH! GREAT, MOM!
NOW WHERE'S THAT NO-GOOD FATHER OF YOURS? I SEE HE HASN'T FINISHED WITH THE VACUUMING.
AND WHAT'S THAT SMELL? DJ, DID ANOTHER ONE OF YOUR PETS DIE?
DINNER IS SERVED!
ALL RIGHT... WHAT DID YOU DO?

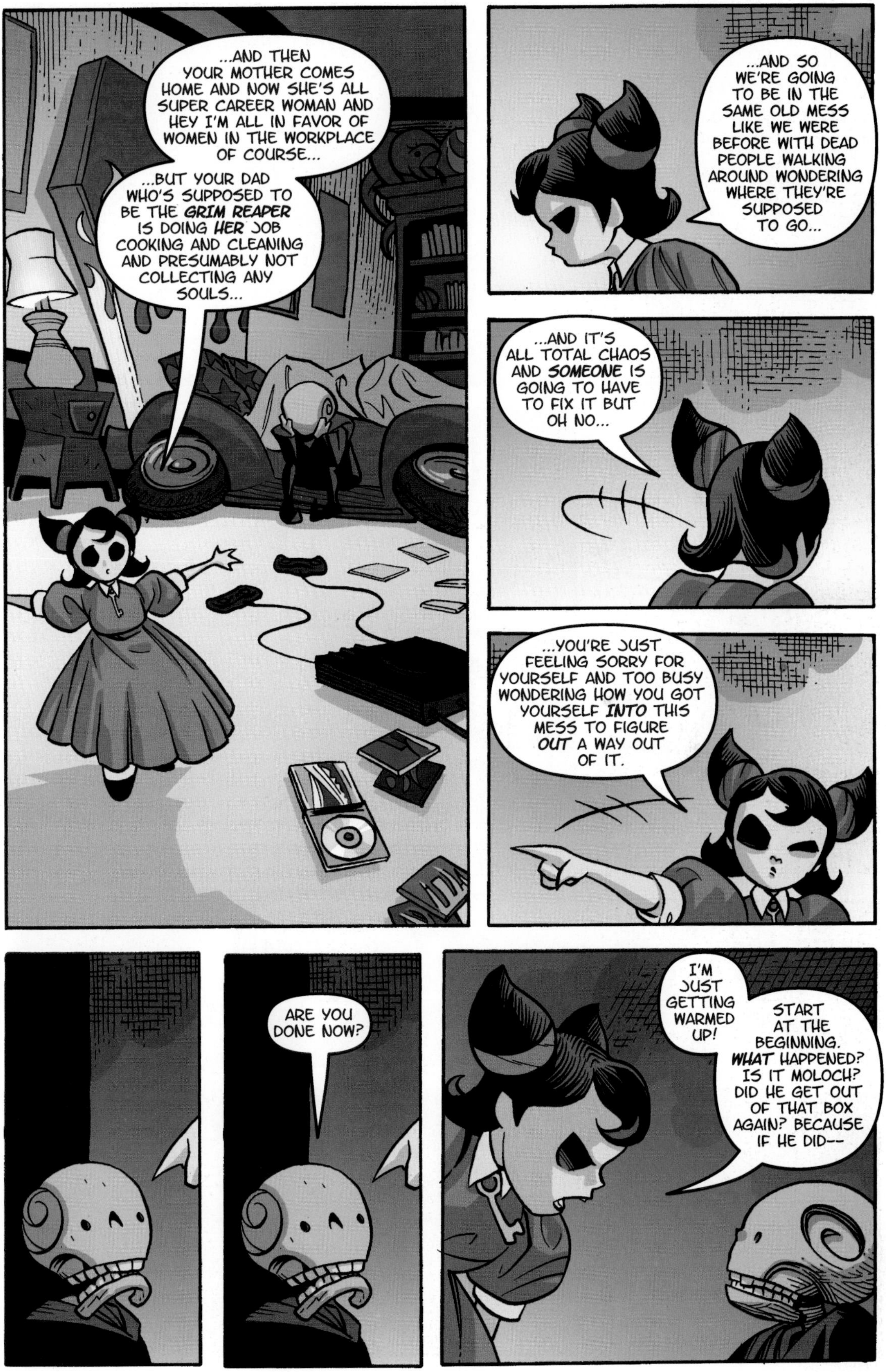
...AND THEN YOUR MOTHER COMES HOME AND NOW SHE'S ALL SUPER CAREER WOMAN AND HEY I'M ALL IN FAVOR OF WOMEN IN THE WORKPLACE OF COURSE...
...BUT YOUR DAD WHO'S SUPPOSED TO BE THE GRIM REAPER IS DOING HER JOB COOKING AND CLEANING AND PRESUMABLY NOT COLLECTING ANY SOULS...
...AND SO WE'RE GOING TO BE IN THE SAME OLD MESS LIKE WE WERE BEFORE WITH DEAD PEOPLE WALKING AROUND WONDERING WHERE THEY'RE SUPPOSED TO GO...
...AND IT'S ALL TOTAL CHAOS AND SOMEONE IS GOING TO HAVE TO FIX IT BUT OH NO...
...YOU'RE JUST FEELING SORRY FOR YOURSELF AND TOO BUSY WONDERING HOW YOU GOT YOURSELF INTO THIS MESS TO FIGURE OUT A WAY OUT OF IT.
ARE YOU DONE NOW?
I'M JUST GETTING WARMED UP!
START AT THE BEGINNING. WHAT HAPPENED? IS IT MOLOCH? DID HE GET OUT OF THAT BOX AGAIN? BECAUSE IF HE DID--

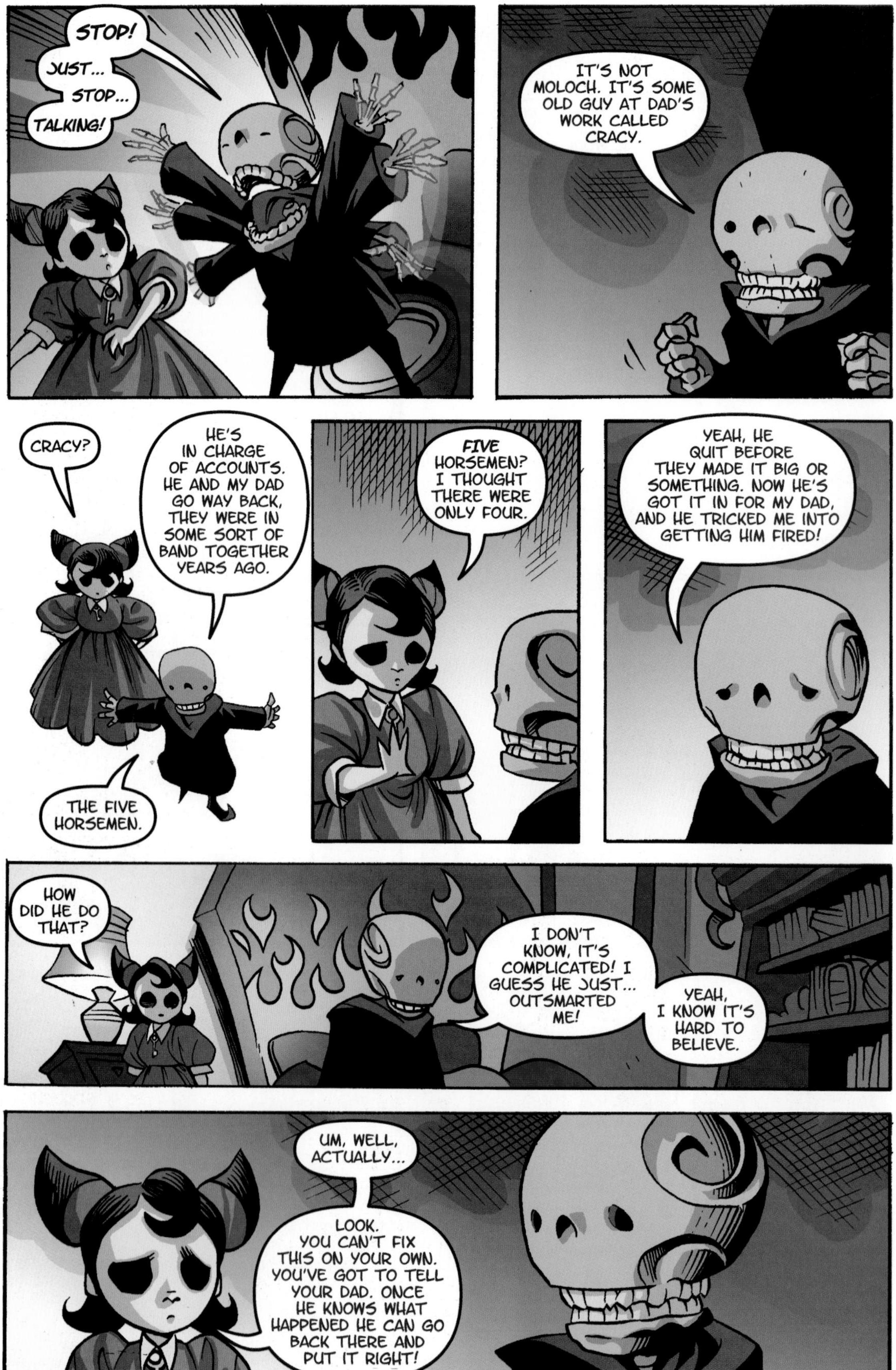
STOP!
JUST... STOP... TALKING!
IT'S NOT MOLOCH. IT'S SOME OLD GUY AT DAD'S WORK CALLED CRACY.
CRACY?
HE'S IN CHARGE OF ACCOUNTS. HE AND MY DAD GO WAY BACK, THEY WERE IN SOME SORT OF BAND TOGETHER YEARS AGO.
THE FIVE HORSEMEN.
FIVE HORSEMEN? I THOUGHT THERE WERE ONLY FOUR.
YEAH, HE QUIT BEFORE THEY MADE IT BIG OR SOMETHING. NOW HE'S GOT IT IN FOR MY DAD, AND HE TRICKED ME INTO GETTING HIM FIRED!
HOW DID HE DO THAT?
I DON'T KNOW, IT'S COMPLICATED! I GUESS HE JUST... OUTSMARTED ME!
YEAH, I KNOW IT'S HARD TO BELIEVE.
UM, WELL, ACTUALLY...
LOOK. YOU CAN'T FIX THIS ON YOUR OWN. YOU'VE GOT TO TELL YOUR DAD. ONCE HE KNOWS WHAT HAPPENED HE CAN GO BACK THERE AND PUT IT RIGHT!

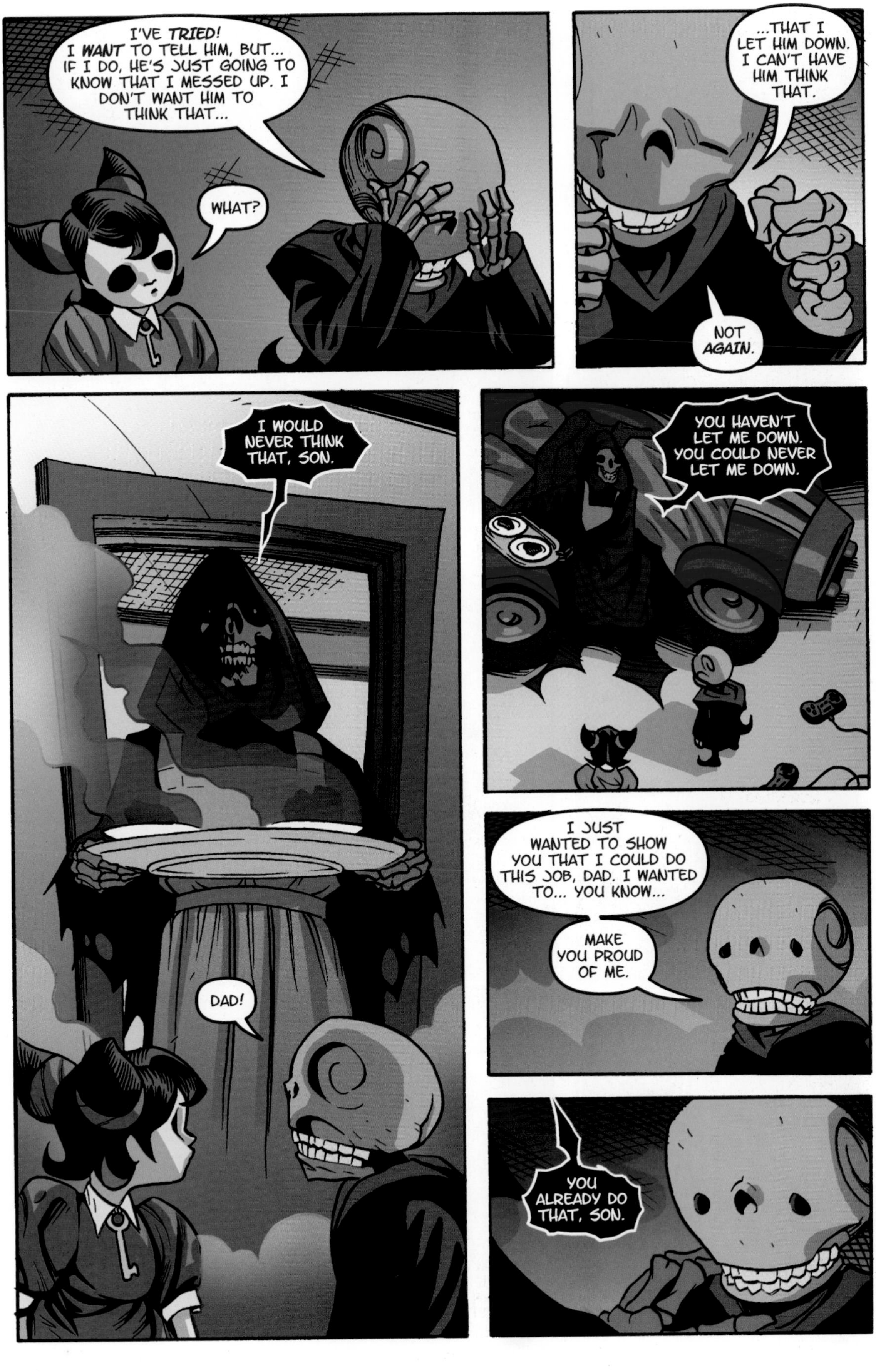
I'VE TRIED! I WANT TO TELL HIM, BUT... IF I DO, HE'S JUST GOING TO KNOW THAT I MESSED UP. I DON'T WANT HIM TO THINK THAT...
WHAT?
...THAT I LET HIM DOWN. I CAN'T HAVE HIM THINK THAT.
NOT AGAIN.
I WOULD NEVER THINK THAT, SON.
DAD!
YOU HAVEN'T LET ME DOWN. YOU COULD NEVER LET ME DOWN.
I JUST WANTED TO SHOW YOU THAT I COULD DO THIS JOB, DAD. I WANTED TO... YOU KNOW...
MAKE YOU PROUD OF ME.
YOU ALREADY DO THAT, SON.

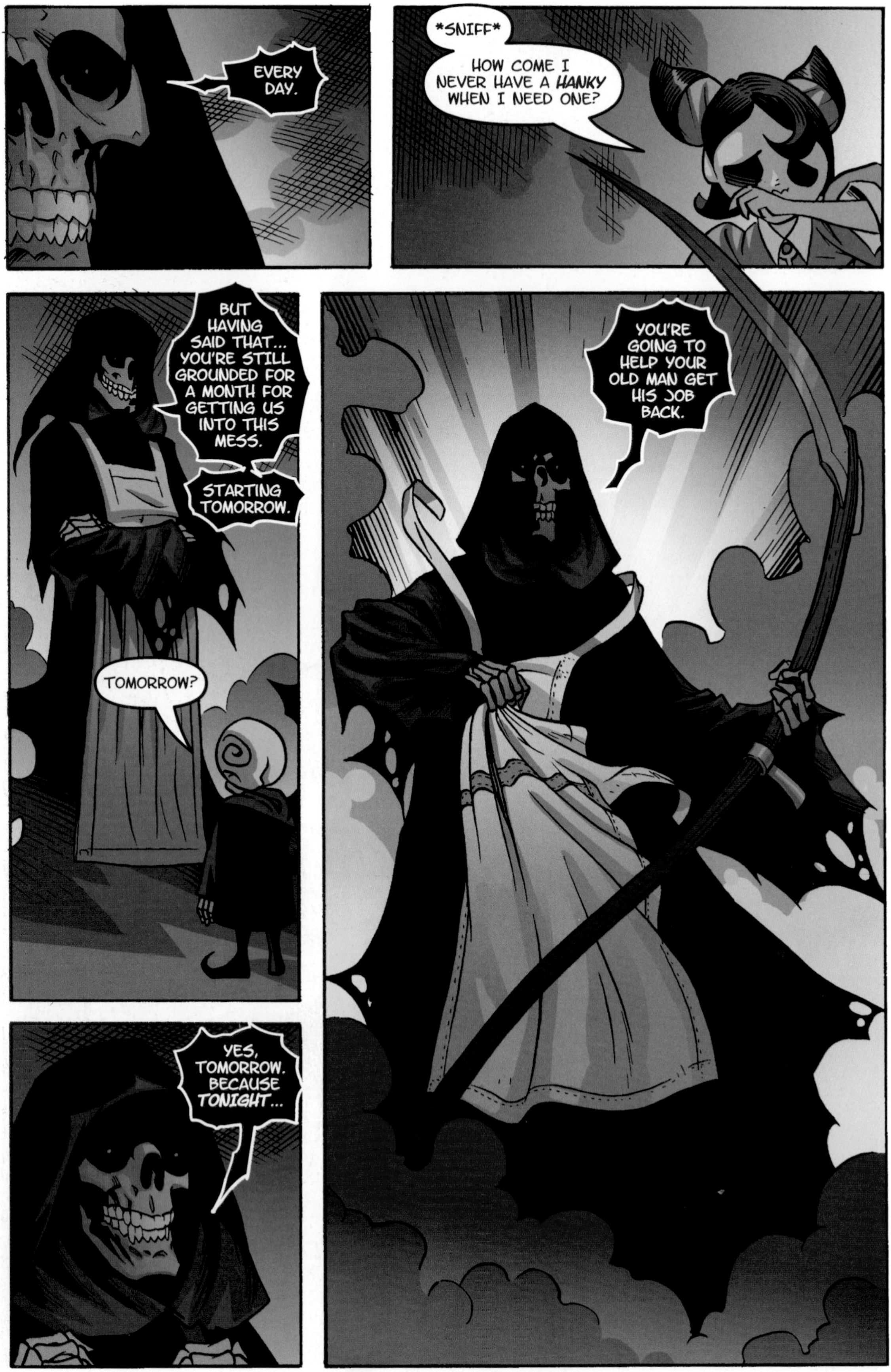
EVERY DAY.
SNIFF
HOW COME I NEVER HAVE A HANKY WHEN I NEED ONE?
BUT HAVING SAID THAT... YOU'RE STILL GROUNDED FOR A MONTH FOR GETTING US INTO THIS MESS.
STARTING TOMORROW.
TOMORROW?
YES, TOMORROW. BECAUSE TONIGHT...
YOU'RE GOING TO HELP YOUR OLD MAN GET HIS JOB BACK.

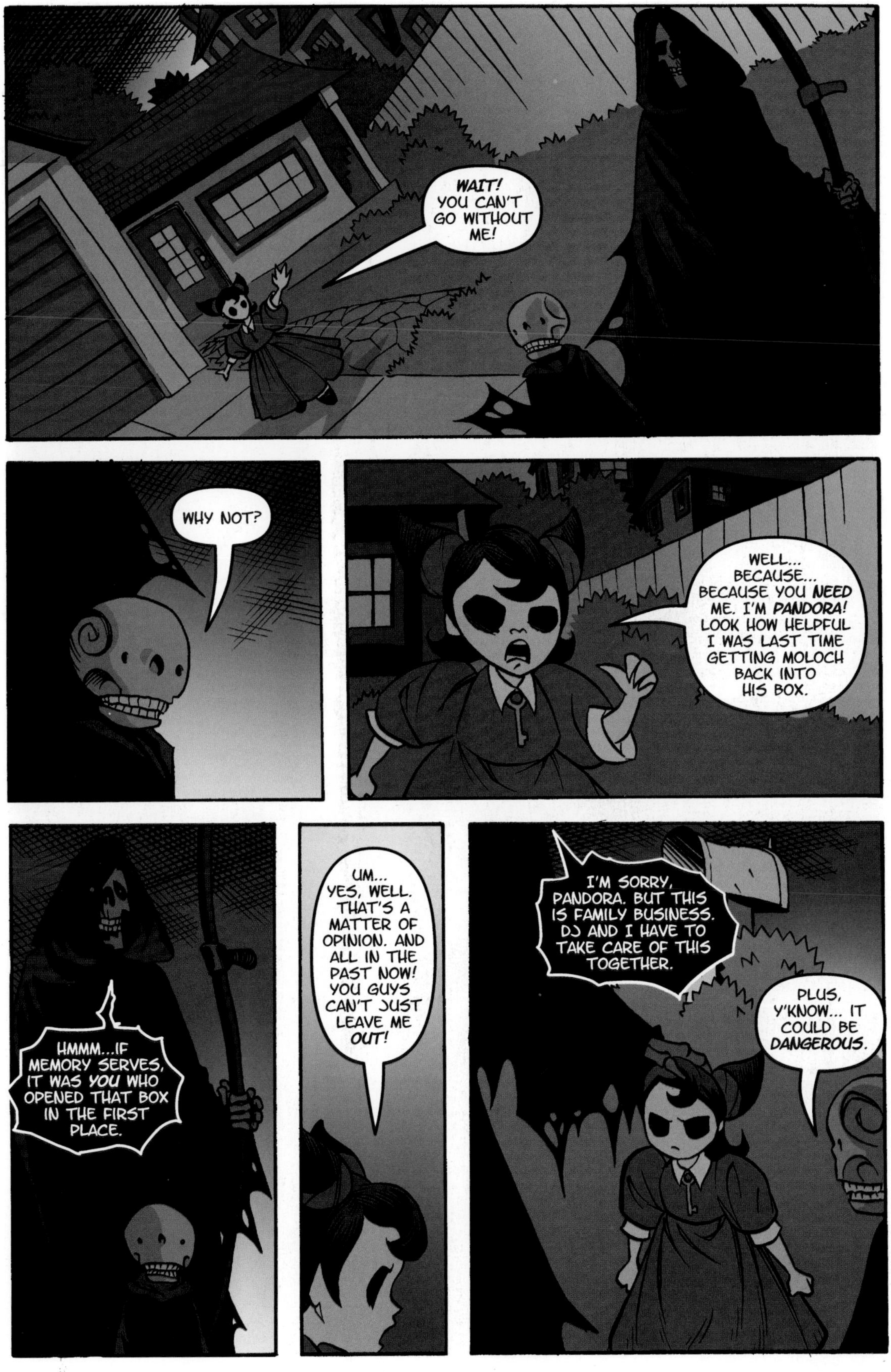
WAIT! YOU CAN'T GO WITHOUT ME!
WHY NOT?
WELL... BECAUSE... BECAUSE YOU NEED ME. I'M PANDORA! LOOK HOW HELPFUL I WAS LAST TIME GETTING MOLOCH BACK INTO HIS BOX.
HMMM...IF MEMORY SERVES, IT WAS YOU WHO OPENED THAT BOX IN THE FIRST PLACE.
UM... YES, WELL. THAT'S A MATTER OF OPINION. AND ALL IN THE PAST NOW! YOU GUYS CAN'T JUST LEAVE ME OUT!
I'M SORRY, PANDORA. BUT THIS IS FAMILY BUSINESS. DJ AND I HAVE TO TAKE CARE OF THIS TOGETHER.
PLUS, Y'KNOW... IT COULD BE DANGEROUS.

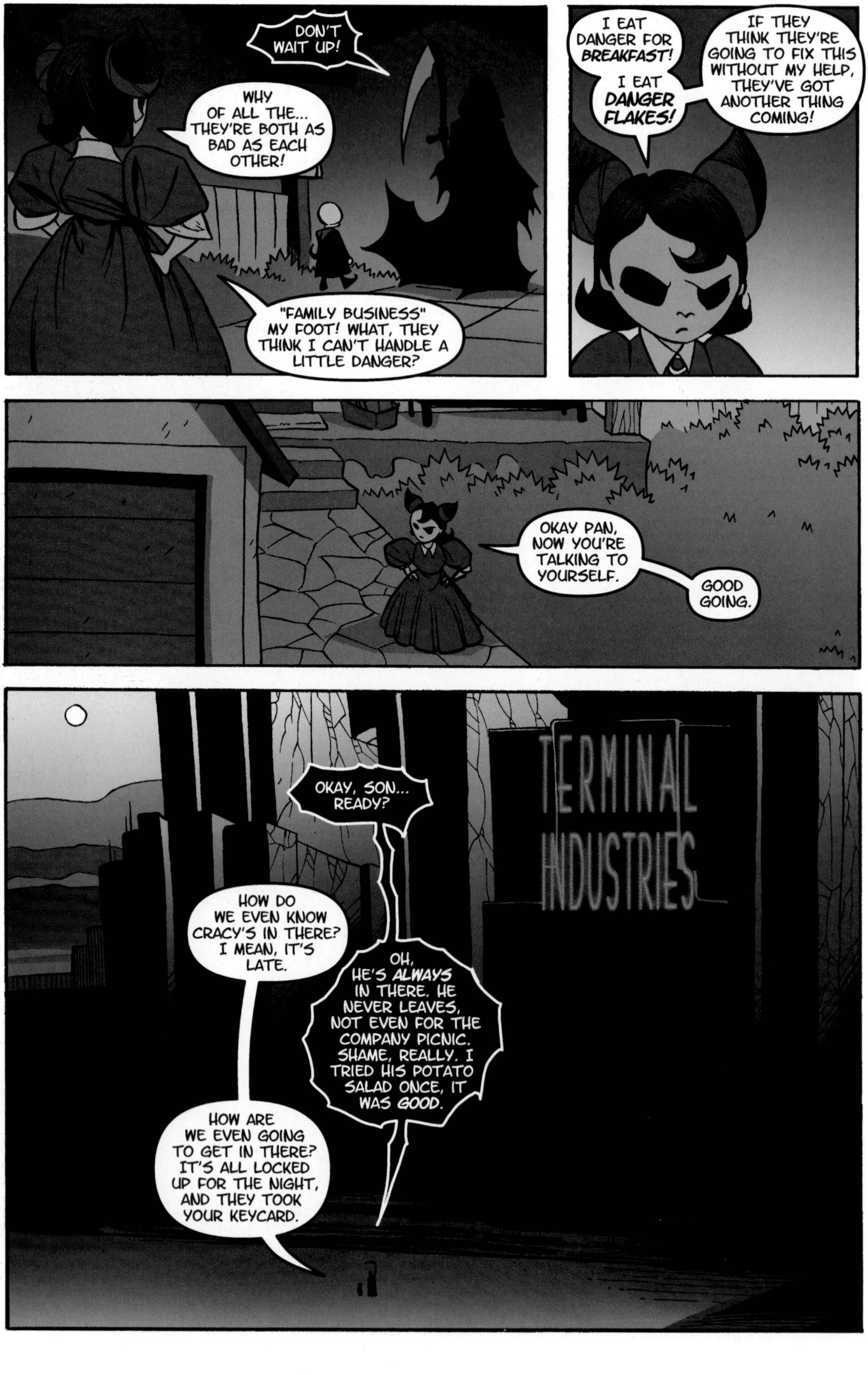
DON'T WAIT UP!
WHY OF ALL THE... THEY'RE BOTH AS BAD AS EACH OTHER!
"FAMILY BUSINESS" MY FOOT! WHAT, THEY THINK I CAN'T HANDLE A LITTLE DANGER?
I EAT DANGER FOR BREAKFAST!
I EAT DANGER FLAKES!
IF THEY THINK THEY'RE GOING TO FIX THIS WITHOUT MY HELP, THEY'VE GOT ANOTHER THING COMING!
OKAY PAN, NOW YOU'RE TALKING TO YOURSELF.
GOOD GOING.
TERMINAL INDUSTRIES
OKAY, SON... READY?
HOW DO WE EVEN KNOW CRACY'S IN THERE? I MEAN, IT'S LATE.
OH, HE'S ALWAYS IN THERE. HE NEVER LEAVES, NOT EVEN FOR THE COMPANY PICNIC. SHAME, REALLY. I TRIED HIS POTATO SALAD ONCE, IT WAS GOOD.
HOW ARE WE EVEN GOING TO GET IN THERE? IT'S ALL LOCKED UP FOR THE NIGHT, AND THEY TOOK YOUR KEYCARD.

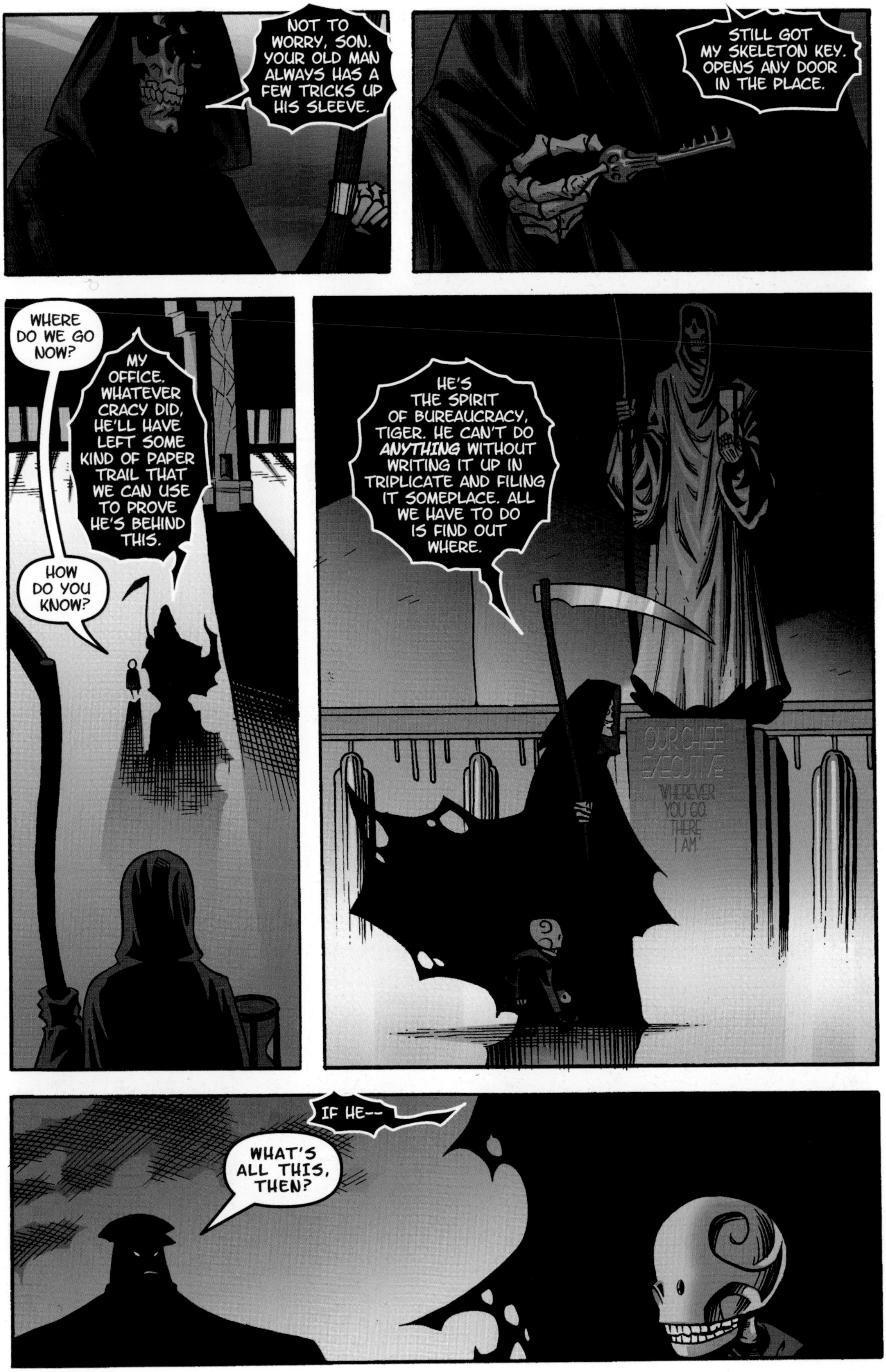
NOT TO WORRY, SON. YOUR OLD MAN ALWAYS HAS A FEW TRICKS UP HIS SLEEVE.
STILL GOT MY SKELETON KEY. OPENS ANY DOOR IN THE PLACE.
WHERE DO WE GO NOW?
MY OFFICE. WHATEVER CRACY DID, HE'LL HAVE LEFT SOME KIND OF PAPER TRAIL THAT WE CAN USE TO PROVE HE'S BEHIND THIS.
HOW DO YOU KNOW?
HE'S THE SPIRIT OF BUREAUCRACY, TIGER. HE CAN'T DO ANYTHING WITHOUT WRITING IT UP IN TRIPLICATE AND FILING IT SOMEPLACE. ALL WE HAVE TO DO IS FIND OUT WHERE.
OUR CHIEF EXECUTIVE
"WHEREVER YOU GO, THERE I AM."
IF HE--
WHAT'S ALL THIS, THEN?

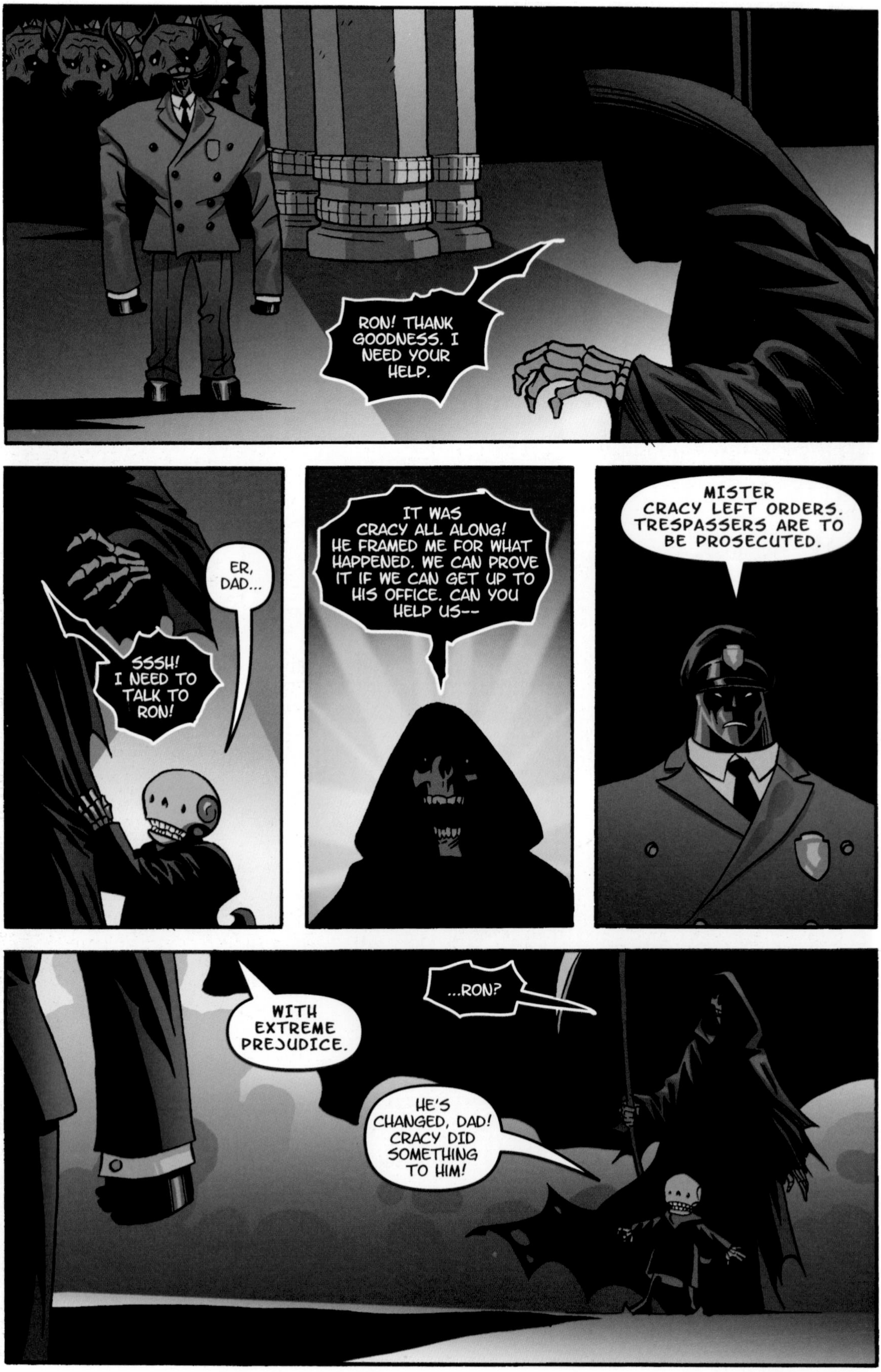
RON! THANK GOODNESS. I NEED YOUR HELP.
ER, DAD...
SSSH! I NEED TO TALK TO RON!
IT WAS CRACY ALL ALONG! HE FRAMED ME FOR WHAT HAPPENED. WE CAN PROVE IT IF WE CAN GET UP TO HIS OFFICE. CAN YOU HELP US--
MISTER CRACY LEFT ORDERS. TRESPASSERS ARE TO BE PROSECUTED.
WITH EXTREME PREJUDICE.
...RON?
HE'S CHANGED, DAD! CRACY DID SOMETHING TO HIM!

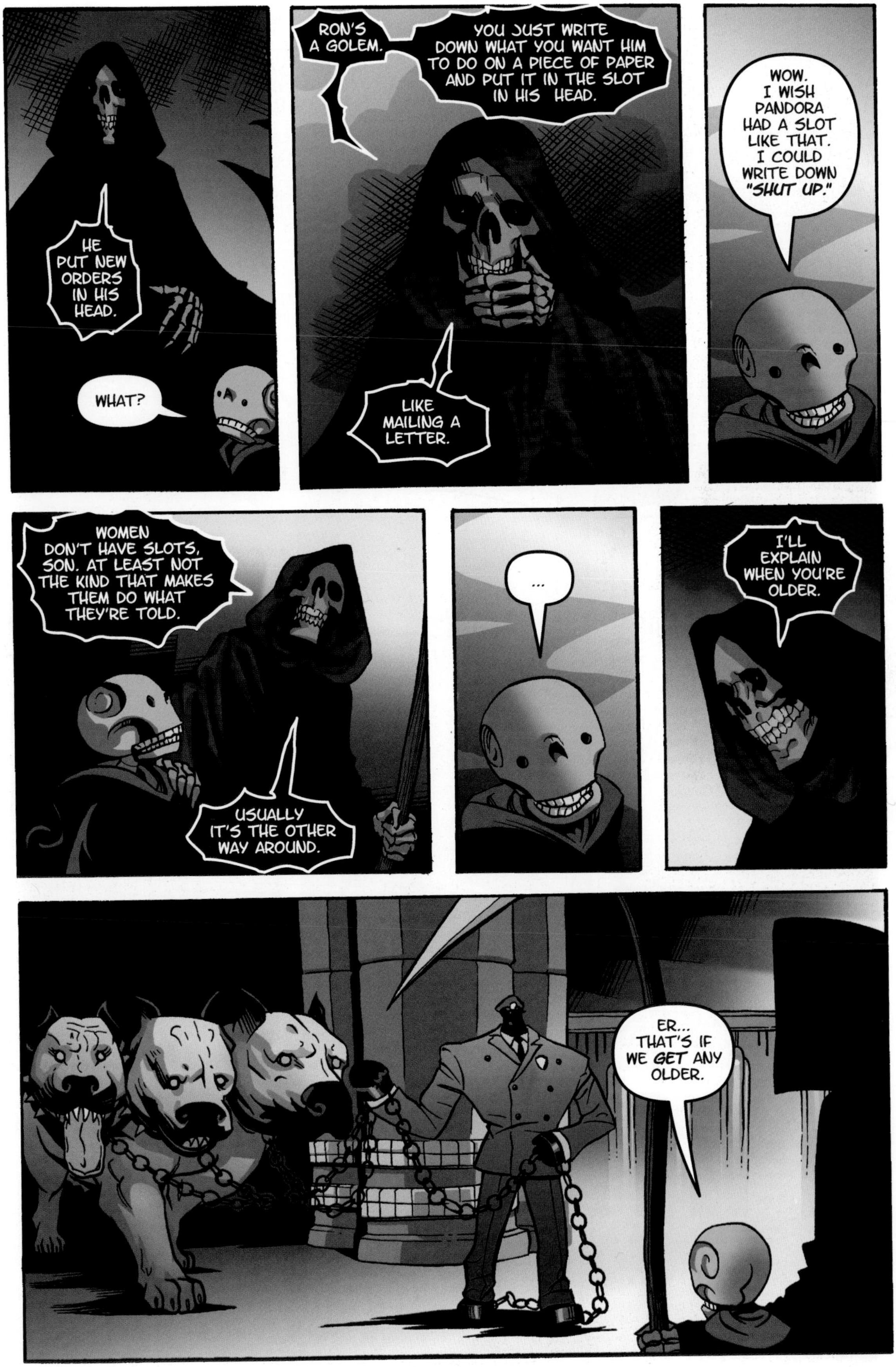
HE PUT NEW ORDERS IN HIS HEAD.
WHAT?
RON'S A GOLEM.
YOU JUST WRITE DOWN WHAT YOU WANT HIM TO DO ON A PIECE OF PAPER AND PUT IT IN THE SLOT IN HIS HEAD.
LIKE MAILING A LETTER.
WOW. I WISH PANDORA HAD A SLOT LIKE THAT. I COULD WRITE DOWN "SHUT UP."
WOMEN DON'T HAVE SLOTS, SON. AT LEAST NOT THE KIND THAT MAKES THEM DO WHAT THEY'RE TOLD.
USUALLY IT'S THE OTHER WAY AROUND.
...
I'LL EXPLAIN WHEN YOU'RE OLDER.
ER... THAT'S IF WE GET ANY OLDER.

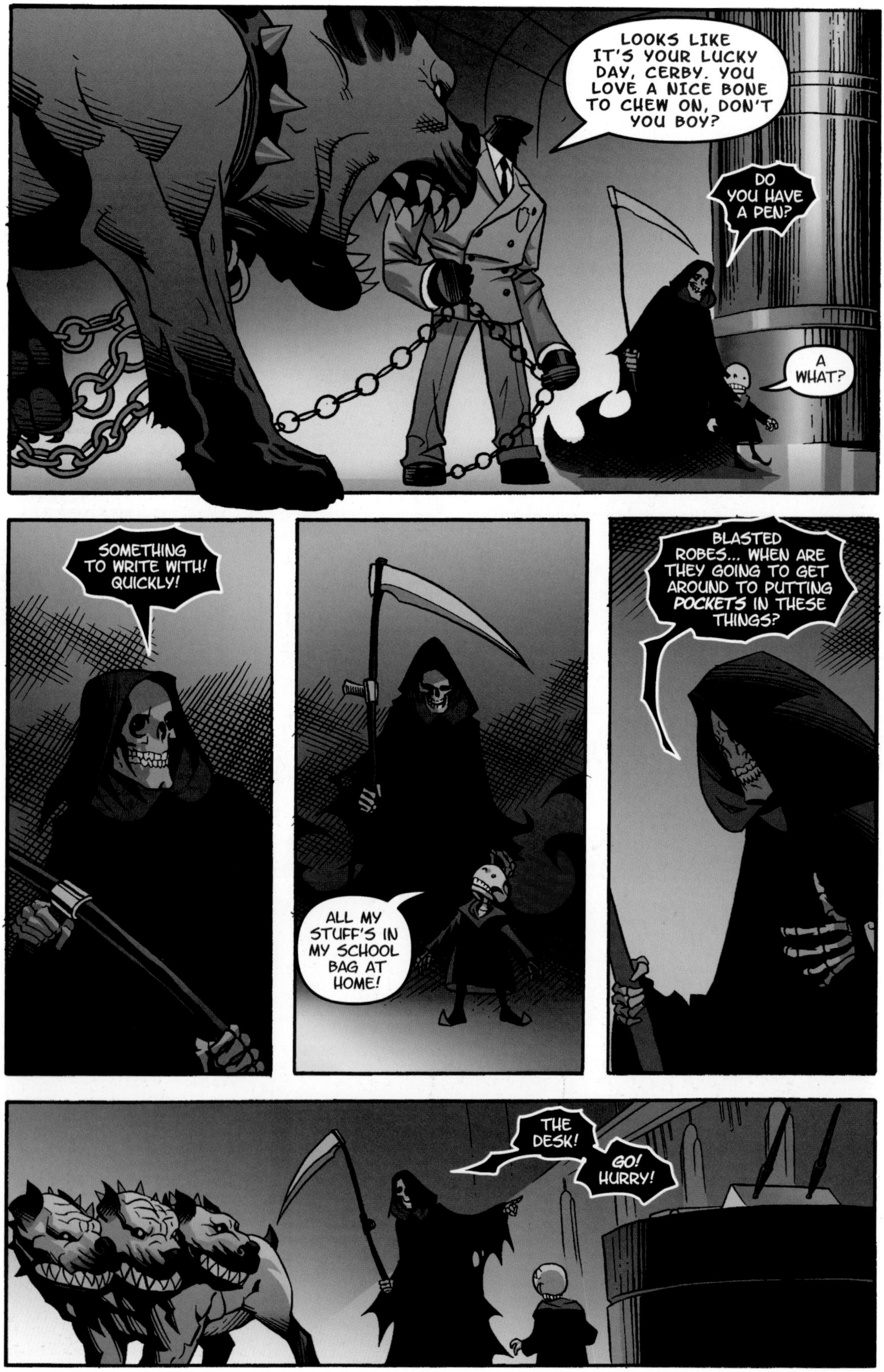
LOOKS LIKE IT'S YOUR LUCKY DAY, CERBY. YOU LOVE A NICE BONE TO CHEW ON, DON'T YOU BOY?
DO YOU HAVE A PEN?
A WHAT?
SOMETHING TO WRITE WITH! QUICKLY!
ALL MY STUFF'S IN MY SCHOOL BAG AT HOME!
BLASTED ROBES... WHEN ARE THEY GOING TO GET AROUND TO PUTTING POCKETS IN THESE THINGS?
THE DESK!
GO! HURRY!

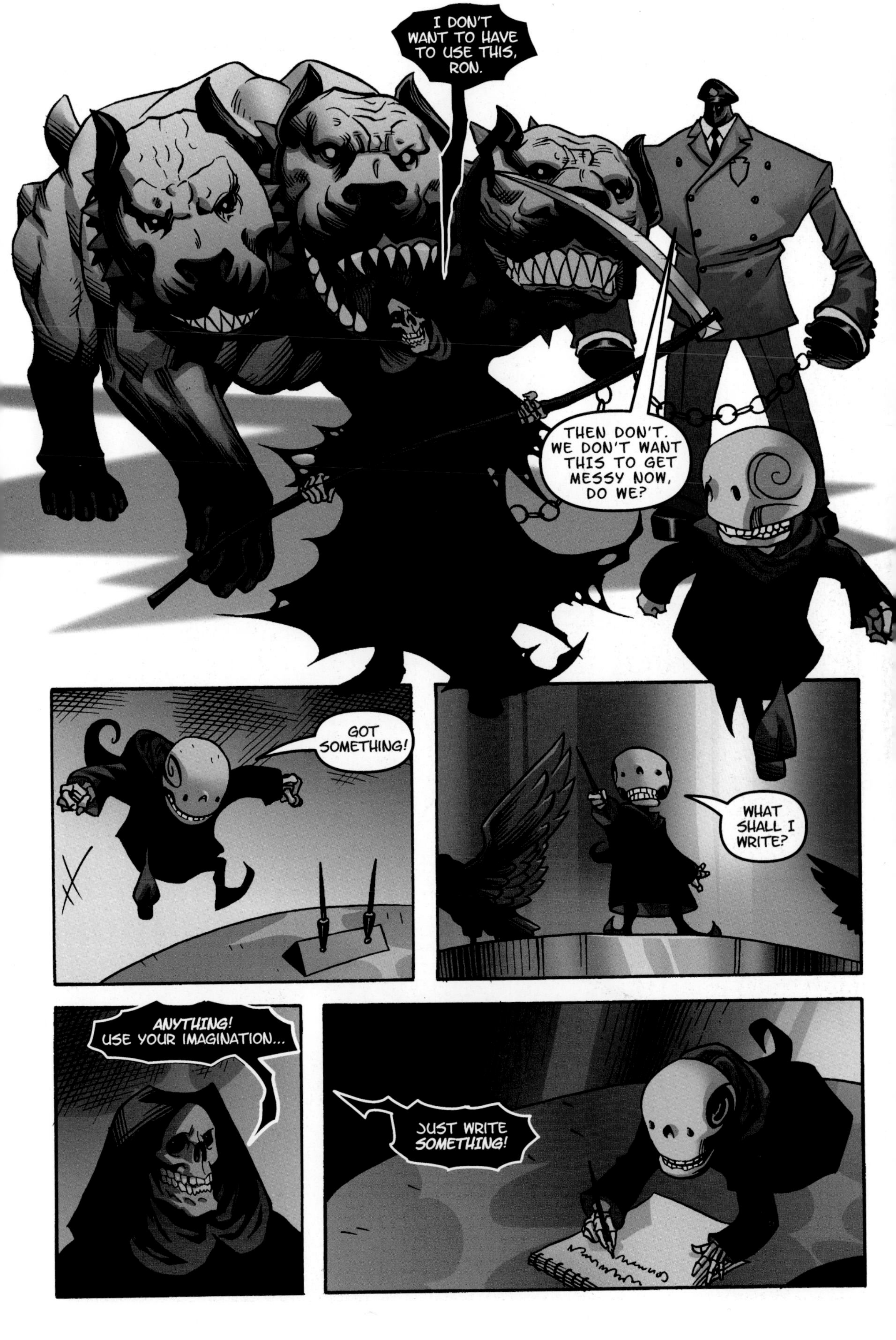
I DON'T WANT TO HAVE TO USE THIS, RON.
THEN DON'T. WE DON'T WANT THIS TO GET MESSY NOW, DO WE?
GOT SOMETHING!
WHAT SHALL I WRITE?
ANYTHING! USE YOUR IMAGINATION...
JUST WRITE SOMETHING!

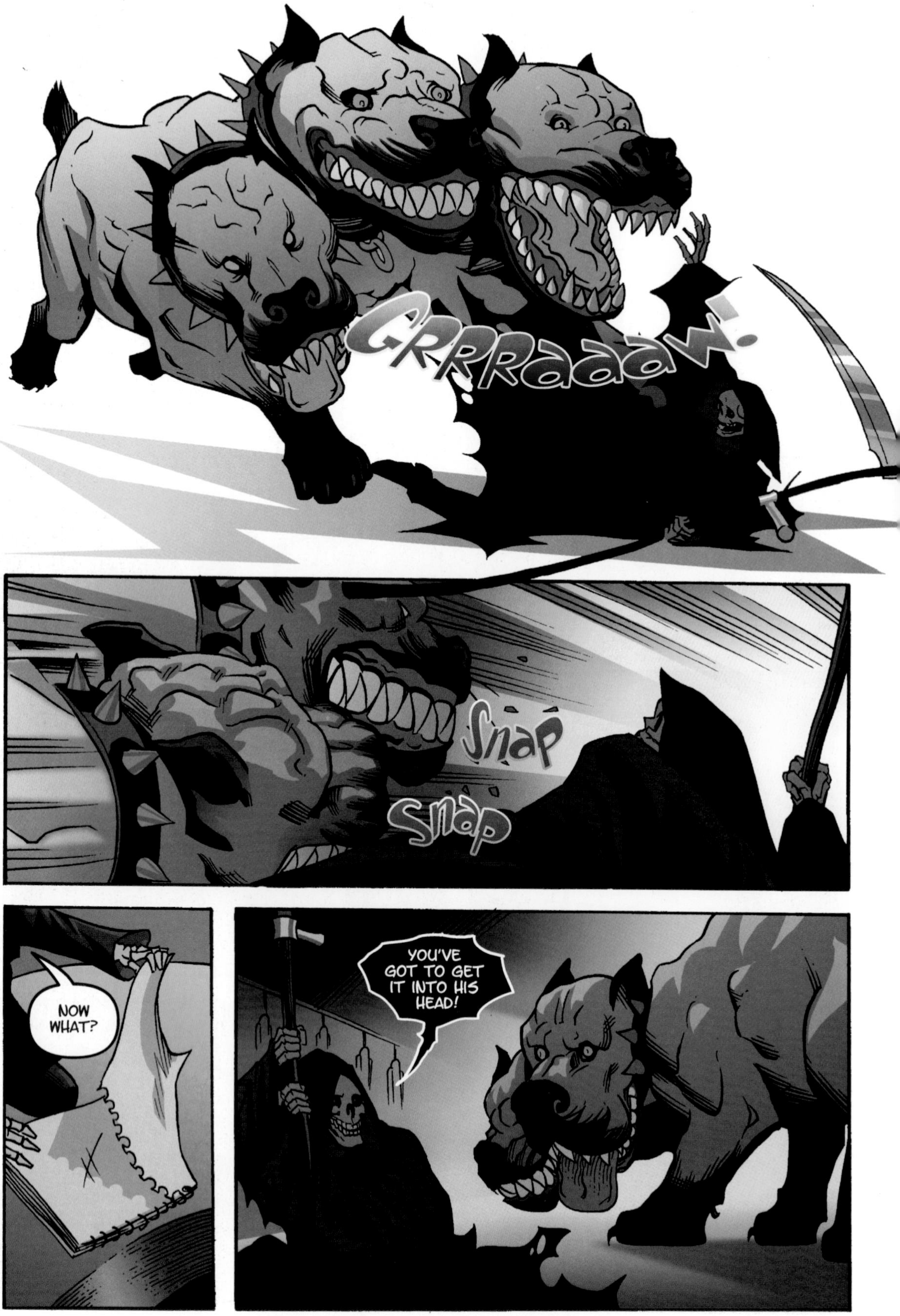
GRRRAAAAW!
SNAP
SNAP
NOW WHAT?
YOU'VE GOT TO GET IT INTO HIS HEAD!

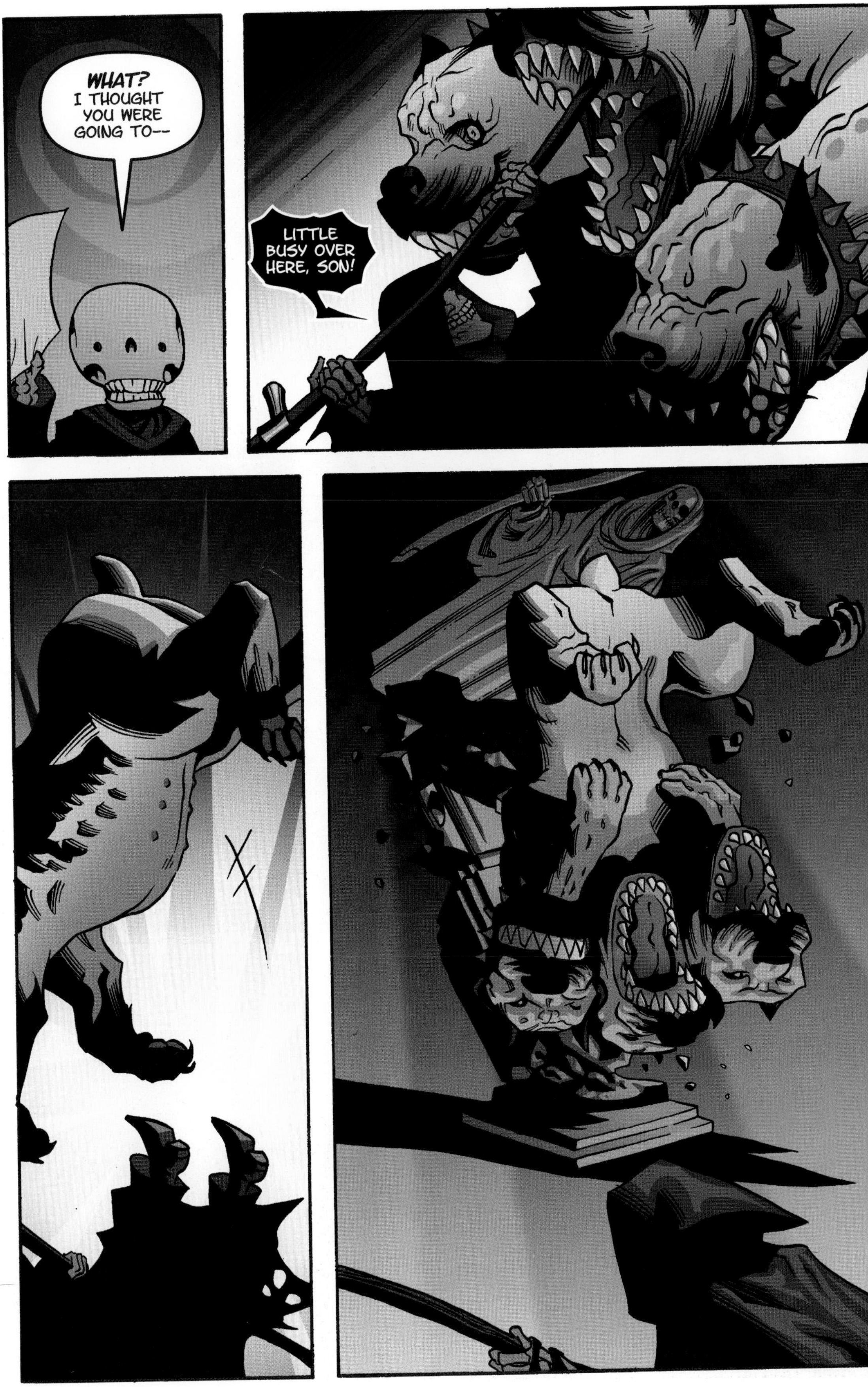
WHAT? I THOUGHT YOU WERE GOING TO--
LITTLE BUSY OVER HERE, SON!

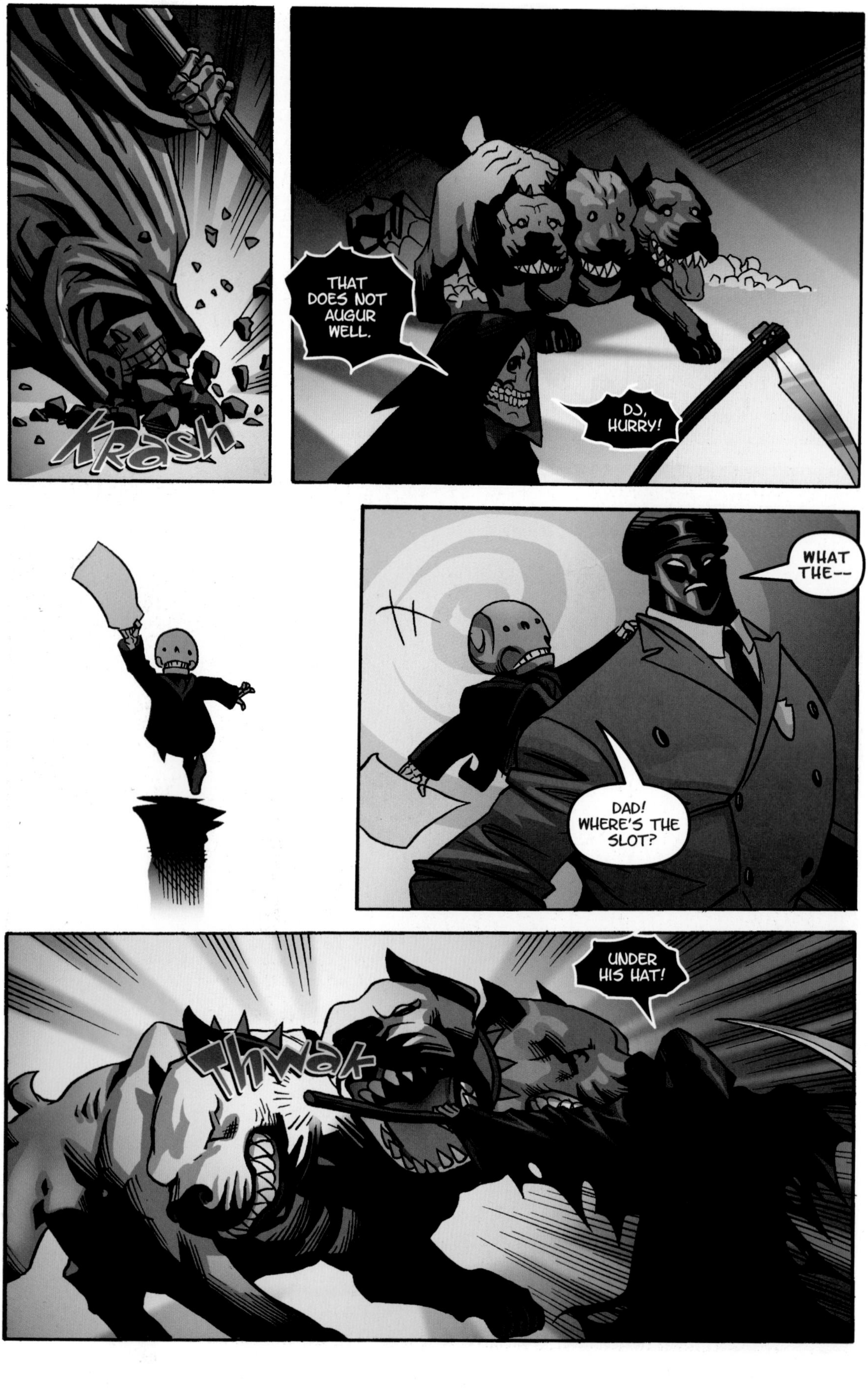
KRASH
THAT DOES NOT AUGUR WELL.
DJ, HURRY!
WHAT THE--
DAD! WHERE'S THE SLOT?
UNDER HIS HAT!
THWAK

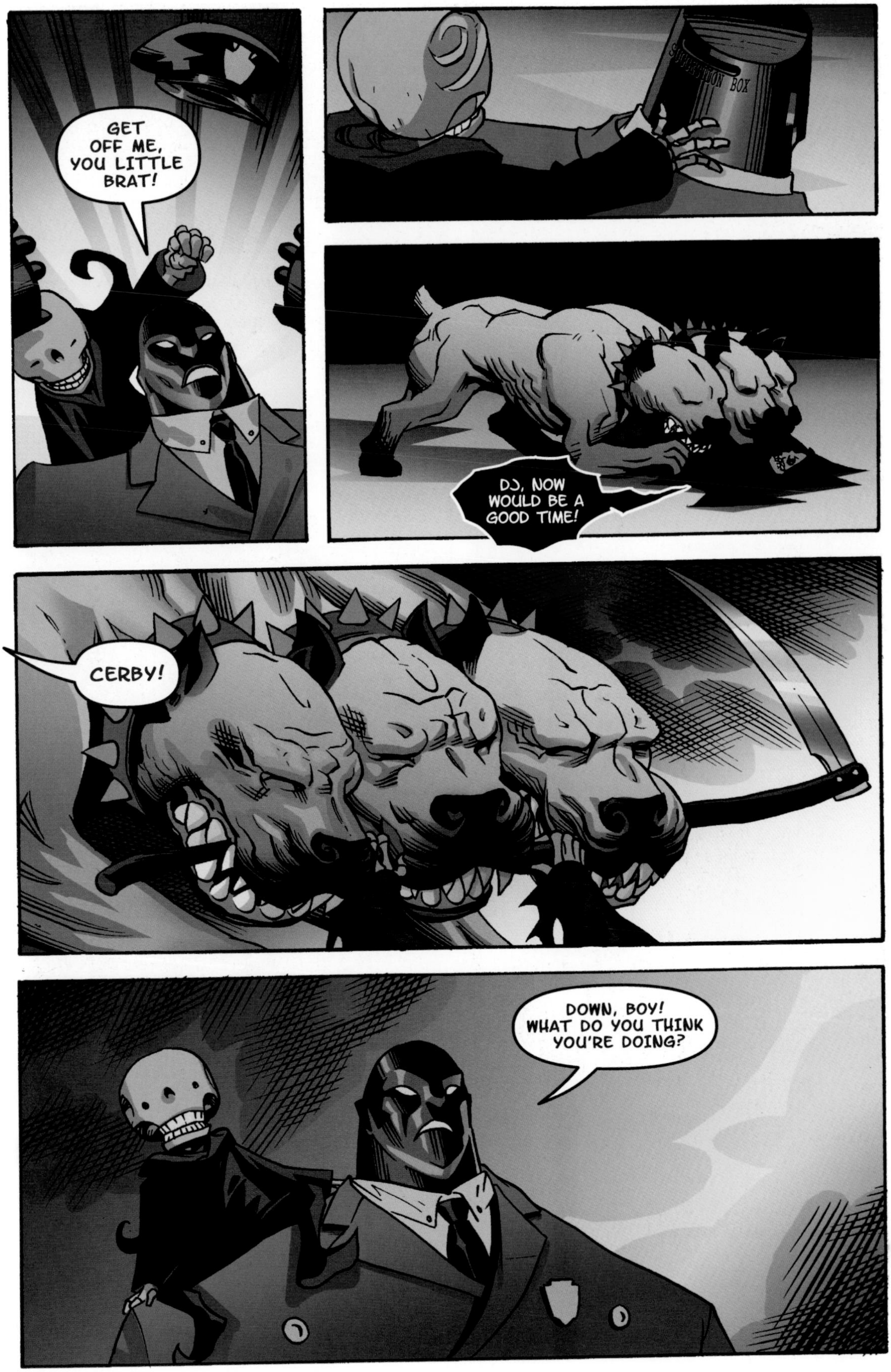
GET OFF ME, YOU LITTLE BRAT!
SUGGESTION BOX
DJ, NOW WOULD BE A GOOD TIME!
CERBY!
DOWN, BOY! WHAT DO YOU THINK YOU'RE DOING?

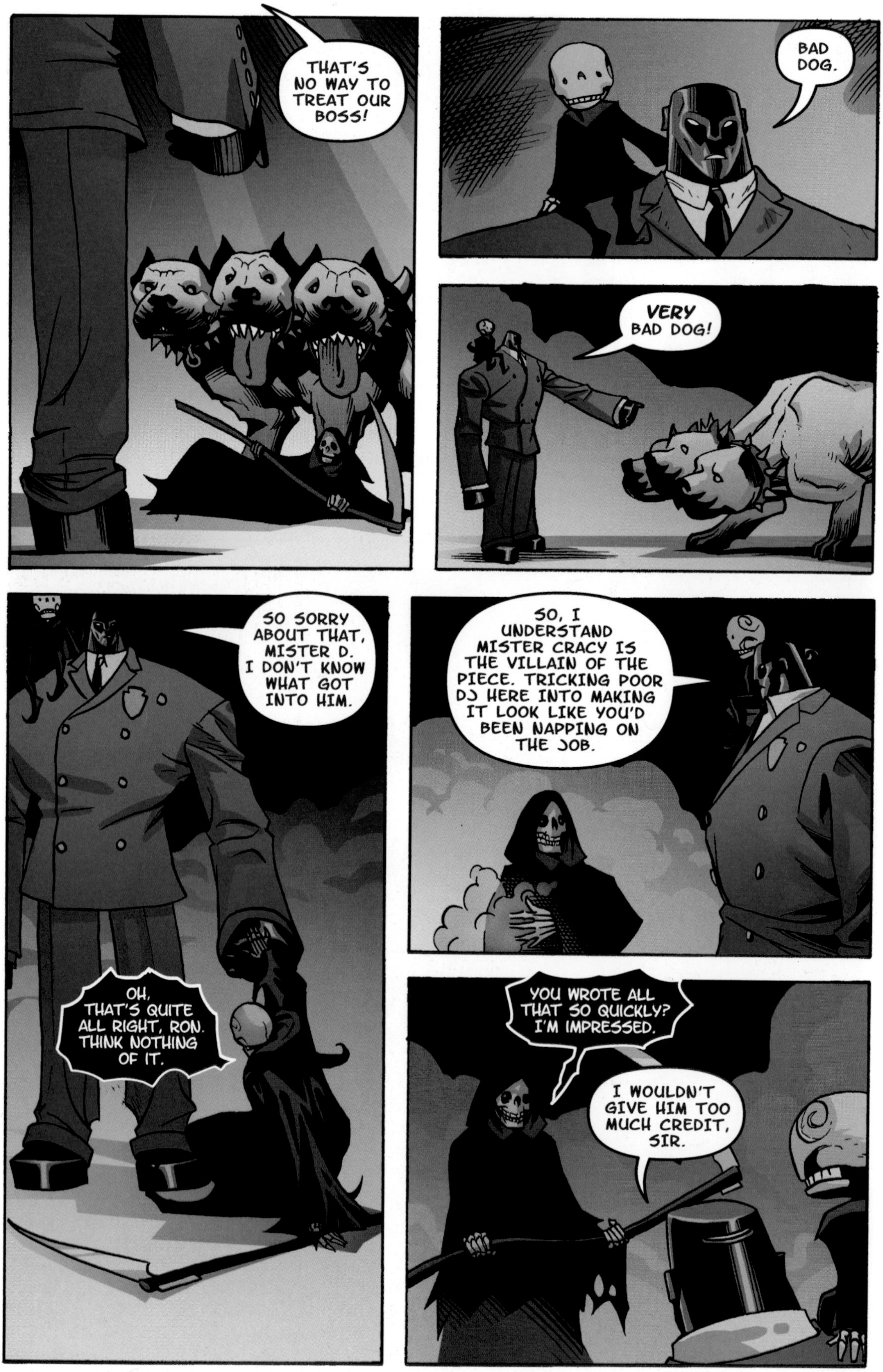
THAT'S NO WAY TO TREAT OUR BOSS!
BAD DOG.
VERY BAD DOG!
SO SORRY ABOUT THAT, MISTER D. I DON'T KNOW WHAT GOT INTO HIM.
OH, THAT'S QUITE ALL RIGHT, RON. THINK NOTHING OF IT.
SO, I UNDERSTAND MISTER CRACY IS THE VILLAIN OF THE PIECE. TRICKING POOR DJ HERE INTO MAKING IT LOOK LIKE YOU'D BEEN NAPPING ON THE JOB.
YOU WROTE ALL THAT SO QUICKLY? I'M IMPRESSED.
I WOULDN'T GIVE HIM TOO MUCH CREDIT, SIR.

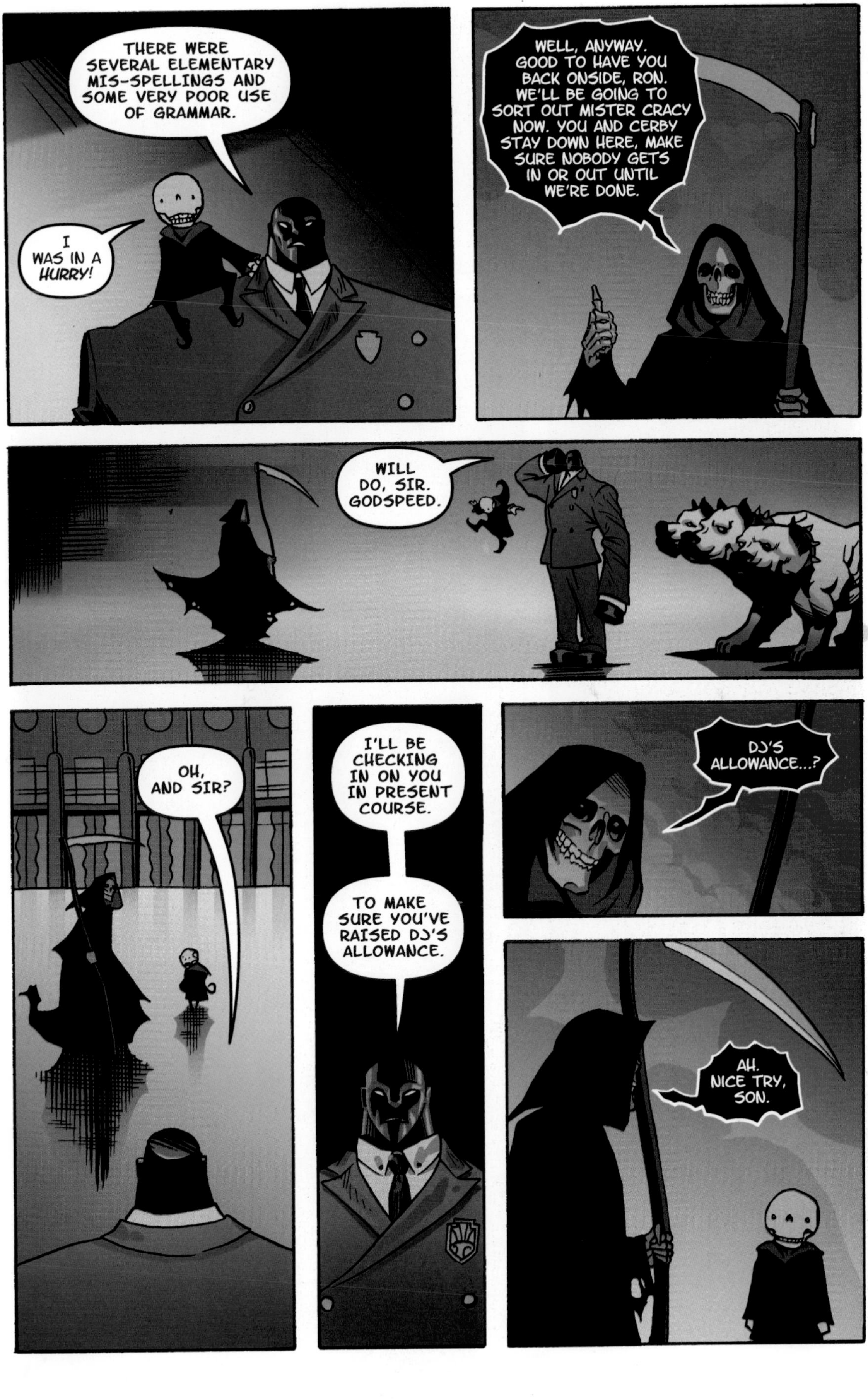
THERE WERE SEVERAL ELEMENTARY MIS-SPELLINGS AND SOME VERY POOR USE OF GRAMMAR.
I WAS IN A HURRY!
WELL, ANYWAY. GOOD TO HAVE YOU BACK ONSIDE, RON. WE'LL BE GOING TO SORT OUT MISTER CRACY NOW. YOU AND CERBY STAY DOWN HERE, MAKE SURE NOBODY GETS IN OR OUT UNTIL WE'RE DONE.
WILL DO, SIR. GODSPEED.
OH, AND SIR?
I'LL BE CHECKING IN ON YOU IN PRESENT COURSE.
TO MAKE SURE YOU'VE RAISED DJ'S ALLOWANCE.
DJ'S ALLOWANCE...?
AH. NICE TRY, SON.

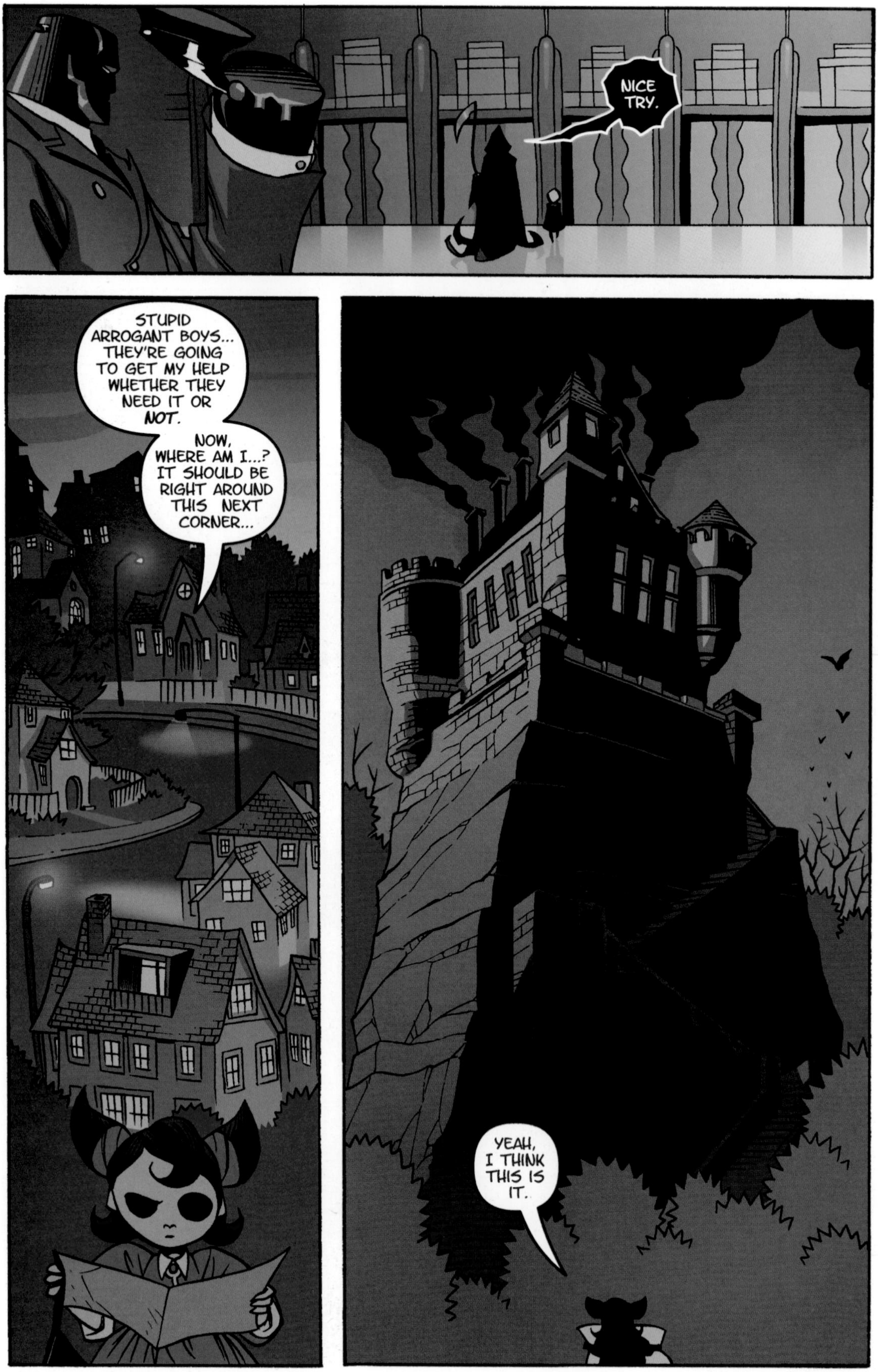
NICE TRY.
STUPID ARROGANT BOYS... THEY'RE GOING TO GET MY HELP WHETHER THEY NEED IT OR NOT.
NOW, WHERE AM I...? IT SHOULD BE RIGHT AROUND THIS NEXT CORNER...
YEAH, I THINK THIS IS IT.

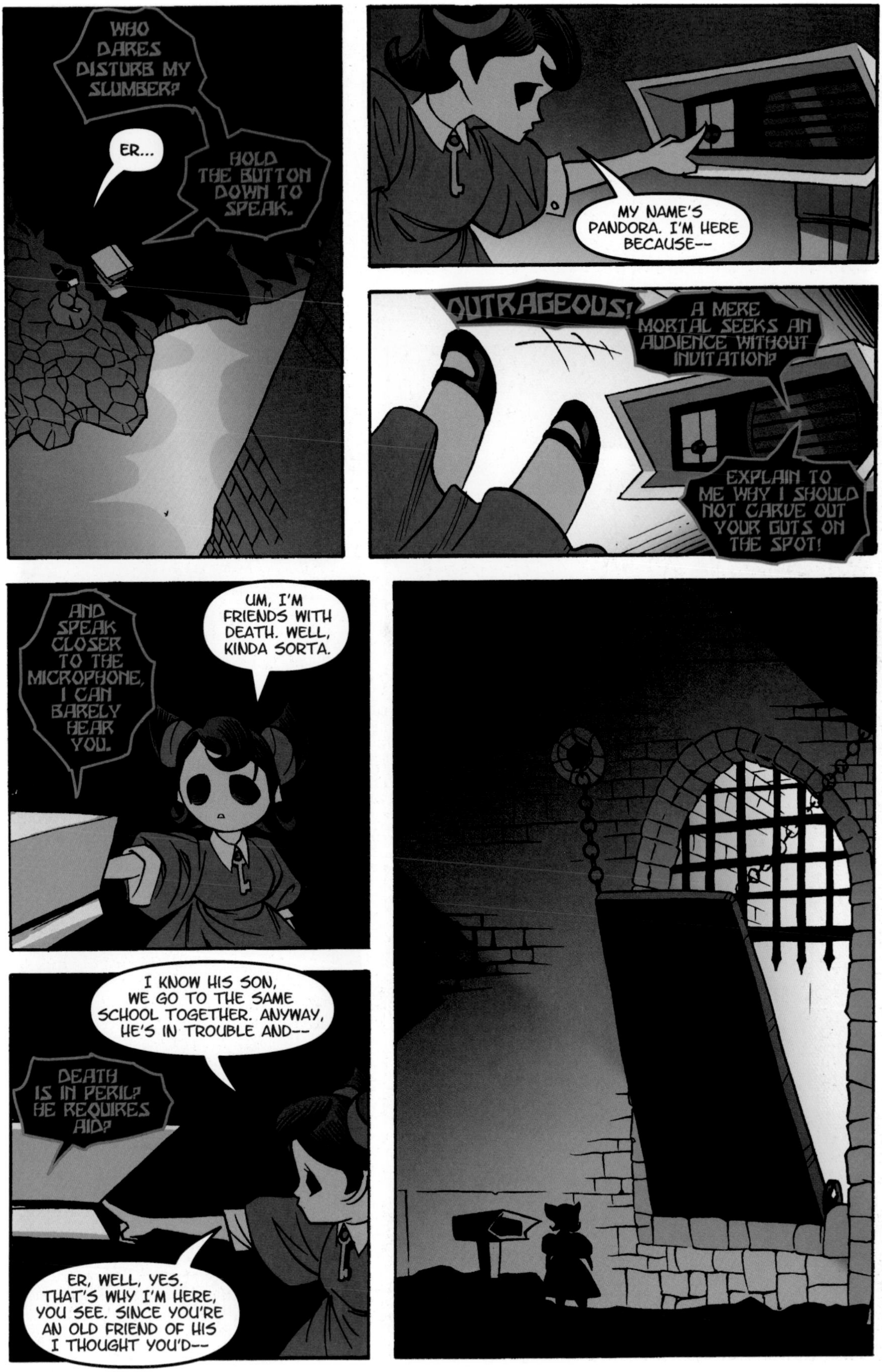

WHO DARES DISTURB MY SLUMBER?
ER...
HOLD THE BUTTON DOWN TO SPEAK.
MY NAME'S PANDORA. I'M HERE BECAUSE--
OUTRAGEOUS!
A MERE MORTAL SEEKS AN AUDIENCE WITHOUT INVITATION?
EXPLAIN TO ME WHY I SHOULD NOT CARVE OUT YOUR GUTS ON THE SPOT!
AND SPEAK CLOSER TO THE MICROPHONE, I CAN BARELY HEAR YOU.
UM, I'M FRIENDS WITH DEATH. WELL, KINDA SORTA.
I KNOW HIS SON, WE GO TO THE SAME SCHOOL TOGETHER. ANYWAY, HE'S IN TROUBLE AND--
DEATH IS IN PERIL? HE REQUIRES AID?
ER, WELL, YES. THAT'S WHY I'M HERE, YOU SEE. SINCE YOU'RE AN OLD FRIEND OF HIS I THOUGHT YOU'D--

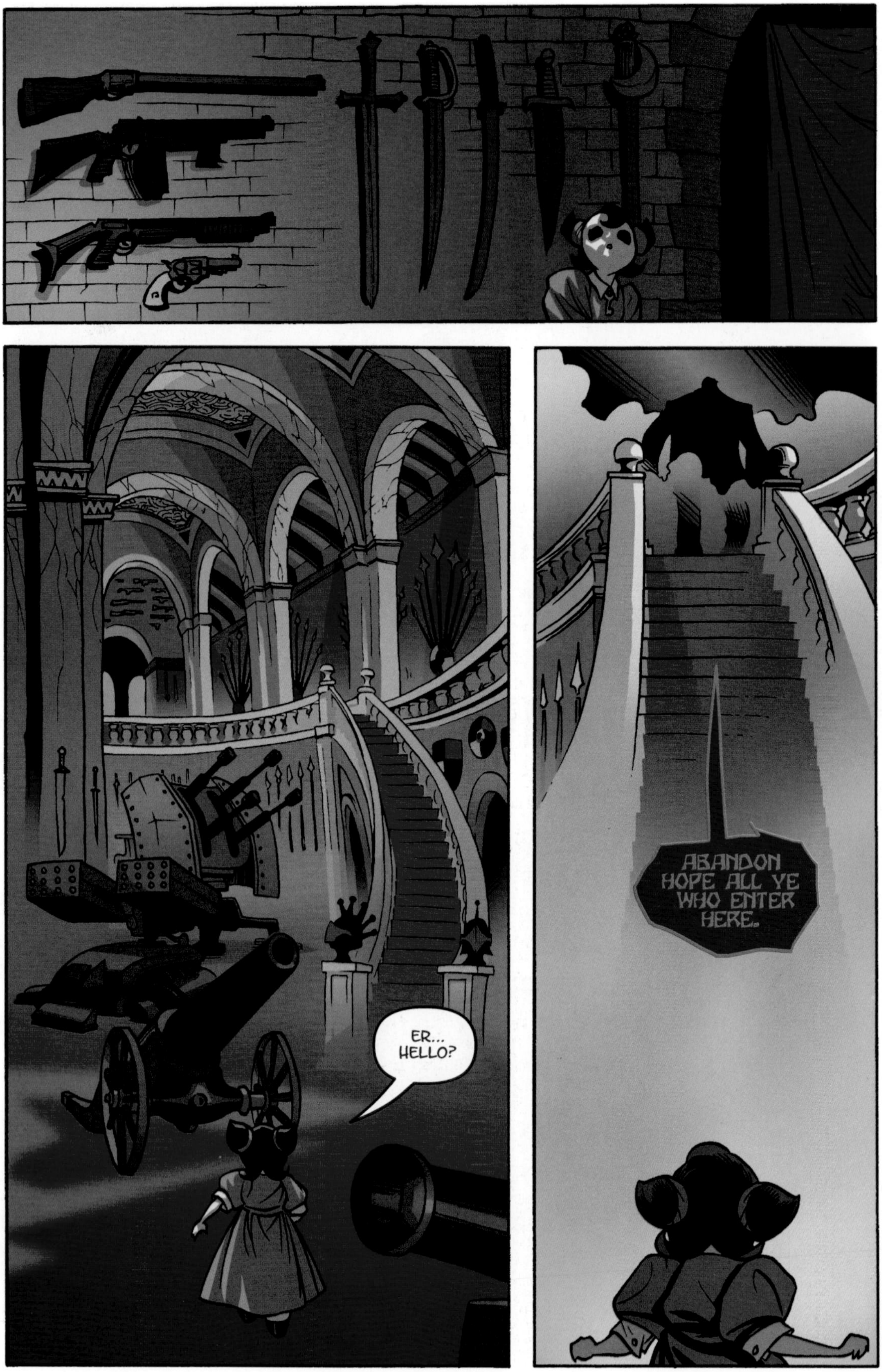
ER... HELLO?
ABANDON HOPE ALL YE WHO ENTER HERE.

AND YOUR SHOES. I JUST HAD NEW CARPET PUT IN.

NOW TELL ME, LITTLE ONE...

WHAT KIND OF TROUBLE HAS "OLD BONY" GOTTEN HIMSELF INTO?

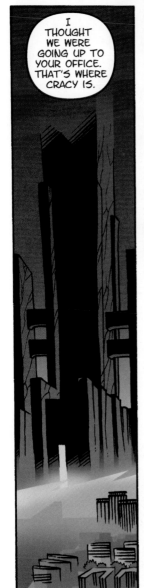

I THOUGHT WE WERE GOING UP TO YOUR OFFICE. THAT'S WHERE CRACY IS.

WE'RE GOING DOWN TO THE SUB-BASEMENT FIRST.

IF I KNOW CRACY, HE WON'T HAVE WASTED ANY TIME.

HE'S PROBABLY BEEN PLANNING THIS FOR YEARS.

I WANT TO SEE HOW MUCH TROUBLE HE'S ALREADY CAUSED...

WELL, DAD...

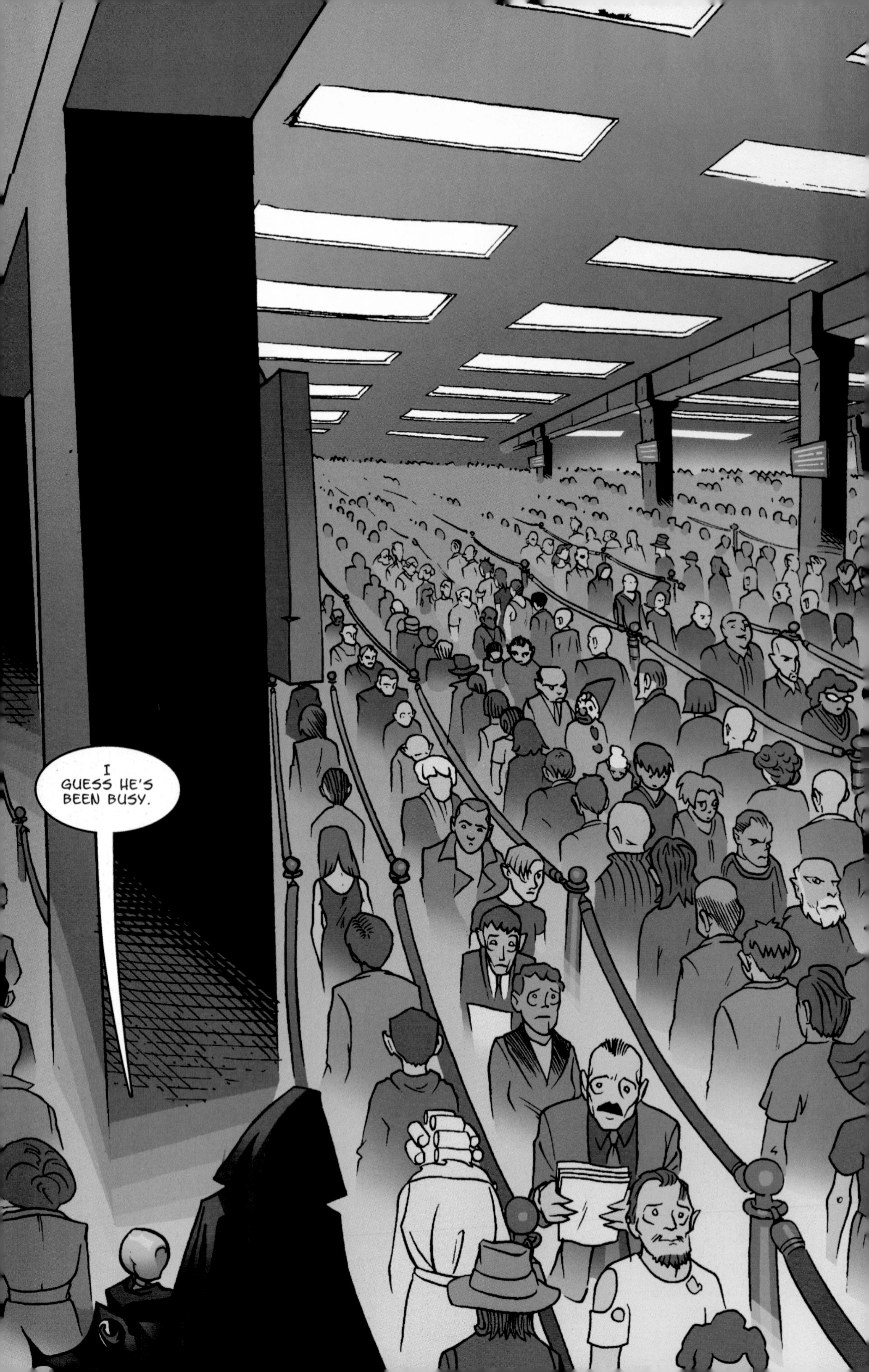
I GUESS HE'S BEEN BUSY.

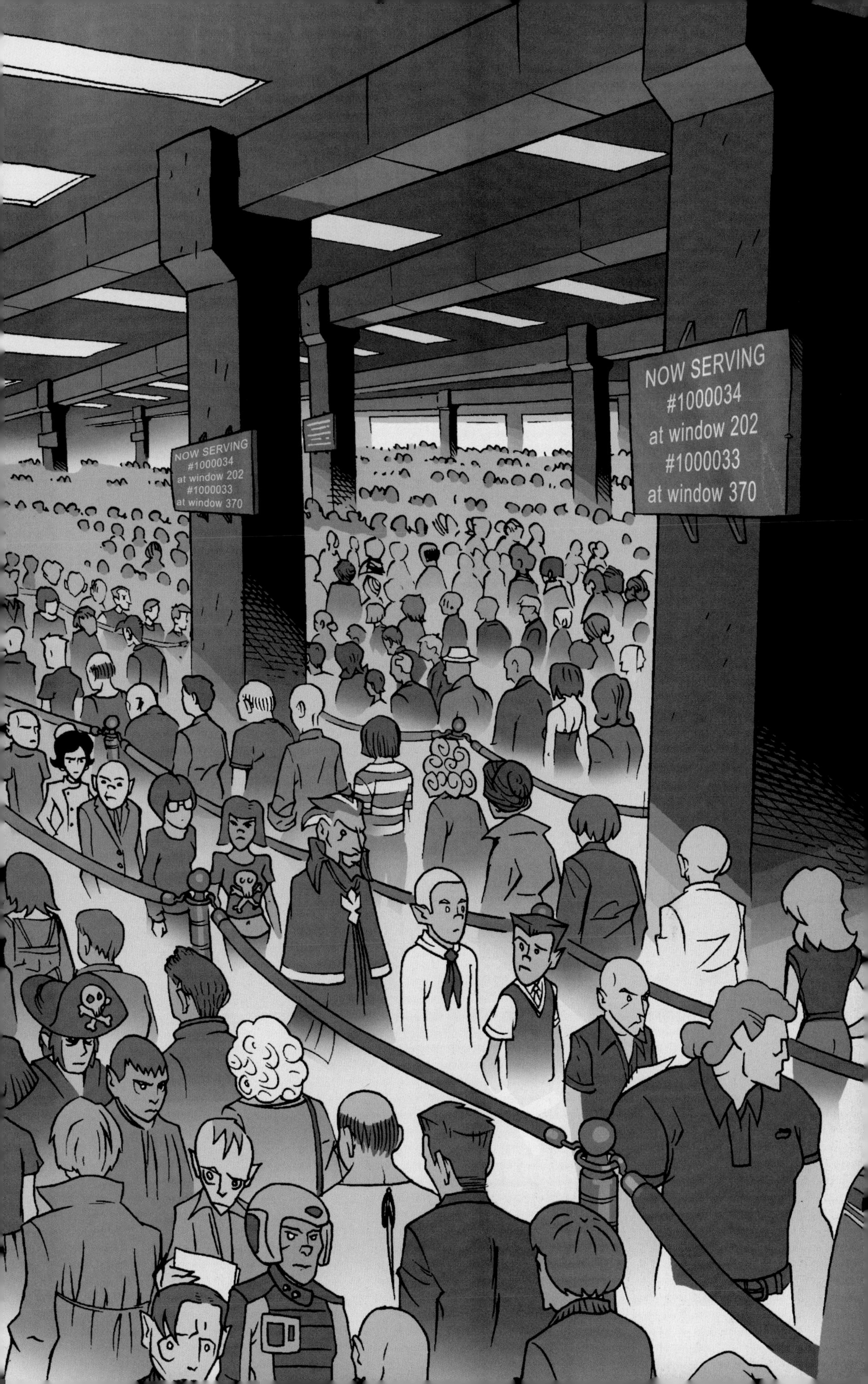
NOW SERVING
#1000034
at window 202
#1000033
at window 370
NOW SERVING
#1000034
at window 202
#1000033
at window 370

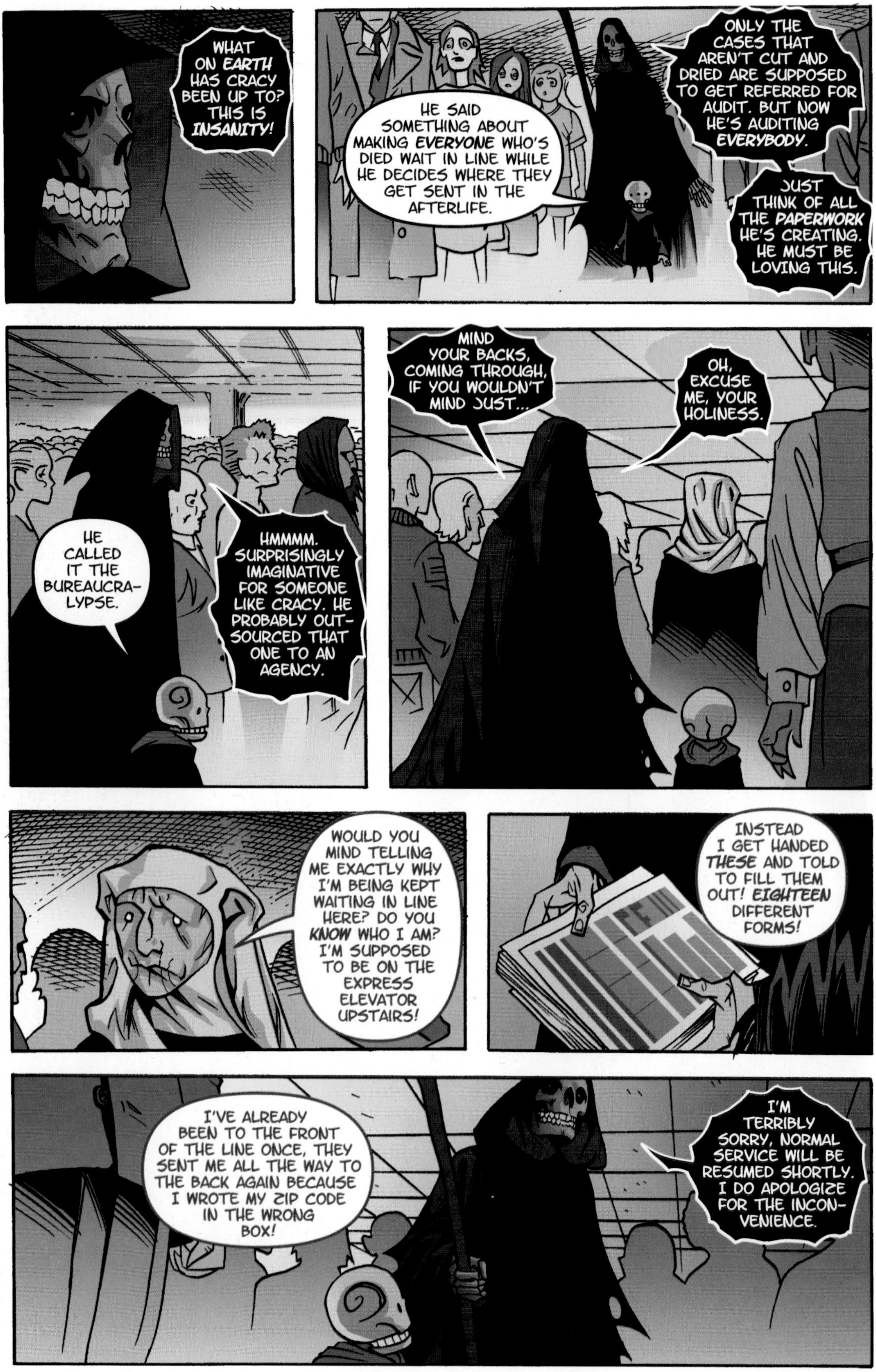
WHAT ON EARTH HAS CRACY BEEN UP TO? THIS IS INSANITY!
HE SAID SOMETHING ABOUT MAKING EVERYONE WHO'S DIED WAIT IN LINE WHILE HE DECIDES WHERE THEY GET SENT IN THE AFTERLIFE.
ONLY THE CASES THAT AREN'T CUT AND DRIED ARE SUPPOSED TO GET REFERRED FOR AUDIT. BUT NOW HE'S AUDITING EVERYBODY.
JUST THINK OF ALL THE PAPERWORK HE'S CREATING. HE MUST BE LOVING THIS.
HE CALLED IT THE BUREAUCRA-LYPSE.
HMMMM. SURPRISINGLY IMAGINATIVE FOR SOMEONE LIKE CRACY. HE PROBABLY OUT-SOURCED THAT ONE TO AN AGENCY.
MIND YOUR BACKS, COMING THROUGH, IF YOU WOULDN'T MIND JUST...
OH, EXCUSE ME, YOUR HOLINESS.
WOULD YOU MIND TELLING ME EXACTLY WHY I'M BEING KEPT WAITING IN LINE HERE? DO YOU KNOW WHO I AM? I'M SUPPOSED TO BE ON THE EXPRESS ELEVATOR UPSTAIRS!
INSTEAD I GET HANDED THESE AND TOLD TO FILL THEM OUT! EIGHTEEN DIFFERENT FORMS!
I'VE ALREADY BEEN TO THE FRONT OF THE LINE ONCE, THEY SENT ME ALL THE WAY TO THE BACK AGAIN BECAUSE I WROTE MY ZIP CODE IN THE WRONG BOX!
I'M TERRIBLY SORRY, NORMAL SERVICE WILL BE RESUMED SHORTLY. I DO APOLOGIZE FOR THE INCON-VENIENCE.

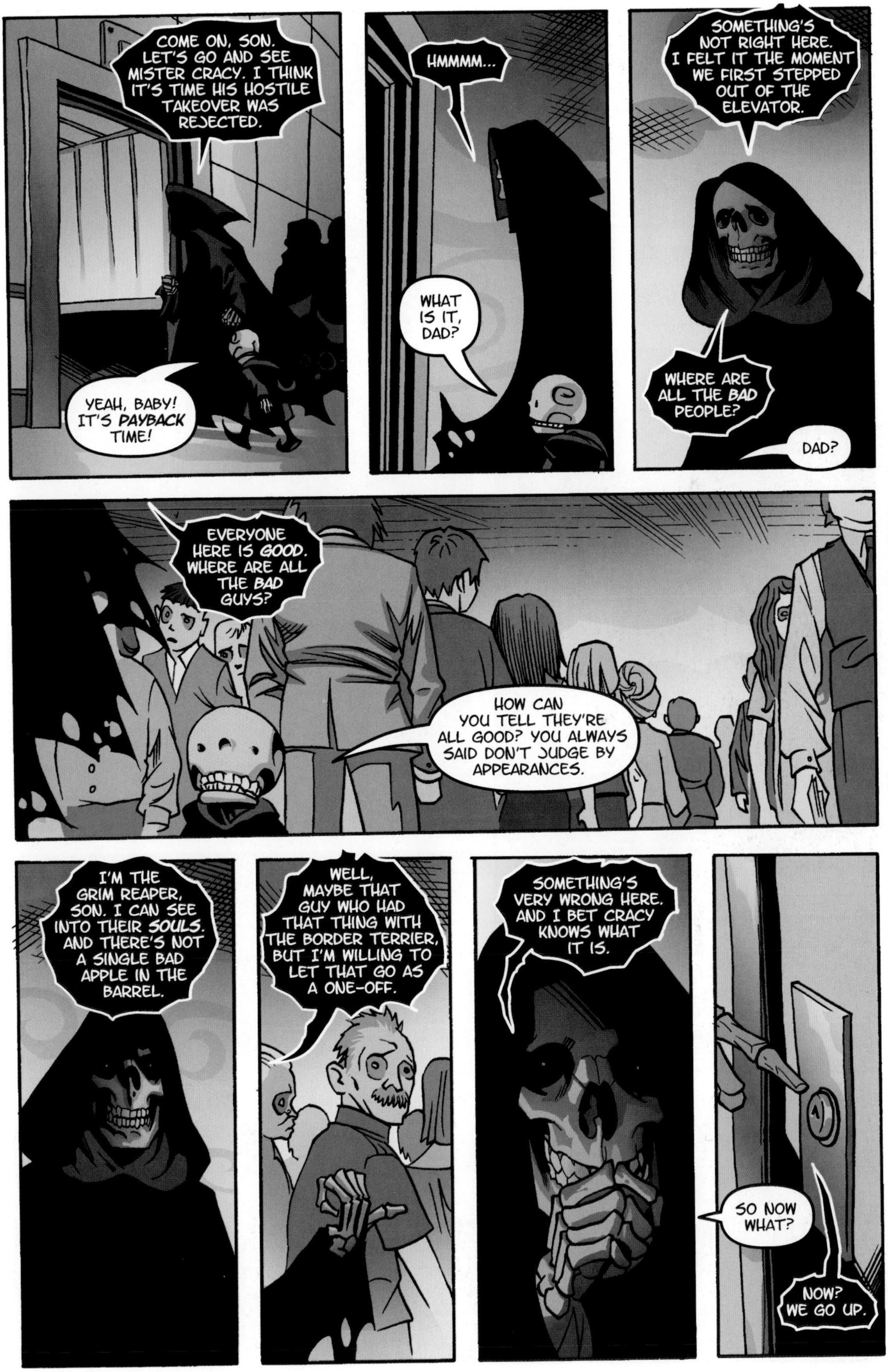
COME ON, SON. LET'S GO AND SEE MISTER CRACY. I THINK IT'S TIME HIS HOSTILE TAKEOVER WAS REJECTED.
YEAH, BABY! IT'S PAYBACK TIME!
HMMMM...
WHAT IS IT, DAD?
SOMETHING'S NOT RIGHT HERE. I FELT IT THE MOMENT WE FIRST STEPPED OUT OF THE ELEVATOR.
WHERE ARE ALL THE BAD PEOPLE?
DAD?
EVERYONE HERE IS GOOD. WHERE ARE ALL THE BAD GUYS?
HOW CAN YOU TELL THEY'RE ALL GOOD? YOU ALWAYS SAID DON'T JUDGE BY APPEARANCES.
I'M THE GRIM REAPER, SON. I CAN SEE INTO THEIR SOULS. AND THERE'S NOT A SINGLE BAD APPLE IN THE BARREL.
WELL, MAYBE THAT GUY WHO HAD THAT THING WITH THE BORDER TERRIER, BUT I'M WILLING TO LET THAT GO AS A ONE-OFF.
SOMETHING'S VERY WRONG HERE. AND I BET CRACY KNOWS WHAT IT IS.
SO NOW WHAT?
NOW? WE GO UP.

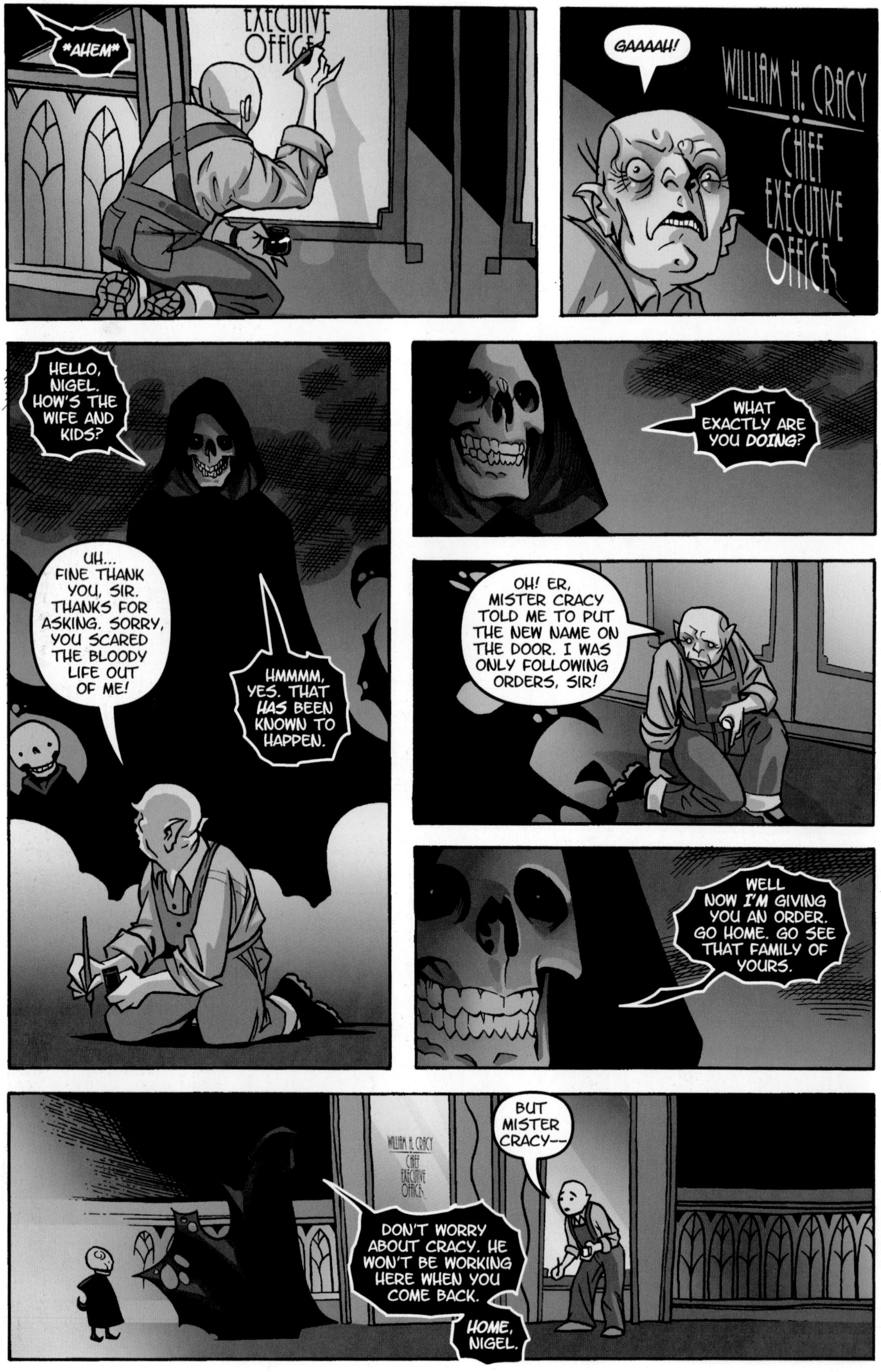
AHEM
EXECUTIVE OFFICE
GAAAAH!
WILLIAM H. CRACY CHIEF EXECUTIVE OFFICE
HELLO, NIGEL. HOW'S THE WIFE AND KIDS?
WHAT EXACTLY ARE YOU DOING?
UH... FINE THANK YOU, SIR. THANKS FOR ASKING. SORRY, YOU SCARED THE BLOODY LIFE OUT OF ME!
HMMMM, YES. THAT HAS BEEN KNOWN TO HAPPEN.
OH! ER, MISTER CRACY TOLD ME TO PUT THE NEW NAME ON THE DOOR. I WAS ONLY FOLLOWING ORDERS, SIR!
WELL NOW I'M GIVING YOU AN ORDER. GO HOME. GO SEE THAT FAMILY OF YOURS.
WILLIAM H. CRACY CHIEF EXECUTIVE OFFICE
BUT MISTER CRACY--
DON'T WORRY ABOUT CRACY. HE WON'T BE WORKING HERE WHEN YOU COME BACK.
HOME, NIGEL.

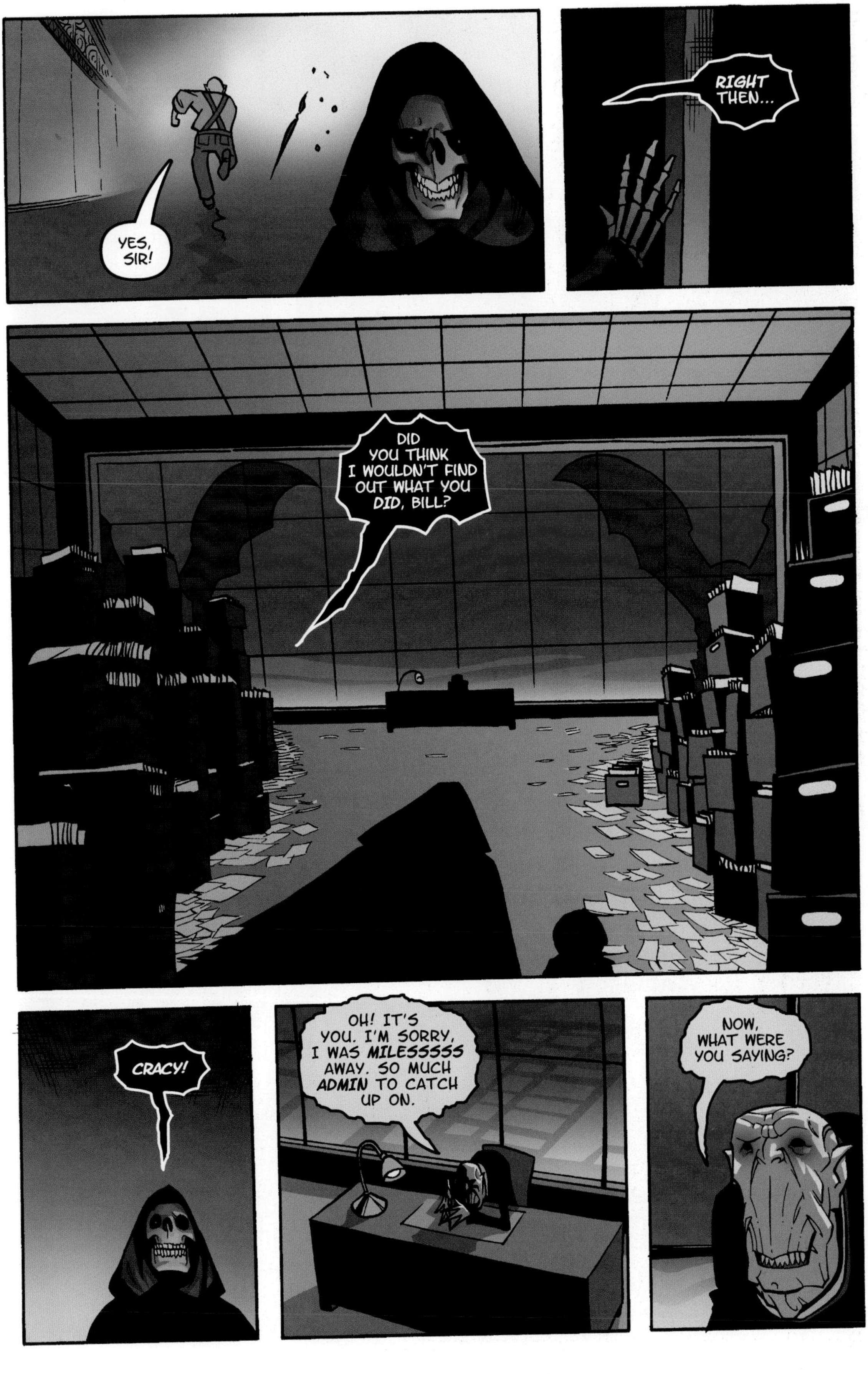
YES, SIR!
RIGHT THEN...
DID YOU THINK I WOULDN'T FIND OUT WHAT YOU DID, BILL?
CRACY!
OH! IT'S YOU. I'M SORRY, I WAS MILESSSSS AWAY. SO MUCH ADMIN TO CATCH UP ON.
NOW, WHAT WERE YOU SAYING?

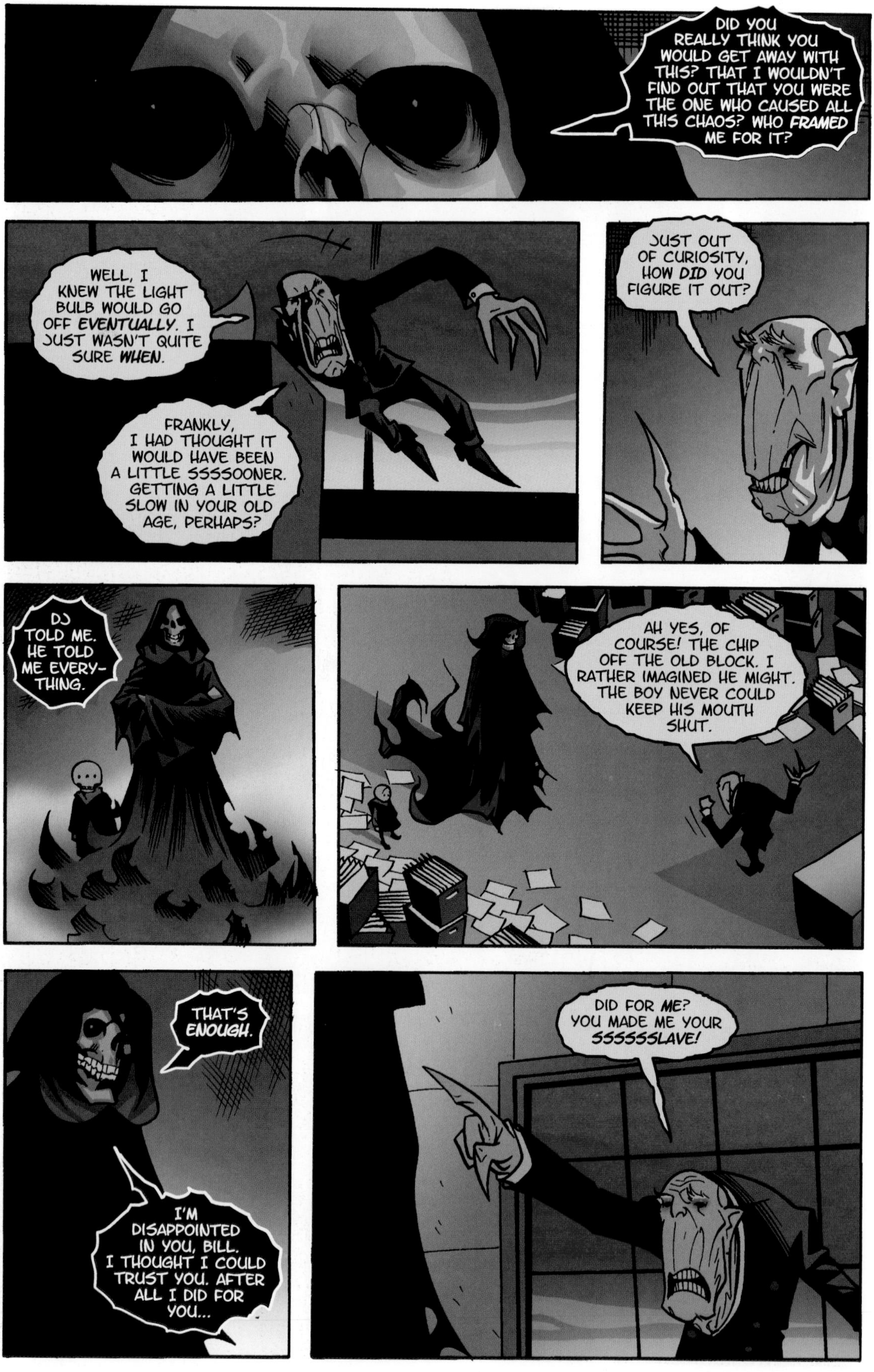
DID YOU REALLY THINK YOU WOULD GET AWAY WITH THIS? THAT I WOULDN'T FIND OUT THAT YOU WERE THE ONE WHO CAUSED ALL THIS CHAOS? WHO FRAMED ME FOR IT?
WELL, I KNEW THE LIGHT BULB WOULD GO OFF EVENTUALLY. I JUST WASN'T QUITE SURE WHEN.
FRANKLY, I HAD THOUGHT IT WOULD HAVE BEEN A LITTLE SSSSOONER. GETTING A LITTLE SLOW IN YOUR OLD AGE, PERHAPS?
JUST OUT OF CURIOSITY, HOW DID YOU FIGURE IT OUT?
DJ TOLD ME. HE TOLD ME EVERY-THING.
AH YES, OF COURSE! THE CHIP OFF THE OLD BLOCK. I RATHER IMAGINED HE MIGHT. THE BOY NEVER COULD KEEP HIS MOUTH SHUT.
THAT'S ENOUGH.
I'M DISAPPOINTED IN YOU, BILL. I THOUGHT I COULD TRUST YOU. AFTER ALL I DID FOR YOU...
DID FOR ME? YOU MADE ME YOUR SSSSSSLAVE!

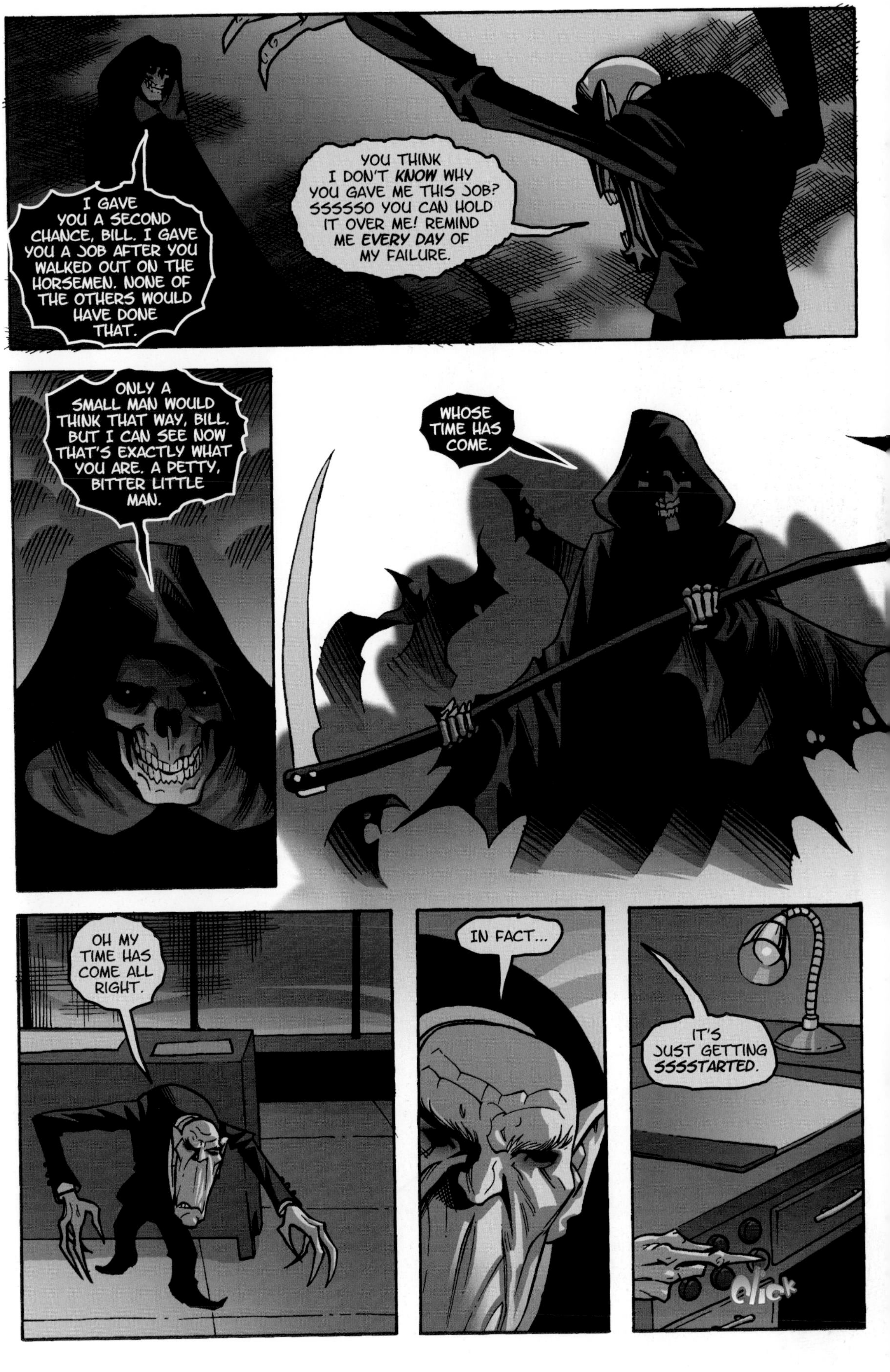
YOU THINK I DON'T KNOW WHY YOU GAVE ME THIS JOB? SSSSSO YOU CAN HOLD IT OVER ME! REMIND ME EVERY DAY OF MY FAILURE.
I GAVE YOU A SECOND CHANCE, BILL. I GAVE YOU A JOB AFTER YOU WALKED OUT ON THE HORSEMEN. NONE OF THE OTHERS WOULD HAVE DONE THAT.
ONLY A SMALL MAN WOULD THINK THAT WAY, BILL. BUT I CAN SEE NOW THAT'S EXACTLY WHAT YOU ARE. A PETTY, BITTER LITTLE MAN.
WHOSE TIME HAS COME.
OH MY TIME HAS COME ALL RIGHT.
IN FACT...
IT'S JUST GETTING SSSSTARTED.
CLICK

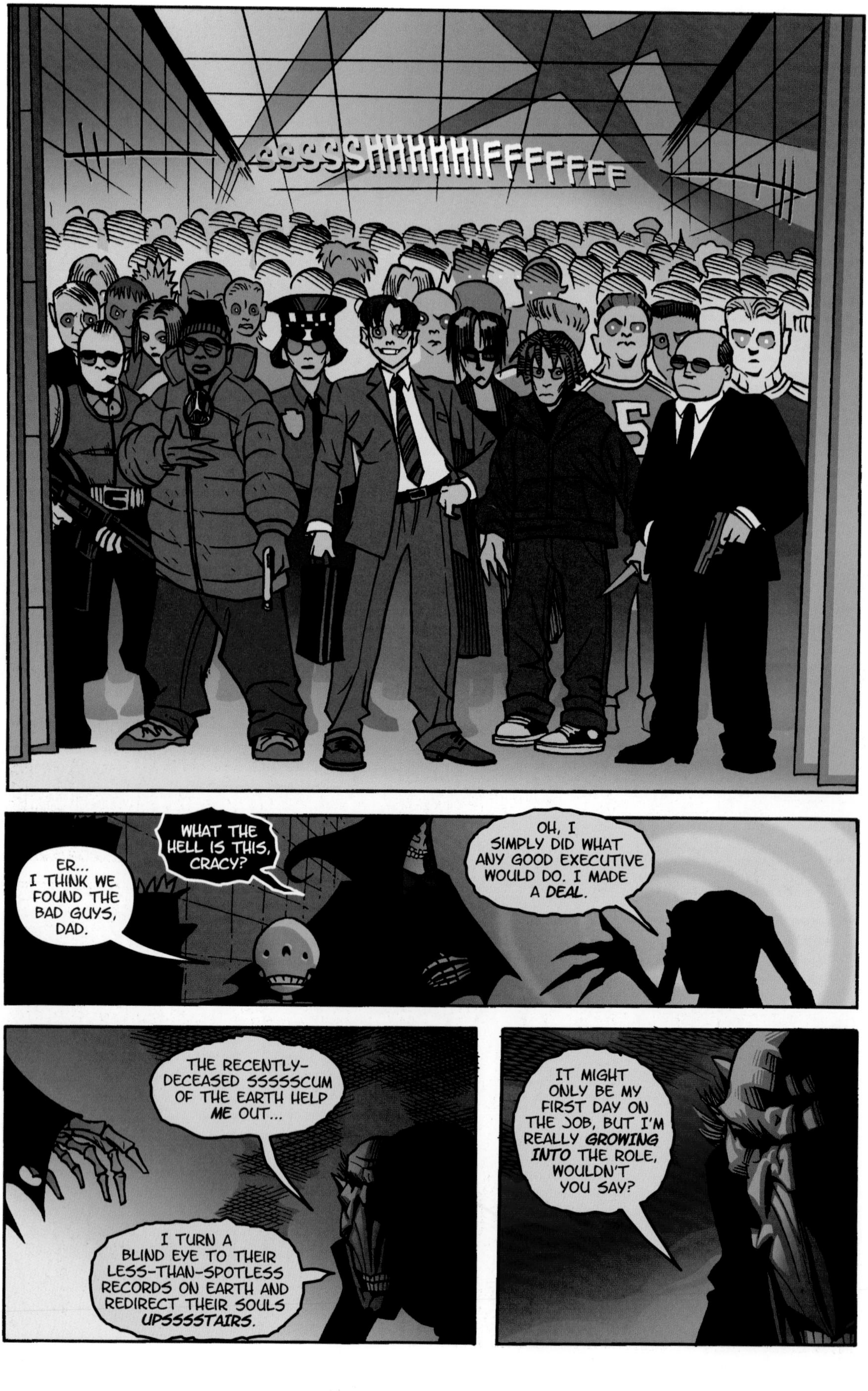
SSSSSHHHHHHIFFFFFFF
ER... I THINK WE FOUND THE BAD GUYS, DAD.
WHAT THE HELL IS THIS, CRACY?
OH, I SIMPLY DID WHAT ANY GOOD EXECUTIVE WOULD DO. I MADE A *DEAL*.
THE RECENTLY-DECEASED SSSSSCUM OF THE EARTH HELP *ME* OUT...
I TURN A BLIND EYE TO THEIR LESS-THAN-SPOTLESS RECORDS ON EARTH AND REDIRECT THEIR SOULS *UPSSSSTAIRS*.
IT MIGHT ONLY BE MY FIRST DAY ON THE JOB, BUT I'M REALLY *GROWING INTO* THE ROLE, WOULDN'T YOU SAY?

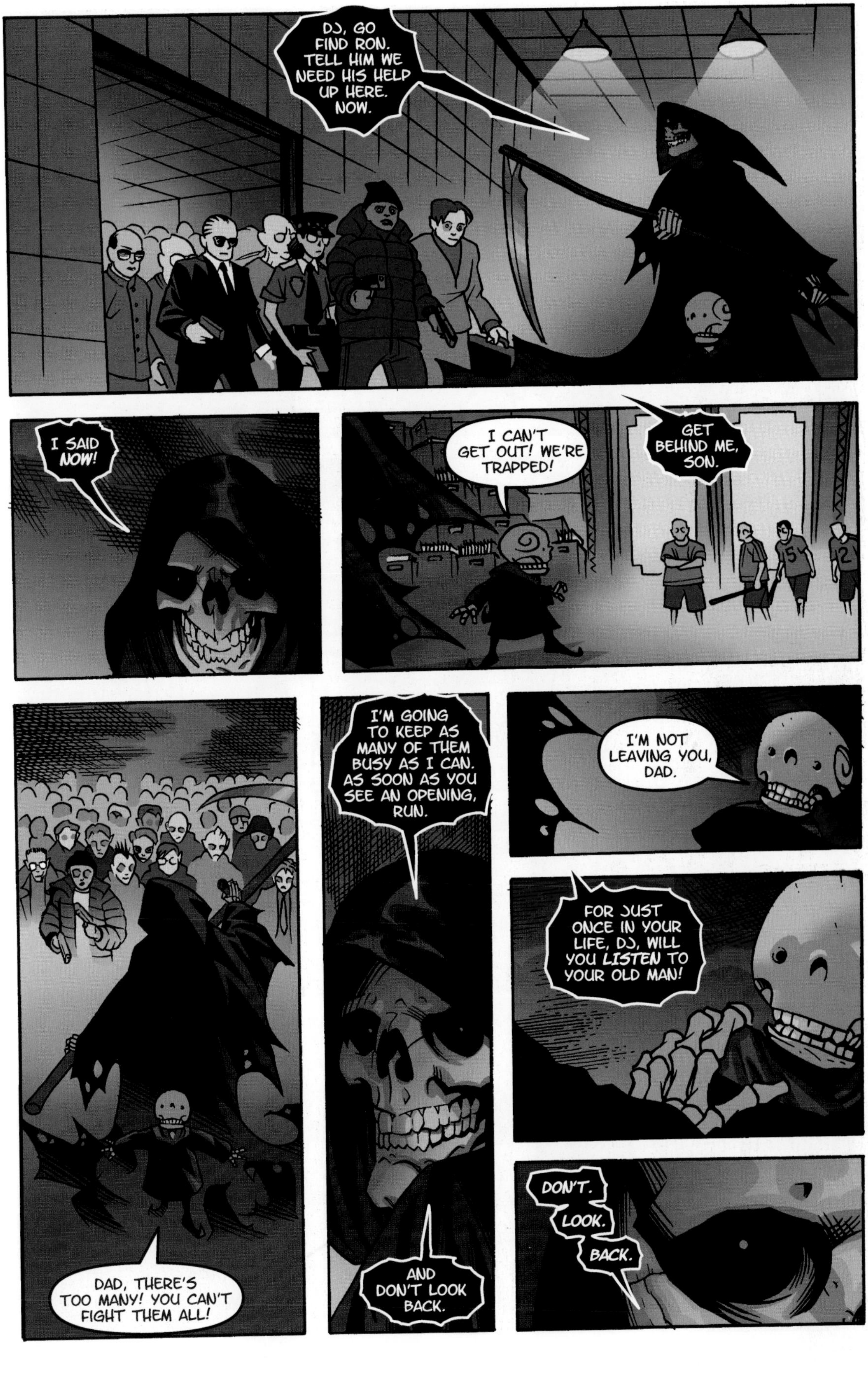
DJ, GO FIND RON. TELL HIM WE NEED HIS HELP UP HERE. NOW.
I SAID NOW!
I CAN'T GET OUT! WE'RE TRAPPED!
GET BEHIND ME, SON.
DAD, THERE'S TOO MANY! YOU CAN'T FIGHT THEM ALL!
I'M GOING TO KEEP AS MANY OF THEM BUSY AS I CAN. AS SOON AS YOU SEE AN OPENING, RUN.
AND DON'T LOOK BACK.
I'M NOT LEAVING YOU, DAD.
FOR JUST ONCE IN YOUR LIFE, DJ, WILL YOU LISTEN TO YOUR OLD MAN!
DON'T.
LOOK.
BACK.

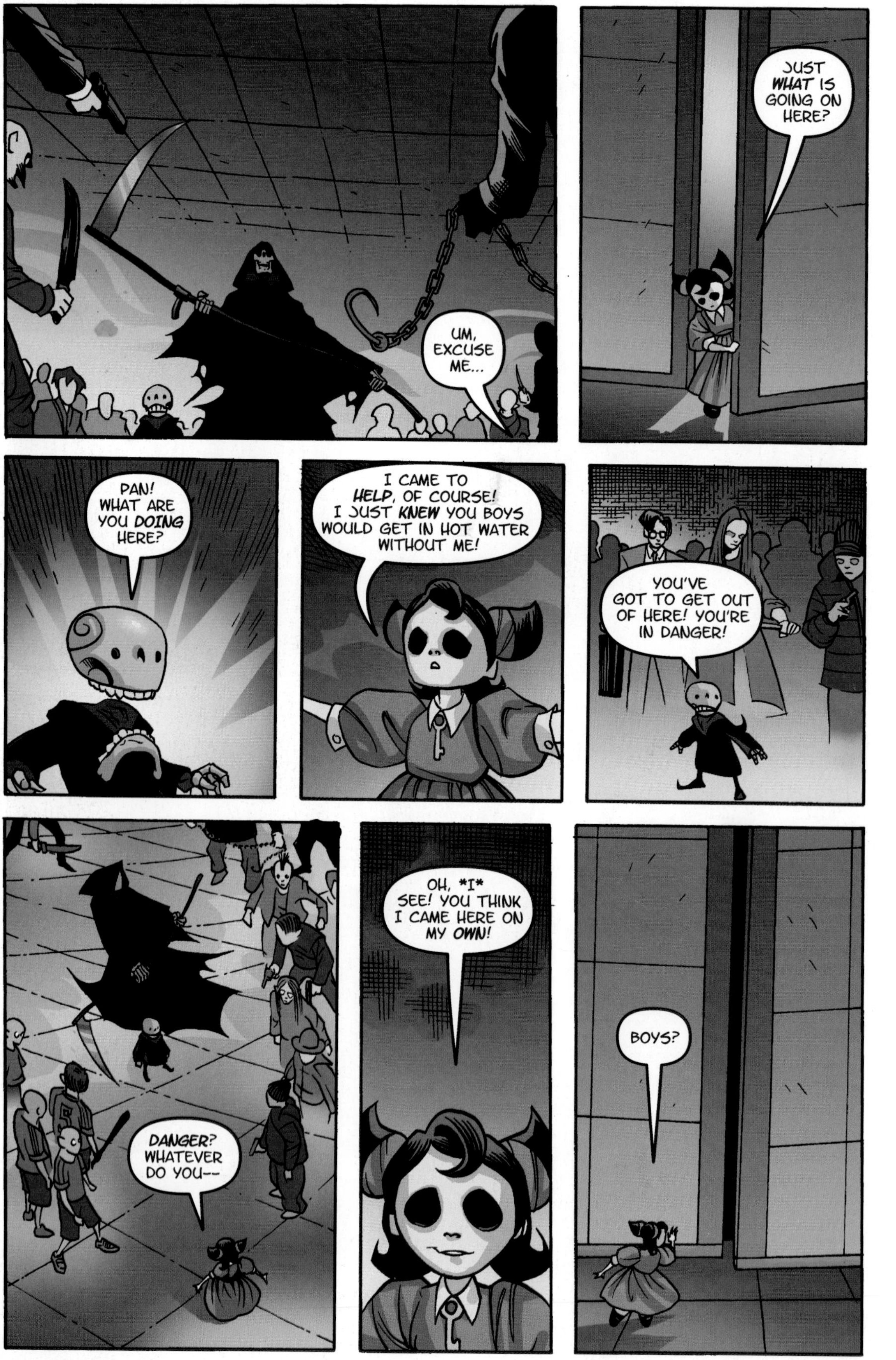
UM, EXCUSE ME...
JUST WHAT IS GOING ON HERE?
PAN! WHAT ARE YOU DOING HERE?
I CAME TO HELP, OF COURSE! I JUST KNEW YOU BOYS WOULD GET IN HOT WATER WITHOUT ME!
YOU'VE GOT TO GET OUT OF HERE! YOU'RE IN DANGER!
DANGER? WHATEVER DO YOU--
OH, *I* SEE! YOU THINK I CAME HERE ON MY OWN!
BOYS?

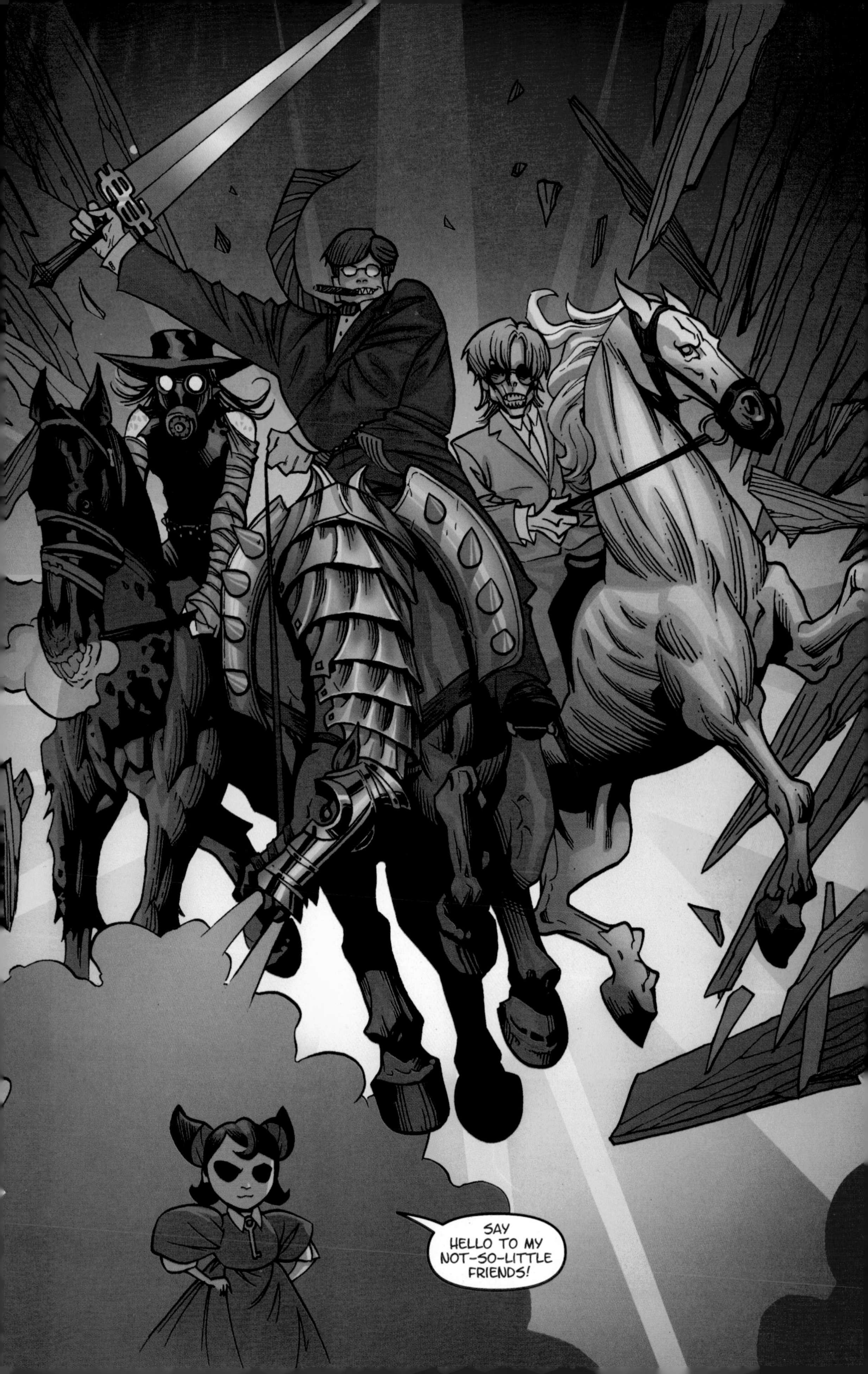
SAY HELLO TO MY NOT-SO-LITTLE FRIENDS!

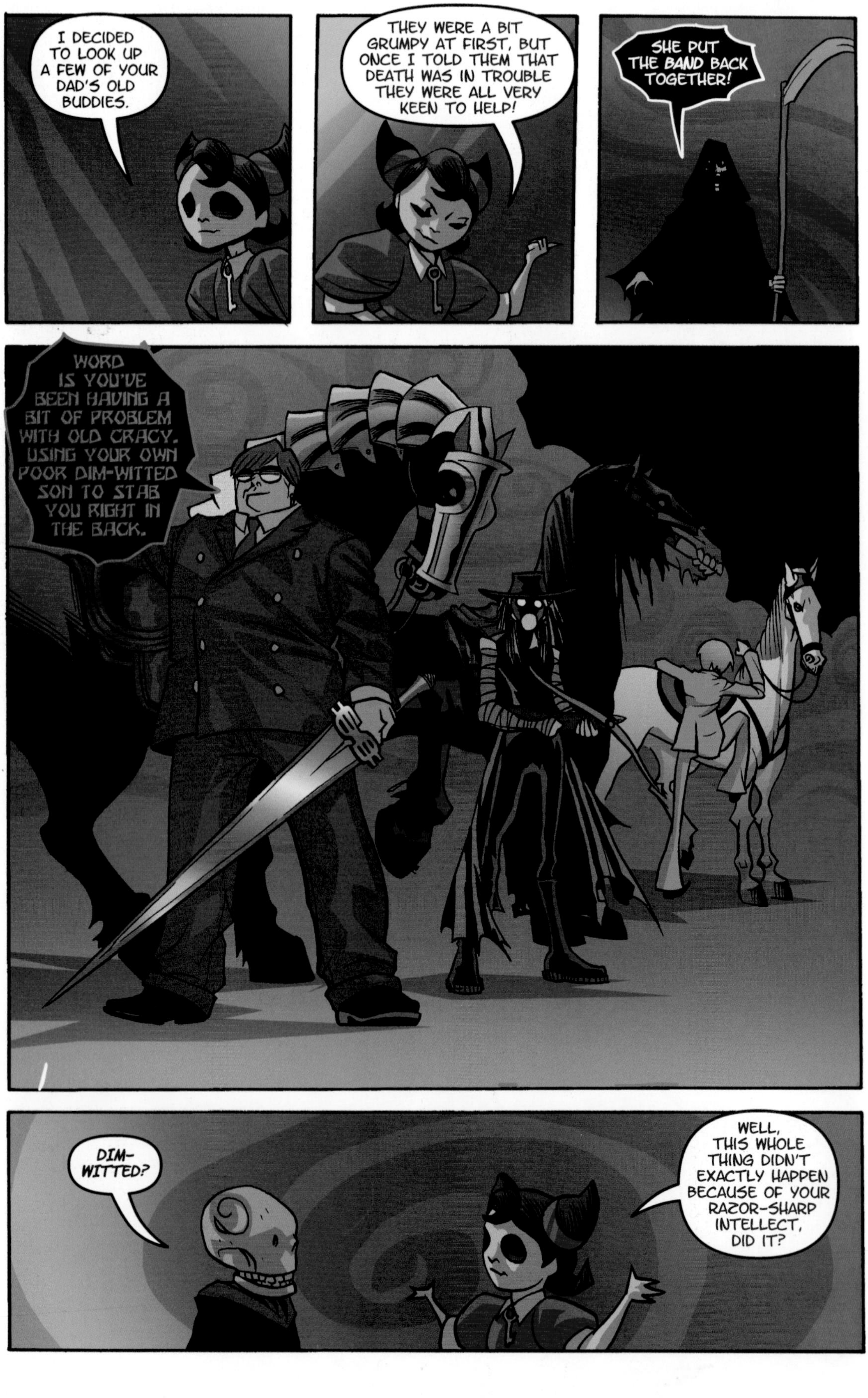
I DECIDED TO LOOK UP A FEW OF YOUR DAD'S OLD BUDDIES.
THEY WERE A BIT GRUMPY AT FIRST, BUT ONCE I TOLD THEM THAT DEATH WAS IN TROUBLE THEY WERE ALL VERY KEEN TO HELP!
SHE PUT THE *BAND* BACK TOGETHER!
WORD IS YOU'VE BEEN HAVING A BIT OF PROBLEM WITH OLD CRACY. USING YOUR OWN POOR DIM-WITTED SON TO STAB YOU RIGHT IN THE BACK.
DIM-WITTED?
WELL, THIS WHOLE THING DIDN'T EXACTLY HAPPEN BECAUSE OF YOUR RAZOR-SHARP INTELLECT, DID IT?

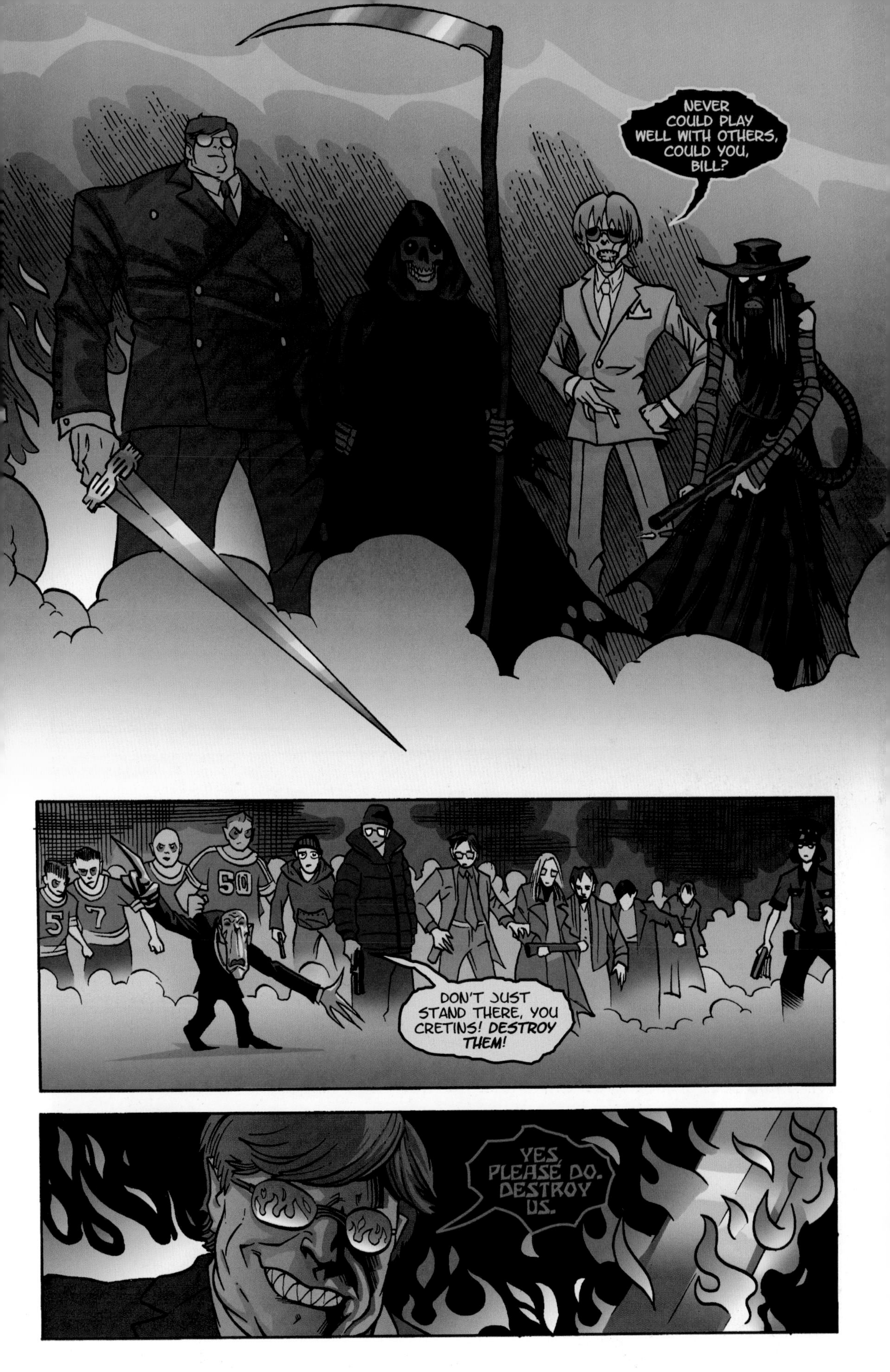
NEVER COULD PLAY WELL WITH OTHERS, COULD YOU, BILL?
DON'T JUST STAND THERE, YOU CRETINS! DESTROY THEM!
YES, PLEASE DO. DESTROY US.

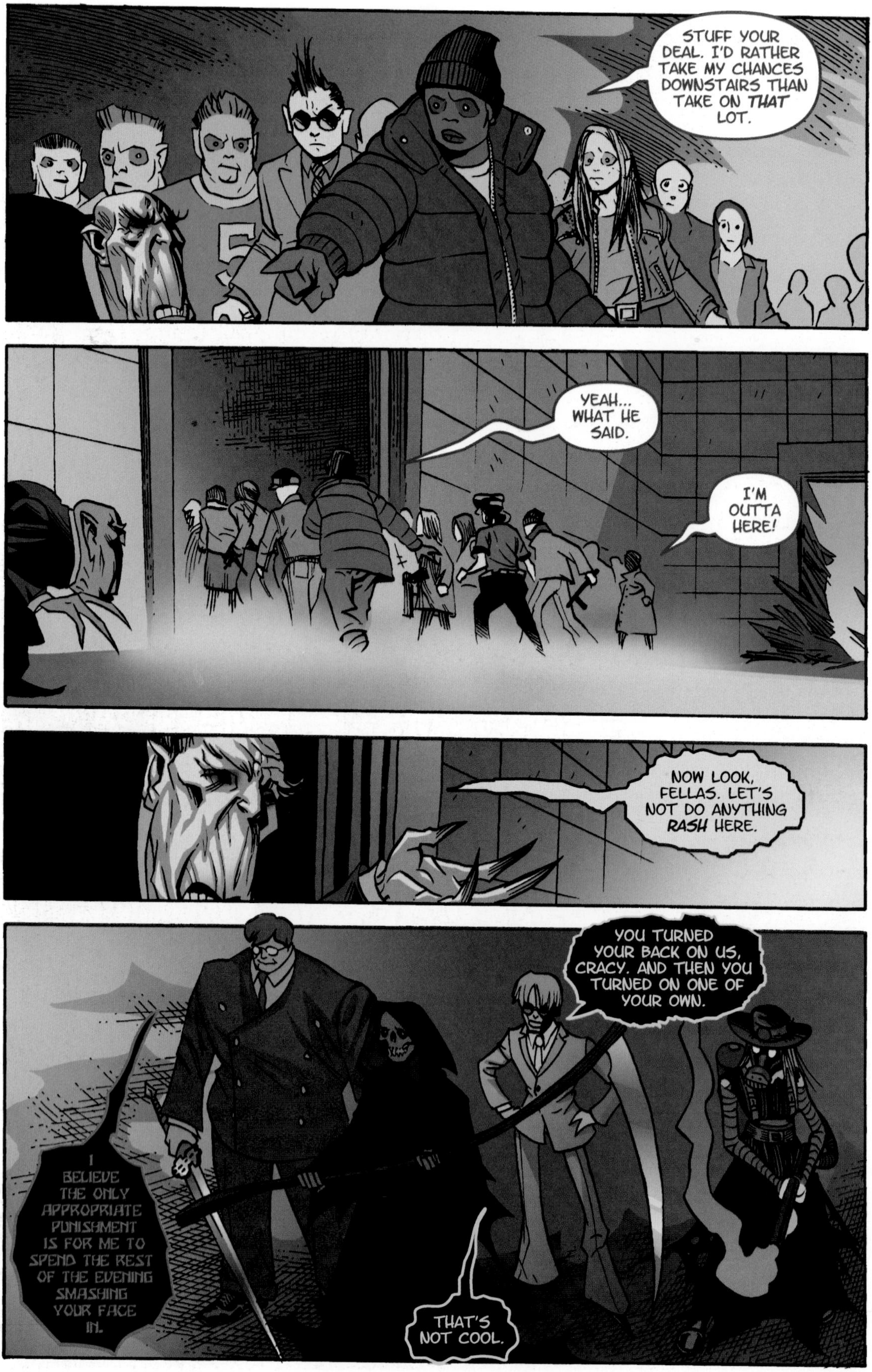
STUFF YOUR DEAL. I'D RATHER TAKE MY CHANCES DOWNSTAIRS THAN TAKE ON THAT LOT.
YEAH... WHAT HE SAID.
I'M OUTTA HERE!
NOW LOOK, FELLAS. LET'S NOT DO ANYTHING RASH HERE.
YOU TURNED YOUR BACK ON US, CRACY. AND THEN YOU TURNED ON ONE OF YOUR OWN.
I BELIEVE THE ONLY APPROPRIATE PUNISHMENT IS FOR ME TO SPEND THE REST OF THE EVENING SMASHING YOUR FACE IN.
THAT'S NOT COOL.

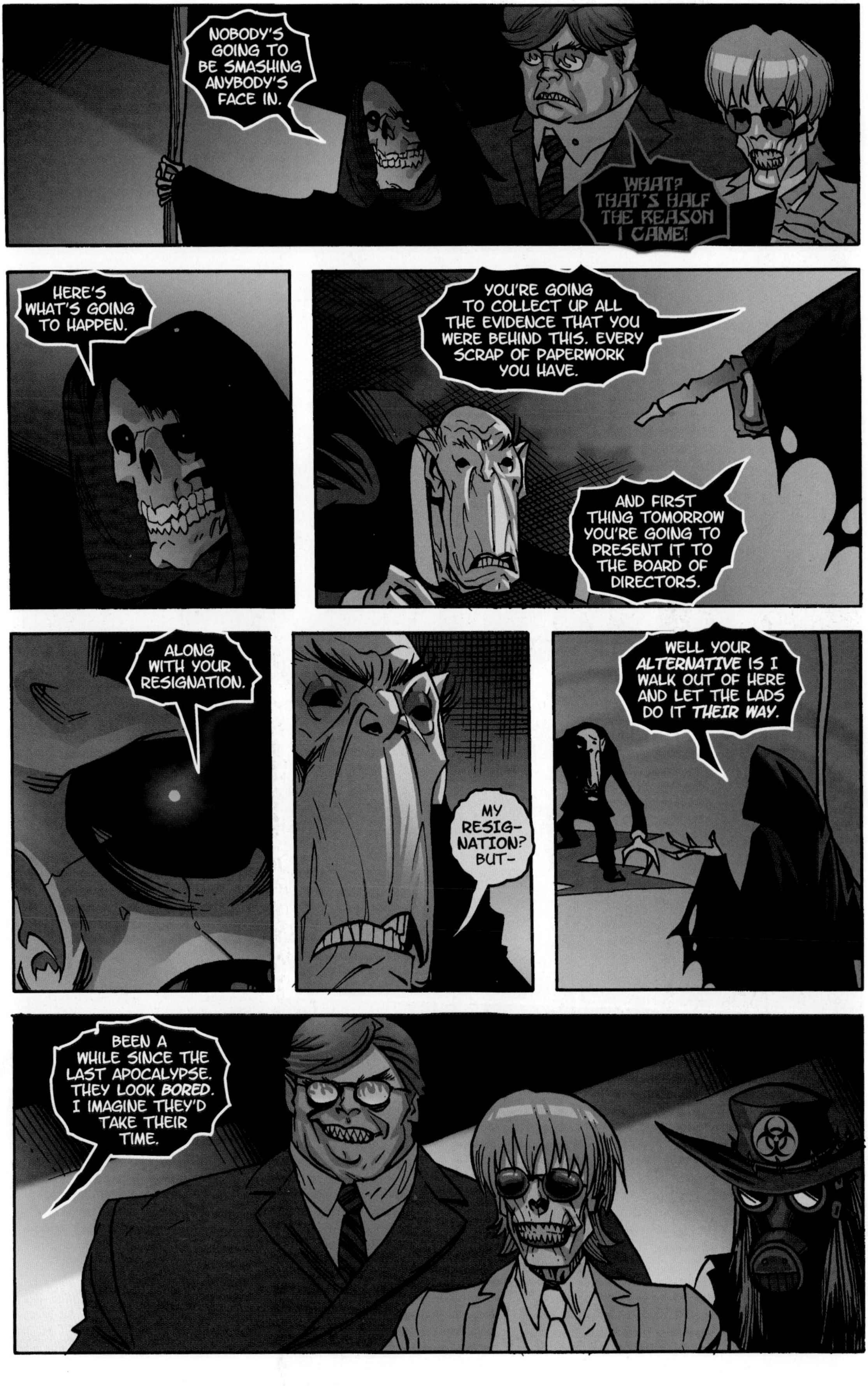
NOBODY'S GOING TO BE SMASHING ANYBODY'S FACE IN.
WHAT? THAT'S HALF THE REASON I CAME!
HERE'S WHAT'S GOING TO HAPPEN.
YOU'RE GOING TO COLLECT UP ALL THE EVIDENCE THAT YOU WERE BEHIND THIS. EVERY SCRAP OF PAPERWORK YOU HAVE.
AND FIRST THING TOMORROW YOU'RE GOING TO PRESENT IT TO THE BOARD OF DIRECTORS.
ALONG WITH YOUR RESIGNATION.
MY RESIG-NATION? BUT-
WELL YOUR ALTERNATIVE IS I WALK OUT OF HERE AND LET THE LADS DO IT THEIR WAY.
BEEN A WHILE SINCE THE LAST APOCALYPSE. THEY LOOK BORED. I IMAGINE THEY'D TAKE THEIR TIME.

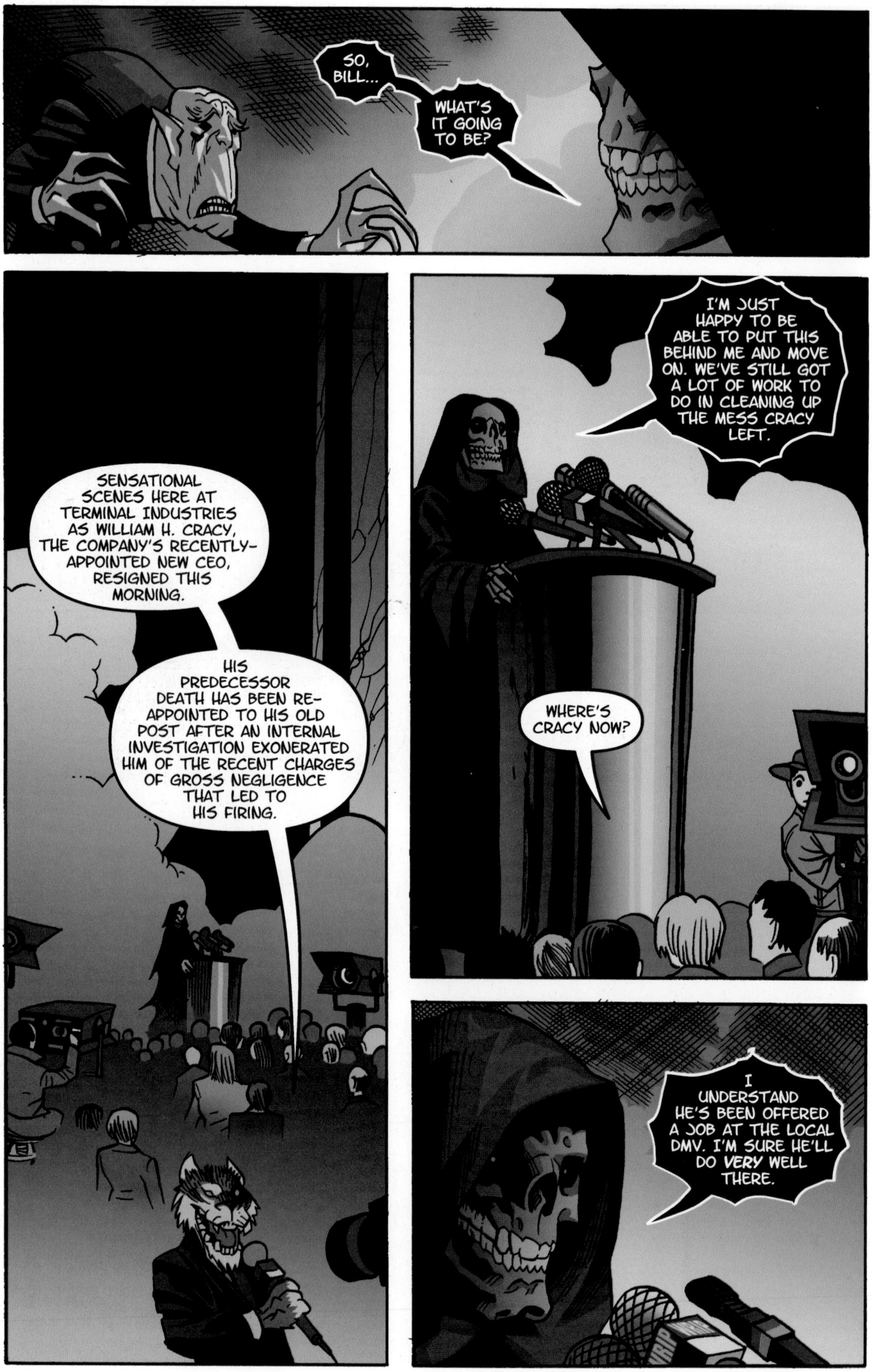
SO, BILL...
WHAT'S IT GOING TO BE?
SENSATIONAL SCENES HERE AT TERMINAL INDUSTRIES AS WILLIAM H. CRACY, THE COMPANY'S RECENTLY-APPOINTED NEW CEO, RESIGNED THIS MORNING.
HIS PREDECESSOR DEATH HAS BEEN RE-APPOINTED TO HIS OLD POST AFTER AN INTERNAL INVESTIGATION EXONERATED HIM OF THE RECENT CHARGES OF GROSS NEGLIGENCE THAT LED TO HIS FIRING.
I'M JUST HAPPY TO BE ABLE TO PUT THIS BEHIND ME AND MOVE ON. WE'VE STILL GOT A LOT OF WORK TO DO IN CLEANING UP THE MESS CRACY LEFT.
WHERE'S CRACY NOW?
I UNDERSTAND HE'S BEEN OFFERED A JOB AT THE LOCAL DMV. I'M SURE HE'LL DO *VERY* WELL THERE.

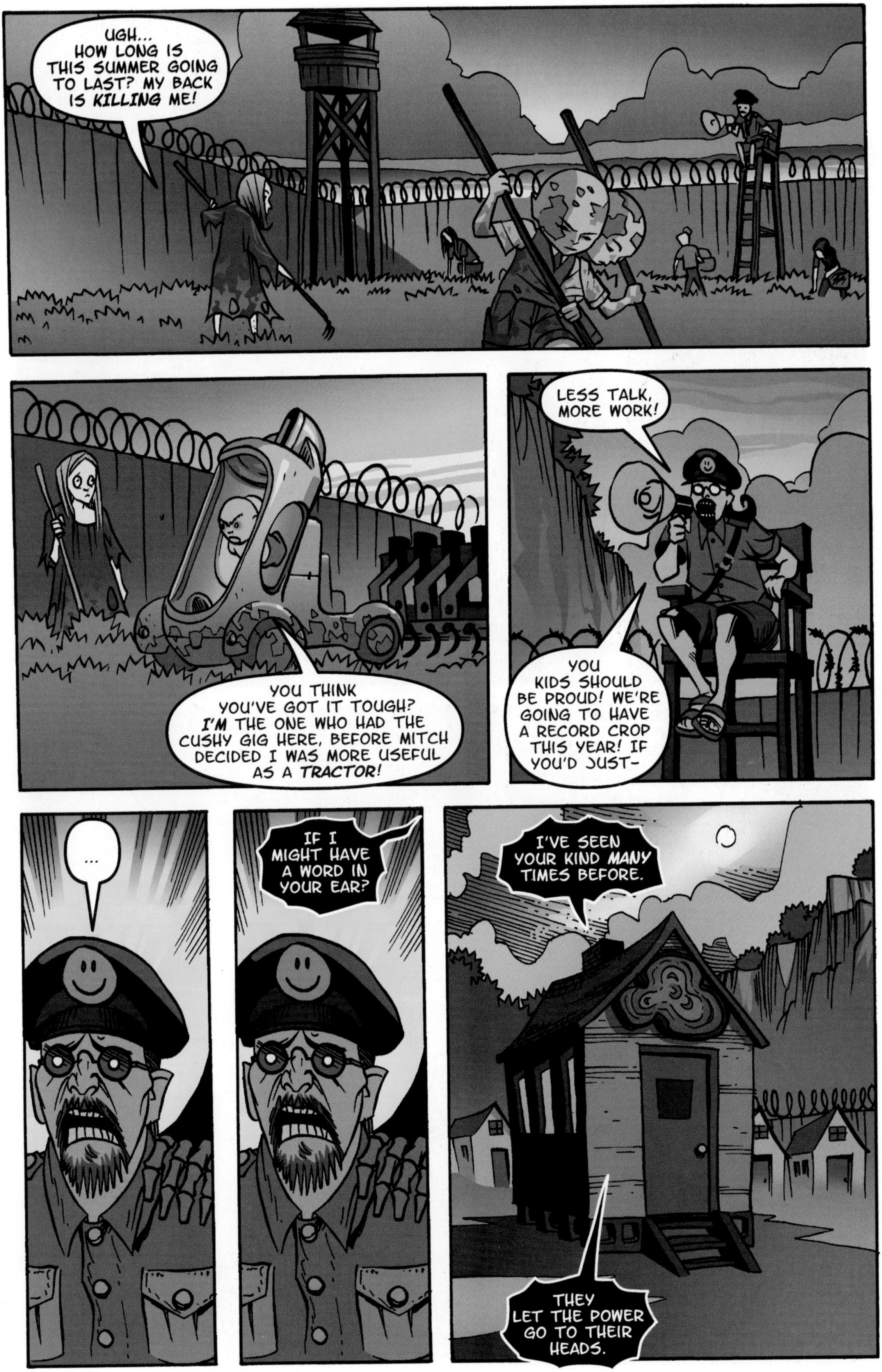
UGH... HOW LONG IS THIS SUMMER GOING TO LAST? MY BACK IS KILLING ME!
LESS TALK, MORE WORK!
YOU THINK YOU'VE GOT IT TOUGH? I'M THE ONE WHO HAD THE CUSHY GIG HERE, BEFORE MITCH DECIDED I WAS MORE USEFUL AS A TRACTOR!
YOU KIDS SHOULD BE PROUD! WE'RE GOING TO HAVE A RECORD CROP THIS YEAR! IF YOU'D JUST-
...
IF I MIGHT HAVE A WORD IN YOUR EAR?
I'VE SEEN YOUR KIND MANY TIMES BEFORE.
THEY LET THE POWER GO TO THEIR HEADS.

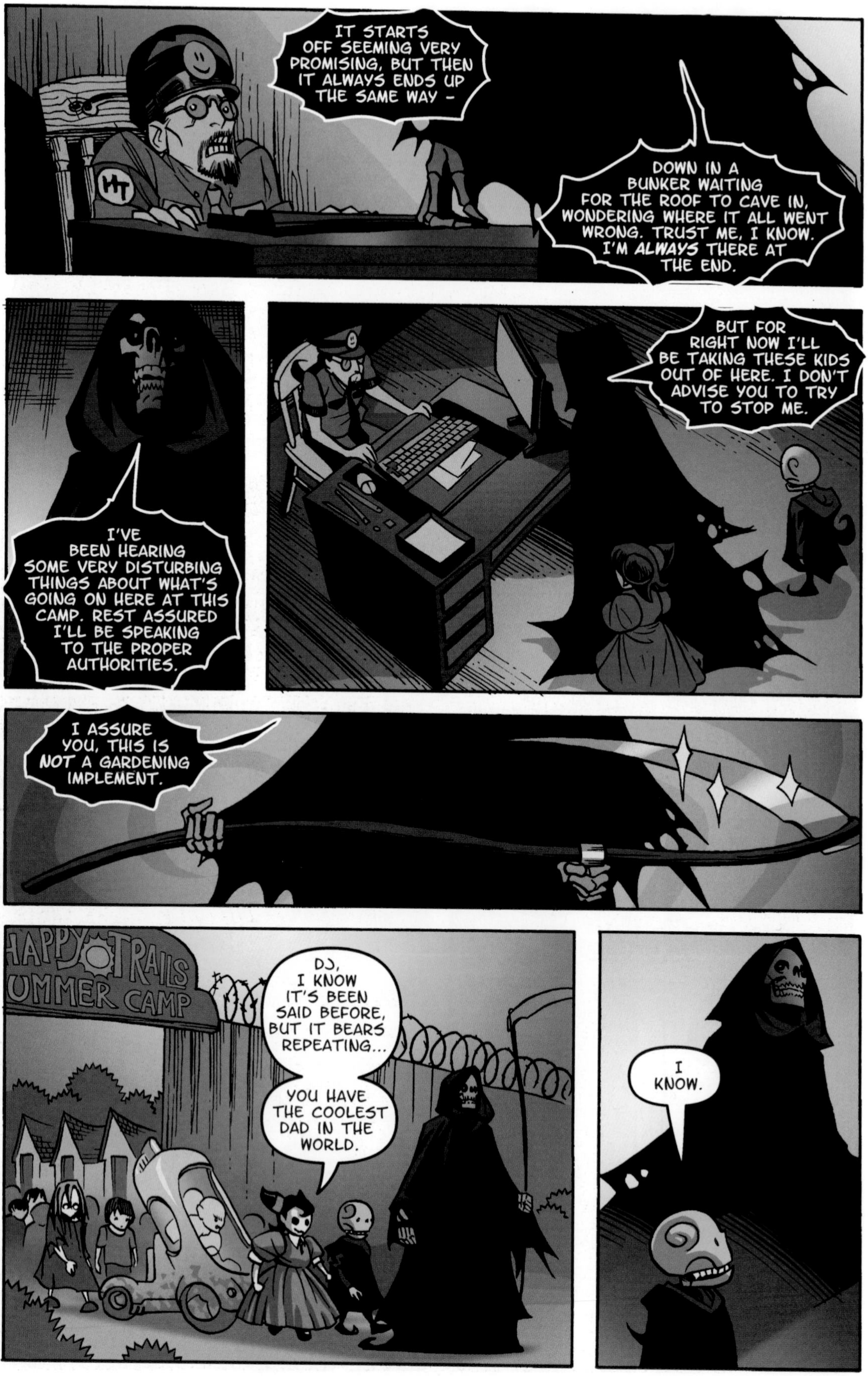
IT STARTS OFF SEEMING VERY PROMISING, BUT THEN IT ALWAYS ENDS UP THE SAME WAY -
DOWN IN A BUNKER WAITING FOR THE ROOF TO CAVE IN, WONDERING WHERE IT ALL WENT WRONG. TRUST ME, I KNOW. I'M *ALWAYS* THERE AT THE END.
I'VE BEEN HEARING SOME VERY DISTURBING THINGS ABOUT WHAT'S GOING ON HERE AT THIS CAMP. REST ASSURED I'LL BE SPEAKING TO THE PROPER AUTHORITIES.
BUT FOR RIGHT NOW I'LL BE TAKING THESE KIDS OUT OF HERE. I DON'T ADVISE YOU TO TRY TO STOP ME.
I ASSURE YOU, THIS IS *NOT* A GARDENING IMPLEMENT.
HAPPY TRAILS SUMMER CAMP
DJ, I KNOW IT'S BEEN SAID BEFORE, BUT IT BEARS REPEATING...
YOU HAVE THE COOLEST DAD IN THE WORLD.
I KNOW.

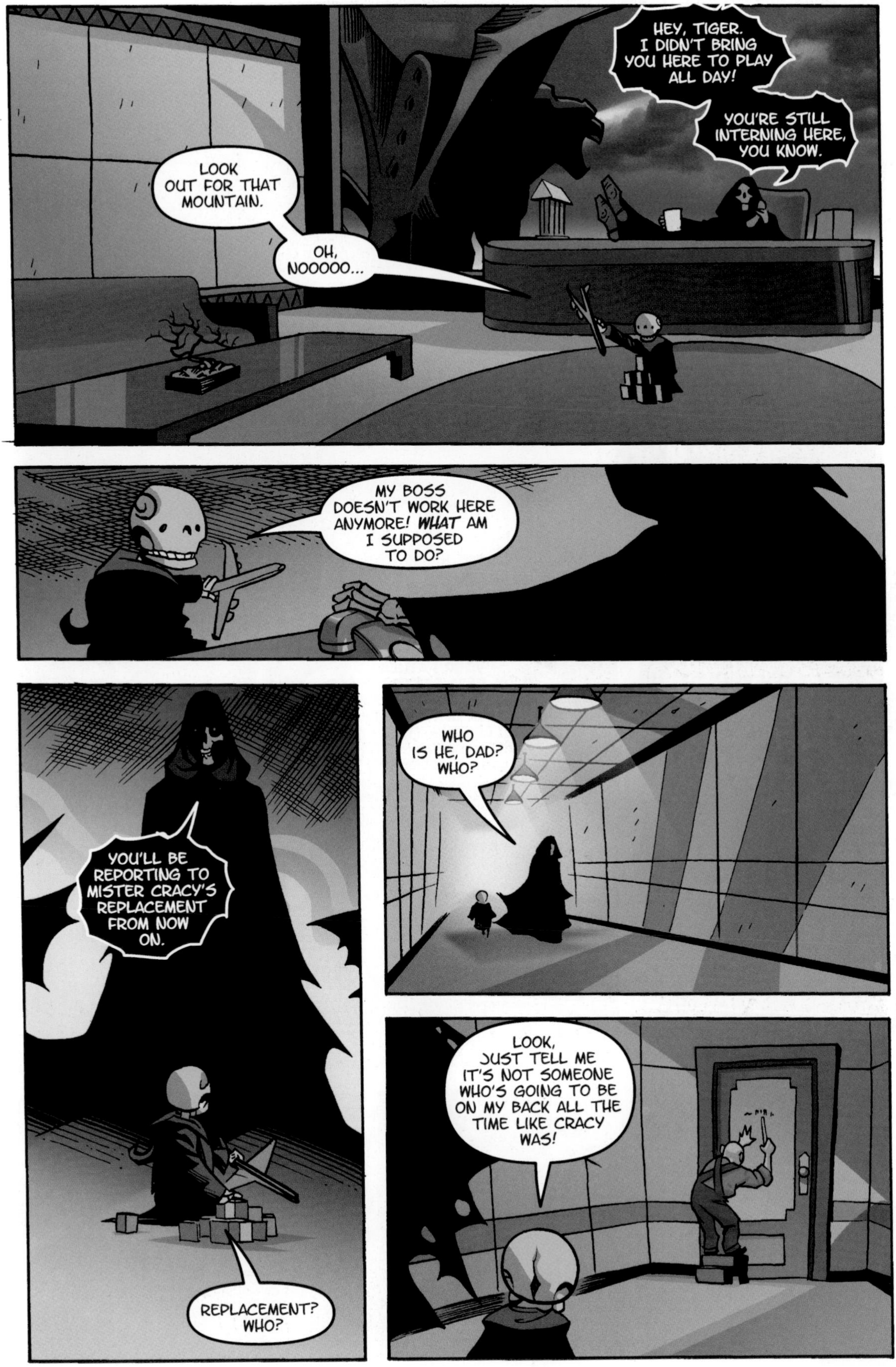
HEY, TIGER. I DIDN'T BRING YOU HERE TO PLAY ALL DAY!
YOU'RE STILL INTERNING HERE, YOU KNOW.
LOOK OUT FOR THAT MOUNTAIN.
OH, NOOOOO...
MY BOSS DOESN'T WORK HERE ANYMORE! WHAT AM I SUPPOSED TO DO?
YOU'LL BE REPORTING TO MISTER CRACY'S REPLACEMENT FROM NOW ON.
REPLACEMENT? WHO?
WHO IS HE, DAD? WHO?
LOOK, JUST TELL ME IT'S NOT SOMEONE WHO'S GOING TO BE ON MY BACK ALL THE TIME LIKE CRACY WAS!

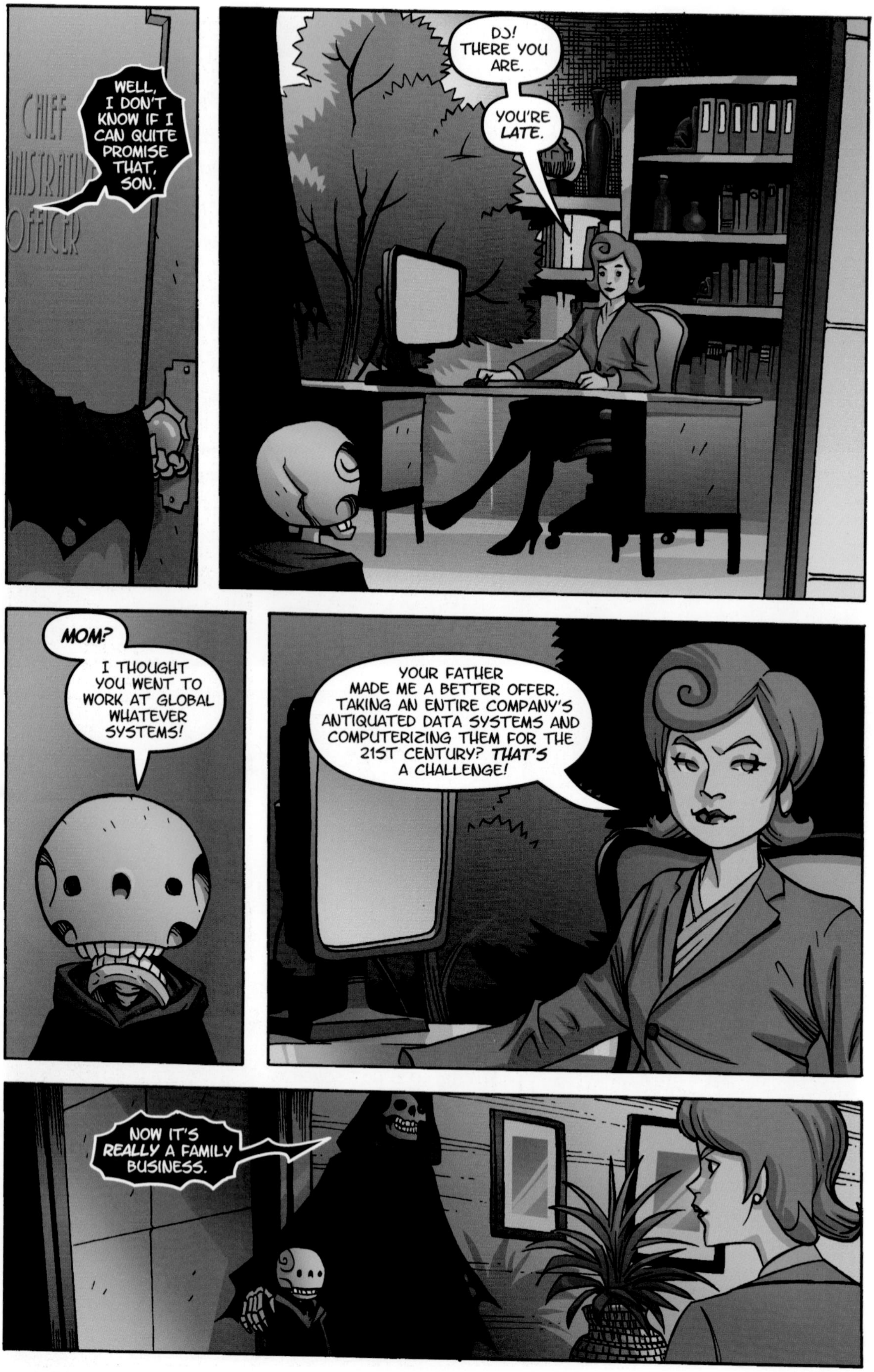

CHIEF ADMINISTRATIVE OFFICER
WELL, I DON'T KNOW IF I CAN QUITE PROMISE THAT, SON.
DJ! THERE YOU ARE.
YOU'RE *LATE*.
MOM?
I THOUGHT YOU WENT TO WORK AT GLOBAL WHATEVER SYSTEMS!
YOUR FATHER MADE ME A BETTER OFFER. TAKING AN ENTIRE COMPANY'S ANTIQUATED DATA SYSTEMS AND COMPUTERIZING THEM FOR THE 21ST CENTURY? *THAT'S* A CHALLENGE!
NOW IT'S *REALLY* A FAMILY BUSINESS.

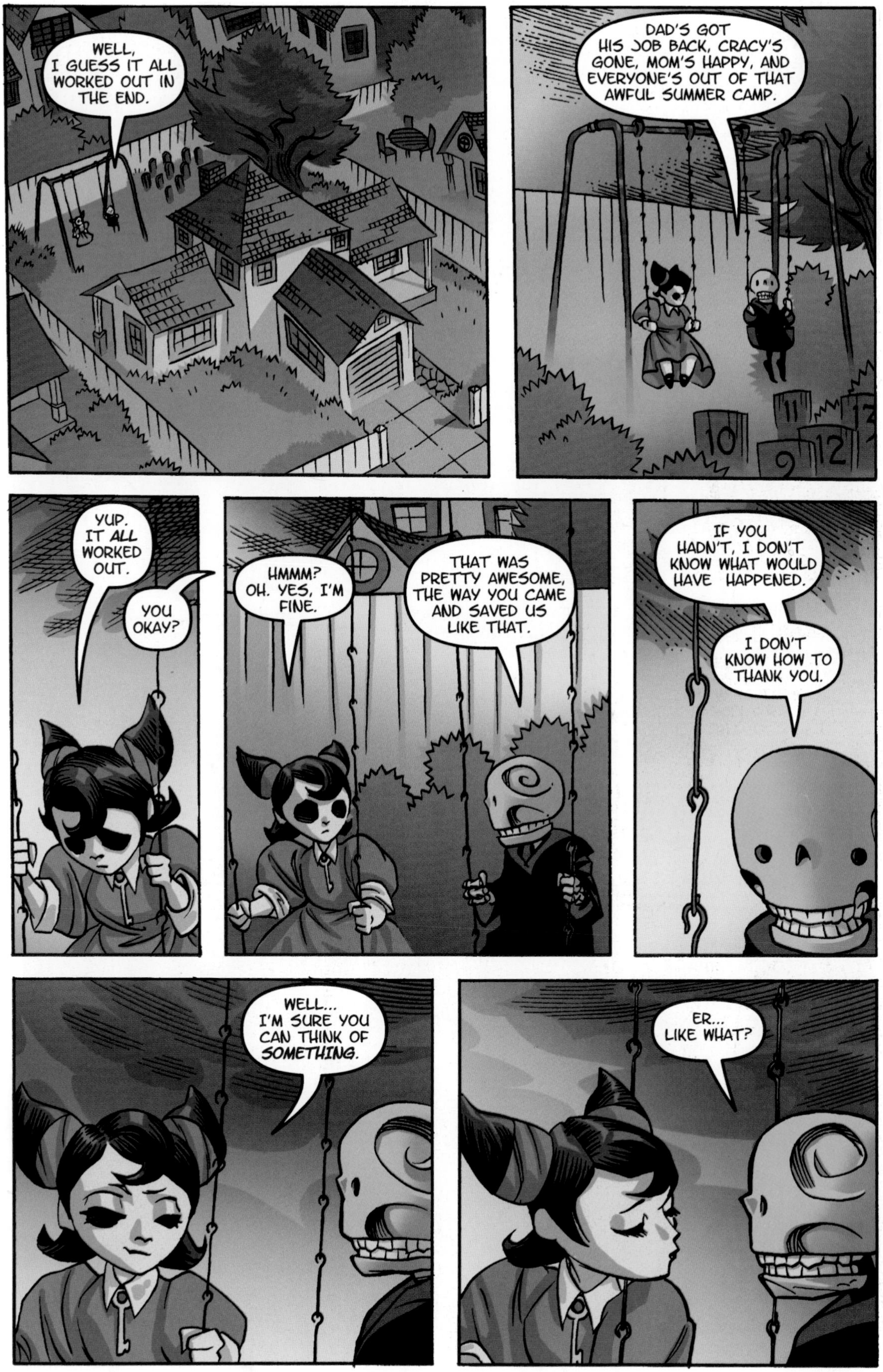
WELL, I GUESS IT ALL WORKED OUT IN THE END.
DAD'S GOT HIS JOB BACK, CRACY'S GONE, MOM'S HAPPY, AND EVERYONE'S OUT OF THAT AWFUL SUMMER CAMP.
10
11
12
13
9
12
YUP. IT *ALL* WORKED OUT.
YOU OKAY?
HMMM? OH. YES, I'M FINE.
THAT WAS PRETTY AWESOME, THE WAY YOU CAME AND SAVED US LIKE THAT.
IF YOU HADN'T, I DON'T KNOW WHAT WOULD HAVE HAPPENED.
I DON'T KNOW HOW TO THANK YOU.
WELL... I'M SURE YOU CAN THINK OF *SOMETHING*.
ER... LIKE WHAT?

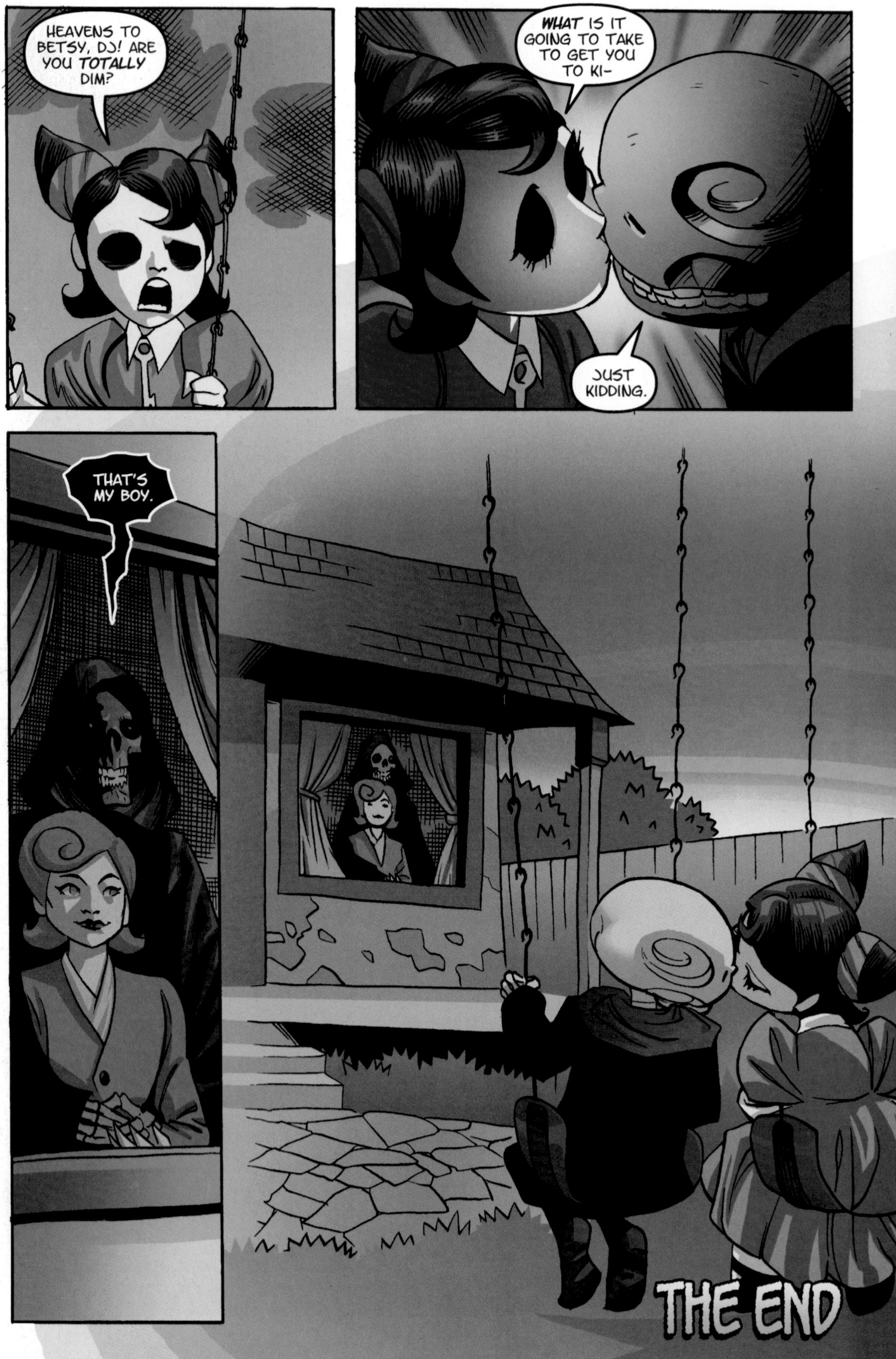
HEAVENS TO BETSY, DJ! ARE YOU TOTALLY DIM?
WHAT IS IT GOING TO TAKE TO GET YOU TO KI-
JUST KIDDING.
THAT'S MY BOY.
THE END

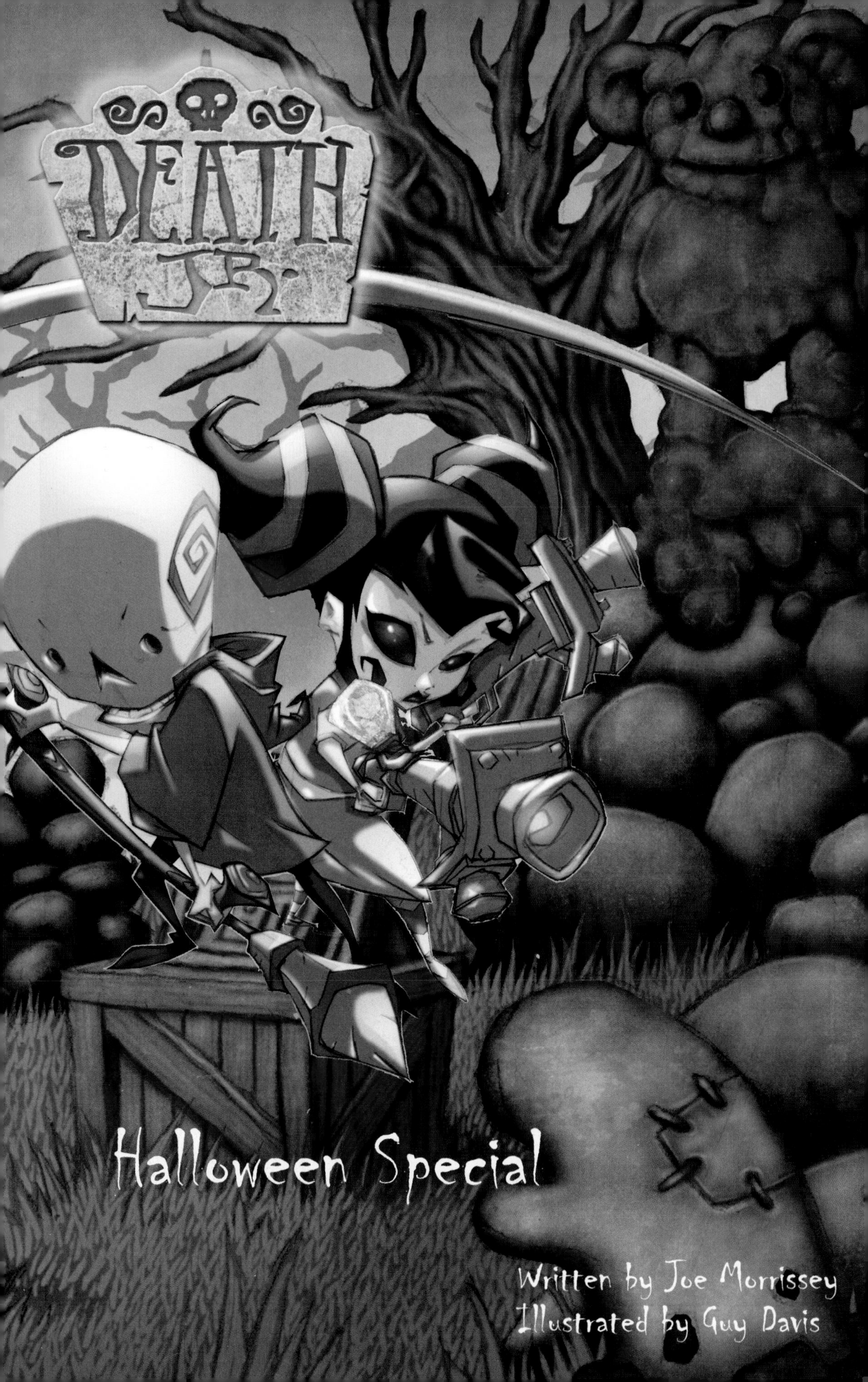
DEATH JR.
Halloween Special
Written by Joe Morrissey
Illustrated by Guy Davis

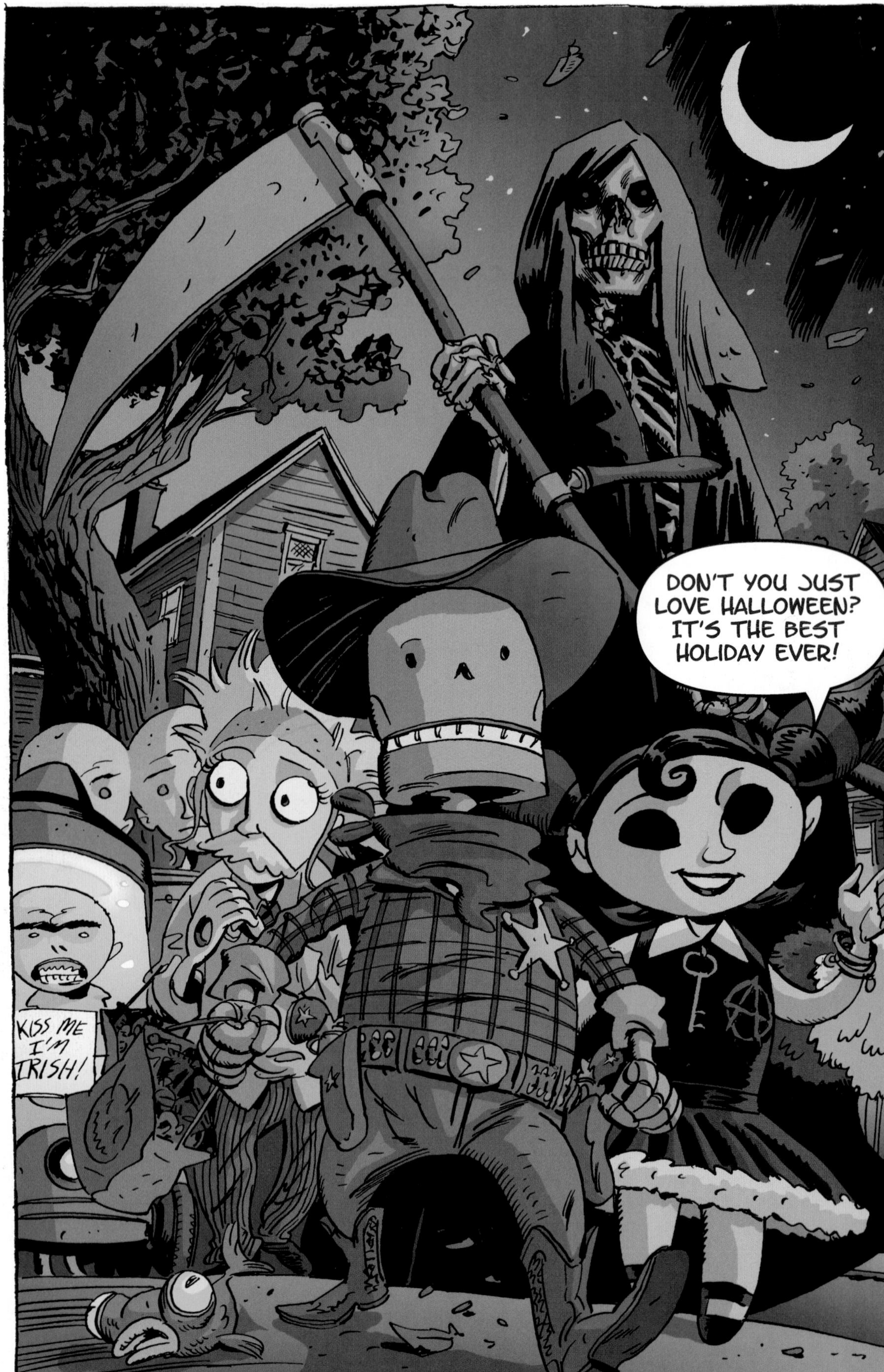
DON'T YOU JUST LOVE HALLOWEEN? IT'S THE BEST HOLIDAY EVER!
KISS ME I'M IRISH!

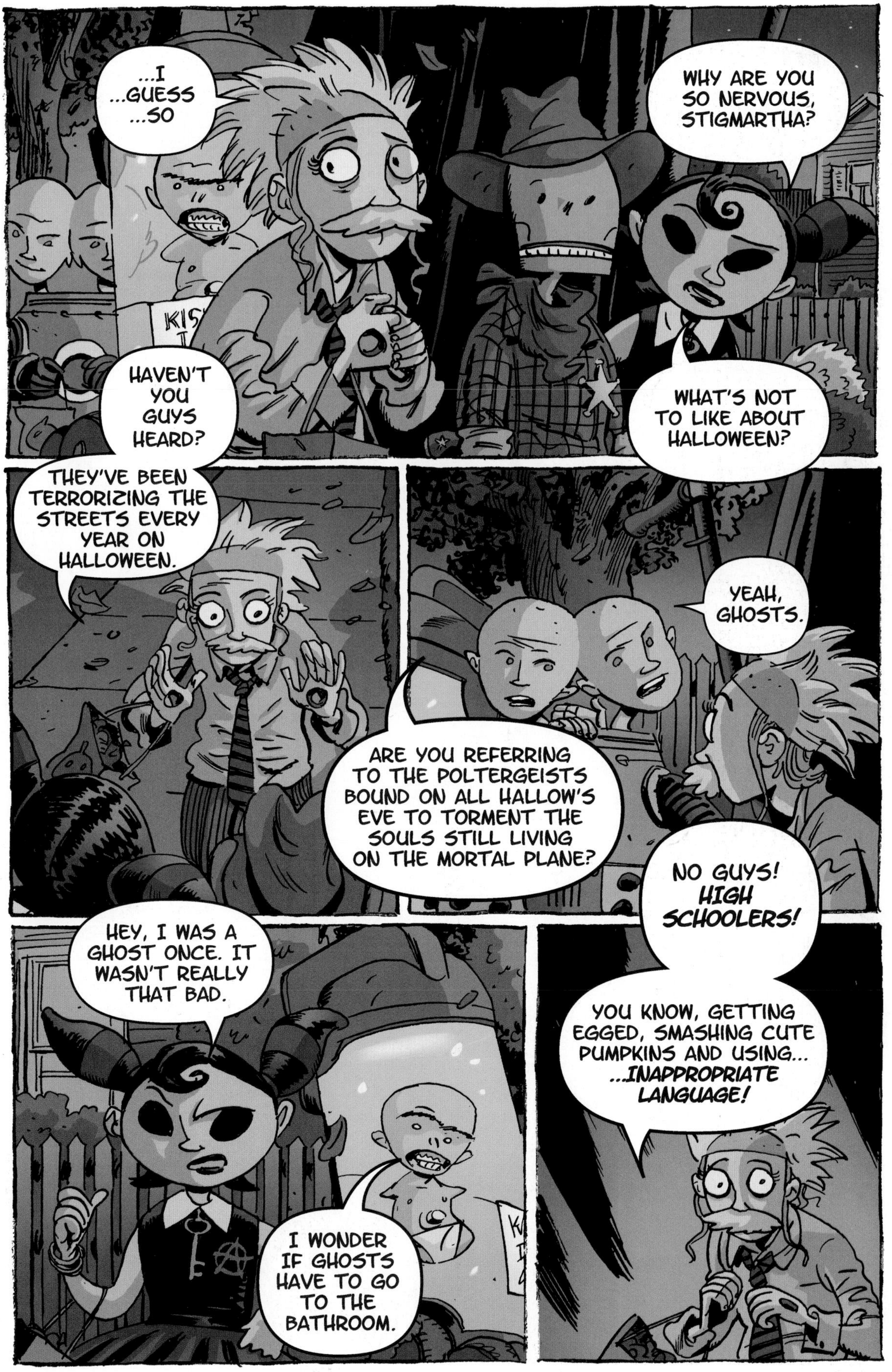

...I ...GUESS ...SO
WHY ARE YOU SO NERVOUS, STIGMARTHA?
HAVEN'T YOU GUYS HEARD?
WHAT'S NOT TO LIKE ABOUT HALLOWEEN?
THEY'VE BEEN TERRORIZING THE STREETS EVERY YEAR ON HALLOWEEN.
YEAH, GHOSTS.
ARE YOU REFERRING TO THE POLTERGEISTS BOUND ON ALL HALLOW'S EVE TO TORMENT THE SOULS STILL LIVING ON THE MORTAL PLANE?
NO GUYS! HIGH SCHOOLERS!
HEY, I WAS A GHOST ONCE. IT WASN'T REALLY THAT BAD.
I WONDER IF GHOSTS HAVE TO GO TO THE BATHROOM.
YOU KNOW, GETTING EGGED, SMASHING CUTE PUMPKINS AND USING... ...INAPPROPRIATE LANGUAGE!

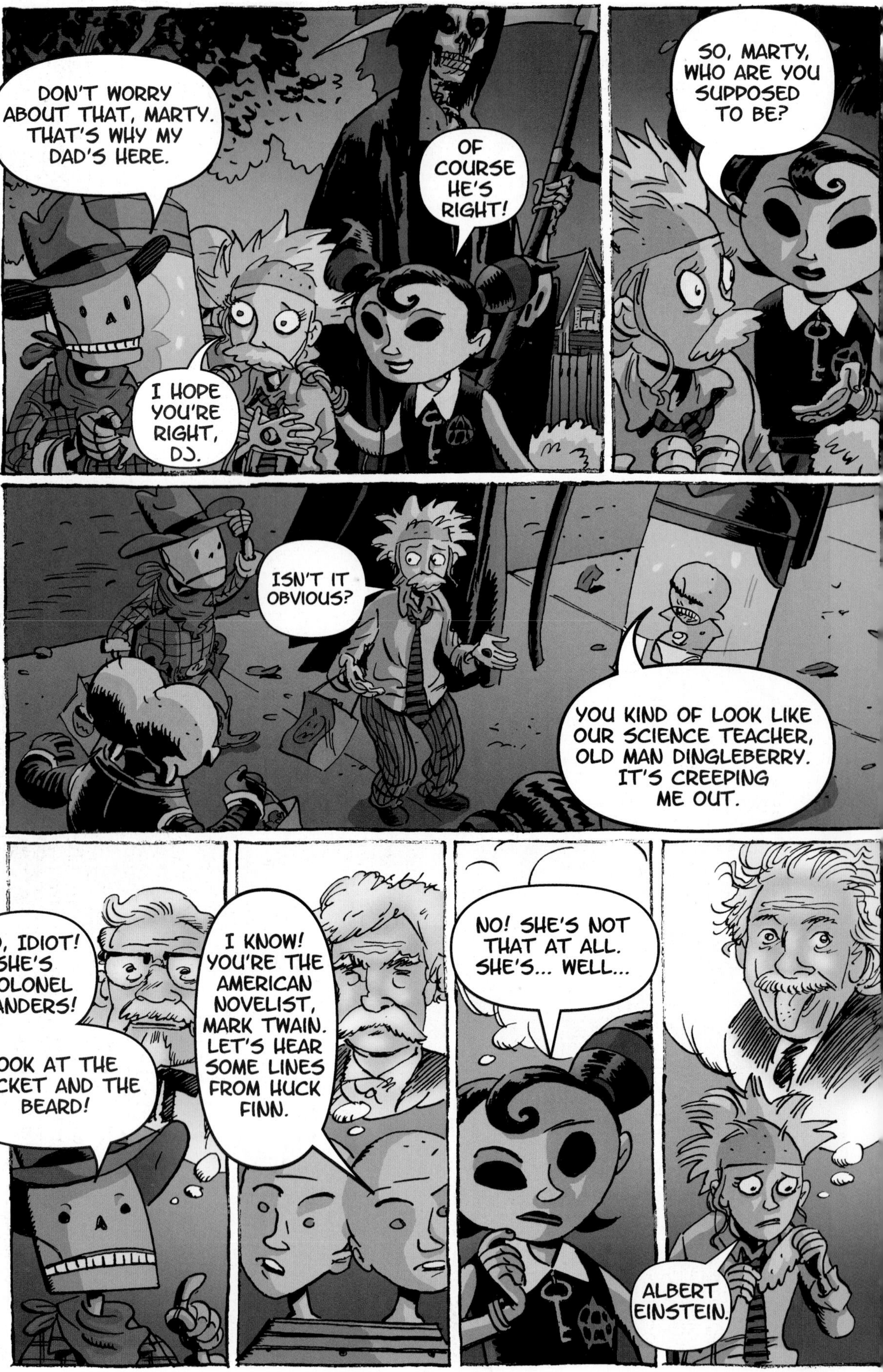
DON'T WORRY ABOUT THAT, MARTY. THAT'S WHY MY DAD'S HERE.
OF COURSE HE'S RIGHT!
I HOPE YOU'RE RIGHT, DJ.
SO, MARTY, WHO ARE YOU SUPPOSED TO BE?
ISN'T IT OBVIOUS?
YOU KIND OF LOOK LIKE OUR SCIENCE TEACHER, OLD MAN DINGLEBERRY. IT'S CREEPING ME OUT.
NO, IDIOT! SHE'S COLONEL SANDERS!
LOOK AT THE JACKET AND THE BEARD!
I KNOW! YOU'RE THE AMERICAN NOVELIST, MARK TWAIN. LET'S HEAR SOME LINES FROM HUCK FINN.
NO! SHE'S NOT THAT AT ALL. SHE'S... WELL...
ALBERT EINSTEIN.

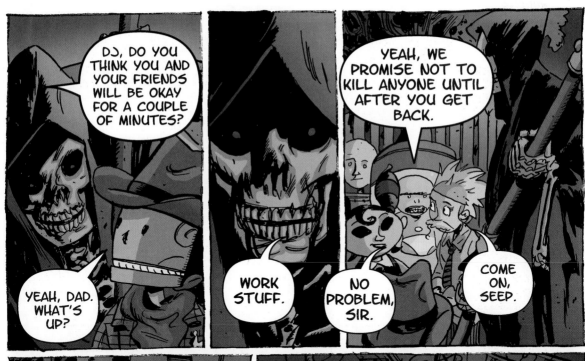

DJ, DO YOU THINK YOU AND YOUR FRIENDS WILL BE OKAY FOR A COUPLE OF MINUTES?

YEAH, DAD. WHAT'S UP?

WORK STUFF.

YEAH, WE PROMISE NOT TO KILL ANYONE UNTIL AFTER YOU GET BACK.

NO PROBLEM, SIR.

COME ON, SEEP.

SWELL. I'LL SEE YOU KIDS IN A FEW MINUTES. REMEMBER, DON'T TAKE ANY CANDY THAT'S NOT INDIVIDUALLY WRAPPED.

I'VE GOT SOME TRICKS TO PREPARE FOR.

UH, DID YOU GUYS SEE THIS PLACE?

DANGER
CONVIENT
POWER
PLANT
INC.

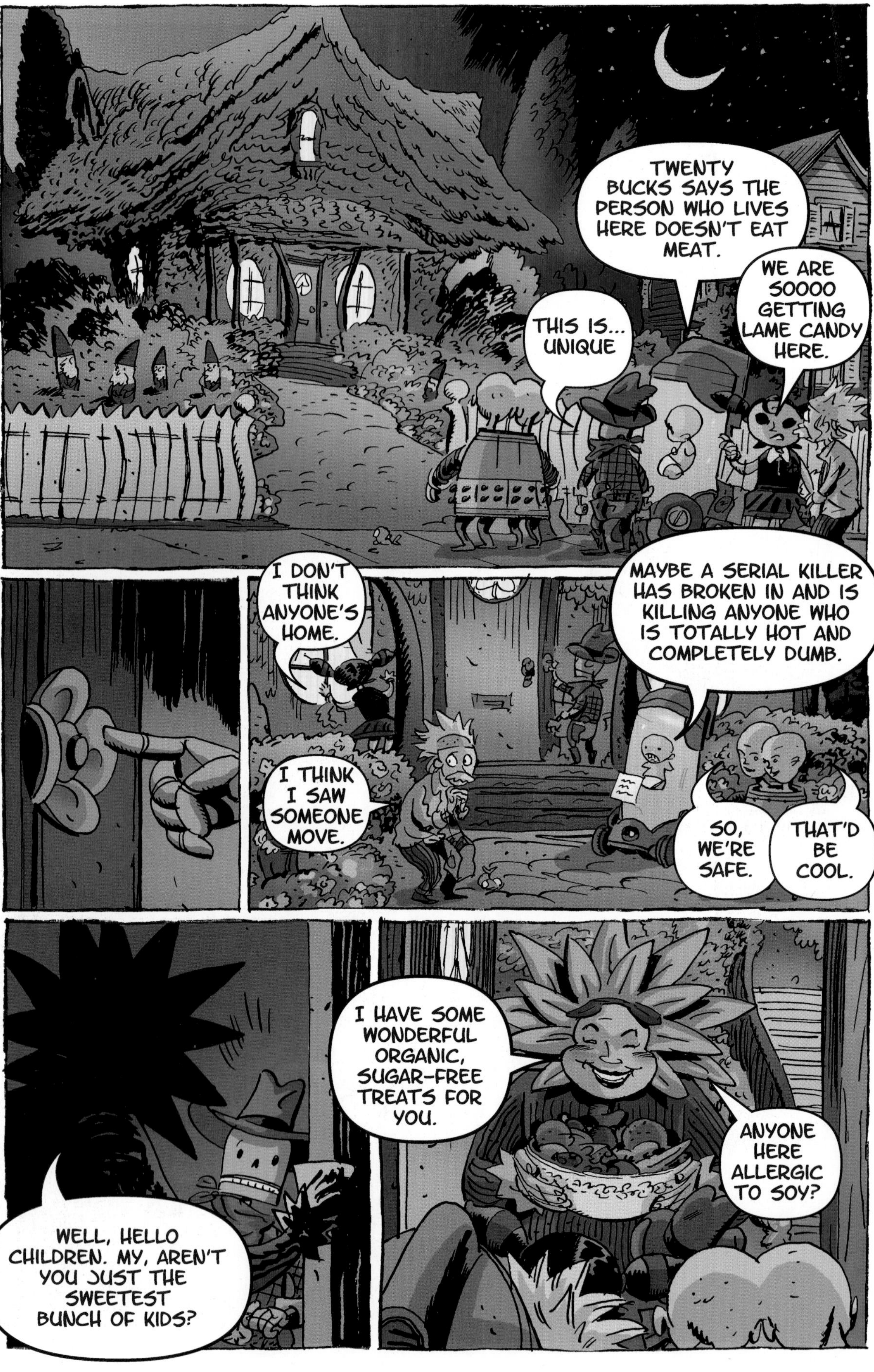
TWENTY BUCKS SAYS THE PERSON WHO LIVES HERE DOESN'T EAT MEAT.
THIS IS... UNIQUE
WE ARE SOOOO GETTING LAME CANDY HERE.
I DON'T THINK ANYONE'S HOME.
MAYBE A SERIAL KILLER HAS BROKEN IN AND IS KILLING ANYONE WHO IS TOTALLY HOT AND COMPLETELY DUMB.
I THINK I SAW SOMEONE MOVE.
SO, WE'RE SAFE.
THAT'D BE COOL.
WELL, HELLO CHILDREN. MY, AREN'T YOU JUST THE SWEETEST BUNCH OF KIDS?
I HAVE SOME WONDERFUL ORGANIC, SUGAR-FREE TREATS FOR YOU.
ANYONE HERE ALLERGIC TO SOY?

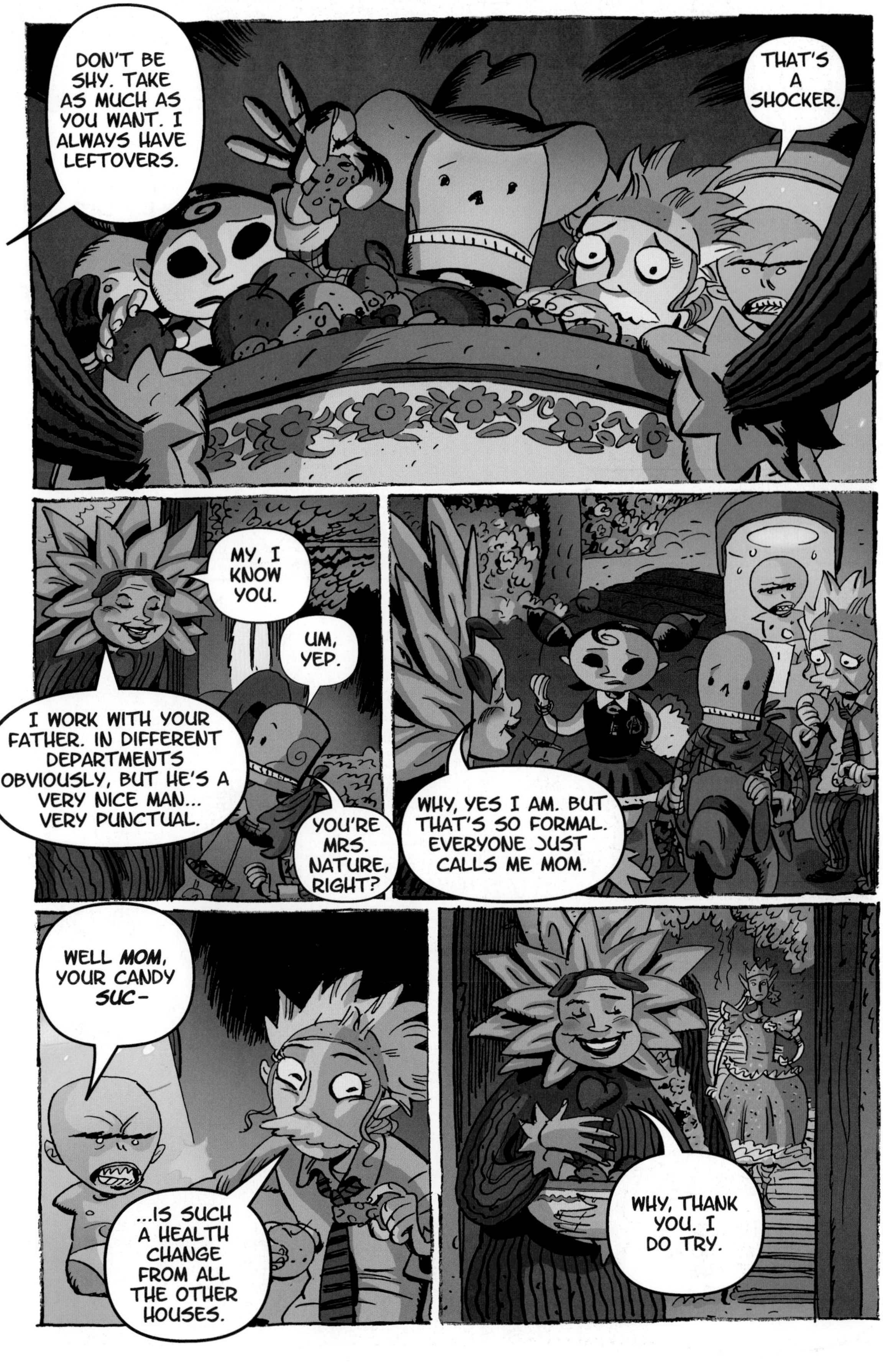
DON'T BE SHY. TAKE AS MUCH AS YOU WANT. I ALWAYS HAVE LEFTOVERS.
THAT'S A SHOCKER.
MY, I KNOW YOU.
UM, YEP.
I WORK WITH YOUR FATHER. IN DIFFERENT DEPARTMENTS OBVIOUSLY, BUT HE'S A VERY NICE MAN... VERY PUNCTUAL.
YOU'RE MRS. NATURE, RIGHT?
WHY, YES I AM. BUT THAT'S SO FORMAL. EVERYONE JUST CALLS ME MOM.
WELL *MOM*, YOUR CANDY *SUC*-
...IS SUCH A HEALTH CHANGE FROM ALL THE OTHER HOUSES.
WHY, THANK YOU. I DO TRY.

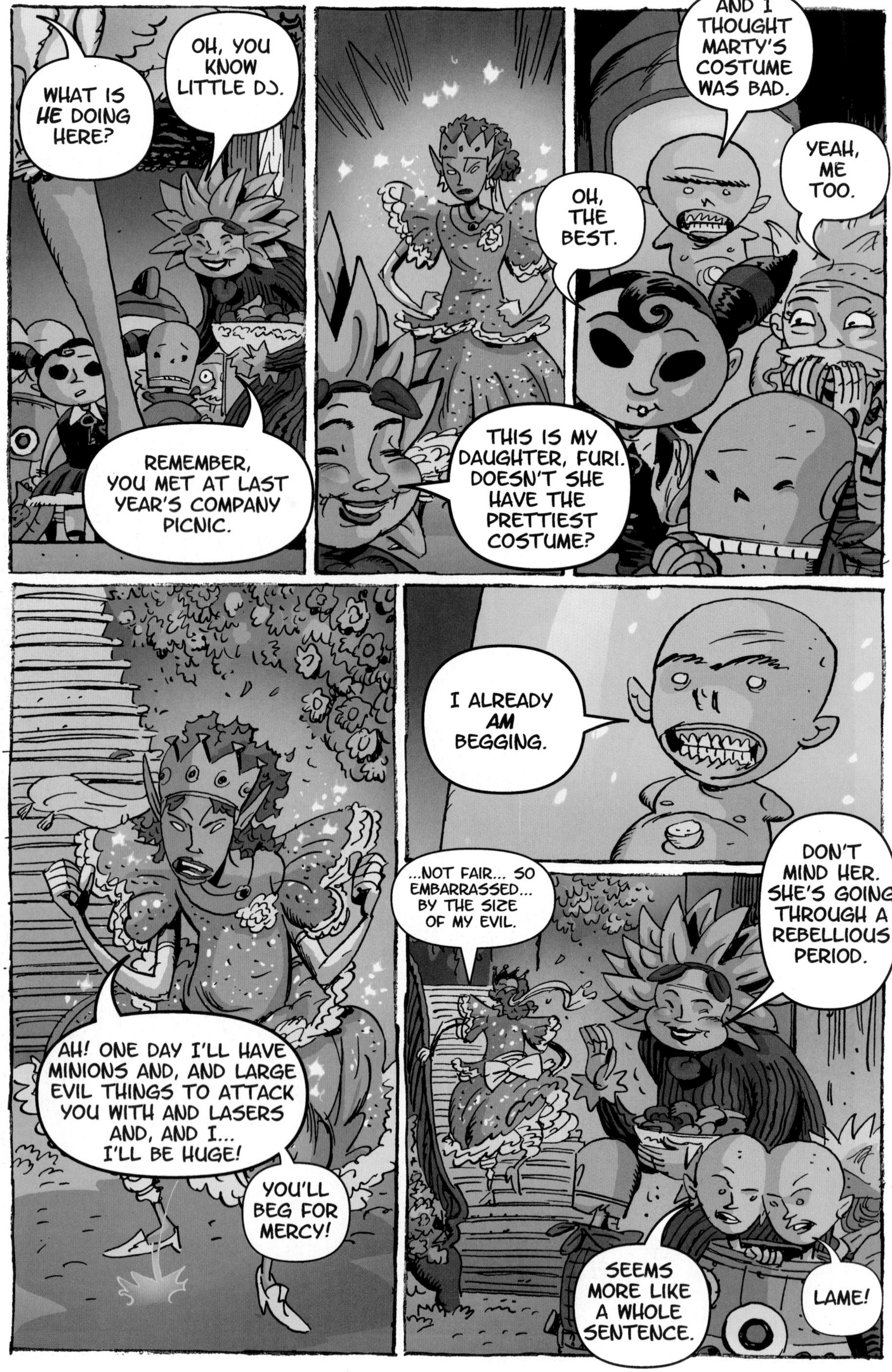
WHAT IS HE DOING HERE?
OH, YOU KNOW LITTLE DJ.
REMEMBER, YOU MET AT LAST YEAR'S COMPANY PICNIC.
THIS IS MY DAUGHTER, FURI. DOESN'T SHE HAVE THE PRETTIEST COSTUME?
AND I THOUGHT MARTY'S COSTUME WAS BAD.
OH, THE BEST.
YEAH, ME TOO.
AH! ONE DAY I'LL HAVE MINIONS AND, AND LARGE EVIL THINGS TO ATTACK YOU WITH AND LASERS AND, AND I... I'LL BE HUGE!
YOU'LL BEG FOR MERCY!
I ALREADY AM BEGGING.
...NOT FAIR... SO EMBARRASSED... BY THE SIZE OF MY EVIL.
DON'T MIND HER. SHE'S GOING THROUGH A REBELLIOUS PERIOD.
SEEMS MORE LIKE A WHOLE SENTENCE.
LAME!

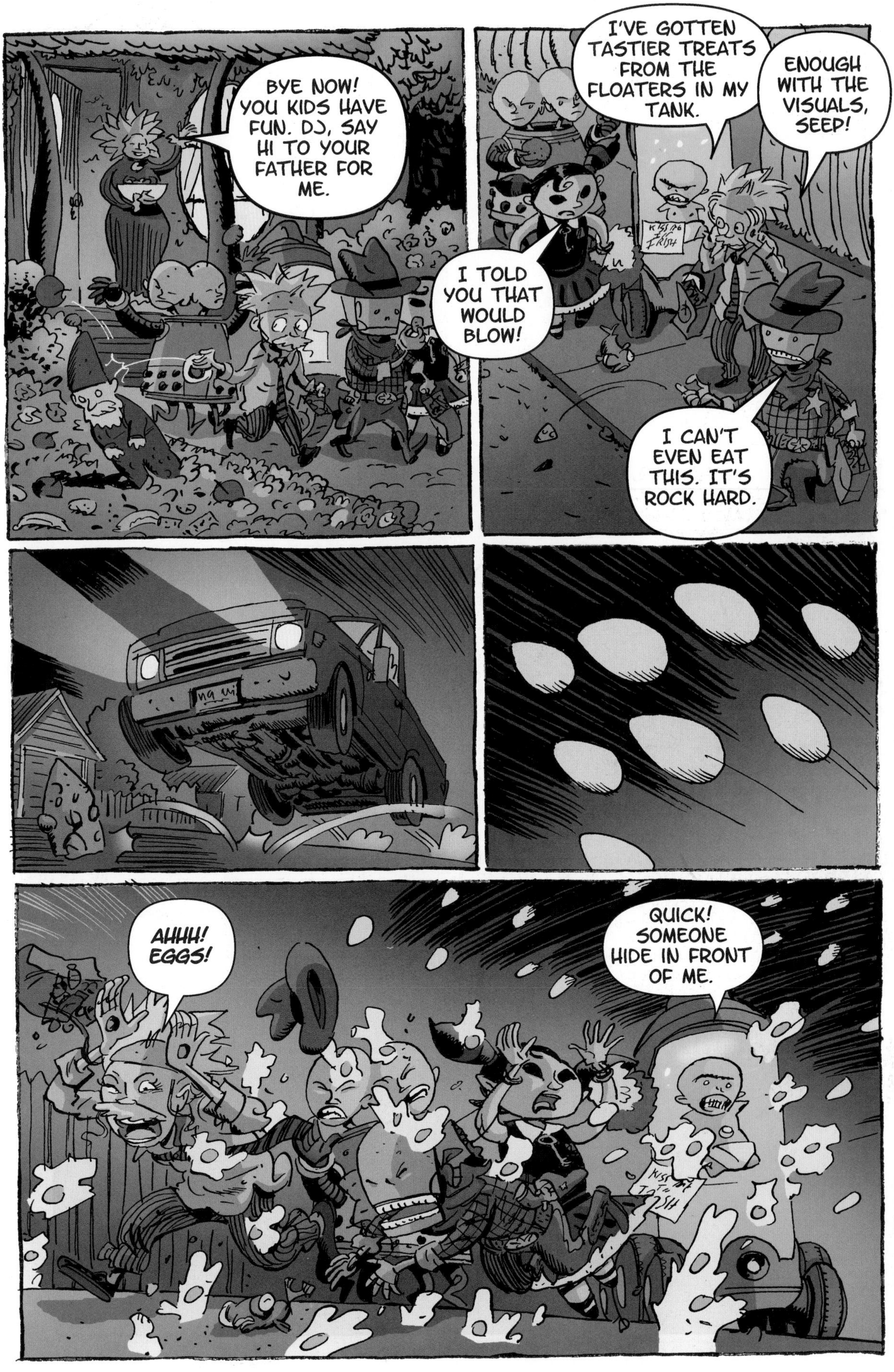
BYE NOW! YOU KIDS HAVE FUN. DJ, SAY HI TO YOUR FATHER FOR ME.
I'VE GOTTEN TASTIER TREATS FROM THE FLOATERS IN MY TANK.
ENOUGH WITH THE VISUALS, SEEP!
I TOLD YOU THAT WOULD BLOW!
I CAN'T EVEN EAT THIS. IT'S ROCK HARD.
AHHH! EGGS!
QUICK! SOMEONE HIDE IN FRONT OF ME.

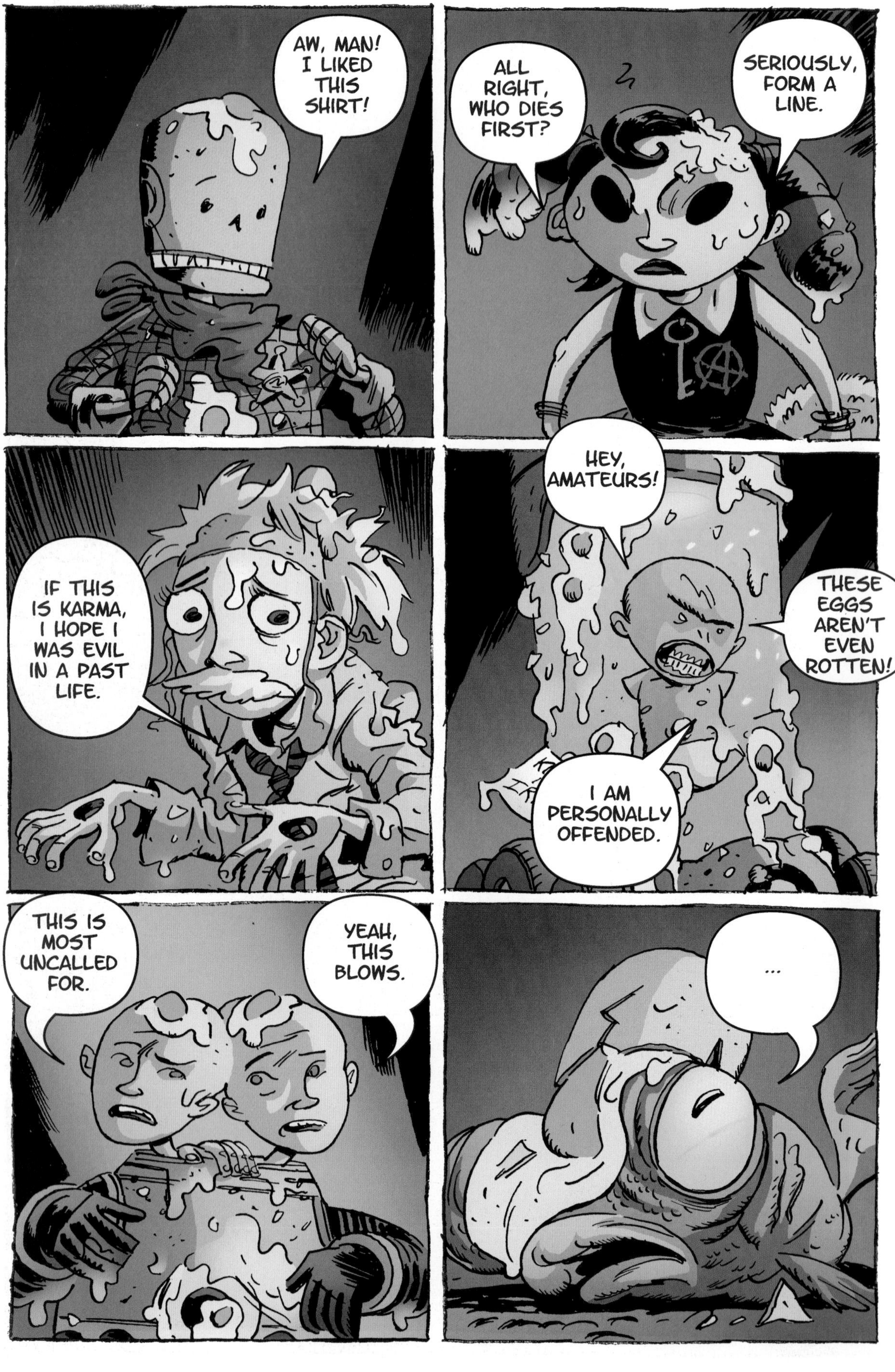
AW, MAN! I LIKED THIS SHIRT!
ALL RIGHT, WHO DIES FIRST?
SERIOUSLY, FORM A LINE.
IF THIS IS KARMA, I HOPE I WAS EVIL IN A PAST LIFE.
HEY, AMATEURS!
THESE EGGS AREN'T EVEN ROTTEN!
I AM PERSONALLY OFFENDED.
THIS IS MOST UNCALLED FOR.
YEAH, THIS BLOWS.
...

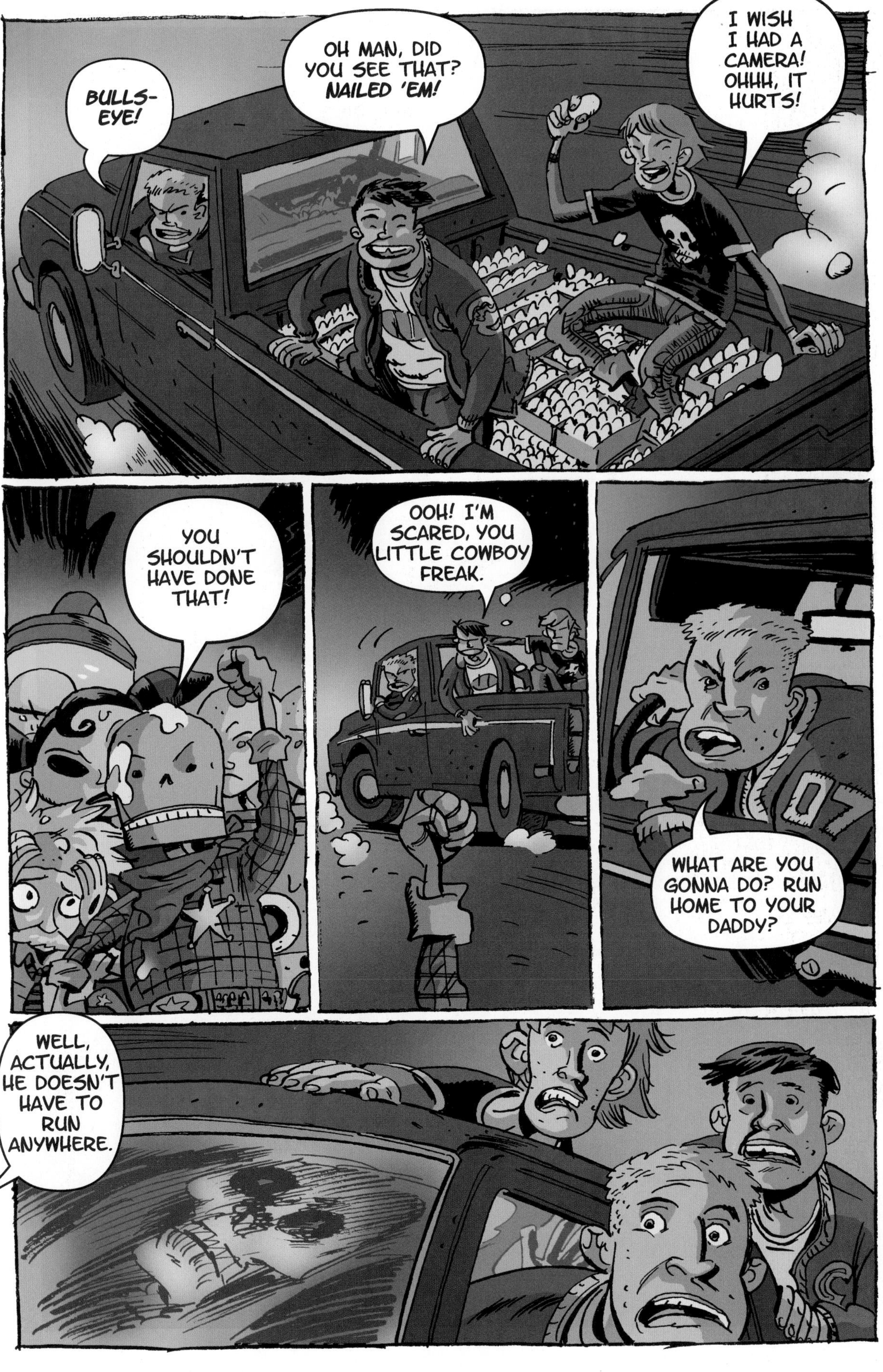
BULLS-EYE!
OH MAN, DID YOU SEE THAT? NAILED 'EM!
I WISH I HAD A CAMERA! OHHH, IT HURTS!
YOU SHOULDN'T HAVE DONE THAT!
OOH! I'M SCARED, YOU LITTLE COWBOY FREAK.
WHAT ARE YOU GONNA DO? RUN HOME TO YOUR DADDY?
WELL, ACTUALLY, HE DOESN'T HAVE TO RUN ANYWHERE.

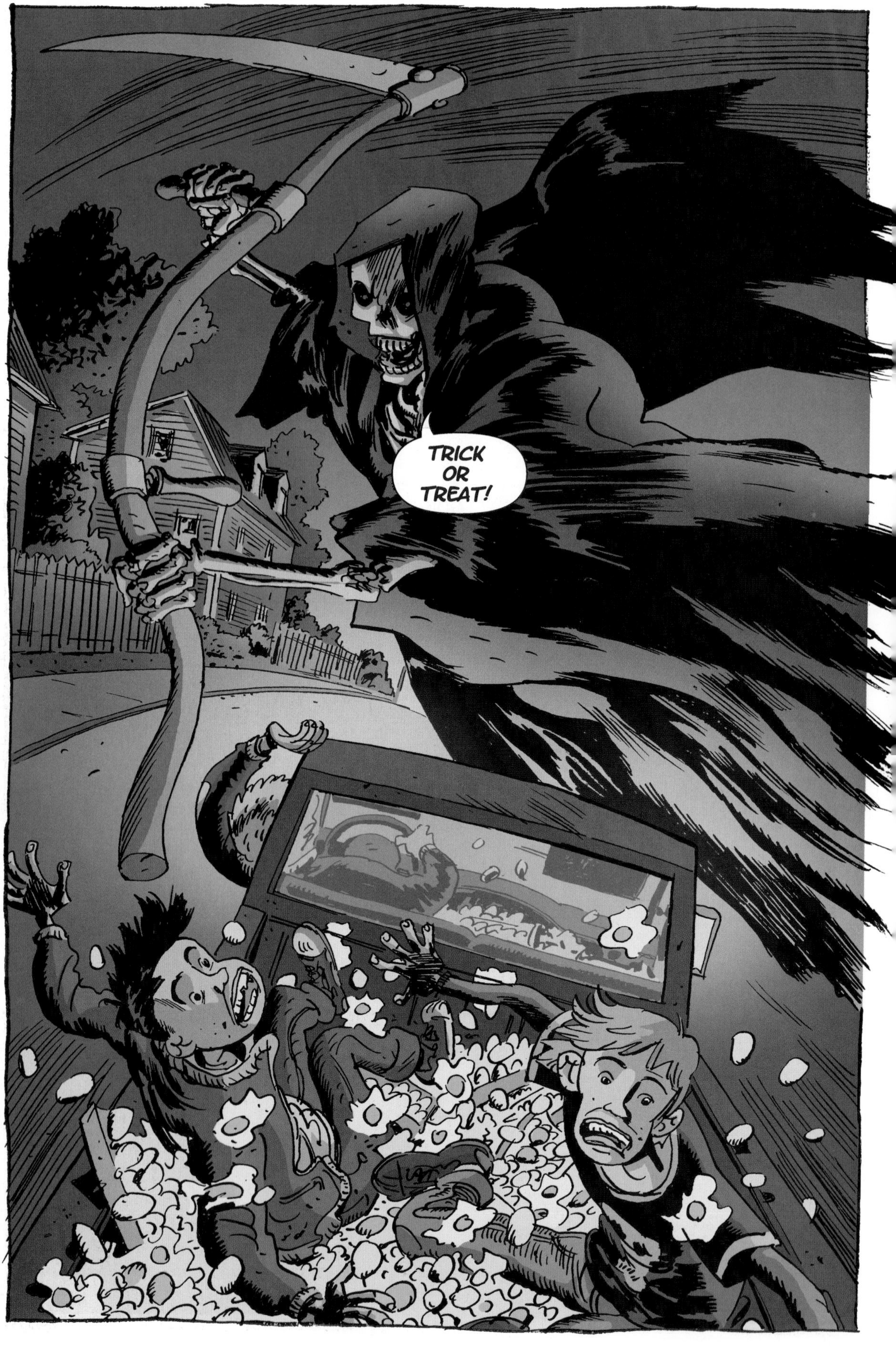
TRICK OR TREAT!

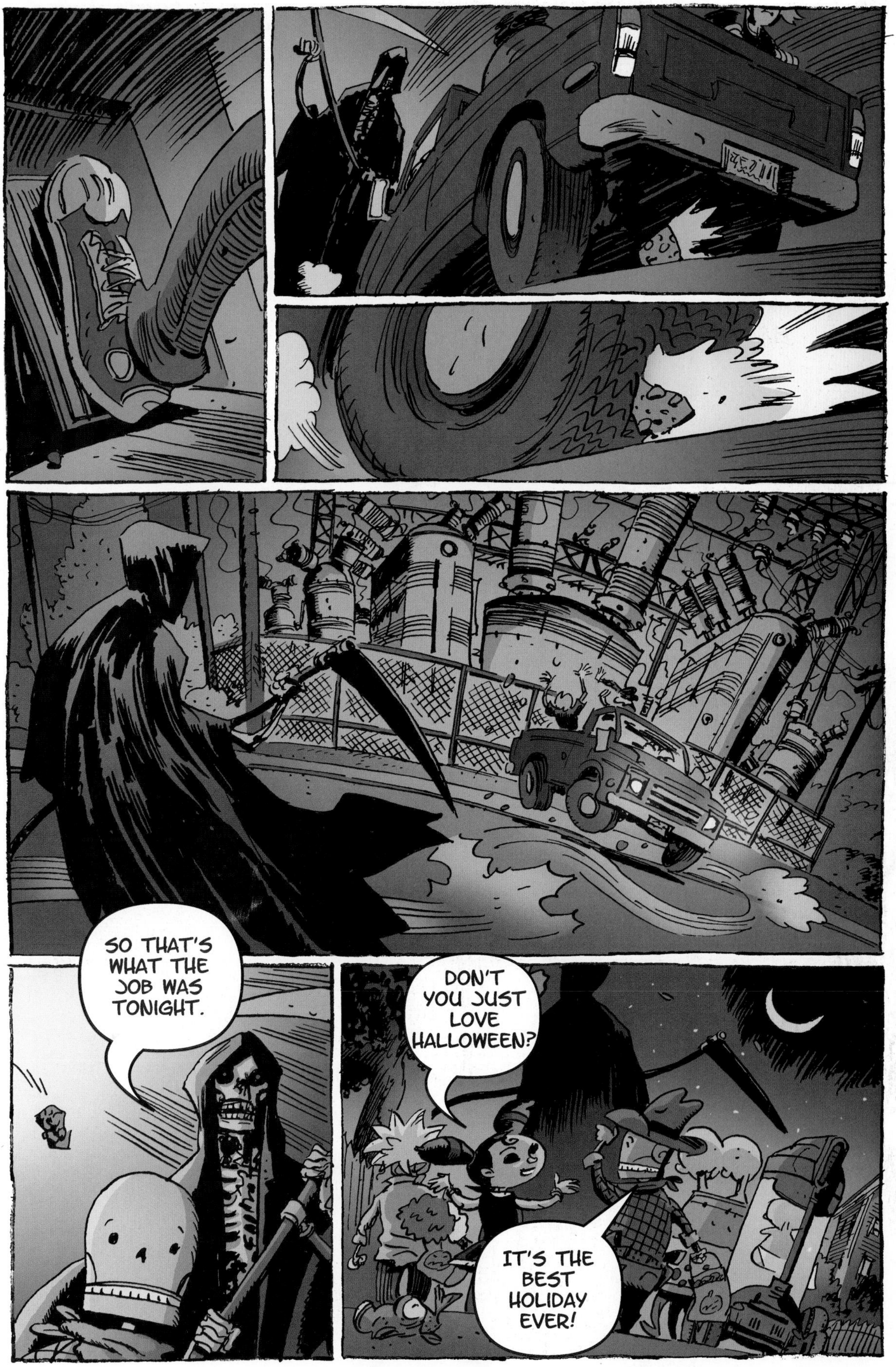
SO THAT'S WHAT THE JOB WAS TONIGHT.
DON'T YOU JUST LOVE HALLOWEEN?
IT'S THE BEST HOLIDAY EVER!

GALLERY

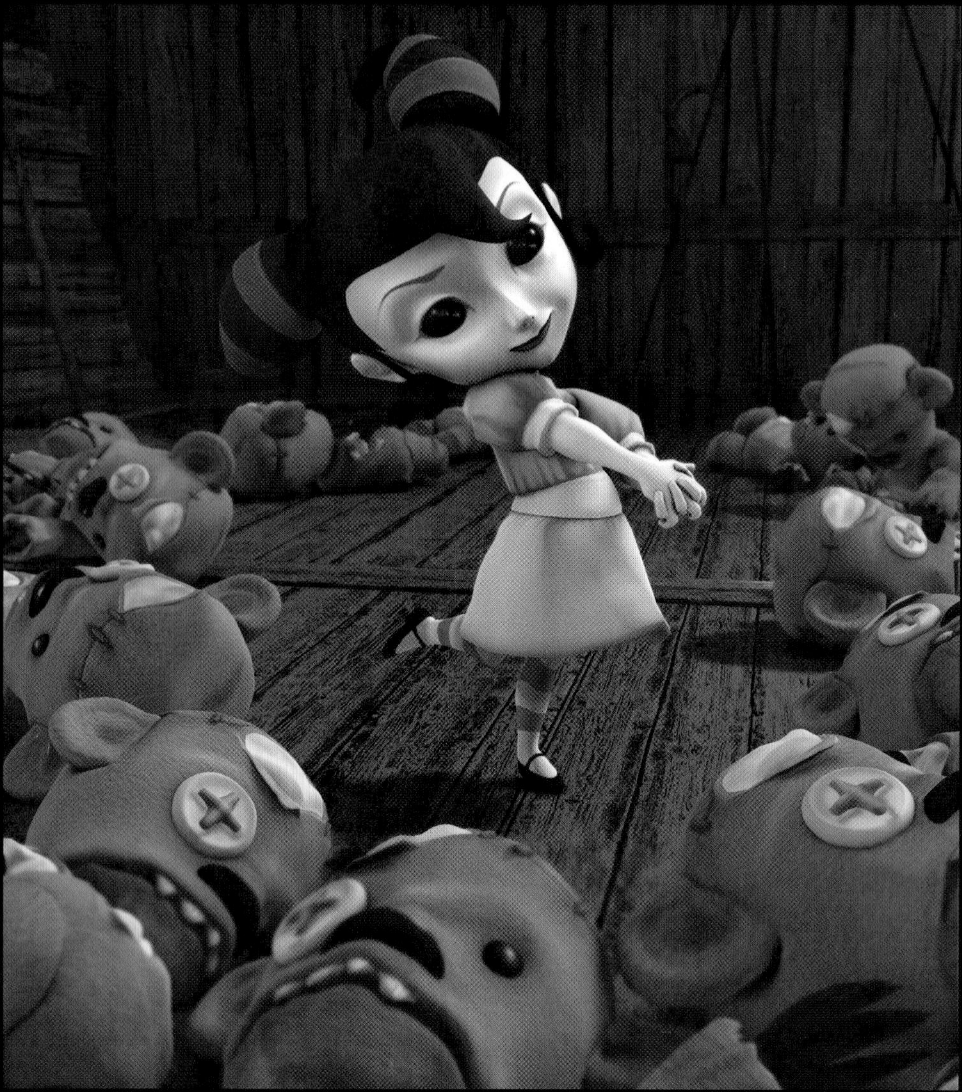

VIDEOGAME RENDER CREATED FOR PLAY MAGAZINE

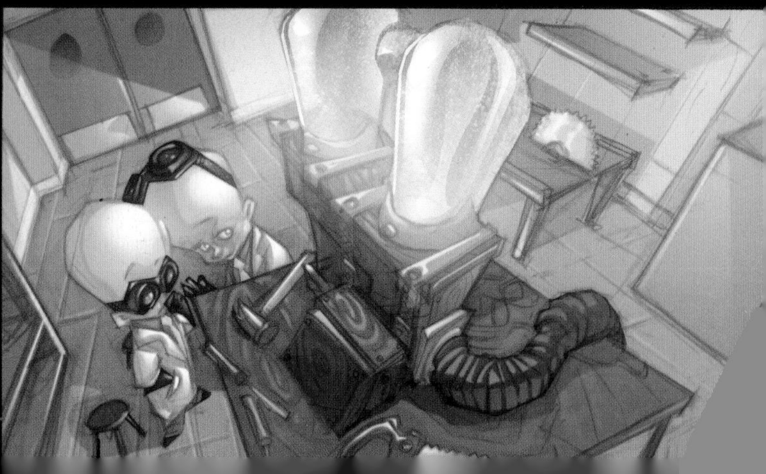

VIDEOGAME CONCEPT ART BY JEFF MATSUDA

PROMOTIONAL POSTER 2006
ART BY TED NAIFEH

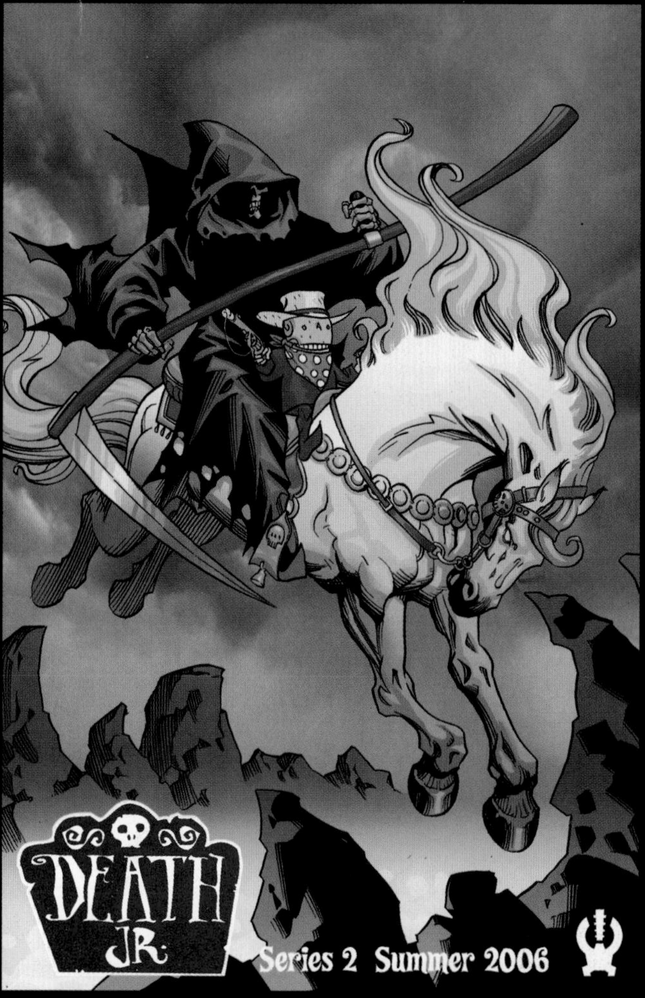

DEATH JR.
Series 2 Summer 2006

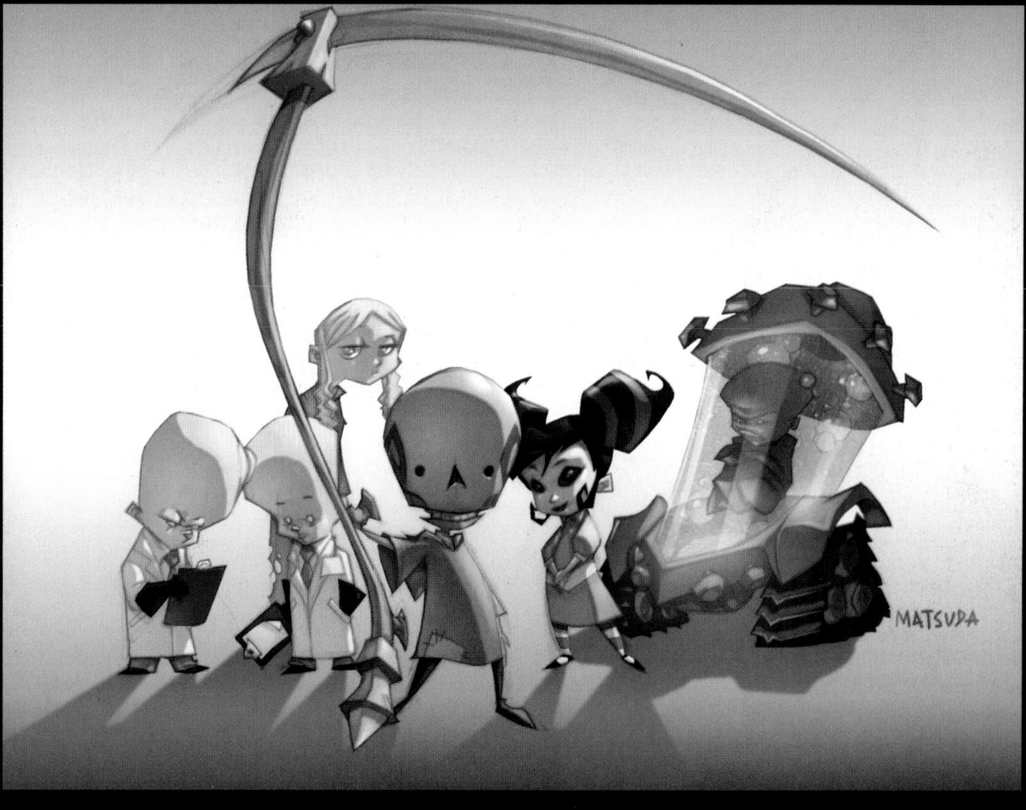

MATSUDA

VIDEOGAME CONCEPT ART BY JEFF MATSUDA

KONAMI

CAN'T GET ENOUGH
DEATH, JR ?

CHECK OUT THE DEATH JR.
VIDEOGAMES AVAILABLE NOW!

BACKBONE
ENTERTAINMENT

NINTENDO DS

© 2007 Konami Digital Entertainment, Inc. Death, Jr., the Death, Jr. Logo and characters are trademarks of Backbone Entertainment. © 2006 Backbone Entertainment. All rights reserved. "KONAMI" is a registered trademark of KONAMI CORPORATION. © 2007 KONAMI CORPORATION. "PSP" is a trademark and "PlayStation" and the "PS" Family logo are registered trademarks of Sony Computer Entertainment Inc. Memory Stick Duo™ may be required (sold separately). TM, ® and Nintendo DS are trademarks of Nintendo. © 2004 Nintendo. The ratings icon is a trademark of the Entertainment Software Association.